Wisdom Christology in the Gospel of John

Wisdom Christology in the
GOSPEL OF JOHN

∽

Dustin R. Smith

WIPF & STOCK · Eugene, Oregon

WISDOM CHRISTOLOGY IN THE GOSPEL OF JOHN

Copyright © 2024 Dustin R. Smith. All rights reserved. Except for brief quotations in critical publications or reviews, no part of this book may be reproduced in any manner without prior written permission from the publisher. Write: Permissions, Wipf and Stock Publishers, 199 W. 8th Ave., Suite 3, Eugene, OR 97401.

Wipf & Stock
An Imprint of Wipf and Stock Publishers
199 W. 8th Ave., Suite 3
Eugene, OR 97401

www.wipfandstock.com

PAPERBACK ISBN: 979-8-3852-1139-5
HARDCOVER ISBN: 979-8-3852-1140-1
EBOOK ISBN: 979-8-3852-1141-8

Scripture quotations are from the New Revised Standard Version Bible, copyright © 1989 National Council of the Churches of Christ in the United States of America; and the New American Standard Bible, copyright © 1995 the Lockman Foundation. Used with permission. All rights reserved worldwide.

To Bethany, Jacob, Nathan, and Talon.

"Wisdom is vindicated by all her children."

Somewhat surprisingly, the thought of Jesus as the Word of God incarnate is not taken up or followed through in the rest of John's Gospel—suggesting to some that the prologue (John 1:1–18) was a later addition to the Gospel, perhaps in the second or third draft of the Gospel as composed by John or by the group around him. However, in Jewish thought there was a more familiar way of speaking of God's interaction with his creation and his people. This was the figure of divine Wisdom, familiar at the time of Jesus particularly in the wisdom literature of Israel's Scriptures.

—James D. G. Dunn

Contents

Abbreviations ix

1 Introduction 1

2 Wisdom's Pilgrimage 11

3 Wisdom in the Prologue 49

4 Wisdom and God in the Narrative of John 81

5 Wisdom and the Mission of Jesus 100

6 Wisdom and Christology 133

7 Wisdom and Her Opponents 162

8 Wisdom and Her Disciples 185

9 Reflections and Conclusions 213

Bibliography 225

Author Index 241

Ancient Document Index 249

III.

Abbreviations

Journals and Reference Works

AB	Anchor Bible
ABD	*Anchor Bible Dictionary*, edited by David Noel Freedman, 6 vols. (New York: Doubleday, 1992)
ABR	*Australian Biblical Review*
ABRL	Anchor Bible Reference Library
ANTC	Abingdon New Testament Commentary
AOTC	Abingdon Old Testament Commentary
ATJ	*Ashland Theological Journal*
ATR	*Anglican Theological Review*
BBR	*Bulletin for Biblical Research*
BDAG	Walter Bauer, Frederick W. Danker, W. F. Arndt, and F. W. Gingrich. *Greek-English Lexicon of the New Testament and Other Early Christian Literature*, 3rd ed. (Chicago: University of Chicago Press, 2000)
BECNT	Baker Exegetical Commentary on the New Testament
BET	Beiträge zur biblischen Exegese und Theologie
BETS	*Bulletin of the Evangelical Theological Society*
BHGNT	Baylor Handbook on the Greek New Testament
BIS	Biblical Interpretation Series
BJS	Brown Judaic Studies
BLS	Bible and Literature Series
BNTC	Black's New Testament Commentary
BZAW	Beihefte zur Zeitschrift für die alttestamentliche Wissenschaft

CBC	Cambridge Bible Commentary
CBQ	*Catholic Biblical Quarterly*
CBQMS	Catholic Biblical Quarterly Monograph Series
CurTM	*Currents in Theology and Mission*
CTQ	*Concordia Theological Quarterly*
DCLS	Deuterocanonical and Cognate Literature Studies
DJD	Discoveries in the Judean Desert
DJG	*Dictionary of Jesus and the Gospels*, edited by Joel B. Green and Scot McKnight (Downers Grove, IL: InterVarsity, 1992)
DLNT	*Dictionary of the Later New Testament and Its Developments*, edited by R. P. Martin and P. H. Davids (Downers Grove, IL: InterVarsity, 1997)
DPL	*Dictionary of Paul and His Letters*, edited by Gerald Hawthorne and Ralph P. Martin (Downers Grove, IL: InterVarsity, 1993)
ECC	Eerdmans Critical Commentary
ETL	*Ephemerides Theologicae Lovanienses*
FOTL	Forms of Old Testament Literature
GOTR	*Greek Orthodox Theological Review*
HALOT	*Hebrew and Aramaic Lexicon of the Old Testament*, by Ludwig Koehler, Walter Baumgartner, and Johann J. Stamm, translated and edited under the supervision of Mervyn E. J. Richardson, 4 vols. (Leiden: Brill, 1994–1999)
HBT	*Horizons in Biblical Theology*
ICC	International Critical Commentary
IECOT	International Exegetical Commentary on the Old Testament
ITQ	*Irish Theological Quarterly*
JBL	*Journal of Biblical Literature*
JBQ	*Jewish Bible Quarterly*
JEHS	*Journal of the Evangelical Homiletics Society*
JESOT	*Journal for the Evangelical Study of the Old Testament*
JSJ	*Journal for the Study of Judaism*

JSJSup	Supplements to Journal for the Study of Judaism
JSNT	*Journal for the Study of the New Testament*
JSNTSup	Supplements to the Journal for the Study of the New Testament
JSOT	*Journal for the Study of the Old Testament*
JSOTSup	Journal for the Study of the Old Testament Supplement Series
JSP	*Journal for the Study of the Pseudepigrapha*
LCL	Loeb Classical Library
LEC	Library of Early Christianity
LNTS	Library of New Testament Studies
NIB	*New Interpreter's Bible*
NICNT	New International Commentary on the New Testament
NICOT	New International Commentary on the Old Testament
NIDB	*The New Interpreter's Dictionary of the Bible*, edited by Katherine Doob Sakenfeld, 5 vols. (Nashville: Abingdon, 2006–2009)
NovT	*Novum Testamentum*
NovTSup	Supplements to Novum Testamentum
NTL	New Testament Library
NTS	*New Testament Studies*
OBO	Orbis Biblicus et Orientalis
OTL	Old Testament Library
OTP	*Old Testament Pseudepigrapha*, edited by James H. Charlesworth, 2 vols. (New York: Doubleday, 1983, 1985)
PRS	*Perspectives on Religious Studies*
RB	*Révue Biblisque*
RBS	Resources for Biblical Study
SBLSBS	Society of Biblical Literature Sources for Biblical Study
SCS	Septuagint and Cognate Studies
SNTSMS	Society for New Testament Studies Monograph Series
SOTSMS	Society for Old Testament Studies Monograph Series
STDJ	Studies on the Texts of the Desert of Judah
TC	*TC: A Journal of Biblical Textual Criticism*

TDNT	*Theological Dictionary of the New Testament*, edited by Gerhard Kittel, translated by Geoffrey W. Bromiley, 10 vols. (Grand Rapids: Eerdmans, 1964)
TNTC	Tyndale New Testament Commentaries
TOTC	Tyndale Old Testament Commentaries
TynBul	*Tyndale Bulletin*
VT	*Vetus Testamentum*
WBC	Word Biblical Commentary

Apocrypha and Septuagint

Bar	Baruch
Sir	Sirach
Wis	Wisdom of Solomon

Old Testament Pseudepigrapha

1 En.	1 Enoch (Ethiopic Apocalypse)

Philo

Cher.	*On the Cherubim*
Congr.	*On the Preliminary Studies*
Det.	*That the Worse Attacks the Better*
Deus	*That God Is Unchangeable*
Ebr.	*On Drunkenness*
Fug.	*On Flight and Finding*
Her.	*Who Is the Heir?*
Leg. 1, 2, 3	*Allegorical Interpretation*
Legat.	*On the Embassy to Gaius*
Mut.	*On the Change of Names*
Post.	*On the Posterity of Cain*
QG 1, 2, 3, 4	*Questions and Answers on Genesis*
Praem.	*On Rewards and Punishments*
Sacr.	*On the Sacrifices of Cain and Abel*

Somn. 1, 2	*On Dreams*

Early Christian Writings

1 Clem.	1 Clement
Comm. Jo.	Origen, *Commentary on the Gospel of John*
Dial.	Justin, *Dialogue with Trypho*
Did.	Didache
Princ.	Origen, *On Principles*

Targumic Texts

Frg. Tg.	Fragmentary Targum
Tg. Neof.	Targum Neofiti
Tg. Ps-J.	Targum Pseudo-Jonathan

Rabbinic Texts

Gen Rab.	Genesis Rabbah
'Abot R. Nat.	'Avot of Rabbi Nathan
m. 'Abot	Avot
m. Ter.	Terumot
m. Qidd.	Qiddushin
b. B. Qam.	Bava Qamma
b. Ber.	Berakhot
b. 'Erub.	Eruvin
b. Git.	Gittin
b. Ned.	Nedarim
b. Qidd.	Qiddushin
b. Sanh.	Sanhedrin

1

Introduction

THE PRIMARY OBJECTIVE OF this book is to demonstrate the Jewish wisdom tradition's impact on the christological portrayal of Jesus within the Fourth Gospel—the Gospel according to John. Scholars have observed a recurring pattern in the New Testament, where the biblical authors apply various attributes, traits, characteristics, and roles that were originally associated with the personified wisdom of Israel's God to the figure of Jesus Christ. This specific christological portrayal is called *Wisdom Christology*, and this book will focus on how the Fourth Gospel extensively employs it to convey the person and significance of Jesus.

DEFINITIONS

We should take the opportunity at the introduction of our study to define what we mean when we refer to God's personified wisdom. Several Jewish texts of poetry offer a window into how the God of Israel has interacted with and instructed his creation in ways that are wise, ordered, and imbued with goodness. A number of key passages describe God as the one who created all things *through* or *with* his wisdom (e.g., Prov 3:19–20; Ps 104:24). The reader of these texts is left with the impression that creation itself must be a reflection of God's wise and ordered ways since God utilized his wisdom in the act of creation. Other poetic texts seek to associate the wisdom of God with the fear of YHWH (e.g., Job 28:28; Prov 1:28–29; 9:10),[1] suggesting that those who revere God are

---

1. YHWH is the personal name of the God of Israel, appearing over 6,800 times

acting and living according to God's wise intentions. We can also find poetic passages that set the wisdom of God in parallel with God's understanding, God's knowledge, and even God's prudence.[2] These passages offer further insight into the meaning of the wisdom of God; it is closely aligned with the concepts of understanding, knowledge, and prudence.

Of crucial importance to our study is the inclination of these Jewish poets to *personify* the wisdom of God. James Paxton's study of poetic personification defines it as the literary act that gives an inanimate object or abstract idea "a consciously *fictional* personality."[3] In other words, the biblical authors employed highly metaphorical language within works of Hebrew poetry to illustrate objects and ideas as if they were conscious persons. Readers of the Hebrew Bible will inevitably encounter a variety of personifications within poetic passages. For example, "goodness" and "mercy" are personified in order to portray these two attributes of YHWH as following behind the psalmist all the days of his life (Ps 23:6). We can observe the personification of God's "light" and God's "truth" in Ps 43:3. Similarly, the poet depicts personified "righteousness" and "peace" as kissing each other (Ps 85:10). Four other attributes of Israel's God (splendor, majesty, strength, beauty) are pictured as standing in his presence within the temple sanctuary (Ps 96:6). In the book of Isaiah, we notice a summons to the "arm" of YHWH to awaken as the author recalls how this arm cut up and pierced the primordial dragon (Isa 51:9). These attributes belonging to the God of Israel are plainly personifications, and it would be a fundamental error to confuse these personifications for actual persons alongside God.[4] The same must be said for God's personified wisdom,[5] and biblical scholars regularly describe her personified form as Lady Wisdom or Woman Wisdom. Burton Mack and Roland Murphy

---

in the Hebrew Bible. Most modern translations of the Bible substitute "LORD" for YHWH.

2. For wisdom parallels with *understanding*, see Job 28:12, 20, 28; Prov 2:2; 3:13, 19; 4:5. For parallels with *knowledge*, see Prov 1:7; 2:6; 3:19–20. For parallels with *prudence*, see Prov 8:5. 12.

3. Paxson, *Poetics of Personification*, 6, emphasis original.

4. Longman, "Woman Wisdom," 172.

5. Hurtado, *One God, One Lord*, 46, arrives at a similar conclusion regarding the importance of recognizing Wisdom as a vivid personification of one of God's attributes. Hurtado criticizes those scholars who interpret these personified attributes literally as actual beings: "This conclusion is a misunderstanding of this particular type of ancient Jewish religious language."

succinctly define the figure of Wisdom: "A poetic personification for God's intimate activity and for his personal summons."[6]

SOURCES

Having established that Wisdom Christology is the portrayal of Jesus Christ in terms of personified wisdom, it is important to identify the Jewish texts from which the New Testament authors drew their inspiration to depict the figure of Jesus as Wisdom. Scholars classify the type of literature in which wisdom themes appear most prominent as Jewish wisdom literature (or sapiential literature). The earliest works of Jewish wisdom literature that bore considerable influence upon the New Testament authors who exhibit Wisdom Christology are the biblical books of Job, Psalms, and Proverbs. These works of Jewish poetry were crucial in defining both the meaning and function of God's wisdom. However, these are not the only works of Jewish wisdom literature that considerably impacted the Wisdom Christology of early Christians. Three other Jewish works were composed chronologically after Job, Psalms, and Proverbs that require our attention. These works (which are sometimes referred to as intertestamental books) are known as Sirach, Baruch, and Wisdom of Solomon.[7] These three are not part of the Protestant canon of Scripture, and as such they are not present within Protestant Bibles, but they are included in some ecumenical translations like the New Revised Standard Version. After closely looking at these three intertestamental texts, it becomes increasingly clear that they are indebted to the portrayals of God's wisdom expressed within the biblical books of Job, Psalms, and particularly Proverbs. Although some readers may be hesitant to study Jewish books outside the Protestant canon, we will nevertheless explore their contents in order to draw attention to the ways in which they influenced New Testament Wisdom Christology. I will offer a detailed treatment of these and several other Jewish texts pertaining to the discussion of God's wisdom in chapter 2 of this book.

While biblical scholars have noticed for well over a century several strands of Wisdom Christology within the Fourth Gospel's depiction of Jesus, these crucial insights have struggled to trickle down to most lay

---

6. Mack and Murphy, "Wisdom Literature," 377.

7. These three Wisdom books are located in the Apocrypha, and they were included in the Greek collection of Old Testament books called the Septuagint (commonly abbreviated LXX).

readers of the New Testament. The average person who reads the Bible, in fact, has little to no idea about the tendency of several authors of the New Testament to illustrate Jesus Christ in terms of God's wisdom. Those few lay readers who do observe Wisdom Christology in the New Testament often, in my experience, struggle to define its meaning, relevance, and importance. This study seeks to shed much-needed light upon what biblical scholars have been saying about the Wisdom Christology in the Gospel of John in order that a wider audience may come to better understand the person, words, and mission of the Johannine Jesus.

It may come as a surprise to some that the Gospel of John was not the first Christian document to express a Wisdom Christology, at least from the perspective of a chronological dating of the various books contained within the New Testament.[8] We can observe this unique christological portrayal in several letters of the Pauline corpus, in the Letter to the Hebrews, and within the three Synoptic Gospels (Matthew, Mark, and Luke).[9] Before diving deep into the Gospel of John's portrayal of Jesus in terms of God's wisdom, it may be helpful to briefly survey the passages in which scholars have discerned Wisdom Christology among these earlier New Testament works.

1 Corinthians

Paul the apostle, one of the first authors of early Christian writings, introduces the figure of Jesus within 1 Corinthians in terms of God's wisdom quite explicitly in the opening chapter. To both Jews and Greeks who are called, Paul preaches Christ as "the power of God and as the wisdom of God" (1 Cor 1:24). Christ Jesus became to us, according to Paul, wisdom from God (1 Cor 1:30). The portrayal of Jesus in terms of wisdom continues in 1 Corinthians, appearing in two further noteworthy instances. When Paul contrasts the so-called gods and so-called lords with his monotheistic Christian faith, he declares that there is only one God, the Father, from whom are all things, and that there is one Lord, Jesus Christ, through whom are all things (1 Cor 8:6). This monotheistic creedal statement sets the one true God—the Father—as the sole Creator of all things,

---

8. The Fourth Gospel as we have it presented in the Bible is a late first-century composition, reaching its final written form in the last decade. See also the discussion of the influence of Wisdom motifs in early Christianity in Hengel, *Studies in Early Christology*, 73–117.

9. Dunn, *Christology in the Making*, 167.

while also, most notably, ascribing to Jesus the instrumental role of God's wisdom—the mediating agent of the God of Israel's creative acts according to texts like Ps 104:24; Prov 3:19; Jer 10:12; 51:15.[10] Paul's thought was not so much that Christ preexisted as the mediator of the Father's creative works, but that preexistent wisdom was now being recognized as Christ.[11] A similar attribution appears in Paul's typological retelling of the Israelite exodus from Egypt and the subsequent wilderness experience in which the rock that followed the children of Israel is identified as Christ (1 Cor 10:4). We have evidence from Jewish sources contemporary to Paul that this rock in the wilderness was being interpreted as God's personified wisdom. This strongly suggests that Paul is interpreting the wisdom of God as a type of Christ.[12] The fact that Paul assigns the characteristics and roles of the wisdom of God to Jesus in such as casual manner, often without explicitly alerting his readers to what he is doing, suggests that he expected them to already possess a general framework to conceptualize and grasp his Wisdom Christology. Within 1 Corinthians, Paul does not demonstrate a need to defend his Wisdom Christology and there does not seem to be any pushback from either his audience or his opponents on this matter.

Colossians

While scholars have pointed to further evidence of Paul's Wisdom Christology scattered throughout 2 Corinthians,[13] Galatians,[14] Romans,[15] and Ephesians,[16] the most dominant expression among the Pauline epistles appears in Colossians. The modern scholarly consensus concerning the Christ-hymn in Col 1:15–20 observes that the passage thoroughly illustrates Christ in terms of Jewish portrayals of God's wisdom. The

---

10. Dunn, *Theology of Paul*, 269, remarks that there are few issues in NT theology that have commanded such unanimity of agreement as the source of the language and imagery in 1 Cor 8:6, namely early Jewish reflection of God's wisdom.

11. Dunn, *Theology of Paul*, 274.

12. See Perriman, *In the Form of a God*, 51–54.

13. See 2 Cor 4:4, 6. On personified wisdom's close association with God's glory, see especially Prov 3:16; 8:17–18.

14. See Gal 4:4-6; cf. Wis 9:10, 17; Schweizer, "Zum religionsgeschichtlichen Hintergrund."

15. See Rom 8:3; 10:6–8; cf. Bar 3:29—4:1.

16. See Eph 1:6, 8–10, 12, 22–23; 3:10, 17–19; 4:10.

christological hymn contains no less than nine characteristics of the wisdom of God (e.g., "image," "firstborn," agent of creation, preceding all things, holding all things together) that are reapplied to the figure of Jesus.[17] This wisdom hymn that was sung about Christ demonstrates the extent to which the early church's understanding of Wisdom Christology came to influence certain strands of Christian liturgy and worship. In addition to the Christ-hymn of Col 1:15–20, we may observe five further passages in which similar portrayals take place within Colossians, such as Christ being the one in whom all the treasures of wisdom are hidden (Col 2:3).[18] The thorough and consistent presentation of Jesus Christ as personified wisdom's embodiment fits well into the letter's overall purpose, which is closely associated with answering the opponents in Colossae, namely those members of the local Jewish synagogue who were almost certainly familiar with the concept of God's wisdom.

Hebrews

The Letter to the Hebrews, written around the time of the destruction of the Jerusalem temple in 70 CE, opens with a catena of descriptive illustrations of Jesus Christ (Heb 1:1–4). Just as we observed in the Pauline letters, scholars have pointed to Jewish portrayals of personified wisdom that appear to have directly influenced the way in which the person of Christ is illustrated in Hebrews. First, the author assigns personified wisdom's role as the instrumental agent through which God made the world to God's son (Heb 1:2).[19] Second, the son is illustrated as the "reflection" of God's glory (1:3), a designation that utilizes a very rare Greek word quoted directly from Wisdom of Solomon's lengthy list of attributes that describe none other than Lady Wisdom.[20] Third, Jesus is displayed as upholding all things with the word of his power (1:4), an example that again draws upon a remarkably similar characterization of personified wisdom.[21] Finally, the son sits down at the right hand of the Majesty on high (1:4), exhibiting a noteworthy resemblance to a portrayal of personified

---

17. Dunn, *Theology of Paul*, 275–77.

18. Col 1:9–10, 28; 2:9; 3:16.

19. The portrayal of Lady Wisdom in Wis 9:1–2 almost certainly lies behind the portrayal of Jesus in Heb 1:1–2.

20. *Apaugasma* ("reflection/radiance") is a direct quote from Wis 7:26, "she is a reflection of eternal light."

21. Wis 1:6–7.

wisdom's position alongside the throne of Israel's God.²² The author of the Letter to the Hebrews is deeply indebted to the representation of Lady Wisdom in Wisdom of Solomon as he aims to present the son of God as the wisdom of God's present and definitive embodiment. Just like the Wisdom Christology in Paul, the roles formerly belonging to the wisdom of Israel's God are now applied to the risen Jesus of Nazareth.

The Gospel of Mark

When we turn to the Synoptic Gospel traditions (Matthew, Mark, and Luke), we have the opportunity to examine sayings concerning the wisdom of God that potentially go back to the historical Jesus himself. Our earliest gospel, Mark does not offer any explicit connections between Lady Wisdom and Jesus. However, several noteworthy moments in the narrative might reflect a subtle Wisdom Christology. At the baptism of Jesus, the voice from heaven addresses the son as "my beloved son" (Mark 1:11). While it is commonplace to interpret this title as a combination of various quotations,²³ the loving intimacy perhaps echoes back to Prov 8:30, where personified wisdom is said to daily be the delight of YHWH.²⁴ For Mark, the loving relationship between YHWH and his wisdom now finds its locus in God and his beloved son, Jesus. The same voice from heaven makes a second announcement at the transfiguration event, again referring to Jesus as "my beloved son" (Mark 9:7). After calling the son "the beloved," the heavenly voice commands those present to listen to the son, and the motif of disciples listening to and obeying personified wisdom is a common trope in Jewish wisdom literature.²⁵ During the transfiguration event, Jesus momentarily appears in dazzling white clothes (Mark 9:3), which may point to descriptions of personified wisdom as possessing radiance.²⁶ Another episode worth exploring appears in Mark 6, where Jesus returns to his hometown, only to suffer an unfortunate rejection. Those in the synagogue who hear Jesus teach begin to ask some pointed questions that might signal a Wisdom

---

22. Wis 9:4.
23. Usually Ps 2:7; Isa 42:1; and Gen 22:2 are presented by specialists of the Gospel of Mark.
24. Cf. also Wis 8:3; "the Lord of all loves her."
25. E.g., Prov 1:33; 8:6, 32–34; Sir 6:22–24.
26. See especially Wis 6:12; 7:26, 29.

Christology. Those present were saying, "Where did this man get these things, and what is this wisdom given to him?" (Mark 6:2). This question concerning wisdom is even more crucial once we recognize that the Greek interrogative pronoun translated "what" could also produce the feminine pronoun "who" (i.e., "*Who* is this Wisdom given to him?"). The hearers wrestle with the content of Jesus' teaching as well as the miraculous deeds performed by his hands, and after considering his origins as Mary's son, they took offense at him. The rejection of the Markan Jesus, who bears the wisdom of God, may recall instances in Jewish literature where personified wisdom is rejected by her intended recipients (e.g., Prov 1:24–25; Bar 3:12). Perhaps Mark intended that the answer to these questions pertaining to Jesus' identity is that Lady Wisdom has made her abode in the person of Jesus, the highly empowered Messiah. In short, a reasonable case can be made that Mark intended for his readers to pick up on the various illustrations of Jesus in terms of the wisdom of God.

Matthew and Luke

When we turn to examine Matthew's and Luke's gospel accounts, we can be far more confident in our search for Wisdom Christology. There are five key passages paralleled between Matthew and Luke's accounts that rather clearly depict Jesus in terms of Lady Wisdom. First, while rebuking "this generation," Jesus recalls how the Queen of the South came from the ends of the earth to hear Solomon's wisdom, concluding that something greater than Solomon is here, namely Jesus himself as the eschatological messenger of wisdom (Matt 12:42; Luke 11:31). Second, when Matthew's Jesus compares "this generation" and its response to the deeds of Christ, he concludes that it is actually personified Wisdom who will be vindicated by "*her deeds*," thereby openly equating Christ with God's wisdom (Matt 11:2, 16–19). In Luke's version of the same account, John the Baptist and Jesus function as the children of Lady Wisdom in whom she will find vindication (Luke 7:31–35). Third, Luke's account of the rejection of Wisdom's messengers consists of Jesus foretelling how the wisdom of God said, "I will send them prophets . . . some of whom they will kill" (Luke 11:49–51); Matthew, however, puts the words of Lady Wisdom on the mouth of Jesus himself: "I am sending you prophets . . . some of whom you will kill" (Matt 23:34–36). In effect, Matthew is making it explicit that the prophetic oracles of the wisdom of God are spoken by none other than Jesus himself—Wisdom's embodiment. Fourth, the lamentation over Jerusalem directly follows Jesus speaking the words of God's wisdom in Matthew's version (Matt 23:37–39), strongly suggesting that the "I" who often wanted to gather the children together is none other than Jesus, who is embodying Wisdom. Luke's account of the Jerusalem lament, however, is set in an entirely different context, following Jesus characterizing his death like other rejected prophets whom Lady Wisdom has sent (Luke 13:33–36). Fifth, Matthew and Luke's depiction of Jesus as the one to whom the Father delivers all things—knowledge that the son mediates—almost certainly reflects the Jewish wisdom tradition. Particularly, this tradition characterizes God's wisdom as *"hidden,"* namely, something only God knows and reveals as a gift to a select few (Matt 11:25–27; Luke 10:21–22). These five parallel Wisdom Christology passages in Matthew and Luke originate from a shared written source that most scholars regard as "Q," a source of Jesus material that may even predate Paul's earliest letters.[27] This shared source would allow us to cautiously date the portrayal of Jesus Christ in terms of God's wisdom to an incredibly early period in the study of Christian origins, sometime around the forties CE.

Independent of the double tradition shared by Matthew and Luke are the individual contributions of these evangelists to Wisdom Christology. Matthew follows up the wisdom saying located in 11:25–27 with an invitation by Jesus for the weary and heavy-laden to come to him. To those who respond to Jesus' invitation, he promises rest, an easy yoke, and a light burden (Matt 11:28–30). Jesus' invitation here shows considerable influence from Sir 51:23–27, where the Jewish sage similarly summons his audience to come, acquire Wisdom, and take upon the yoke of her instruction so that they may find rest in her. By employing many of the same Greek words, Matthew appears to have transformed the yoke and rest promised to Lady Wisdom's disciples from the book of Sirach into the yoke and rest that Christ himself promises to his followers, thus further enhancing Matthew's Wisdom Christology.

The Gospel of Luke offers a few additional noteworthy instances where the figure of Jesus is closely associated with the wisdom of God. Luke closely associates Jesus with wisdom from an early age, noting in two passages that as a child Jesus continued to learn, grow, and increase in wisdom (Luke 2:40, 52). As a child/disciple of personified wisdom

---

27. The Wisdom Christology would still stand in Matthew and Luke if it turned out that the Farrer hypothesis was the correct solution to the Synoptic problem.

(Luke 7:35), Jesus can provide his own disciples with a mouth to speak forth wisdom that their oppressors will be unable to refute or withstand (Luke 21:15). Presumably, followers of the Lukan Jesus would similarly grow in wise teachings in order that they may be equipped to carry out wisdom-enabled evangelism. As such, both Matthew and Luke build upon the Wisdom Christology outlined in the shared source Q with their individual emphases.

THE POTENTIAL RESPONSE OF THIS BOOK

Elisabeth Schüssler Fiorenza's assessment that the "earliest Christian theology was sophialogy"[28] (the close study of God's personified wisdom) appears to be quite appropriate, based on the several strands of New Testament data that we briefly surveyed. The Gospel of John came into its final form at a date later than Paul's letters, the Letter to the Hebrews, the Synoptic Gospels, and Q. The express aim of this book is to establish the extent to which John's Gospel illustrates the figure of Jesus Christ by assigning to him the roles and characteristics formerly belonging to the personified wisdom of Israel's God. It will soon become apparent that the Fourth Gospel offers the most complete and thorough Wisdom Christology in the New Testament, with more passages describing the Johannine Jesus as the embodiment of Lady Wisdom than all the other New Testament authors combined.[29]

Although biblical scholars who work closely with the Gospel of John have been aware of its Wisdom Christology since the late nineteenth century, there has been little effort made to pass along these insights to the wider audience of adult readers of the Bible. Even my experience in teaching the Gospel of John to both undergraduate and graduate divinity students has confirmed this matter of unfamiliarity about this crucial component of the christological portrayal within the Fourth Gospel. If this present volume succeeds in its overall objective, then I will consider my humble contribution worthwhile.

---

28. Schüssler Fiorenza, *In Memory of Her*, 134.
29. Brown, *Introduction to New Testament Christology*, 210.

2

Wisdom's Pilgrimage

BEFORE WE CAN BEGIN our study of Wisdom Christology in the Gospel of John, we must first look backward and take stock of the origins and journey of the concept of the wisdom of God within Jewish sapiential literature. Our survey will attempt to move from source to source within a reasonable assessment of chronology, particularly by following the standard dates of composition that modern scholars offer for these various texts. This pilgrimage of sorts begins with the biblical wisdom literature within the Hebrew Bible, focusing specifically on the book of Job, the Psalms, and the book of Proverbs. From there we will move to Jewish Second Temple literature relevant to our study, specifically the surviving works of Aristobulus, Ben Sirach, Baruch, Wisdom of Solomon, the Qumran documents entitled Genesis Apocryphon and Hymn to the Creator, the works of Philo, and the *Parables* of 1 Enoch. Last, we will give attention to the Tannaitic and Amoraic literature belonging to the Jewish exegetes of 10–500 CE. Once we have surveyed the pilgrimage of God's wisdom, we will be in a better position to responsibly interpret and situate the Fourth Gospel in the context of Jewish wisdom speculation, albeit from a distinctly Christian perspective.

THE BOOK OF JOB

Our study of the pilgrimage of wisdom begins with the book of Job, written in the postexilic period probably between the sixth and fourth centuries BCE. Although wisdom is a concept that the narrative of Job mentions frequently, we should take notice of the beautiful wisdom poem found in chapter 28, which functions as an interlude Job's last discourse of self-defense.[1] The second half of the poem (28:12–28) concentrates on the subject of wisdom, particularly on the attempt to locate wisdom's whereabouts in the midst of a search for precious stones within the deepest recess of the earth (28:1–11).[2] The poem begins by asking an important question that the rest of the passage sets out to answer: "Where can wisdom be found? And where is the place of understanding?" (28:12). This search for wisdom reappears with slight rewording in 28:20: "Where then does wisdom come from? And where is the place of understanding?" The pairing of wisdom and understanding suggests that the poet's pursuit has expanded to a cosmic level—far beyond the earthly quest for minerals and stones.[3] The poem offers a variety of responses to these closely related questions: "She is not found in the land of the living" (28:13) and "She is hidden from the eyes of all living" (28:21). Wisdom, the poem insists, is inaccessible, concealed, and hidden from humanity.[4]

Throughout this poem dedicated to locating the wisdom of God, we can detect multiple occurrences of personification.[5] Offering a reply to the initial question regarding wisdom's location, the personified deep and the sea both speak in the first person, reporting that wisdom is not within "me" (28:14). Further personification takes place with Abaddon[6] and its parallel, death, both possessing ears and collectively saying that they indeed have heard a report of wisdom (28:22). It is no surprise, therefore, that the personification of God's wisdom also occurs within this poem. After surveying the living, the deep, the sea, the birds of the sky, Abaddon, and death, God authoritatively declares to understand her way and to know her place (28:23).[7] Alice Sinnott argues that this statement of personified wisdom implies a more clearly defined identity than that of

---

1. Meyers et al., *Women in Scripture*, 548.
2. Newsom, "Job," 530.
3. Jones, *Rumors of Wisdom*, 38–39; Newsom, "Job," 531.
4. Brueggemann, *Theology*, 343; Clines, *Job 21–37*, 925–26; Pope, *Job*, 183.
5. Burkes, "Choosing Life," 258.
6. *Abaddon* is the Hebrew word for the realm of the dead, making it a suitable parallel for death.
7. Habel, *Book of Job*, 393; and Balentine, *Job*, 425. Both draw attention to the personification of death and of Abaddon.

a mere attribute of God.[8] Wisdom—like the deep, the sea, Abaddon, and death—is personified by the author of Job in this poem.[9]

Although Job 28 depicts personified wisdom as hidden from humanity, she is not wholly absent. The poem continues by speaking about the creative acts of God in former times (28:24–27). When God imparted weight to the wind, meted out the waters, and set a limit for the rain and a course for the bolt of thunder, then he saw personified wisdom. When God created the heavens and set forth the details therein, he declared wisdom, established her, and searched her out (28:27).[10] By "declaring" wisdom from the mouth of God, we may begin to observe a close association between God's wisdom and God's word.[11] Personified wisdom is closely tied to the created order belonging to the Creator God. Since God knows wisdom's location—which is unseen by the living—God can reveal how to attain her: "The fear of the Lord, that is wisdom" (28:28). Humanity may only attain wisdom by submitting to God, the only one who has direct access to her.

To summarize, Job 28 describes a postexilic Jewish perspective on wisdom's whereabouts. This wisdom poem emphasizes her elusive nature as hidden and inaccessible to humanity.[12] In doing so, the poem gives personality to the concept of wisdom, thus making wisdom a poetic female figure. This personified wisdom is manifest in creation because God wisely ordered his creative works. Those who seek wisdom will only succeed in finding her by fearing the Lord.

THE BOOK OF PSALMS

The concept of the wisdom of God appears fairly infrequently in the Psalms, with the noun occurring in only six instances. Despite the popular speculation of wisdom within Judaism, there is no evidence of a wisdom cult within the psalter. One striking passage worth considering

---

8. Sinnott, *Personification of Wisdom*, 88.

9. Murphy, *Tree of Life*, 34; Johnson, "Jesus, the Wisdom of God," 264; Habel, *Job*, 394. For an alternative interpretation that suggests that wisdom is depicted in a process of objectification, abstraction, and reification, see Jones, *Rumors of Wisdom*, 235–36.

10. Perdue, *Wisdom & Creation*, 186, helpfully remarks that by God searching personified wisdom out, he is "indicating his intimate knowledge of her very being." Meyers et al., *Women in Scripture*, 549, tease out of the text a hint of wisdom's personification.

11. Epp, "Wisdom, Torah, Word," 132.

12. Murphy, *Wisdom Literature*, 37.

as we trace wisdom's pilgrimage within Judaism is Psalm 104, a wisdom psalm praising creation and its Creator.[13] Verse 24 states: "How great are your works, O YHWH! In wisdom you have made all of them; the earth is full of your possessions." While the unnamed psalmist has gone to great lengths to catalog the powerful acts of YHWH, verse 24 indicates that YHWH's role as Creator involved his wisdom as an instrumental agent. YHWH made his great works with his wisdom, not unlike the role of the creative and powerful utterance of God (Gen 1:3; Ps 33:6).[14]

The passage raises some interesting questions regarding wisdom, its identity, its role, and its relationship to YHWH. First, what sort of interpretation might we offer regarding wisdom's identity? There are no other clues from which to gather further data within Psalm 104. Without any evidence that wisdom is personified, talking, or acting independently of YHWH in this passage, it appears that wisdom is simply functioning as an attribute of God. As an attribute, wisdom highlights the wise ordering and knowledgeable skill characterizing the Creator's works.[15] In other words, creation manifests the quality of wisdom in that it is well crafted and logical.[16] The psalmist is careful not to confuse the Creator YHWH with his wisdom. Grammatically, the works and possessions in verse 24 belong to YHWH, not to wisdom. Even the Hebrew verb *asa* ("to make") in this passage is second-person masculine singular, referring to YHWH, rather than to the grammatically feminine wisdom. YHWH alone is the Creator,[17] but he wisely made all things with his wisdom. There is sufficient reason, therefore, to aptly categorize this psalm as a wisdom psalm.[18]

In summing up Psalm 104, we noted that wisdom appears in an undeveloped form, as an impersonal agent of YHWH's creative works. The psalmist depicts God making all things through his wisdom in a manner that closely resembles similar illustrations of the creative word of God. By stressing wisdom's preexistent role in the act of creation, the psalmist

---

13. Gammie, "From Prudentialism to Apocalypticism," 481–82; Whybray, *Intellectual Tradition in the Old Testament*, 154.

14. Scholars regularly point out the similarities between the creation motifs in Genesis 1 and Psalm 104. See van Wolde, "Separation and Creation," 611–47; Gottlieb, "Creation Theme," 29–36.

15. Goldingay, *Psalms 3*, 191; McCann, "Book of Psalms," 1098.

16. Berlin, "Wisdom of Creation," 71.

17. Allen, *Psalms 101–150*, 32–34.

18. Hossfeld and Zenger, *Psalms 3*, 54.

intends to portray the Creator God as wisely making and actively ordering all his good works.

THE BOOK OF PROVERBS

Within the Hebrew Bible, there is no larger hub of wisdom material than within the book of Proverbs. Structurally, the editors of Proverbs bookended the collection with noteworthy sections pertaining to personified wisdom, beginning with chapters 1–9 and concluding with the acrostic poem describing the Woman of Substance in 31:10–31. Although it is difficult to ascertain a firm date for the original compilation of Proverbs, the Jewish sages responsible for chapters 1–9 and 31 probably composed them during the Persian period, between 539 and 333 BCE.[19] It will be prudent for this study to examine the portrayal of personified wisdom in each of the relevant passages.

Proverbs 1 introduces the whole collection by declaring its intent to impart wisdom to its readers. In doing so, wisdom is associated with instructions for discipline, understanding, wise behavior, prudence, knowledge, and discretion (1:2–4). The household father and mother are those trying to commit these wise precepts to the readers (1:8). In verses 1:20–33, however, the concept of wisdom has moved beyond the royal father's mere wise instructions into a heavily personified female figure.[20] Wisdom—depicted as a lady who speaks in the first person—now stands openly in the public arena: in the streets, in the town square, and at the entrance of the city gates (1:20–21). Lady Wisdom's speech and behavior resemble that of an inspired prophet.[21] She speaks forth prophetic condemnations to those who refuse to listen to her wise sayings (1:24–25, 28–30).[22] She utters prophetic threats that are to follow as judgment upon those who do not heed her words (1:26–27, 31–32).[23]

---

19. For a thorough treatment on the dating of Prov 1–9 and 31:10–31, see Yoder, *Wisdom as a Woman*, 39–91.

20. Treier, *Proverbs*, 18, observes: "This personal character of biblical teaching manifests a new dimension beginning in 1:20, as Wisdom—personified—cries out in the public square."

21. Teh, "Images of Personified Wisdom," 108–15; Meyers et al., *Women in Scripture*, 549.

22. Lady Wisdom's prophetic condemnations draw upon the earlier biblical prophets in form and language (see Isa 1:15; 50:2; 65:12; 66:4; Jer 7:13; 11:10–11; 17:23; 29:19; Hos 5:6; Mic 3:4).

23. In these prophetic threats, Lady Wisdom resembles threats uttered by other

Although Lady Wisdom speaks as an authorized prophetess, she talks in the first person; "I will pour out my spirit on you, I will make my words known to you" (1:23). This illustration of Wisdom herself making known God's words suggests a close association between the concepts of the wisdom of God and the word of God. She situates herself publicly as accessible, particularly as she shouts, lifts her voice, cries out, and utters her sayings. However, she will become inaccessible to those who refuse to repent: "They will call on me, but I will not answer; they will seek me, but they will not find me" (1:28). The chapter concludes with Lady Wisdom promising a life of security and ease to those who faithfully listen to her wise oracles (1:33).[24]

The ways that the Jewish sages portrayed wisdom in Proverbs as both God's wise commands and a personified female figure are clear in 2:1–12. On one hand, the wisdom of God is likened to the words, commandments, understanding, and discernment that the ideal readers should strive to receive (2:1–3). On the other, wisdom is almost instantly personified as an active figure who takes the initiative to enter the heart of the upright (2:10).[25] The author then offers synonyms to wisdom—knowledge, discretion, and understanding—as additional personifications that actively guard and watch over those walking in integrity (2:10–11). Since Lady Wisdom is the personification of God's wise interaction with his creation, God and his wisdom are often interchangeable in their actions (2:6–11).[26] As such, Wisdom continues to appear accessible and openly available to those who diligently search for her (2:2–7).

Proverbs 3 stresses the unparalleled value of the wisdom of God, and this chapter encourages its readers to acquire her at all costs. Her economic worth is incredible; she is greater than silver, gold, and jewels (3:14–15). Personified wisdom holds long life, riches, and glory in her hands (3:16).[27] Her ways, which are meant to provide a contrast with the crooked ways leading to the personified strange woman (2:15–19),[28] are characterized as pleasant and peaceful (3:17). Furthermore, Wisdom is

---

biblical prophets (see Isa 1:15; Jer 11:11; Hos 5:6; Ps 2:4).

24. Rad, *Old Testament Theology*, 443.

25. Murphy, *Proverbs*, 16.

26. Murphy, *Proverbs*, 16.

27. These three benefits were also given to Solomon by God (1 Kgs 3:13; 2 Chr 1:11–12), further indicating that wisdom offers by extension that which God himself offers.

28. Yoder, "Personified Wisdom," 277.

likened to a tree of life that is to be grasped and held fast (3:18), a stark contrast from the inaccessible tree of life as described in Gen 3:22–24. Readers interested in wealth, life, and glory would do well to diligently seek after wisdom. In order to further heighten the value of wisdom, the sages depict YHWH as having utilized her as an instrumental agent when he founded the earth,[29] meaning that God wisely ordered the good creation (3:19).[30] Wisdom thus brings order to the heavens and the earth, while simultaneously restraining potential chaos.[31] However, wisdom is not to be confused with a conscious female figure alongside God, as the sages carefully parallel wisdom with the regular synonyms "understanding" and "knowledge" (3:19–20).[32] If the Creator used his priceless wisdom to make all things, then it is no wonder that the household father implores his son to keep wisdom and never let her vanish from sight (3:21).[33]

The personification of wisdom reaches its poetic climax in Proverbs 8, where Lady Wisdom utters her longest speech. Taking the role of a teacher, Wisdom encourages her listeners to take hold of her instruction, counsel, and discipline (8:10, 14, 33). Wisdom again presents herself openly and publicly, indicating her accessibility to those who listen to her and keep her ways (8:2–3). Her wise sayings come forth from her personified mouth (8:6–8), which suggests another close connection between God's wisdom and word. To those who love her, she again reciprocates her love in addition to offering both riches and glory (8:17–18). She can reward those who love her with wealth (8:21) because Wisdom herself is valuable, and within her speech, she spends a considerable amount of time describing the extent of her preeminence in terms of her ancient origins (8:22–31).[34] By employing the use of several prepositions and phrases ("in the beginning," "before," "from everlasting," "from the

---

29. Martin, *Proverbs*, 37.

30. Goldingay, *Biblical Theology*, 138; Wilson, *Proverbs*, 87. Compare the similar expression in Jer 10:12; 51:15, a prophetic work distinct from the Jewish wisdom literature: "[YHWH] established the world with his wisdom."

31. Treier, *Proverbs*, 26.

32. Bauckham, *Jesus*, 16–17, insists on this very point: "The texts in question make it quite clear that they are not infringing the standard monotheistic insistence that God created without assistance of any kind."

33. Longman, *Proverbs*, 138.

34. Clifford, *Wisdom Literature*, 61. Longman, *Proverbs*, 213, offers an important reminder to interpreters: "Woman Wisdom is not a preincarnate form of the second person of the Trinity."

earliest times") the sages illustrate Lady Wisdom as preexistent. However, she is not coeternal with YHWH; she declares that YHWH created her (8:22),[35] established her (8:23), and brought her forth as a child (8:24, 25).[36] She details the extent to which she witnessed creation alongside God, but she never claims to be the Creator. That role she is incredibly careful to reserve for YHWH alone: "he made the earth and the fields" (8:26); "he established the heavens" (8:27); "he made firm the skies above" (8:28); "he set a boundary for the sea" (8:29). As a joyful child, personified wisdom delights in YHWH, and that love is reciprocated: "I was daily his delight" (8:30).[37] Having proven her preeminent value, she displays her accessibility to anyone who listens to her, keeps her ways, and heeds her instructions, resulting in life and favor (8:32–36).

Personified wisdom gains yet another role in chapter 9 as she acts as the head of the household—a house that she built (9:1). The passage focuses on the dinner she prepares and the invitation she openly offers to whoever lacks understanding. Her table of nourishment consists of meat, bread, and wine (9:2, 5).[38] Lady Wisdom's request to dine at her table is a summons to forsake folly and walk in the path of understanding that only wisdom offers. In doing so, the naïve will surely find life (9:6). The table fellowship that personified wisdom offers is set in contrast to the dinner that personified folly offers (9:13–18).[39] While the two dinner hosts bear some parallels—both are homeowners, invite the naïve, and offer food and drink—Lady Wisdom's invitation is clearly the better choice. She offers wine to drink, while Lady Folly can only provide stolen water (9:17). Lady Wisdom is affluent enough to have female servants whom she sends (9:3), while Lady Folly has no servants. Those who partake of personified wisdom's meal are offered life, but the personified folly's guests are in the depths of Sheol (9:18). By juxtaposing the invitation of Wisdom

---

35. The Hebrew verb *qana* can mean "to create" and "to acquire" (*HALOT*, 1111–12). Both definitions seem to be intended here, as it would be difficult to argue persuasively that the author intended one but did not intend the other. See the discussion in Yoder, *Proverbs*, 94–95. In private correspondence, Yoder suggested that the ambiguity in the verb's meaning was likely intentional on the part of the sage.

36. Brown, "Proverbs 8:22–31," 286.

37. Despite the lack of scholarly consensus on the meaning of *amon* (architect, faithful, nurse, child?), the close intimacy between YHWH and personified wisdom remains intact. For a recent survey of meanings of *amon* and a new proposal, see Anthonioz, "Amon," 73–93.

38. Sandelin, *Wisdom as Nourisher*, 19–24.

39. Davis, *Proverbs*, 70, 74.

and the invitation of Folly, the sages highlight the value and necessity of Wisdom's life-giving teachings and instructions.

Although the authors of the collection of Proverbs intended that their primary audience be young males,[40] the final passage is clearly directed at Jewish females who incorporate Wisdom's teachings into their daily lives.[41] In 31:10–31, the poem of the Woman of Substance[42] stands out as a noteworthy passage[43] that pertains to Lady Wisdom, where in particular several of her traits, qualities, and descriptions expressed in chapters 1–9 are recapitulated in the portrayal of ideal Jewish wives.[44] The poem is outlined in an acrostic arrangement, with each line beginning with a sequential letter of the Hebrew alphabet. The purpose of arranging the poem acrostically is that it would set forth an all-encompassing description of Jewish women in the Persian period who embody personified wisdom. When the reader of the poem compares the Hebrew text with the descriptions of wisdom in chapters 1–9, it becomes immediately apparent that this ideal woman is being deliberately illustrated as exemplifying the wisdom of God.[45] The similarities are striking. The Woman of Substance, like personified wisdom, is more valuable than jewels (31:10; 3:15). Both women offer good things (31:12; 2:8–9), despise evil (31:12; 8:13), are delightful (31:13; 3:15), bring forth profit (31:14; 3:14), offer bread (31:14; 9:5), are homeowners (31:15; 9:1), have female servants (31:15; 9:3), bear fruit (31:16; 8:19), speak at the gates of the city (31:23; 8:3), and laugh (31:25; 8:30–31).[46] In fact, the sages responsible for the poem of the Woman of Substance make a bilingual pun in 31:27, where the Hebrew verb *tsofiya* ("she watches over") is almost

---

40. Yoder, "Personified Wisdom," 277; Martin, *Proverbs*, 80–81.

41. Waltke, *Proverbs: Chapters 15–31*, 299, 518, concludes from this passage an ideal interpretation where wise people "aim to incarnate the wisdom she embodies."

42. For a detailed discussion on the translation "Woman of Substance," see Yoder, *Proverbs*, 292.

43. The LXX separates Prov 31:1–9 from 31:10–31, demonstrating that the latter was recognized as a distinct composition from a very early period of interpretation.

44. Fox, *Proverbs 10–31*, 908–9, records eleven different ways in which the woman in 31:10–31 is portrayed with the same language and characteristics as personified wisdom, wisdom, and wise women. See also Horne, *Proverbs-Ecclesiastes*, 359–65; Ringe, *Wisdom's Friends*, 34; McCreesh, "Wisdom as Wife," 30–46.

45. Fox, *Proverbs 10–31*, 890, observes that the Hebrew alphabet denotes "totality" in its ability to encompass all words. See also the helpful diagram in Horne, *Proverbs-Ecclesiastes*, 360–61.

46. Camp, *Wisdom and the Feminine*, 188–89.

certainly an intentional bilingual pun with the Greek word for wisdom, *sophia*.[47] There is an emerging consensus among specialists of Proverbs who draw attention to the poem in 31:10–31 and describe its depiction of these Jewish women in the Persian period[48] as the embodiment and incarnation of personified wisdom.[49] Leo Perdue, noting that the characteristics of personified wisdom are applied to the Woman of Substance, observes that she "becomes the human incarnation of what Woman Wisdom teaches."[50] Pauw follows Perdue in this line of interpretation: "The 'woman of substance' is in some ways a real-life incarnation of Woman Wisdom."[51] Ernest C. Lucas echoes this reading of the wife in 31:10–31: "She is a portrait of Woman Wisdom because she incarnates the attributes of wisdom presented in Proverbs."[52] Proverbs 31 appears to be the origin of the doctrine of incarnation—an incarnation of a personification coming down to earth to become flesh in the Woman of Substance.[53]

To sum up, the book of Proverbs presents personified wisdom in a variety of roles: she is a prophetess, teacher, child, and homeowner. These roles contribute to her summons to listen to her wise teachings and instructions. The teachings of Wisdom come forth from her mouth, thereby strongly associating the words of God with the wisdom of God. Wisdom is the instrumental agent of creation, indicating that God created wisely and orderly. Lady Wisdom, naturally, preexisted creation, while making it absolutely certain that YHWH alone is the Creator. She makes herself available to those who diligently seek her and even becomes incarnate

---

47. Murphy, *Proverbs*, 244, argues that this play on words was deliberate and suggestive of a relationship between the woman of the poem and personified wisdom.

48. Yoder, "Personified Wisdom and Feminist Theologies," 276, defines these woman as "real, albeit exceptional, women in the early post-exilic or Persian period." She adds that these women are skillful, managers of business, and possess thriving households.

49. Perdue, *Proverbs*, 229. Yoder, *Proverbs*, 299, succinctly states that the woman of substance is identified with personified wisdom; McKinlay, *Gendering Wisdom the Host*, 127, "Wisdom herself in human form;" Witherington, *Jesus the Sage*, 34–35, "This woman is indeed the very embodiment of Wisdom . . . she is Wisdom truly embodied." See also Kwon, "Wisdom Incarnate," 181, 187–88; Shaw, "Wisdom Incarnate," 47–48; Schroer, *Wisdom*, 21–24; Treier, *Proverbs*, 108; Meyers et al., *Women in Scripture*, 303–4; Longman, *Proverbs*, 542.

50. Perdue, *Proverbs*, 63. Horne, *Proverbs-Ecclesiastes*, 357, comes to the same conclusion: "Readers are challenged to associate the wife with Woman Wisdom herself."

51. Pauw, *Proverbs and Ecclesiastes*, 32.

52. Lucas, *Proverbs*, 197.

53. Perdue unpacks this theology by calling the Jewish woman "the incarnation of wisdom in female form" (*Proverbs*, 280). It is no surprise that Prov 19:14 describes the prudent wife as coming from YHWH.

in the Woman of Substance, a strikingly early reference to the concept of incarnation within Judaism.[54] Nevertheless, those who spurn her will find her inaccessible, resulting in judgment and calamity.

ARISTOBULUS

The Alexandrian Jew Aristobulus is the earliest example of a Hellenistic Jewish theologian writing about Moses and the Torah, based on our surviving sources.[55] Aristobulus lived during the reign of the Egyptian king Ptolemy VI Philometor—the intended recipient of his written works. Having identified the recipient, we can date the works of Aristobulus to the first half of the second century BCE. The works of Aristobulus are now lost, but Clement of Alexandria and Eusebius of Caesarea fortunately preserved several of his writings in the form of fragmentary quotes.

In one particular quote, Aristobulus offers his understanding of God's wisdom based on his reading of Genesis and the book of Proverbs. In Fragment 5, preserved in Eusebius's *Praeparatio Evangelica*, Aristobulus discusses the God of Israel, creation, the seventh day, and the bringing into existence of light:

> And the same thing might be said metaphorically about wisdom also. For all light has its origin in it. And some belonging to the Peripatetic school have said that wisdom holds the place of a lantern; for as long as they follow it unremittingly, they will be calm through their whole life. And one of our ancestors, Solomon, said more clearly and better that wisdom existed before heaven and earth, which indeed agrees with what has been said.[56]

Aristobulus demonstrates the influence of the portrayal of personified wisdom in Proverbs upon his theological outlook. To him, the wisdom of God preexisted the formation of the heavens and the earth. He associates this wisdom with light and he indicates that wisdom is the source of all light.[57] This strongly suggests that Aristobulus viewed the wisdom of God as the agent of creation, the means through which God originated

---

54. Several scholars whose works attempt to trace the development of God's wisdom throughout Jewish literature overlook Proverbs 31 and its portrayal of Lady Wisdom's incarnation entirely—e.g., O'Boyle, *Wisdom Christology*, 20–24; Willett, *Wisdom Christology*, 11–13.

55. Collins, *Between Athens and Jerusalem*, 177; Bowley, "Aristobulus," 378.

56. *Praeparatio Evangelica* 13.12.10–11, in Collins, "Aristobulus," 2:841.

57. Kuschel, *Born before All Time?*, 201; Tobin, "Logos," 350.

all light. Furthermore, Aristobulus compares wisdom with the light that a lantern gives off and argues that those who follow wisdom will experience a calm life.

As the passage continues, Aristobulus closely associates the seventh day of God's creation with the activity of his sevenfold *logos*: "For, having set all things in order, he maintains and alters them so (in accordance with that order). And the legislation has shown plainly that the seventh day is legally binding for us as a sign of the sevenfold *logos* which is established around us, by which we have knowledge of human and divine matters."[58] God thus orders his creation with his *logos*, not unlike how he brings forth creation through his wisdom. Both *logos* and wisdom, for Aristobulus, perform similar functions of ordering God's cosmos.[59]

Since he depicts people following wisdom as well as assigning wisdom's existence before creation, it appears that Aristobulus regarded wisdom as a personification—a conclusion he likely derived from his reading of the book of Proverbs alongside the creation account in Genesis 1, where the act of creation takes place with the help of God's creative word.

THE BOOK OF SIRACH

The book of Sirach (otherwise known as Ben Sira or Ecclesiasticus) belongs to the Jewish intertestamental literature included in the Septuagint. Most scholars date Sirach to the beginning of the second century BCE, around the year 180.[60] One thing that becomes clear upon reading Sirach is that it is deeply indebted to the book of Proverbs, drawing upon its theology and structure quite heavily.[61] Several of the key themes expressed in Proverbs reappear in Sirach's portrayal of the subject of God's wisdom. Sirach interprets the wisdom of God in terms of the Torah's commandments and the fear of the Lord; "If you desire wisdom, keep the commandments, and the Lord will lavish her upon you" (1:26; see

---

58. *Praeparatio Evangelica* 13.12.12, in Collins, "Aristobulus," 2:841. Collins translated the noun *logos* as "principle" in her translation.

59. Tobin, "Logos," 350.

60. Crenshaw, "Book of Sirach," 613; Rybolt, *Sirach*, 5–6; Sinnott, *Personification of Wisdom*, 112.

61. Yoder, *Proverbs*, xxiv; Fox, *Proverbs 1–9*, 6; Sandelin, *Wisdom as Nourisher*, 27. Beentjes, "Full Wisdom," 149, remarks that scholars are unanimous in their observation that Proverbs can be detected in every portion of Sirach.

1:10). Wisdom is hidden with God, but available to all who obey the law (1:1–10).[62] The theme of wisdom dominates the book of Sirach, appearing in various forms more than ninety times in the document.[63]

Like the book of Proverbs, Sirach also personifies the wisdom of God as a female figure.[64] Lady Wisdom is a bride and nourishing mother (15:2); her children are those whom she teaches (4:11).[65] As a personification of God's wise interaction with creation, Lady Wisdom often blurs the lines between herself and God, so much that those who serve her serve the Holy One (4:14).[66] Even so, she portrays herself as obedient to the commands of the Creator (24:8). In addition to playing the role of bride and mother, personified wisdom is a teacher who utilizes strict discipline and testing (6:18–31). Those who take on her yoke are rewarded with rest (4:15), long life (1:12; 4:12), peace (1:18), and desirable goods (1:17).[67] Showing influence from Proverbs 9, Sirach describes the benefits of Lady Wisdom in terms of nourishing bread, water (15:3), and fruit (1:16; 24:19).[68]

One of the notable contributions to Wisdom's pilgrimage offered by Sirach is the portrayal of Wisdom as the law of the commandments: "All these are the book of the covenant of the Most High, the law that Moses commanded us" (24:23).[69] Wisdom, who remains personified throughout Sirach 24,[70] requests of Israel's God where she should abide, resulting

---

62. Beentjes, "Full Wisdom," 149; and Ceresko, *Old Testament Wisdom*, 127–28, rightly detect the influence of Job 28 and Proverbs 8 in Sir 1:1–10.

63. Rad, *Wisdom in Israel*, 242, argues that wisdom is the most prominent theme in the book of Sirach, even more prominent than the fear of the Lord.

64. Sinnott, *Personification of Wisdom*, 120–34; Harrington, *Jesus Ben Sira*, 103; Witte, "Key Aspects and Themes," 26; Dunn, *Christology in the Making*, 172.

65. Meyers et al., *Women in Scripture*, 551.

66. Ellis, *Gender in Ben Sira*, 80, draws attention to the Hebrew original of Sirach which states, "To serve God is to serve Wisdom herself" (4:14), thereby reinforcing the theology that personified wisdom is akin to God wisely interacting with his servants.

67. On the personification of wisdom in 1:17, wisdom's relationship with God, and the influence of Prov 9:1–6, see especially Di Lella, "Fear of the Lord as Wisdom," 124.

68. Sandelin, *Wisdom as Nourisher*, 27, observes that the fruit that Wisdom offers in Sir 24:17–21 has developed the imagery of Wisdom as a nourisher in Prov 9:1–6.

69. Rogers, "Overflows," 114–21. Perdue, "Cosmology," 461–62, astutely notes that Ben Sira is not the first to interpret wisdom as Torah, noting how the Torah psalms of Psalms 19 and 119 predate Ben Sira.

70. Muraoka, *Wisdom of Ben Sira*, 366, draws comparisons between personified wisdom's first-person speech in Sirach 24 and the portrayal of personified wisdom in Proverbs 8.

in her Creator commanding her to come down out of heaven so that she may pitch her tabernacle among Jacob, on earth (24:7–8).[71] Taking the role of the law of Moses, Wisdom promises whoever obeys her will not be put to shame (24:22).[72] While this gives the impression that, as the law of commandments, the wisdom of God is accessible to Israel, Sirach creates tension by asking, "Who can search out Wisdom?" (1:2–3). In fact, Lady Wisdom acknowledges that she held sway over every people and nation, not just the children of Israel (24:6).

Like the depictions of wisdom in Job 28, Psalm 104, and Proverbs, Sirach portrays wisdom's preexistence. She was created before all other things, making her the firstborn of God (1:4, 9; 24:9). Personified wisdom declares, "I came forth from the mouth of the Most High" (24:3), which likens her to God's word.[73] Wisdom refers to God as "my Creator" and "the Creator of all things" (24:8; 43:33).[74] She possessed a throne in heaven (24:4), indicating a ruling position. Having taken root in Zion, Lady Wisdom likens herself to a variety of plants/vegetation: a cedar, a cypress, a palm tree, rosebushes, an olive tree, a plane tree, cassia and camel's thorn, myrrh, a terebinth, and even a vine (24:12–17).[75] Even so, all wisdom is with God (1:1), since God is the source of wisdom.[76]

In a similar vein to how the book of Proverbs concludes its collection with a portrait of personified wisdom becoming incarnate in the Woman of Substance,[77] Sirach also ends with a depiction of Wisdom's incarnation, specifically in the high priest Simon ben Onias (50:1–24).[78] Simon,

71. Di Lella, "God and Wisdom," 13, argues that the depiction of personified wisdom in Sirach 24 draws upon Prov 8:4–36.

72. Reiterer, "Interpretation of the Wisdom Tradition," 225.

73. John Snaith observes that Ben Sira refers to the opening chapters of Genesis, where the creation of the universe by God occurs through a series of creative words. See his *Ecclesiasticus*, 121. See also Schmidt, *Wisdom, Cosmos, and Cultus*, 252–53; and Gilbert, "Ben Sira," 93–94, who both detect allusions to and influence from Genesis 1.

74. Schmidt, *Wisdom, Cosmos, and Cultus*, 238, astutely notes that Wisdom is a created entity, despite preexisting everything else. For an excellent overview of God in his role as Creator within Sirach, see Di Lella, "God and Wisdom," 4–8.

75. Burkes, "Choosing Life," 64, observes that the association of personified wisdom with the trees evokes the tree of life imagery from Proverbs, where the life-giving tree is another way of speaking about Lady Wisdom's value and benefits.

76. Skehan and Di Lella, *Wisdom of Ben Sira*, 138.

77. McKinlay, *Gendering Wisdom the Host*, 152, insists that the high priest Simon in Sirach 50 has particularly taken the place of the Woman of Worth of Proverbs 31.

78. Himmelfarb, "Wisdom of the Scribe," 97, argues that the high priest Simon "appears . . . almost as Wisdom's double." The most thorough study of the high priest Simon

by faithfully carrying out the temple functions, manifests the very same Wisdom who tabernacled among Jacob. In a way that is remarkably similar to the sages in Proverbs, who portrayed the Woman of Substance with intentional echoes to Wisdom's descriptions, Sirach deliberately illustrates the high priest with the very same language formerly used for personified wisdom.[79] For example, Simon the high priest pronounces glory (50:20; 24:1); situates himself in the midst of the people (50:5; 24:12); and is likened to a rosebush (50:8; 24:14), incense (50:9; 24:15), an olive tree (50:10; 24:14), a cypress tree (50:10; 24:13),[80] a cedar tree (50:12; 24:13), and a pleasing fragrance (50:15; 24:15).[81] What is noteworthy to consider is that while Lady Wisdom is incarnated into Jewish females in Proverbs 31, Sirach displays the incarnation of Wisdom in a prominent cultic figure of history—the high priest Simon.[82] Fletcher-Louis acknowledges that incarnational language is appropriate when concluding the theology of Sirach 50: "She is 'incarnate' in her avatar, Israel's high priest."[83] In his exhaustive study of Simon in Sirach, Schmidt draws a similar conclusion that the high priest is "the preeminent embodiment of Wisdom in the world."[84] In his recent commentary, Wilson argues that Simon's priestly role helps illustrates his portrayal as the incarnation of Lady Wisdom: "In performing his duties, the high priest essentially embodies wisdom, which according to 24:10 not only was established in Zion but also 'ministers' before God in the holy place."[85] By characterizing personified wisdom as becoming incarnate in Simon the high priest, Sirach underscores

---

as the incarnation of personified wisdom is Schmidt, *Wisdom, Cosmos, and Cultus*, 408–39. See also the helpful comments connecting the high priest with Lady Wisdom's activity in Perdue, *Wisdom Literature*, 152–55.

79. See the discussion in Mulder, *Simon the High Priest*, 333, 340.

80. Skehan and Di Lella, *Wisdom of Ben Sira*, 549.

81. For further parallels between personified wisdom and Simon, see the chart and discussion in Ellis, *Gender in Ben Sira*, 81–86.

82. See Schmidt, *Wisdom, Cosmos, and Cultus*, 439: "Ben Sira sees the high priest as one who transmits wisdom by his own embodiment of Wisdom." Gathercole, "Wisdom (Personified)," acknowledges Wisdom's incarnation in Simon, but attempts to play down her significance. See also the helpful exegesis in Kirk, *Man Attested by God*, 127–28.

83. Fletcher-Louis, "Cosmology," 112.

84. Schmidt, *Wisdom, Cosmos, and Cultus*, 439.

85. Wilson, *Wisdom of Sirach*, 523.

the importance of God's wise interactions among the daily temple service and priestly activities.[86]

To summarize, Sirach is a Jewish work that draws upon the influence of the book of Proverbs in order to impress the importance of God's wisdom, particularly identified as the law of Moses. Wisdom continues to be personified in Sirach, taking the roles of a bride, mother, and strict teacher. She existed before all creation—which she attributes to her Creator—and now she is obtainable in the form of the law. Her ongoing presence and involvement with Jacob are observable in the cultic activities of the high priest Simon ben Onias,[87] the human being in whom she became incarnate. Those who accept her discipline will find security, peace, and life.

BARUCH

The book of Baruch, like Sirach, is in the intertestamental collection of Jewish writings preserved in the Greek Septuagint. Baruch, which frames the destruction of the Jerusalem temple by the Babylonians in terms of Israel's rejection of wisdom, is a composite document that likely arrived at its final form sometime between the second century BCE and the first century CE.[88] While the unknown authors write from the perspective of what they think Baruch, the scribe of the sixth-century prophet Jeremiah, would have said in light of the events surrounding the temple's destruction,[89] they offer an important glimpse into their understanding of theodicy as it pertains to the acceptance or rejection of the wisdom of God.

Within this short five-chapter document, the relevant discussion of wisdom occurs in chapters 3 and 4. The third chapter records Baruch's prayer that laments the sins of Israel. Once the prayer reaches its conclusion, Baruch turns to address the children of Israel, summoning them to "hear the commandments of life ... give ear and learn wisdom" (3:9). Baruch rhetorically asks why Israel is in exile and counted among the dead (3:10–11), to which he firmly answers, "You have forsaken the fountain

---

86. On the support that Ben Sira offers towards the temple and the priesthood, see Wright, "Fear the Lord," 189–96.

87. McKinlay, *Gendering Wisdom the Host*, 153.

88. See the helpful discussion on dating in Saldarini, "Book of Baruch," 931–33.

89. Wacker, *Baruch*, 2.

of wisdom" (3:12).⁹⁰ Ascertaining wisdom's location is the next order of business, and Baruch facilitates this by encouraging his listeners to learn where wisdom is, where understanding is, and where strength is (3:14). What follows is a search for wisdom that seemingly echoes the structure of the wisdom poem in Job 28.⁹¹ Baruch asks, "Who has found her place? And who has entered her storehouses?" (3:15). The answer appears to be, unfortunately, that no one has found wisdom (3:31), no one has understood her paths or laid hold of her (3:20).⁹² Even those who sought after understanding did not learn the way to wisdom, nor give thought to her paths (3:23).⁹³ The language the author employs in order to illustrate the pursuit of wisdom indicates that she is a personification.⁹⁴

However, there is one who knows wisdom—the God of Israel. As the Creator of all things and he who knows all things, he found wisdom (3:32–35). Baruch then explains that God gave personified wisdom to Jacob, and she appeared on earth and lived among humanity (3:36–37). Like Sirach 24, Baruch unambiguously defines the way in which Wisdom was given to Jacob: "She is the book of the commandments of God, the law that endures forever" (4:1). Baruch's rhetorical goal appears to be that by encouraging readers to hold the law fast and walk in its commandments, they will encounter the elusive wisdom of God and come to possess life in the community.⁹⁵

In sum, Baruch equates God's personified wisdom with the law's commandments. By obeying the law, Israel will find access to wisdom, but she is inaccessible apart from this narrow focus. By framing wisdom in this manner, the author of Baruch can portray God's wisdom as both unavailable and available, while at the same time defining the strict means by which wisdom may be found—through the law of Moses. The wisdom

90. Wacker, *Baruch*, 43.

91. See the helpful chart in Henderson, "Inter-textual Dialogue," 44–45. Meyers et al., *Women in Scripture*, 552, argue that Baruch's presentation of wisdom is strongly reminiscent of Job 28 and the wisdom poems in Proverbs and Sirach.

92. On the rhetorical effect of this language and the manner in which the God of Israel has created an exception for his elect people, see Tibbertsma, "Bright Ecological Wisdom in Baruch," 158.

93. Wacker, *Baruch*, 52, observes that Baruch's perspective is different from Ben Sira, who portrays personified wisdom as gaining influence among the peoples of the world before taking root in Jerusalem.

94. Nemes, *Trinity and Incarnation*, 161.

95. Burkes, "Choosing Life," 275, notes the subtle yet important distinction between the individual life available through wisdom (according to Ben Sira) and the national life of the law-abiding community (in Baruch).

of God within Baruch shows discernable signs of personification,[96] although she has now coalesced with the commandments that God gave to Israel.

WISDOM OF SOLOMON

The final noteworthy book dealing with the wisdom of God within the intertestamental collection of Septuagintal Jewish works is the Wisdom of Solomon, also known as the Book of Wisdom. The unknown author of Wisdom of Solomon composed it in Greek, probably in Alexandria, Egypt. It was written sometime between the first century BCE and the early first century CE, with most modern scholars favoring the earlier date.[97] Among all the Jewish wisdom books surveyed thus far, the depiction of personified wisdom is at its fullest within the Wisdom of Solomon, taking the central focus even at the expense of the God of Israel.[98] Not only is Lady Wisdom active in the present among the friends of God and prophets (7:27), but her activity throughout Jewish history is documented. She was present in the lives of Adam, Cain, Noah, Abraham, Lot, Jacob, Joseph, and the generation of the wilderness as recounted in the books of Exodus and Numbers (Wis 10–19).[99] The author of Wisdom of Solomon seems intent on conveying the notion that the wisdom for which King Solomon prayed is the same wisdom that the God of Israel has been using to interact with his people from the beginning.[100]

In fact, Wisdom of Solomon traces the interaction of wisdom and the people of God to the moment of creation. In 9:1–2, Solomon prays to the Creator God and praises him for making all things with his word

---

96. Pace Tibbertsma, "Ambiguous Way to Wisdom," 95.

97. Zurawski, "Wisdom of Solomon," 338–40; Sinnott, *Personification of Wisdom*, 142. Mazzinghi, *Wisdom*, 28–30, has quite recently argued for a composition date toward the end of the reign of the emperor Augustus (30 BCE–14 CE).

98. Collins, *Between Athens and Jerusalem*, 182. Witherington, *Jesus the Sage*, 109, describes the figure of Wisdom in Wisdom of Solomon as a moving beyond personification "to a hypostasis," but this is blatant historical anachronism, reading fourth-century Christian definitions of an independent hypostatization into a Second Temple Jewish work. Sinnott, *Personification of Wisdom*, 154, offers a more level-headed assessment: "Wisdom as delineated in the Wisdom of Solomon is a product of the Hebrew tradition. She remains firmly grounded in the Hebrew tradition while being transformed into a Jewish-Hellenistic figure in keeping with the setting in which she now functions."

99. Rybolt, *Wisdom*, 34–37.

100. Sinnott, *Personification of Wisdom*, 159.

(*logos*) and making humanity with his wisdom (*sophia*). In doing so, word and wisdom effectively function as synonymous categories when referencing God's instrumental agents of creation (Pss 33:6; 104:24; Prov 3:19–20; Jer 10:12; 51:15; Wis 18:14–16).[101] The role of personified wisdom in creation is expressed in ways that clarify her overlapping role with the word through which the God of Israel created all things. Lady Wisdom is the "fashioner of all things" (Wis 7:22), "the active cause of all things" (8:5), and "the fashioner of what exists" (8:6; 14:2). Despite all these grand declarations concerning her role as an agent in creation, the author of Wisdom of Solomon is careful to attribute the role of Creator to God alone: "He created all things so that they might exist" (1:14); "God created humanity . . . he made him to be his image" (2:23); and "the author of beauty created them" (13:3).[102] Like Proverbs and Sirach, the Wisdom of Solomon portrays Israel's God as the Creator who used personified wisdom as his agent in the wise ordering of all things.[103]

The personification of wisdom into a female figure is a regular feature in the Wisdom of Solomon.[104] Drawing on her role in creation as an agent, personified wisdom functions as a mother of all good things (7:12). Solomon describes her as a figure whom he loved, sought after, and took as a bride (8:2). Since the Creator God gave her a noble birth, she is also a daughter (8:3). Additionally, she plays the role of a teacher who conveys self-control, prudence, justice, and courage to her pupils (8:7). Lady Wisdom is one with whom one may find rest and companionship (8:16). When the author portrays the involvement of wisdom throughout the history of Israel in chapter 10, she is emphatically expressed in the Greek text with the intensive use of the third-person pronoun ("She herself").[105] The agency to which God gives personified wisdom is evident in the various descriptions of her activity. It was Lady Wisdom who saved the earth

---

101. Nemes, *Trinity and Incarnation*, 160; Tobin, "Logos," 350. For discussion and several examples of the overlapping functions between *logos* and *sophia* in Wisdom of Solomon, see Webster, "Sophia: Engendering Wisdom," 76.

102. The author of Wisdom of Solomon is careful to describe the Creator with the masculine title *technitin* ("fashioner"), but when God's title is shared with personified wisdom, she bears the feminine title *techynitis*.

103. Kolarcik, "Book of Wisdom," 516; Sinnott, *Personification of Wisdom*, 155.

104. Sinnott, *Personification of Wisdom*, 142, observes that personified wisdom in the Wisdom of Solomon would be a familiar figure from the biblical wisdom texts of Job 28; Prov 1:20–33; 8:1–36; 9:1–6; Sir 24:1–33; Bar 3:9—4:4.

105. Winston, *Wisdom of Solomon*, 212; Rybolt, *Wisdom*, 34; Reider, *Book of Wisdom*, 132. The intensive use of the third-person feminine pronoun appears in Wis 10:1, 5, 6, 10, 13, 15.

during the flood (10:4), who delivered the righteous man (10:6), and who descended with Joseph into the pit (10:13). Her involvement is indicative of her role as a savior among the people of God.[106]

When it comes to describing the relationship between the Creator God and personified wisdom, the author spares no expense or effort. In 7:22–23, there is a list of twenty-one attributes of wisdom, which is triple the number seven, suggesting that this list was intended as an all-encompassing portrayal of a personification expressing God's wise interactions.[107] Here are some of her most noteworthy attributes: intelligent, holy, unique (*monogenes*), mobile, loving the good, steadfast, all-powerful, and overseeing all. Shortly after this list is another catena of metaphors closely associating Wisdom and the wise God whom she personifies.[108] She is the breath of the power of God, a pure emanation of the Almighty's glory, a reflection of eternal light, a mirror of God's work, and an image (*eikon*) of his goodness (7:25–26).[109] Lady Wisdom is enthroned alongside God, indicating that she is with God and comes from God as a gift (9:4, 9). Reminiscent of God giving Solomon wisdom as an answer to prayer in 1 Kings 3, Israel's God may send Lady Wisdom forth from heaven in order that she may labor and teach whoever is willing to learn (Wis 9:10). Last, personified wisdom shares remarkably similar functions with God's Spirit (1:7; 7:23–24, 27; 8:1; 9:2; 12:1), she stands in parallel to the Spirit (9:17), and Wisdom is even occasionally designated as the Spirit: "wisdom is a kindly spirit" (1:6; 7:7, 22).

To summarize, the author of Wisdom of Solomon portrays personified wisdom as active throughout the history of the people of God. She is the agent of the act of creation, and she continues to play a role in rescuing, saving, and delivering creation from peril. She takes on the roles of bride, daughter, mother, teacher, and savior. As the personification of the active God, Lady Wisdom shares his attributes, as well as the characteristics of God's word and God's Spirit. Wisdom of Solomon is indicative

---

106. Sinnott, *Personification of Wisdom*, 152, remarks: "By personifying Wisdom as savior, [the author] is interpreting their sufferings in the light of the sufferings of their Israelite ancestors."

107. Clarke, *Wisdom of Solomon*, 54. The number seven regularly symbolizes completeness in Jewish literature.

108. Geyer, *Wisdom of Solomon*, 31, notes that personified wisdom is "so closely connected to the being of God."

109. Meyers et al., *Women in Scripture*, 551, insightfully point out: "If Woman Wisdom is not quite God ... neither is there any way for the reader to distinguish her from God."

of a growing effort to increasingly personify the wisdom of God within Second Temple Jewish literature.

GENESIS APOCRYPHON (1Q20)

Among the earliest scrolls recovered from the caves near Qumran between 1947 and 1956 was the Aramaic text that scholars designate as 1Q20, the Genesis Apocryphon. Attempts to date this document are complicated by arguments proposing 1Q20's possible relationship with earlier portions of 1 Enoch and the book of Jubilees. Therefore, a safe range of possible dates of its composition extends between the second and first centuries BCE.[110] The Genesis Apocryphon is a nonbiblical scroll that retells many stories from the book of Genesis, including accounts of Lamech, Noah, and Abraham. In the scroll's retelling of Abraham's life, we can clearly discern the influence of the book of Proverbs, particularly the poetic tradition in which personified wisdom becomes incarnate in exceptional human women (Prov 31:10–31). Of particular interest for our current study is the way in which the Genesis Apocryphon illustrates Sarah—Abraham's wife—as Lady Wisdom's incarnation in three separate instances over the course of the reimagination of the Genesis account.[111]

First, the Genesis Apocryphon portrays Sarah embodying the characteristic of Lady Wisdom from Prov 3:13–18, where she offers and extends life, specifically involving the imagery of a tree. In 1Q20 column 19, the author of the Apocryphon recounts one of Abraham's dreams in which Sarah is illustrated as a date palm and Abraham as a cedar tree. Within the dream, the date palm symbolizing Sarah speaks out and rescues Abraham when some men attempt to chop down the cedar (19.15–17). Thus, Sarah's decisive boldness and courage save the life of Abraham with remarkable similarity to the earlier portrayal of Lady Wisdom in Proverbs as a life-giving tree. The wisdom of God formerly identified as a tree of life is now recognized to be Sarah.

Second, the author of the Genesis Apocryphon confers upon Sarah a catena of praises indicating her greatness and surpassing value (1Q20 20.2–7). This description of Sarah recalls the superlative of personified wisdom in Prov 3:14–15, where Lady Wisdom is illustrated as more

---

110. For a detailed discussion of the Apocryphon's dating and its relationship with Jubilees and 1 Enoch, see Machiela, *Genesis Apocryphon*, 7–17.

111. I am indebted to the insights of Lipscomb, "She Is My Sister," 319–47.

profitable than silver and gold, more precious than jewels, and greater than anything desirable. Craig Evans and Anthony Lipscomb have convincingly identified the lengthier passage in Proverbs where several praises are heaped upon the Woman of Substance (Prov 31:10–31) as the biggest influence on the Apocryphon's portrayal of Sarah here.[112] The author notes how the Egyptian ruler Hirqanos admires several of Sarah's features, including her pretty face, her lovely hair and eyes, the pleasantness of her nose, the beauty of her face and arms, the perfection of her hands, and similar compliments of her feet and thighs (1Q20 20.2–6). Furthermore, he lauds Sarah's beauty in comparable language to the praise of Wisdom in Prov 3:15: "No virgin or bride entering the bridal chamber is more beautiful than her" (1Q20 20.6). At the conclusion of his list of praises of Sarah, he acknowledges that despite her beauty, "she possesses great wisdom" (20.7). Sarah is thus able to embody the superlatives that formerly described personified wisdom because Sarah has that very wisdom in herself.

Last, the Apocryphon depicts Sarah acting as the sister of Abraham, greatly elaborating on the story in Gen 12:13. The trick wherein Sarah plays the part of Abraham's sister is alluded to on three separate occasions in the Genesis Apocryphon's retelling (1Q20 19.18–20; 20.9–10, 26–27). In the first two occurrences, Sarah refers to Abraham as her brother, while the final occurrence contains the king's rebuke to Abraham because "You told me, 'She is my sister.'" The reason the author of 1Q20 gives such heightened attention to the sister motif is best explained when we observe the father instructing his son in Proverbs to "say to Wisdom, 'You are my sister'" (Prov 7:4). In this way, Abraham's ruse in which he refers to Sarah as his sister effectually identifies her with Lady Wisdom herself; Sarah is human incarnation of the wisdom of God. Since Sarah already possesses the characteristics of personified wisdom, the Genesis Apocryphon has essentially put a positive spin on the original story in Genesis, which appeared to be morally questionable.

In sum, the Genesis Apocryphon demonstrates the impact of the portrayal of personified wisdom within the book of Proverbs by illustrating the wife of Abraham, Sarah, as the embodiment of wisdom. The author of the Apocryphon draws upon several characteristics of Lady Wisdom in Proverbs: the ability to impart life through the symbolism of a tree, Wisdom's incomparable value, and her identification as a sister.

---

112. Evans, "Genesis Apocryphon," 163; Lipscomb, "She Is My Sister," 335.

The author has applied each of these descriptors to the person of Sarah. In doing so, Sarah imitates the Woman of Substance from Prov 31:10–31, where Jewish women in the Persian period appear as the incarnation of wisdom. The portrayal of Sarah also explicitly indicates that she is the bearer of great wisdom, for wisdom is in her. By recapitulating the theology of personified wisdom's incarnation from the book of Proverbs, 1Q20 is the first Aramaic text in which the doctrine of the incarnation appears in Jewish sources.

HYMN TO THE CREATOR (11Q5)

The eleventh cave near Qumran that bore a cache of manuscripts contained a particularly interesting document that pertains to our study of Wisdom's pilgrimage. Within the twenty-eight-columned text that scholars have categorized as 11Q5 (also known as 11QPs^a) is a nonbiblical hymn in column 26, written in Hebrew. Specialists have dubbed this short passage as "Hymn to the Creator." There seems to be a consensus in dating 11Q5 to the first half of the first century CE.[113] The hymn drew heavily on the language and structure of poetry within the Hebrew Bible. After the author of the hymn offers praise to YHWH and addresses him as the Holy One to each generation, we can observe the personification of several of God's attributes. God's "majesty" goes on before him (line 9). Following God's majesty are his grace and truth, which surround his presence (line 10). A further trio of personifications function as the foundation of God's throne, namely truth, justice, and righteousness (lines 10–11). While these poetic descriptions of God bear a recognizable influence from similar personifications within the book of Psalms, the Hymn to the Creator offers a description of how the earth came to be formed that is drawn from a different book of the Hebrew Bible. In lines 13–14, we read: "Blessed is the one who makes the earth by his power, establishing the world *with his wisdom*, with his understanding he stretched out the heavens."[114] This is yet another reference to YHWH bringing creation into existence by means of his wisdom functioning as an instrumental agent.

---

113. Sanders, *Psalms Scroll*, 89–91; more recently in "Modern History," 404; Grant, "Hymn to the Creator," 1.

114. My translation.

What makes this text noteworthy is that the portrayal of God creating with his wisdom is not drawn from early Jewish wisdom texts like Job, Psalms, or Proverbs, but rather lines 13–14 are a direct quote from the Hebrew text of Jer 10:12. Since God's wisdom is set in parallel with his understanding and his power, this suggests that we are still in the interpretive realm of personified attributes.[115] The proximity of the earlier personifications (majesty, grace, truth, justice, and righteousness) strengthens the likelihood that the author understood God's wisdom along the same vein, as *personified* wisdom.

In sum, the Hymn to the Creator in 11Q5 demonstrates that the influence of portrayals of the wisdom of God acting as an agent of the formation of the universe was not limited to the sapiential Jewish wisdom texts. Even the prophetic work of Jeremiah was drawn upon in order to express the function of personified wisdom as the instrumental agent of YHWH's creative acts.

PHILO

The collective works of Philo Judaeus—the Greek-speaking Jew living in Alexandria, Egypt—are more voluminous than all the books of the New Testament combined. Philo's authorial prowess, demonstrated in his fifty-two extant treatises,[116] is even more impressive when we acknowledge that he uses the Greek noun for "wisdom" (*sophia*) more than two hundred times. The necessity, therefore, to examine Philo's writings as they pertain to his understanding of the wisdom of God in the first half of the first century CE is rather apparent.

Since wisdom comes from God, Philo portrays wisdom's personification as a female figure as it relates to the God of Israel.[117] Wisdom is the wife of the Creator God—the father of all things. She is also a personified mother, parent, daughter of God, and nurse.[118] When Philo allegorically comments on why a man shall leave his father and mother in order to cleave to his wife, he describes how this father actually is to be identified as "the God of the universe, and the mother of all things, namely, the

---

115. Brewer-Boydston, "They Walk in Wisdom or Folly," 330.
116. Sterling, "Philo," 1065.
117. Mattila, "Wisdom," 108.
118. *Cher.* 49; *Ebr.* 30–31; *Det.* 54; *Fug.* 51, 109.

virtue and wisdom of God."[119] Upon taking the role of a mother, Lady Wisdom offers nourishment and divine food in the form of nursing.[120] Humanity regards Wisdom as their mother and as the spouse within the family.[121] She offers the necessary and sweet drink to those who will drink from her goodness and virtue.[122] She is the delight of God, and the feeling is mutual since God also is the delight of wisdom.[123]

When detailing Lady Wisdom's role in creation, Philo draws upon the influence of Proverbs, Sirach, and perhaps the Wisdom of Solomon in order to portray God creating through the agency of his wisdom.[124] In doing so, Philo continues to depict personified wisdom as a female figure.[125] For example, Wisdom takes upon the role of a mother "through whom the universe was brought to completion."[126] Since the Creator God is the father of all things, personified wisdom functions as a mother "through whom the universe arrived at its origin."[127] Lady Wisdom, however, never creates on her own; Philo is careful to reserve the role of Creator of all things for God the Father.[128] As the personified agent through whom God made all things, Philo naturally regards wisdom as preexisting and with the Father in the beginning.

Being a Jewish interpreter of Scriptures, Philo often comments on the activity of the wisdom of God within the history of Israel. One of the ways in which Philo finds wisdom present and active is in the exodus from Egypt narratives when God gave the Israelites manna from heaven. For example, Philo writes that "God, the only cause and giver, rains down food from heaven without the cooperation of any other person," followed

---

119. *Leg.* 2.49.

120. *Det.* 115–16.

121. *Praem.* 59–61.

122. *Ebr.* 112.

123. E.g., *Somn.* 2.242.

124. On the influence of biblical wisdom literature on Philo, see Cohen, *Maccabees to the Mishnah*, 42. Both Beentjes, "Philo of Alexandria," 63–78, and Sterling, "Interpreter of Moses," 415–35, find evidence that Philo had thoroughly read Sirach. On the influence of the Alexandrian Wisdom of Solomon on Philo's thinking, see Schäfer, *Jewish Mysticism*, 159.

125. Hadas-Lebel, *Philo of Alexandria*, 188, points to *Ebr.* 31 where Philo explicitly personifies Wisdom as one who speaks for herself, followed by a direct quote from Prov 8:22.

126. *Det.* 54.

127. *Fug.* 109.

128. *Leg.* 3.10; *Her.* 205.

by a quote from Exod 16:4. Philo immediately explains his motivation for citing the book of Exodus: "Now what nourishment can the Scriptures properly say is rained down except heavenly wisdom?"[129] Peder Borgen, in his examination of Philo's argument, observes in this passage that Philo combines wisdom, Torah, and manna: "The manna that rains down from heaven is the heavenly Sophia, sent from above."[130] The same theme reappears when Philo again cites Exod 16:4 and follows the quotation by saying, "You see that the soul is nourished not on earthly and corruptible food, but on the reasons that God rains down out of his sublime and pure nature."[131] This all-nourishing food, Philo elsewhere states, is the "food of wisdom."[132] Essentially, Philo regards the bread from heaven that nourished the children of Israel in the past and continues to nourish humanity in the present as none other than the wisdom of God.

Although Philo has much to say about God's personified wisdom, he speaks far more frequently about the *logos*, the intermediary between God and the material realm.[133] Many scholars rightly note that Philo seems to intentionally depict the *logos* with characteristics and attributes similar to the wisdom of God.[134] Having already pointed out that wisdom is the personified agent through whom God made the universe, the *logos* shares the same functions: God "created the universe and raised up the first human being from the earth with the same word."[135] God created this world, according to Philo, through the agency of his *logos*.[136] Sometimes Philo will go so far as to outright identify wisdom and word: "Now the wisdom of God is the word of God."[137] In other places, however, Philo illustrates wisdom and word as coming forth from one another. In one instance, the *logos* is said to proceed forth from wisdom: "And the divine word, like a river, flows forth from wisdom as from a spring."[138] Yet, in

---

129. *Mut.* 259.

130. Borgen, *Gospel of John*, 62.

131. *Leg.* 3.162.

132. *Congr.* 174.

133. Niehoff, *Philo of Alexandria*, 217, remarks that this definition of Philo's *logos* is the broad consensus among modern scholars specializing in the literature of Philo.

134. E.g., Cohen, *Maccabees to the Mishnah*, 82; Harris, *Prologue and Gospel*, 151; Tobin, "Logos," 350.

135. *Sacr.* 8.

136. *Cher.* 127.

137. *Leg.* 1.65.

138. *Somn.* 2.242.

another instance, the *logos* is described as the fountain of wisdom.¹³⁹ Ultimately, Philo's obsession with discussing the *logos*, which appears more than 1,400 times in his works, overshadows his interest in the personified wisdom of God. For Philo, the *logos* not only overlaps God's wisdom but also shifts the emphasis in the way that a Greek-speaking Jew speaks about the interaction of God in the world in the first century CE.

Philo not only presents the wisdom of God as a personification and agent in creation, but he also identifies several females figures within the history of Israel as Wisdom in ways that indicate an understanding of Wisdom's incarnation.¹⁴⁰ Without any discernable awareness of the Genesis Apocryphon, Philo illustrates Sarah, the wife of Abraham and the mother of Isaac, as Wisdom herself on numerous occasions.¹⁴¹ Philo discusses the meaning of Isaac's name, and in doing so his mother, Sarah, is called *Sophia*: "When God eradicated the pain from wisdom, he gave rejoicing as an offspring."¹⁴² The identification of personified wisdom with Sarah is even more explicit when Philo declares, "Do you not see that dominant Wisdom Sarah says, 'For whosoever shall hear it will rejoice with me.'"¹⁴³ Sarah is here clearly acknowledged to be God's wisdom to the point where wisdom does the speaking for virtuous Sarah. Elsewhere, Philo describes the mother of Isaac as "motherless wisdom"¹⁴⁴ and even "wisdom from heaven above."¹⁴⁵ In another example, Philo recalls Sarah telling Abraham to bear children with her handmaiden: "And here we are to admire Wisdom . . . she brought forth no child."¹⁴⁶ Within the same tractate, Philo characterizes this handmaiden as "the handmaiden of Wisdom."¹⁴⁷ Furthermore, God can calls the names of the wise man and Wisdom "Abraham and Sarah."¹⁴⁸ When Philo quotes Gen 15:10, where

---

139. *Fug.* 1.97. Johnson, "Jesus, the Wisdom of God," 287, summarizes Philo's use of personified wisdom and personified *logos*: "At times Philo identified them; at times Sophia was the source of Logos; and at times it was the other way around."

140. Laporte, "Philo in the Tradition of Wisdom," 117; Dunn, "Incarnation," 34.

141. Sly, *Philo's Perception of Women*, 151–52; Sandelin, *Wisdom as Nourisher*, 97–98; Laporte, "Philo in the Tradition of Wisdom," 117. Tobin, "Logos," 355, appears tone deaf when he suggests that Philo never identified wisdom with a human being.

142. *Det.* 124; *Ebr.* 59–62.

143. *Leg.* 2.82.

144. *QG* 4.145.

145. *Fug.* 166–67.

146. *Congr.* 12–13.

147. *Congr.* 9.

148. *Cher.* 9–10; *Her.* 61–62; *QG* 3.21–22. See also the comments on the marriage of

God says that Sarah shall bring forth a son, Philo immediately interprets this passage by replacing Sarah with the wisdom from heaven: "Wisdom shall bring forth joy."[149] Even the death of Sarah, who Abraham mourned, is understood by Philo as the mourning of wisdom.[150] Based on this evidence, Hadas-Lebel summarizes Philo's portrayal of the matriarch Sarah as the embodiment and representation of the wisdom of God.[151]

Sarah is not the only woman in whom Philo articulates Wisdom's incarnation. Another woman, Rebekah, appears to also function as the embodiment of the wisdom of God, according to Philo. The figure of Rebekah is said to have "taken the vessel of wisdom into her arm from a higher place" to the point where Philo can outright call her "the daughter of God, Wisdom."[152] This identification appears again when Philo names the wisdom that God sends from above as the queen and mistress Rebekah.[153] Dorothy Sly has drawn attention to the way that Philo illustrates Rebekah like Sarah/Wisdom and concluded that Rebekah "sometimes represents... wisdom itself."[154]

In addition to depicting Sarah and Rebekah as human incarnations of God's wisdom, Philo identifies the figures of Leah and Zipporah with the same theology. Leah and Zipporah are characterized as the wives of loving husbands who are "the lovers of Wisdom."[155] On one occasion, Philo associates Leah with the person of Sarah/Wisdom, suggesting that the wisdom of God can become incarnate in successive women.[156] Jean Laporte aptly summarizes the appearances of the personified wisdom embodied in these noteworthy women from Israel's history as the

---

Abraham with Wisdom in Hadas-Lebel, *Philo of Alexandria*, 191.

149. *Mut.* 264.

150. *QG* 4.73. See the discussion in Niehoff, *Philo of Alexandria*, 133.

151. Hadas-Lebel, *Philo of Alexandria*, 178.

152. *Post.* 146; *Fug.* 51; *QG* 4.97. Laporte, "Philo in the Tradition of Wisdom," 118. Sly, *Philo's Perception of Women*, 158.

153. *Congr.* 36–37; *Fug.* 166. See also the discussion in Sandelin, *Wisdom as Nourisher*, 99.

154. Sly, *Philo's Perception of Women*, 157–58.

155. *Cher.* 41; *Post.* 77–78. In *Cher.* 41 Philo names all four ladies as the wives of male lovers of Wisdom, their husbands: "Sarah is princess and guide, Rebecca is perseverance in what is good; Leah again is virtue, fainting and weary at the long continuance of exertion, which every foolish man declines, and avoids, and repudiates; and Zipporah, the wife of Moses, is virtue, mounting up from earth to heaven."

156. *Congr.* 22–33; Sly, *Philo's Perception of Women*, 166. See also *Post.* 135.

"extra-temporal existence" of wisdom.[157] With this nuanced and well-developed understanding of the wisdom of God, Philo demonstrates his indebtedness to the portrayals of the incarnation of Wisdom in Proverbs 31 and Sirach 50. The portraits of Sarah, Rebekah, Leah, and Zipporah act as sequential incarnations of Lady Wisdom.

To summarize, Philo Judaeus speaks frequently about the wisdom of God in his writings. Demonstrating influences from the previous Jewish wisdom books, Philo personifies wisdom as a wife, daughter, parent, and nurse. She shares many characteristics with the *logos*, and the two are often identified. Philo is far more interested in the *logos* than the wisdom of God, but both concepts are extremely meaningful to Philo's outlook concerning the way Israel's God interacts with creation. Personified wisdom is the bread from heaven that offers true nourishment. Although personified wisdom is a mother through whom God created all things, she has also come down to earth to embody several virtuous women: Sarah, Rebekah, Leah, and Zipporah—all of whom Philo identifies as *sophia*. His theology offers an important glimpse into first-century Jewish speculation of the wisdom of God as it pertains to God the Father on one hand and to humanity on the other.

THE *PARABLES* OF 1 ENOCH

The pilgrimage of the wisdom of God is not limited to the wisdom literature of Judaism, for the authors of 1 Enoch utilize the genre of Jewish apocalyptic in order to convey their understanding of wisdom's significance. The composite document 1 Enoch was written over the course of hundreds of years, and the relevant section for our study is the *Book of Parables* (1 En. 37–71).[158] Scholars argue for a composition date of the *Parables* sometime around the turn of the era but not limited to the period after the destruction of the Jerusalem temple in 70 CE.[159] The Enochic *Book of Parables* offers an apocalyptic perspective on wisdom,

---

157. Laporte, "Philo in the Tradition of Wisdom," 116; followed by Sandelin, *Wisdom as Nourisher*, 99.

158. The alternative designation that scholars use for this section of 1 Enoch is "The Similitudes."

159. See Knibb, "Enoch, Similitudes of," 587; Isaac, "1 (Ethiopic Apocalypse of) Enoch," 7; Bautch, "Enoch, First Book of," 263. More recently, Bauckham, *Son of Man*, 1:267–85, argues that the *Parables* of Enoch are to be more accurately dated between the late first century to the early second century CE.

particularly as it relates to speculation surrounding the figure called "son of man."

In 1 Enoch 42, the author details personified wisdom's descent from heaven and her subsequent ascent back into the heavens. Wisdom was unable to find a place for her to dwell (42:1). She came down out of heaven in order that she might find a dwelling among humanity, but she found no such place to reside, concluding with her return to heaven (42:2).[160] As a result, another personification, Iniquity, left her rooms and comfortably resided among the people (42:3). The author of 1 Enoch 42 conveys with this descent and ascent motif the rejection of personified wisdom by the children of humanity, resulting in the inaccessibility of wisdom and a consequential judgment in the form of iniquity personified. Wisdom—once available—is now residing permanently in heaven among the angels, suggesting that she is out of humanity's reach.

The next significant section concerning the wisdom of God (1 En. 48–49) details her close association with a figure called the "son of man."[161] Within these chapters, Enoch describes the events that he witnessed taking place in the heavenly throne room. Wisdom takes the form of numerous fountains of water that surround another fount, the fountain of righteousness (48:1). The author depicts God's wisdom not only as a fountain but also as actively flowing like water, an image suggesting a revelatory intention (49:1).[162] Those who drink of this water will be filled with God's wisdom. Where are these fountains of wisdom to be located? It is the "son of man" figure who reveals this wisdom to the righteous, namely, those who hate the world and its ways of life (48:7). Wisdom is even illustrated as embodying that "son of man": "In him dwells the spirit of wisdom" (49:3).[163] Nickelsburg and VanderKam carefully observe that

---

160. Nickelsburg and VanderKam, *1 Enoch 2*, 140, rightly note that Wisdom's return to heaven is later explained—she is residing in the person of the Son of Man, indicating that this initial reference to wisdom in 1 Enoch 42 anticipates the further discussion in chapters 48–49.

161. I am careful not to treat "son of man" as a title in the context of 1 Enoch 37–71. Ethiopic has no definite article nor emphatic state, so it is unlikely that the author of the *Parables* intended the "son of man" figure to be anything more than a reference to a mortal, a human being. See the thorough study of the meaning of "son of man" in 1 Enoch in Bauckham, *Son of Man*, ch. 4.

I do regard "Son of Man" as having solidified into a functional title within the Gospel of John.

162. Macaskill, *Revealed Wisdom*, 63–64.

163. We are probably dealing with an *empowering* function of God's wisdom rather than the sort of *incarnation* that we observed in Proverbs, Sirach, Genesis Apocryphon,

while the passage does not identify the "son of man" *as wisdom*, the two are closely associated.[164] Bearing the empowerment of God's wisdom, the "son of man" figure exercises insight, instruction, and strength, all prerogatives that formerly belonged to God but are now shared with this "son of man." Furthermore, the "son of man" figure can know secret things and issue forth judgment, two further prerogatives that God imparts to his chosen one (49:4).[165] Enoch even likens an unfailing glory in the presence of that "son of man" with the Wisdom who has been poured out like water (49:1).

As we have observed, the *Book of Parables* in 1 Enoch offers two relevant passages concerning the activity of the wisdom of God. On one hand, personified wisdom came down to earth, was rejected by humanity, and returned to heaven, thereby making herself inaccessible. On the other hand, the wisdom-empowered "son of man" reveals God's wisdom to righteous persons. This indicates that the wisdom of God is indeed available, but only through God's authorized human intermediary—Enoch's "son of man." The author of the *Book of Parables* seems to be comfortable with these two paradoxical emphases regarding the availability of the wisdom of God, being in one sense inaccessible to those who reject her and available through the highly authorized "son of man," in whom wisdom dwells.

JUDAISM IN THE TANNAITIC AND AMORAIC PERIODS

The Jewish Tannaitic period covers the years 10–220 CE and the subsequent Amoraic period extends until the year 500. These two eras will serve as our final body of Jewish literature pertaining to the pilgrimage of the wisdom of God. During this period, the rabbis continued to speculate about the role of personified wisdom in accounts of creation, but at this stage in the development, they also stressed the identification of wisdom with the Torah.[166] Since the study of the Torah was a regular part

---

and Philo.

164. Nickelsburg and VanderKam, *1 Enoch 2*, 170.

165. Villiers, "Revealing the Secrets," 54, notes that although the Son of Man is exceptionally wise, he receives his wisdom from God.

166. Kittel, "λέγω, λόγος, κτλ.," 136; Epp, "Wisdom, Torah, Word," 133. The seeds of this identification were already laid in Sir 24:23 and Bar 4:1–2, where these authors portrayed personified wisdom as embodying herself in the law of the commandments.

of Jewish life, it is only natural that the wisdom of God that is identified as Torah is perceived as readily available to all who seek it.[167]

The portrayal of personified wisdom in Proverbs 8 functioned as the most influential text in linking wisdom with Torah. It became commonplace for Jewish exegetes during this period to read Prov 8:22 ("YHWH made me the *beginning* of his work") and detect a subtle allusion to the word *beginning* in Gen 1:1 ("In the *beginning* God created the heavens and the earth.").[168] This led to the rabbis granting the Torah the qualities and characteristics of wisdom, including preexistence, the role as an intermediary in creation, and a prehistory.[169] The Torah even underwent a personification, just like the personification of wisdom. The Torah also took the role of the heavenly bride who sought the love of humanity.[170] Although Proverbs portrays personified wisdom as a tree of life, "The Law is the tree of life for everyone who studies it," according to the Targum Neofiti. This theme also appears in Sipre Deuteronomy, a document produced by the school of Rabbi Ishmael around 100 CE: "As water gives life to the world, so do the words of Torah give life to the world" (84a).[171] Hillel, the first-century founder of a pharisaical school bearing his name, offered a summation of personified wisdom's purpose in Proverbs 3: "More Torah? More life!"[172] According to Genesis Rabbah, a fifth-century Palestinian document drawing upon earlier traditions, the proselyte to Judaism will find the "bread of Torah" in Israel, which develops the imagery from Prov 9:5 where personified wisdom offers bread in the form of her teachings (Gen. Rab. 54:1).

Just as personified wisdom preexisted the creation that God brought into existence through her, so too did the Tannaitic sages depict the Torah as preexisting and functioning as the blueprint of creation. After noticing that the word "beginning" appeared in both Prov 8:22 and Gen 1:1, some Jews speculated that the law of Moses, which was closely associated with God's wisdom, could justifiably be read into the opening verse of Genesis. The important work Genesis Rabbah preserves a noteworthy midrashic reading on Gen 1:1:

---

167. Tropper, "Wisdom in Rabbinic Interpretation," 205–7.
168. Strawn, "Bĕ-rē' šît," 358–87.
169. Schechter, *Aspects of Rabbinic Theology*, 127.
170. Schechter, *Aspects of Rabbinic Theology*, 135.
171. Maher, "Some Aspects of Torah," 318.
172. m. 'Abot 2:7; Maher, "Some Aspects of Torah," 320.

> In human practice, when a mortal king builds a palace, he builds it not with his own skill but with the skill of an architect. The architect, moreover, does not build it out of his head, but he employs plans and diagrams to know how to arrange the chambers and the wicket doors. So, God consulted the Torah and created the world, while the Torah declares, "In the beginning God created (Gen 1:1)," 'beginning' is referring to the Torah, as in the verse, "The Lord made me at the beginning of his way (Prov 8:22)."[173]

Proverbs 8:22 continued to be highly influential in the Tannaitic identification of preexistent wisdom with the Torah.[174] Genesis Rabbah 1:4 lists the six things that preexisted the creation of the world, and then the author divides these six into two important distinctions: things that were actually created and things that were only contemplated in God's plans.[175] The things that literally preexisted were the throne of glory and the Torah, while the things that preexisted in God's contemplations were the patriarchs, the nation of Israel, the temple, and the name of the Messiah. In order to justify the argument that the Torah preexisted as an actual creation, the sage cites the passage about personified wisdom in Prov 8:22: "The Lord made me at the beginning of his way, prior to his works of old." When exactly did God create the Torah? The midrash answers, "Torah preceded the creation of the world by two thousand years."[176] Rabbi Akiba, who died in the year 132 CE, gave an interpretation preserved in the Mishnah regarding the Torah as the agent of creation: "In that [the Torah] was disclosed to them that they had been given a desirable tool through which the world was created."[177] Akiba's reading demonstrates one way in which the roles and characteristics of personified wisdom were given over to the Torah during this period.

Speculation on wisdom as the instrumental agent of creation was not completely eliminated during this period, as evidenced by such examples as the Fragmentary Targum on Gen 1:1. Within this Aramaic targum, the sage interprets the phrase "In the beginning God created" as "God

---

173. Urbach, *Sages*, 199.

174. Urbach, *Sages*, 198.

175. These refer to the two types of preexistence commonly recognized by New Testament scholars: literal preexistence and ideal (notional) preexistence.

176. Gen Rab. 8:2.

177. m. 'Abot 3:14; Tropper, "Wisdom in Rabbinic Interpretation," 209.

created with wisdom."[178] Philip Alexander observes that several important Jewish targums interpreted Gen 1:1 along these lines—in terms of God creating through his wisdom.[179] Another important example, which was discovered in 1949, Targum Neofiti, interprets Gen 1:1 by combining wisdom and word as intermediaries: "From the beginning, with wisdom, the word of the Lord created and perfected the heavens and the earth."[180] Brent Strawn has shown that the traditions contained within Targum Neofiti that closely associate God's wisdom and God's word with the creation in Genesis 1 may in fact be as early as the late first century CE.[181] Furthermore, the Christian document *Apostolic Constitutions* preserves a synagogal prayer from sometime between the second and third centuries CE. In this prayer that was prayed among the Jewish synagogues, God began to create, but only after issuing an order to his wisdom.[182] Henry Fischel has drawn important attention to the inclusion of portrayals of Wisdom as God's instrumental agent in creation in the daily prayers of Tannaitic Jewish liturgy.[183] Before reciting the *Shema*, Psalm 104:24 ("How great are your works, in wisdom you have made them all") was recited during the morning prayer. The evening liturgical prayer that preceded the recitation of the *Shema* praised God with this line: "With wisdom you open the gates." Similarly, this liturgy, which pious Jews recited after their ritualistic washing of hands, included a reference to God as the one "who created humanity with wisdom." The theological concept that the God of Israel made all things by means of his personified wisdom thus continued in several strands of Judaism during the rabbinic period.

In short, the trajectory of wisdom's close association with the commandments of the Torah, beginning from Proverbs and moving through Sirach and Baruch, finds its landing spot among the Tannaitic sages and

178. The date of fragmentary targums could be as early as the second century CE. See Strawn, "*Be-reʾsit*," 365; Klein, *Fragment-Targums*, 43.

179. Alexander, "In the Beginning," 11, cites as evidence the Fragmentary Targum [Vatican], Fragmentary Targum [Paris], and Targum Neofiti 1. Anderson, "Interpretation of Genesis 1:1," 23, astutely observes that these Aramaic targums retain the Hebrew spelling of "wisdom" as evidence of the exegetical process taking place with Gen 1:1.

180. English translation provided by McNamara, *Targum Neofiti 1: Genesis*, 52. For discussion on the discovery and dates of its publication, see Vries, "Targumim as Background," 98–99. The Aramaic word for "word" (*memra*), like *sophia*, is grammatically feminine.

181. Strawn, "*Bĕ-rēʾ šît*," 365.

182. The "Hellenistic Synagogal Prayer" is preserved in *Apostolic Constitutions* 7.34.6.

183. Fischel, "Wisdom in the World," 68.

the Amoraic rabbis. These Jewish exegetes understood God's wisdom to be accessible only through the study and application of the Torah. Since the Jews in this era illustrated the Torah's significance by drawing upon the portrayal of personified wisdom in Proverbs 8, Torah became personified, it preexisted creation, it functioned as the blueprint of creation, and it embodied the qualities formerly attributed to God's wisdom. The sages did not completely lose sight of wisdom as God's personified agent of creation; in fact, the tradition of God creating the heavens and the earth with his personified wisdom appears to have existed alongside the wisdom-infused-Torah traditions.

CONCLUSION

Christine Roy Yoder articulates well the vast journey of Lady Wisdom by saying, "Wisdom who walked into Proverbs and built her house came to stay."[184] As this lengthy yet important exploration of wisdom's pilgrimage draws to a close, it is prudent that we create a profile of the wisdom of God that appears in the relevant sources of Jewish literature spanning the Second Temple period and the subsequent Amoraic period.[185] This profile will help set the context in which we may responsibly discern references to Jewish concepts of wisdom within the Gospel of John. This summary is not meant to be exhaustive but rather intends to highlight the most noteworthy qualities of wisdom within the literature we have just surveyed.

1. Wisdom is the *personification* of the God of Israel's wise interaction with and instruction to his creation, frequently taking the role of a female figure (Job, Proverbs, Aristobulus, Sirach, Baruch, Wisdom of Solomon, "Hymn to the Creator," Philo, 1 Enoch, Tannaitic and Amoraic literature).

2. Wisdom acts as the instrumental *agent of creation*, which characterizes God the Father—the maker of heaven and earth—as wisely ordering all things (Psalms, Proverbs, Aristobulus, Sirach, Wisdom of Solomon, "Hymn to the Creator," Philo, Tannaitic and Amoraic literature).

---

184. Yoder, "Personified Wisdom and Feminist Theologies," 273.

185. For similar lists, albeit leaving off some key data relevant to our study of the Fourth Gospel, see Murphy, *Tree of Life*, 145–46; Witherington, *Jesus the Sage*, 114–15.

3. Wisdom *instructs* humanity (sometimes Israel alone) with precepts of wise living, often referring specifically to the fear of the Lord and the precepts of Torah (Job, Proverbs, Sirach, Baruch, Wisdom of Solomon, Philo, 1 Enoch, Tannaitic and Amoraic literature).

4. The qualities of wisdom frequently overlap and closely resemble *the word of God*—the creative and powerful utterance of YHWH (Job, Psalms, Proverbs, Aristobulus, Sirach, Wisdom of Solomon, Philo, Tannaitic and Amoraic literature).

5. Similarly, the wisdom of God is sometimes associated with the role and functions of *the Spirit of God* (Proverbs, Wisdom of Solomon, 1 Enoch).

6. Personified wisdom *descends to earth on a mission*, often accompanied by the offering of blessings, prosperity, and life (Proverbs, Sirach, Baruch, Wisdom of Solomon, Genesis Apocryphon, Philo, 1 Enoch, Tannaitic and Amoraic literature).

7. The response of those who interact with the wisdom of God determines the nature of her subsequent *accessibility* (Job, Proverbs, Sirach, Baruch, Wisdom of Solomon, 1 Enoch, Tannaitic and Amoraic literature).

8. Wisdom, as a personification, *becomes incarnate in human beings*, resulting in these noteworthy individuals being identified with Wisdom, sharing her qualities, and speaking forth her words (Proverbs, Sirach, Genesis Apocryphon, Philo).[186]

9. The wisdom of God was eventually closely identified with *the Torah of Moses* (Proverbs, Sirach, Baruch, Wisdom of Solomon, Philo, Tannaitic and Amoraic literature).

It is crucial at this juncture of the study to grasp an adequate understanding of the wisdom of God as it is presented in these Jewish sources. Normally, it would be apt to simply define God's wisdom as an attribute describing God's ability to act skillfully with knowledge and

---

186. Dunn, "Incarnation," 47, provides a helpful summary: "The recognition that Wisdom Christology is the most obvious root of incarnation Christology also has an important corollary, particularly when it is recalled that in Jewish thought Wisdom is not a being independent of God but is God's self-manifestation." Fuller, *New Testament Christology*, 75, offers a similar conclusion: "The concept of *sophia* . . . made an important contribution to the doctrine of incarnation."

understanding.[187] The Jewish sages who composed the biblical wisdom literature went a step further than simply portraying God's wisdom as a wise attribute; they sought to deeply *personify* wisdom as a female figure, based upon the grammatical gender of the Hebrew noun *hokmah*. It would be, however, going beyond the evidence to interpret God's wisdom in a more developed fashion than a personification of an attribute.[188] To reckon the wisdom of God as a distinct, conscious person—whether it be an individual being, a goddess, or a hypostasis alongside the God of Israel—would be to fundamentally misread the Jewish sages responsible for wisdom literature.[189] The conclusions reached by James D. G. Dunn seem appropriate here: "Thus far we can say with confidence that it is very unlikely that pre-Christian Judaism ever understood Wisdom as a divine being in any sense independent of Yahweh. The language may be the language of the wider speculation of the time, but within Jewish monotheism and Hebraic literary idiom Wisdom never really becomes more than a personification."[190] Ben Witherington urges similar caution: "It is clear from the flexibility of what is predicated of Wisdom in all this material that the sages are not dealing with a person and certainly not with a goddess, but with a personification of an idea, concept, attribute, or quality that was seen as desirable for humans to obtain and was already something that characterized God and God's orderly creation."[191] Alice Sinnott draws analogous conclusions: "In Judaism Wisdom is personified but never apotheosized."[192] If we are to responsibly set the Johannine Jesus in his Jewish context, we must take care to understand Lady Wisdom as she is presented in the Jewish sources—as a personification.

Having established a working definition and collection of attributes pertaining to the wisdom of Israel's God, we are now in a better place to venture into the New Testament and begin exploring the Fourth Gospel. How does the Gospel of John, which does not use the noun "wisdom" (*sophia*) even once, portray the person of Jesus in terms of Wisdom

---

187. *HALOT*, 314.

188. See esp. Dunn, *Christology in the Making*, 210, "Wisdom never became more than a personification of God's own activity."

189. It is admitted by several scholars that that Wisdom Christology exists within the New Testament, but many fail to adequately define the meaning of this wisdom based on the relevant sources in Jewish wisdom literature, namely, as a personification.

190. Dunn, *Christology in the Making* 176.

191. Witherington, *Jesus the Sage*, 115–16.

192. Sinnott, *Personification of Wisdom*, 178.

Christology?[193] In order to offer a plausible answer to this question, we must first explore the Johannine Prologue—the famous opening christological hymn that serves to introduce the contents of the Gospel of John. It is to this sophisticated, complex, and controversial hymn that we shall now turn.

---

193. O'Boyle, *Towards a Contemporary Wisdom Christology*, 151, makes the case that while no word in the *sophia/sophos* family appears in John, Wisdom Christology is unquestionably fundamental to the book.

3

Wisdom in the Prologue

THE PROLOGUE OF JOHN covers the first eighteen verses of the Fourth Gospel. Of the four New Testament gospel accounts, the Gospel of John possesses the lengthiest introduction to its narrative. More than one hundred years ago, James Rendel Harris argued that the Johannine Prologue was originally a hymn dedicated to Wisdom, and Harris provided invaluable parallels with Jewish wisdom literature to substantiate his point.[1] Since then, scholars have increasingly grown to recognize the influence of personified wisdom texts upon the Prologue of the Gospel of John, so much so that this position has reached such a dominant consensus that virtually all modern commentaries acknowledge the influence of wisdom parallels.[2] The conclusions of Raymond Brown well illustrate this dominant scholarly opinion: "In the OT presentation of Wisdom, there are good parallels for almost every detail of the Prologue's description of the

---

1. Harris, *Origin of the Prologue*. Harris's research is built upon in Dodd, *Interpretation*, 274–76. Scholars continue to find Harris's observation of the Wisdom hymn convincing; see Painter, "Christology and the History," 465–66; Epp, "Wisdom, Torah, Word," 130; Culpepper, *Gospel*, 111.

2. See the summary from Cory, "Wisdom's Rescue," 99: "Johannine scholars long have noted the manner in which sapiential traditions have shaped the Fourth Gospel's portrayal of Jesus as the Wisdom of God." Talbert, "Descending-Ascending Redeemer," 109, notes that the background for the logos in the prologue "is almost certainly the Wisdom myth assimilated with the logos." Kümmel, *Theology*, 280, remarks: "Striking parallels undoubtedly exist" between the *logos* in the Prologue and Wisdom. See also Tobin, "Logos," 353; Stanton, *Gospels and Jesus*, 108–9; Achtemeier et al., *New Testament*, 182; Freed, *New Testament*, 352; Casey, *Jewish Prophet*, 157, 159. Two defectors from this dominant consensus are Michaels, *Gospel of John*, and Ridderbos, *John*.

Word."[3] Gail O'Day summarizes the impact of personified wisdom on the Prologue: "The Jewish wisdom tradition, both biblical and extra-biblical, has emerged as the governing view of the provenance of the language of the Prologue."[4] Warren Carter points to at least twelve connections in the Prologue between Jesus and personified wisdom as it is portrayed in the Jewish wisdom literature.[5] Even Rudolf Bultmann, who famously argued—unconvincingly by modern standards—that the Prologue was rooted in a Gnostic Redeemer myth, nevertheless admitted: "There can be no doubt . . . that a connection exists between the Judaic Wisdom myth and the Johannine Prologue."[6] More recently, Mary L. Coloe, in her 2021 two-volume commentary on John, has brilliantly put her finger on the issue as to why lay readers of the Bible have not widely recognized these wisdom parallels: "Christianity has moved away from its Jewish roots, and many Christians are not familiar with the wisdom literature."[7] It is no wonder that most adult readers of the Gospel of John are unaware of its indebtedness to the traditions of God's personified wisdom.

This chapter aims to thoroughly explore the contents of John 1:1–18 and demonstrate the ways in which it offers a christological portrayal of Jesus Christ in terms of the wisdom of God. This task will involve carefully setting the contents of the Prologue in the context of Jewish speculation surrounding God's wisdom in the literature that we surveyed in the previous chapter. Before we can begin our exegesis of the Prologue proper, we need to provide answers to three preliminary questions. First, what is the function of the Johannine Prologue in relation to the rest of the Gospel of John? The answer to this question will help determine the character and quality of our exegesis of the contents of the Prologue. Second, why does the author of the Prologue use "word" (*logos*) to explain what was in the beginning with God, instead of using "wisdom" (*sophia*)? If the Prologue truly demonstrates the influence of the Jewish wisdom literature, then there must be a convincing reason the author opted to frame the Prologue around the *logos* instead of *sophia*. Last, why did the

---

3. Brown, *John I–XII*, 523. MacRae, "Fourth Gospel," 22; and Culpepper, "Christology," 72–73, echo Brown's position.

4. O'Day, "Gospel of John," 517.

5. Carter, *John: Storyteller, Interpreter, Evangelist*, 136–39.

6. Bultmann, *John: A Commentary*, 22.

7. Coloe, *John 1–10*, 8. Schüssler Fiorenza, *Jesus*, 143–44, expresses a similar observation concerning the Christian tradition involving Wisdom that "has been almost completely erased from the memory of Western Christianity."

author of the Prologue choose to begin the Fourth Gospel with a hymn as opposed to other more traditional ways of introducing Greco-Roman biographies? By exploring the conceptual links between the opening hymn and Jewish portrayals of Lady Wisdom, we may gain some insight into the author's literary, narrative, and theological motivations.

The Prologue's Function

What is the relationship, if any, between the opening eighteen verses and the subsequent chapters of the Gospel of John? Some scholars have suggested that the Prologue serves as a *summary* of the contents of the Fourth Gospel. While it is true that the Prologue contains many subjects that are present later in the Gospel of John, it lacks some key features that we would expect if the Prologue was intended to fully summarize its contents. For example, the new commandment to "love one another just as Jesus as loved the disciples" is a significant feature in the Farewell Discourse (chapters 13–17) but is completely absent from the Prologue. Similarly, the role of the Paraclete—the Holy Spirit—is certainly emphasized in chapters 14–16, but it is also missing from the Prologue. One of the distinctive christological portrayals found in the Fourth Gospel when compared to the Synoptics is the insistence that Jesus is the sacrificial Lamb of God. One can find this portrayal in various places within the narrative of the Gospel of John, but it is not mentioned anywhere in the opening Prologue. Therefore, it seems unlikely that the Prologue is an intentional summary of the rest of the Gospel of John's contents.

Other scholars have made the argument that during the process of editing the Gospel of John, the Prologue was a *late addition*—completely unrelated to the overall narrative—and was tacked on to the beginning. Although it is fairly certain that multiple hands contributed to the final edition of the Gospel of John[8] (as evidenced, for example, by chapter 21 serving as an epilogue and appendix after the formal conclusion in 20:30–31), it is difficult to clearly demonstrate that the Prologue is an independent addition, unrelated to the main narrative.

A more likely solution is to view the Prologue as an *introduction* that aims to prepare readers to read the rest of the Gospel of John but not

---

8. See Carter, *John*, 155–74, for an excellent survey of scholars developing the evidence for multiple hands working on the Gospel of John.

necessarily as a summary.[9] The contents of the Prologue contain themes that appear later in the narrative, such as the relationship of the *logos* to God, the purpose of John the Baptist, the contrast of light and darkness, the rejection and acceptance of the *logos*, the necessity for readers to believe in Jesus' name, the revelation of glory among Jesus' followers, and the way the unique son functions as the authoritative revealer of the unseen God. It may be, as Craig Keener proposes, that John added the Prologue after completing the first draft of the gospel, having meditated on the fruits of its contents.[10] Since the Prologue acts as an introduction, it means that any evidence of Wisdom Christology within the opening eighteen verses would naturally serve to direct the attention of the reader to further portrayals of Jesus as the wisdom of God that would be embedded in the narrative of the Gospel of John.[11]

Why Does the Prologue Use *Logos* Instead of *Sophia*?

The Prologue details the pilgrimage of the *logos* in a way that suggests the passage is itself a hymn celebrating Jesus as God's wisdom made flesh.[12] Why did the author of the Prologue choose to portray Jesus as the embodiment of the *logos* when, as we will demonstrate, the Prologue is heavily indebted to the influence of Jewish wisdom traditions?[13] Although Jesus of Nazareth was a male, there is no hint that it would have been out of place to depict him as the embodiment of the grammatically feminine *sophia*. Ben Sira certainly had no trouble describing Simon ben Onias, the high priest, as the incarnation of Lady Wisdom in Sirach 50. Any consideration that the author preferred the masculine *logos* over the feminine *sophia* due to a sexist disregard for females would overlook the overwhelmingly positive portrayal of female disciples throughout

---

9. Painter, "Christology," 461; Culpepper, *Gospel*, 116–20; Thompson, *John*, 16.

10. Keener, *Gospel of John*, 1:334.

11. O'Boyle, *Wisdom Christology*, 159. Martin Scott, *Sophia*, 88, makes the same observation: "If the Prologue is to be seen as an integral part of the Gospel and not merely a kind of preface stuck on at the beginning of a book as an afterthought, the one would expect the motifs contained in it to be worked out to some extent at least within the Gospel as a whole." Lincoln, *Gospel*, 82, notes that the Fourth Gospel uses Jewish wisdom traditions in both the prologue and in Jesus' discourses.

12. Smith, *John*, 51, correctly observes that "wisdom and word can be used interchangeably." See also Schneiders, *That You May Believe*, 49, 70.

13. Davies, "Reflections," 44, forcefully argues, "It is evident that John thought as a Jew."

the Gospel of John, particularly with the faith of the Samaritan woman, Mary, Martha, Mary Magdalene, and Jesus' mother.[14] A proposed answer that takes into account the teachings and deeds of Jesus is this: the *logos*, rather than *sophia*, was a more appropriate way to portray the Johannine Jesus, who obediently *speaks forth the words and commands of God*—a regular christological feature in the Fourth Gospel's narrative.[15] In fact, Jesus insists that his words are not his own; rather they belong to the Father who commissioned him. As the embodiment of God's word, Jesus naturally speaks forth the words of God as an authorized spokesman. Stated differently, the human Jesus in whom the *logos* became flesh functions as the mouthpiece of God's words and commands, and the masculine *logos* was a far more suitable metaphor than feminine wisdom in order to achieve this particular christological portrayal.[16] This is not to suggest that the author did not think of Jesus as the embodiment of wisdom, as we will soon demonstrate. Rather, the flexibility of the word of God being a recognized synonym for the wisdom of God, particularly as the two relate to the ways in which the God of Israel interacted with his creation through a personified intermediary, allowed the author of the Prologue to begin the gospel with a more appropriate metaphor to frame Jesus as the authorized agent who speaks forth the Father's words, without excluding the influences and echoes from Jewish wisdom texts.[17]

---

14. Beirne, *Women and Men*, 219, concludes that "the Gospel text gives support to the equality of women and men with respect to the nature and value of their discipleship . . . there is a consistent balancing of the female and male characters." For an alternative perspective behind the motivation to refer the feminine wisdom as the masculine *logos*, see especially Douglas, *Early Church Understandings*, 47–48.

15. Furthermore, the noun *logos* possesses a meaning within the Synoptic Gospel presentations as the spoken good news about the kingdom of God, which Jesus preached (e.g., Matt 13:19–23; Mark 1:45; 2:2; Luke 5:1; 8:11).

16. Haenchen, *John 1*, 102, put it succinctly: "He needed only to substitute the masculine Logos for the feminine Wisdom in order to create a coherent poem."

17. Scott, *Sophia*, 94, makes the same point: "By the time of the writing of the Fourth Gospel the concepts Logos and Sophia had become more or less synonymous in at least some areas of Jewish thought." Several scholars have voiced their support of this conclusion: Hurtado, *One God, One Lord*, 42–47; Painter, "Christology," 468; Ladd, *Theology*, 240; Bhaldraithe, "Johannine Prologue," 66–67; Manns, "Jewish Approach," 267; Culpepper, *Gospel*, 93; Cullmann, *Christology*, 257; Burnett, "Wisdom," 876.

Why Is the Prologue Arranged as a Hymn?

Many commentators continue to point to remarkable similarities between the Johannine Prologue and Jewish literary hymns, particularly hymns celebrating God's wisdom.[18] Rudolf Schnackenburg suggests that the Prologue has incorporated an earlier wisdom hymn that was familiar to the Johannine community.[19] This raises the interesting question as to why the author of the Gospel of John chose to arrange the Prologue with a hymnic structure in order to introduce his work. A readily available solution, having explored the relevant Jewish wisdom literature in which personified wisdom's pilgrimage is set forth, is to interpret the hymnic Prologue in light of the former hymns and poems that celebrate the wisdom of God.[20] We observed wisdom hymns and poems in the books of Job (28:1–28), Proverbs (1:20–33; 8:1–36), Sirach (1:1–10; 24:1–34), Wisdom of Solomon (7:22—8:1), Baruch (3:9—4:4), and 1 Enoch (42:1-2). The author of the Prologue likely felt that a more poetic hymn would better serve the introductory needs of his community,[21] as opposed to the introductions fully composed of prose used by authors like Luke and Plutarch.[22]

The Prologue's Chiasm

The wisdom-inspired hymnic Prologue contains what scholars identify as a chiastic structure.[23] A chiasm is a literary arrangement common among oral cultures that sets various themes in descending and ascending parallel lines, creating an intentional mnemonic device. The paralleled topics within the structural arrangement of the chiasm repeat in a reversed order (e.g., A, B, B, A). The meeting point of the chiasm and the topic placed therein by the author functions as a crucial climactic part of

---

18. E.g., Bernard, *Gospel*, 1:1; Gordley, "Johannine Prologue," 781–802.

19. Schnackenburg, *Gospel*, 1:225–26.

20. Lincoln, *John*, 93.

21. Epp, "Wisdom, Torah, Word," 129.

22. Luke 1:1–4; Plutarch, *Alexander*, 1:1–3. The Johannine Prologue does contain two small sections of prose in which John the Baptist is mentioned in relation to the wisdom-embodied Jesus.

23. Pryor, "Jesus and Israel," 201.

the passage. The following is my proposed chiasm of John 1:1–18, drawing heavily on the work of R. Alan Culpepper:[24]

(A) The *logos* was with God (1:1–2)

  (B) Creation through the *logos* (1:3)

    (C) Received life and light (1:4–5)

      (D) John the Baptist's testimony (1:6–8)

        (E) Negative response to the *logos* (1:9–11)

          (F) Those who received the *logos* become children of God (1:12–13)

        (E') Positive response to the *logos* (1:14)

      (D') John the Baptist's testimony (1:15)

    (C') Received grace (1:16)

  (B') Grace and truth through Jesus (1:17)

(A') The unique son is with God (1:18)

Many scholars offer their own chiastic reconstruction of the Prologue with some slight nuances and alterations to the above proposal.[25] Nearly every scholarly chiasm identifies John 1:12–13, or a particular phrase within this section, as the climax of the Prologue,[26] since it is the obvious meeting place of the topics sorted by the parallel lines.[27] Therefore, the Prologue is not only a hymnic celebration of the *logos*/wisdom that introduces the narrative for readers, but it also bears a stylistic arrangement in the form of a chiasm that finds its climactic highlight in the transformation of those who receive the *logos* into children of God.

(A) THE *LOGOS* WAS WITH GOD (1:1–2)

As we move to the text of the Prologue in order to assess its indebtedness to Jewish wisdom writings, we will consider the merits of the chiastic

---

24. Culpepper, "Pivot of John's Prologue," 9–17.

25. See especially Kim, *Sourcebook of the Structures*, 25

26. Lund, "Influence of Chiasmus," 43–44, suggested that 1:13 is the center point. Boismard, *St. John's Prologue*, 79–80, proposes 1:12–13. Culpepper, "Pivot," 16, argues for a more precise center/pivot at 1:12b ("he gave to them authority to become children of God").

27. Aune, "Chiasmus," 94.

arrangement as well as the various ways in which themes unfold and receive elaboration as the passage progresses. We begin with the opening two verses that describe the *logos* that was with God. This *logos* was "in the beginning" (*en arche*), which recalls the Genesis creation by quoting Gen 1:1 LXX verbatim.[28] According to Genesis 1, God made all things by speaking them into existence with his powerful and creative utterance,[29] with the refrain "and God said" repeated several times.[30] Since Genesis 1 and the Johannine Prologue both discuss the themes of God creating with his powerful speech, bringing light to darkness, and making life, we can be confident that the author of the Prologue is quite deliberate in his attempt to point his readers to remember the Genesis creation by positioning the *logos* "in the beginning."[31]

Personified wisdom was also in the beginning, preexisting all that the Creator made.[32] As we have observed in many Jewish wisdom texts, the wisdom of God—regularly personified as a female figure—preexisted in creation.[33] Proverbs 8, in particular, uses the same Greek phrase translated as "in the beginning" (*en arche*) when describing Lady Wisdom's preeminent position (Prov 8:22–23 LXX).[34] Personified wisdom herself acknowledges her activity was "before [God's] works of old" (Prov 8:22),[35] "when there were no depths" (Prov 8:24), and "while he had not yet made the earth" (Prov 8:26). In Wisdom of Solomon, the author

---

28. It is the dominant consensus of biblical scholars that John 1:1 deliberately cites the opening line of Gen 1:1. See Bruce, *Gospel and Epistles*, 30–31; Brown, *John I–XII*, 4; Beasley-Murray, *John*, 10; McHugh, *John 1–4*, 6; Haenchen, *John 1*, 109; Von Wahlde, *Gospel and Letters of John*, 2:2; Carson, *John*, 114; Gaston, *Dynamic Monarchianism*, 14.

29. Robinson, *Priority of John*, 379.

30. Gaston, "High Christology," 131, points out that the creative word in Genesis 1 is not a person but rather the activity of God. Boyarin, *Border Lines*, 96, observes that the "saying" of God that makes everything is in both Genesis 1 and John 1.

31. Myers, *Characterizing Jesus*, 40–41, 62. See further the references listed in Keener, *Gospel of John*, 1:365; Witherington, *John's Wisdom*, 52.

32. Tobin, "Logos," 353; Brown, *John I–XII*, cxxiii; Charlesworth, "Lady Wisdom," 113–14; Coloe, "Structure," 46; *John 1–10*, 4; Witherington, *Jesus the Sage*, 284; Brant, *John*, 25. Carter, *John and Empire*, 93; Ceresko, *Old Testament Wisdom*, 178; Kysar, *John*, 25. Von Wahlde, *John*, 2:2–3, observes that the thought world that gave rise to the conception of personified Word has the Jewish wisdom writings among its closest parallels.

33. Job 28:26–27; Ps 104:24; Prov 8:22–31; Wis 6:22; 9:9. Wisdom functions as the agent of creation in the prophetic literature as well—e.g., Jer 10:12; 51:15.

34. Vries, "Targumim," 114, argues from his study of Targum Neofiti and the Fragmentary Targum that the connection between Gen 1:1 and Prov 8:22 was already observed by Jewish interpreters prior to 70 CE.

35. Dillon, "Wisdom Tradition," 276; Talbert, *Reading John*, 68.

traces the course of personified wisdom from the beginning of creation (Wis 6:22). Similarly, the Fragmentary Targum interpreted Gen 1:1 as God creating the heavens and the earth with wisdom—a reading that occurred "in the beginning." Similarly, Targum Neofiti interprets Gen 1:1 as the creative word of the Lord using Wisdom to make the heavens and the earth.[36] Daniel Boyarin summarizes the data succinctly: "The Logos of the Prologue . . . is the product of a scriptural reading of Genesis 1 and Proverbs 8 together."[37] While some Jewish wisdom texts indicate that wisdom was the first created personification (Prov 8:22; Sir 1:4, 9; 24:9), the Johannine Prologue insists that the *logos* simply "was" in the beginning (John 1:1–2).

Since God created the heavens and the earth in the beginning (Gen 1:1), it is no surprise that the Prologue similarly positions the *logos*, the personified creative and powerful utterance,[38] *with* God (literally "the God"). The Greek preposition *pros* can here mean towards, with, by, at, or near—all indicating close proximity between God and his creative utterance.[39] In the poetic speeches within the book of Job, the author similarly portrays words and decrees as being "with" God (Job 23:14). The things concealed in the heart of God are those that are "with" him (Job 10:13). Furthermore, the author of Job can speak about "what is with the Almighty" (Job 27:11).

The parallels with personified wisdom are more numerous than the references to a word being with God. For example, in Proverbs 8, Lady Wisdom herself declares that she was with YHWH before creation (Prov 8:22–23).[40] "When he established the heavens," personified wisdom says, "I was there" (Prov 8:27), "I was beside him . . . rejoicing before him"

---

36. Anderson, "Genesis 1:1 in the Targums," 28–29, insists that the parallels between Targum Neofiti and John 1:1 need to be seriously considered by New Testament scholars. Coloe, "Structure," 53, correctly draws attention to the relevance of Neofiti in her discussion of wisdom's role in John 1:1.

37. Boyarin, *Border Lines*, 95. Boyarin notes that this reading is not particularly Christian, due to its Jewish flavor.

38. BDAG, 601 defines the *logos* in John 1:1 as "the independent personified expression of God." On the author intending that the *logos* was a personification, see Boer, "Original Prologue," 448–49. Dunn, *Christology in the Making*, 219, persuasively points out G. F. Moore's observation, "Nowhere either in the Bible or in extra-canonical literature of the Jews is the word of God a personal agent or on the way to become such." Witherington, *John's Wisdom*, 52, provides much clarity here: "Gen 1 is not about a personified attribute, much less a person assisting God in creation."

39. BDAG, 874–75.

40. Von Wahlde, *John*, 2:3.

(Prov 8:30).⁴¹ Sirach opens his book by explicitly declaring that all wisdom is from the Lord and it is "with him" forever (Sir 1:1). Similarly, the Wisdom of Solomon records a prayer to God in which personified wisdom is "with you . . . and was present when you made the world" (Wis 9:9).⁴² Martin Scott concludes from his study of the prepositions connecting Wisdom with God that "we can see in these Wisdom parallels a precise correspondence to the Johannine Logos."⁴³ The Prologue, by positioning the preexistent *logos* with God, demonstrates the influence of Jewish texts portraying Israel's God being with his personified wisdom.⁴⁴

The third and final phrase in the opening verse of the Prologue brings with it some translational difficulties. Most English versions render the phrase, "and the word was God." Since the previous phrase in the passage clearly distinguished God from his *logos*, it seems rather unlikely that the author intended to then identify the two as one and the same.⁴⁵ Grammarians regularly point out that the anarthrous "God" in this phrase seems to be functioning adjectively, indicating that the *logos* was fully expressive of God or "divine" in quality.⁴⁶ The adjectival use of "God" is appropriate because spoken words naturally reflect the character of the person who speaks them forth. Moloney observes in his commentary on this final phrase in John 1:1 that the author of the Prologue has gone to "considerable trouble to indicate that an identification between the Word and God is to be avoided."⁴⁷ The observation that the *logos* qualitatively expresses God finds its parallel in John 1:18—the final line of the chiasm—where the embodied *logos* is the unique son, who reveals and explains the unseen God.

---

41. Bernard, *Gospel*, 1:2; McHugh, *John 1–4*, 9; Talbert, *Reading John*, 68; Brant, *John*, 25; Barrett, *Gospel*, 155; Lincoln, *John*, 93, 96; Boyarin, *Border Lines*, 96.

42. Boyarin, *Border Lines*, 96.

43. Scott, *Sophia*, 96–97.

44. Robert and Feuillet, *Introduction*, 874; Carter, "Prologue and John's Gospel," 38; O'Day and Hylen, *John*, 24; Tobin, "Logos," 353; Charlesworth, "Lady Wisdom," 115–16.

45. See Thompson, *John*, 29; Davies, *Rhetoric and Reference*, 81; Phillips, *Prologue*, 153–54.

46. Zerwick and Grosvenor, *Grammatical Analysis*, 285; Wallace, *Greek Grammar*, 269; Novakovic, *John 1–10*, 2–3; Phillips, *Prologue*, 154; Barclay, *Gospel of John*, 17. Moloney, *John*, 42, correctly notes that the *logos* is "divine" and that it should not be equated with God.

47. Moloney, *Gospel of John*, 35. See also Kümmel, *Theology*, 281.

Like the personified word, personified wisdom reveals God's wise interactions and self-expression with creation. Ben Sira depicted Lady Wisdom as expressing the God of Israel by writing that those who serve Wisdom will serve the Lord, and that the Lord loves those who love Wisdom (Sir 4:14). Wisdom's detailed expression in Wisdom of Solomon indicates her revelatory function: "She is the breath of the power of God . . . a pure emanation of the glory of the Almighty" (Wis 7:25).[48] Furthermore, wisdom is "a reflection of eternal light, a spotless mirror of the working of God, and an image of his goodness" (Wis 7:26). Elizabeth Johnson aptly summarizes the monotheistic implications of wisdom's personification: "The Wisdom of God in late Jewish thought was simply God, revealing and known."[49]

John 1:2 repeats the information provided in 1:1a and 1:1b; "This one was in the beginning with God." In doing so, the Prologue reemphasizes the preexistence of the *logos*, its close ties with the opening chapter of Genesis, and its distinction from Israel's God.[50] The translation "*He* was in the beginning" gives special observation to the personification of the *logos*, which draws influence from similar depictions of God's word within poetic passages of the Hebrew Bible. Psalm 107:20 indicates that God sends his word out on a mission in order to heal and deliver. We can also note a similar illustration in Ps 147:15, where God commissions forth his spoken command to the earth, and the parallel line states that God's personified word "runs very swiftly." This imagery appears again in Isa 55:11, in which God associates the word being sent forth from his mouth with the accomplishing of "what I desire." John A. T. Robinson carefully argues that it is crucial to recognize the *logos* as a preexisting personification, not as a person.[51]

We have already demonstrated that wisdom, the near-synonym of God's personified word, is quite regularly portrayed as the personification of God's wise actions within the Jewish wisdom literature that predates the Gospel of John. Urban C. von Wahlde argues that Wisdom's depiction as preexistent and as a female person "was never intended (or apparently

---

48. Talbert, *Reading John*, 68.
49. Johnson, "Wisdom Was Made Flesh," 99.
50. Scott, *Sophia*, 97–98.
51. Robinson, *Priority of John*, 380–81. Similarly, Collins and Collins, *King and Messiah*, 176, express doubt that John 1 is compatible with the views of the second person of the Trinity.

taken) literally among the Jews."[52] Within the book of Proverbs, Lady Wisdom talks, shouts in the streets, calls forth, issues summons, builds a house, prepares a meal, mixes wine, and sends forth maidens. Various Jewish writers personify the grammatically feminine wisdom as a woman, a wife, a bride, a mother, a nurse, a prophetess, and even more generally as a teacher, an owner of a house, and a child. Personified wisdom's close ties with the word of God can be detected in the Prologue's insistence that he—the personified *logos*—was in the beginning with God.[53]

(B) CREATION THROUGH THE *LOGOS* (1:3)

John 1:3 illustrates the instrumental role of the *logos* in bringing creation into existence. The quotation of Gen 1:1 in John 1:1, combined with the reference to "all things" and the aorist tense of the verb "to become," again indicates that the Genesis creation is in view here.[54] Just as God brought about all things through the agency of his creative utterance in Genesis 1, the Prologue indicates that God made all things through his word—the personified *logos*. In a comment that reinforces the all-encompassing role of the personified *logos* in creation, John 1:3 states that not one thing came into being apart from him. The author is careful to identify the *logos* as the personified agent of creation, not as the Creator himself. The Prologue's portrayal of the God of Israel fashioning all things by means of his powerful and creative utterance draws influence from the Hebrew Bible. Within the book of Psalms, we observe that the God of Israel made the heavens and all their host "by the word of YHWH" (Ps 33:6).[55] The parallel line places the breath of God's mouth as the synonym for his creative word. The psalm continues by defining the word of YHWH in terms of God *speaking* and *commanding* (33:9). This portrayal of God creating with his powerful word shows dependence upon the account of

---

52. Von Wahlde, *John*, 1:429.

53. Lincoln, *John*, 96, highlights the importance of recognizing the act of personification in the Prologue: "Such talk involves a personification of a divine function, a way of speaking of God's immanence in the creation, God's active engagement in the world and with Israel, without compromising God's transcendence."

54. Boer, "Original Prologue," 463–64, observes that the first Christians to argue against the consensus view of the opening verses recalling the creation account of Genesis 1 are Origen, Hilary, and Ambrose.

55. Bernard, *Gospel*, 1:3.

creation in the opening chapter of Genesis, where the phrase "and God said" is a constant refrain.

Wisdom too acts as the instrumental agent of the Creator God in several Jewish texts.[56] YHWH made all his works by using his wise agent, wisdom (Ps 104:24). Proverbs depicts YHWH as having founded the earth with his wisdom, which is immediately set in parallel with God's understanding and his knowledge (Prov 3:19-20). In the prophetic literature, we can similarly observe wisdom as YHWH's creative agent: "He established the world with his wisdom" (Jer 10:12; 51:15). The portrayals of the one God creating through his word and wisdom influenced the author of Wisdom of Solomon, who described Solomon's prayer as praising God for making all things with his *logos* and creating humanity with his *sophia* (Wis 9:1-2).[57] In communicating how God made all things through an agent, Wisdom of Solomon indicates an awareness that personified wisdom is the appropriate synonym for the creative word/speech of God.[58] On more than one occasion, Philo portrays God the Father creating the universe through personified wisdom, creation's mother.[59] Furthermore, the Tannaitic literature reflects the understanding that Gen 1:1 was being read through the lens of wisdom acting as the agent of God's creative acts: "God created through wisdom" (Frag. Tg. of Gen 1:1).[60] The Johannine Prologue therefore demonstrates the impact of the Jewish wisdom traditions upon its depiction of God having made all things through his instrumental agent—the personified *logos*.[61]

(C) RECEIVED LIFE AND LIGHT (1:4-5)

Continuing to draw upon themes from the act of creation depicted in Genesis 1, John 1:4-5 describes how that which came into being in the

---

56. Haenchen, *John 1*, 112; Carter, *John and Empire*, 116; Charlesworth, "Lady Wisdom," 114-15; Tobin, "Logos," 353-54; Kruse, *John*, 61.

57. Sidebottom, *Fourth Gospel*, 203; Gaston, "High Christology," 132; Perkins, "John," 944.

58. Morris, *John*, 121; Hurtado, *Lord Jesus Christ*, 366.

59. *Fug.* 109; *Det.* 54.

60. Anderson, "Genesis 1:1 in the Targums," 28-29.

61. Scott, *Sophia*, 98; Thomas Aquinas, *John 1-5*, 33; Dunn, *New Testament Theology*, 63; Carter, "Prologue," 38; Talbert, *Reading John*, 68; Barrett, *Gospel*, 157; Coloe, *John 1-10*, 4.

logos was life, and how this life was the light of humanity.[62] This light is then set in contrast to darkness, with darkness being unable to overtake the light. Again, we can discern the echoes of Genesis 1, where God calls the light "good" and separates the light from the darkness.[63] These three themes—life, light, and darkness—continue throughout the narrative of the Gospel of John as major metaphors within Jesus' discourses, so their introduction in the Prologue is noteworthy. The creation account in Genesis 1 expresses many ways in which God brings forth living things through his creative word ("and God said"), including living creatures, birds, cattle, creeping things, beasts, and even humanity (Gen 1:20, 24, 26–27).

Like the *logos*, personified wisdom brings forth life according to the Jewish wisdom tradition.[64] Within the book of Proverbs, she is a tree of life for those who take hold of her (Prov 3:18) and she offers life to those who find her (Prov 8:35).[65] Baruch assures its readers that all who hold Wisdom fast will live (Bar 4:1).[66] According to the author of Wisdom of Solomon, Lady Wisdom offers a form of life that is special—she offers immortality (Wis 6:18–20). "Because of her," the author declares, "I will have immortality" (Wis 8:13). Both the word of God and the wisdom of God offer life as agents of creation as well as agents of redemption (Wis 9:1–2, 18). Readers of the Prologue familiar with the Jewish wisdom literature would readily associate the life located in the *logos* with the summons to come to Lady Wisdom to find life.

Additionally, God uses his word and wisdom to bring forth light in a manner that illuminates darkness.[67] During creation, God spoke forth his word "Let there be light" when darkness had covered the surface of

---

62. The last three critical editions of the Nestle-Aland Greek text punctuate John 1:4 in this manner, followed by the NRSV and NAB. Boer, "Original Prologue," 465, observes that this was the uncontested reading of all interpreters of John 1:4 (both "orthodox" and "heretic") until the fourth century CE.

63. Boyarin, *Border Lines*, 98; Coloe, *John 1–10*, 10.

64. Coloe, "Structure," 47; Carter, *John and Empire*, 116; Charlesworth, "Lady Wisdom," 116–17; Collins and Collins, *King and Messiah*, 177; Tobin, "Logos," 354; Burnett, "Wisdom," 876.

65. Scott, *Sophia*, 98, and Lincoln, *John*, 99, note that Prov 8:35 is a direct parallel to John 1:4.

66. Talbert, *Reading John*, 68.

67. Tobin, "Logos," 354; Charlesworth, "Lady Wisdom," 117; Achtemeier et al., *New Testament*, 182; Collins and Collins, *King and Messiah*, 177–78.

the deep (Gen 1:2-3).⁶⁸ There is a surfeit of evidence from the Jewish wisdom literature indicating that the wisdom of God gives off an illuminating light.⁶⁹ Personified wisdom enters into the heart of the righteous to deliver them from paths of darkness (Prov 2:10-13), while the path of the righteous is, by contrast, likened to the dawn's light shining brighter and brighter until the full day (Prov 4:18). Similarly, the instruction from Lady Wisdom shines forth like the dawn (Sir 24:25-27, 32). The author of Baruch urges Jacob to turn, take Lady Wisdom, and walk towards the shining of her light (Bar 4:2).⁷⁰ Those who find wisdom will discover light for their eyes and life (Bar 3:14). Wisdom herself is radiant and unfading (Wis 6:12), a reflection of eternal light (Wis 7:26),⁷¹ more beautiful than the sun that shines light, and she is superior to the light (Wis 7:29).⁷² The next verse (Wis 7:30) explains that while the darkness of night overtakes the sun at the end of each day, evil is unable to overtake wisdom. Scholars regularly identify this passage as directly influencing the Prologue's insistence that the darkness did not overtake the light (John 1:5).⁷³ Both Wisdom of Solomon and the Prologue of John juxtapose light and darkness in terms of good and evil, particularly in terms describing personified wisdom. John 1:5 also makes an important shift in tense, going from the past, where the light *was* the light of humanity, to the present, where the light *is currently* shining in the darkness. The Prologue, therefore, sets the tone for the rest of the Gospel of John by introducing the personified *logos* actively shining amid evil darkness.

(D) JOHN THE BAPTIST'S TESTIMONY (1:6-8)

As the Prologue shifts from the poetic illustration of creation themes (1:1-5) toward a short section of prose containing the testimony of John the Baptist (1:6-8), the characterization of the personified *logos*/wisdom

---

68. Bernard, *Gospel*, 1:5; Scott, *Sophia*, 101.

69. Talbert, *Reading John*, 68; Carter, *John and Empire*, 116; Burnett, "Wisdom," 876.

70. Morris, *John*, 83-4, notes that Bar 4:1-2 connects the themes of light and life in a manner that creates a parallel to John 1:4.

71. Dillon, "Wisdom Tradition," 276; Witherington, *Jesus the Sage*, 285; Sidebottom, *Fourth Gospel*, 203; Lincoln, *John*, 99.

72. Schnackenburg, *Gospel*, 1:241-42.

73. Bernard, *Gospel*, 1:6; Thomas Aquinas, *John 1-5*, 45-46; Brown, *John I-XII*, 8; Tobin, "Logos," 354; Talbert, *Reading John*, 68; Brant, *John*, 30; Von Wahlde, *John*, 2:4-5, 29; Carter, *John and Empire*, 116.

as light continues.[74] The Baptist functions as an authorized prophet, commissioned by God in order to offer witness about the light—the new designation for the *logos* in its life-giving and darkness-illuminating activities. The Prologue stresses the fact that John the Baptist was not the light and that his purpose was to testify in order that all might believe through the light (1:7–8). The *logos* that shone light in the beginning continues to shine light during the present within the narrative of the Gospel of John.

(E) NEGATIVE RESPONSE TO THE *LOGOS* (1:9–11)

The Prologue pivots from the figure of the Baptist who witnesses to the content of that witness. The light, now defined as "true," enters the realm of humanity by coming into the world in order to continue God's light-giving purposes (1:9). This description portrays the light in its power to both enlighten darkness and enlighten the insights of humanity. Verse 10 returns to specifically discussing the *logos*, as indicated by the masculine pronouns, rather than the neuter pronouns referring to the light. The mission of the *logos* to the world is, unfortunately, met with rejection, which is ironic since the world was made through the *logos* (1:3).[75] This ironical rejection is repeated in 1:11; the *logos* embodied in Jesus the Jew was not accepted by his own Jewish people.[76]

While the word of God comes to God's people on occasion (e.g., when the word of YHWH comes to a prophet), personified wisdom has a rich history in the Jewish wisdom literature of visiting Israel.[77] Ben Sira details how the Creator commanded Lady Wisdom to come down

---

74. Boyarin, *Border Lines*, 97, remarks: "The material about the Baptist has thus been tightly woven into the old Wisdom myth."

75. Pryor, "Jesus and Israel," 218. Thomas Aquinas, *John 1–5*, 58, nevertheless observes the indebtedness of this reference to earlier passages concerning Wisdom—e.g., Sir 1:10.

76. Pryor, "Jesus and Israel," 207–18, makes a compelling case that 1:11 and the reference to Israel is a more specific view of the lack of acceptance of the *logos* by the world in 1:10. Pryor's argument confirms the interpretation that 1:10–13 refers to the ministry of Jesus as it is presented in the Gospel of John. Boyarin, *Border Lines*, 99, argues convincingly that verse 11 expands on 1:5.

77. McHugh, *John 1–4*, 42; Tobin, "Logos," 354; Coloe, "Structure," 48; *John 1–10*, 4; Talbert, *Reading John*, 68–69; Thompson, *John*, 31; Kuschel, *Born before All Time?*, 382; Perkins, "John," 944; Carter, *John and Empire*, 116; Ringe, *Wisdom's Friends*, 50; Brown, *John I–XII*, 29, who follows Schnackenburg, *Gospel*, 1:88.

from heaven and make a dwelling in Jacob (Sir 24:4–8).[78] Along the same lines, Baruch tells of how God gave personified wisdom to Israel, resulting in her appearance on earth, where she lived with humankind (Bar 3:36–37).[79] The same concept is picked up by the author of Wisdom of Solomon. Wisdom is portrayed as reaching mightily from one end of the earth to the other in Wis 8:1. Solomon prayed that God would send forth Lady Wisdom from the heavenly throne of glory so that she may labor at his side (Wis 9:10).[80]

Just as there are many traditions speaking of personified wisdom coming down from heaven to be among the children of Israel, the sages regularly lament the fact that wisdom was principally rejected by God's people.[81] Lady Wisdom, after making herself publicly accessible, pronounces judgment on those who neglect her counsel (Prov 1:20–31). Ben Sira, the wisdom theologian, offers his own reasons Wisdom is rejected: "The people *without understanding* will not obtain her, and *sinners* will not see her" (Sir 15:7). Baruch confesses that the reason the children of Israel are in the land of their enemies and counted among those in the grave is that they have forsaken the fountain of wisdom (Bar 3:10–12). They have strayed far from the way of Wisdom (Bar 3:21) to the point where no one knows the way to her (Bar 3:31). The author of 1 Enoch 42 laments that personified wisdom tried to dwell among the children of the people, but she found no suitable place, resulting in her return to heaven (1 En. 42:1–2).[82] Raymond Brown directly states that John 1:11 is "a reflection of the Johannine theology that Jesus is personified Wisdom."[83] The Prologue's insistence that the *logos* came into the world only to suffer rejection clearly demonstrates the impact of the Jewish wisdom literature wherein Lady Wisdom descends to earth and subsequently experiences rejection by Israel.[84]

78. Davies, *Rhetoric and Reference*, 82.

79. Boyarin, *Border Lines*, 97.

80. Schnackenburg, *Gospel*, 1:257.

81. Scott, *Sophia*, 102; Haenchen, *John 1*, 117; Talbert, *Reading John*, 69; Carter, *John and Empire*, 116; Tobin, "Logos," 354; Burnett, "Wisdom," 876.

82. Bernard, *Gospel*, 1:14; Brown, *John I-XII*, 30; Witherington, *Jesus the Sage*, 288; Lincoln, *John*, 96; Perkins, "John," 944; Charlesworth, "Lady Wisdom," 117; Beasley-Murray, *John*, 12.

83. Brown, *John I-XII*, 30."

84. Holladay, *Critical Introduction*, 209; Scott, *Sophia*, 104; Manns, "Jewish Approach," 267; Davies, *Rhetoric and Reference*, 82; Boyarin, *Border Lines*, 99; Cullmann, *Christology*, 257. Brown, *John I-XII*, 30, bluntly states that this passage is "a reflection

(F) THOSE WHO RECEIVED THE *LOGOS* BECOME CHILDREN OF GOD (1:12-13)

Although Israel rejected the *logos* of God, some accepted him by believing in his name. To these believers, the *logos* gave the right to become children of God (1:12). This special status is indicative of a newfound familial relationship with Israel's God.[85] In the works of Philo, the *logos* reveals God as the father of the universe, suggesting that the people of God are his children.[86] When we examine Jewish literature that discusses the wisdom of God alongside familial language, we find an abundance of parallels to the language of the Johannine Prologue. The book of Proverbs, which encourages its readers to "make your ear attentive to wisdom" (Prov 2:2; 5:1), frequently regards them as children (Prov 1:8, 10, 15; 2:1; 3:1, 11), even portraying the reader as a child whom a father—YHWH—reproves (Prov 3:12). Personified wisdom summons the children to listen to her and offers a blessing to those who keep her ways (Prov 8:32). Sirach draws influence from Proverbs as it depicts its readers as "children" (Sir 2:1; 3:1, 17: 4:1; 6:32) and even promises "my child" that they will find wisdom if they choose discipline from their youth (Sir 6:18-22). Many wisdom texts even portray personified wisdom as a "mother" (Sir 15:1-2; Wis 7:12). If Lady Wisdom teaches "her children"—those who seek her—then she functions as a mother figure to them (Sir 4:10-11). Philo similarly identifies the mother of all things as the wisdom of God who nurses her children.[87] When Philo speaks of God creating all things through the agency of personified wisdom, Philo calls her a mother.[88] Furthermore, those who take upon wisdom become "wise" children of God (Prov 1:2-3). The Prologue draws upon these Jewish wisdom images in portraying those who accept the *logos*, Wisdom's synonym, as children of God.[89]

---

of the Johannine theology that Jesus is personified Wisdom."

85. Tobin, "Logos," 354, draws attention to Wis 7:27, where personified wisdom makes those through whom she passes into *friends* and *prophets*, but the passages involving children receiving God's wisdom make for a stronger parallel to John 1:12.

86. *Her.* 1.205; *Somn.* 1.70; 190; *QG* 2:62.

87. *Leg. All.* 2.49; *Det.* 115-16.

88. *Det.* 54; *Fug.* 109.

89. Carter, "Prologue," 38-39; *John and Empire*, 116; Talbert, *Reading John*, 69; Coloe, *John 1-10*, 17.

John 1:12 carefully clarifies what it means to accept the *logos* as "believing in his name."[90] The act of believing (*pisteuo*) is a vital behavior that describes those who respond appropriately to the personified *logos* as newly identified children of God. The Jewish wisdom literature similarly depicts those who seek after Lady Wisdom with faithful and believing characteristics. Ben Sira describes the children of wisdom as those who "remain faithful" (*empisteuo*) while promising that these believers will inherit her (Sir 4:11, 16). Additionally, whoever fears the Lord will obtain wisdom, and the recipient will "lean on her" and "rely on her" (Sir 15:1, 4). The sensible person believes (*pisteuo*) and faithfully trusts (*empisteuo*) in the law (Sir 32:24; 33:3), which Sirach formerly identified with Lady Wisdom (Sir 24:1–23). It is only natural that John's Prologue depicts those who accept the *logos*, Lady Wisdom's close synonym, as believers.

Structurally, it is important that we remind ourselves that the center point of the Prologue's chiastic arrangement is 1:12–13, and a chiasm's center point is the intended climax of the argument. This climax consists of the new birth as children of God that is offered to those who accept the *logos* by demonstrating acts of belief and faithfulness. Not only do these points show considerable influence from former depictions of personified wisdom in Jewish literature, but they also function as important themes within the narrative of the Gospel of John and in the book's own purpose statement (20:31).[91] We should be careful to not allow the description of the word's incarnation in the following verse (1:14) to overshadow the rightful climax of the Prologue's purposeful arrangement.[92]

(E') POSITIVE RESPONSES TO THE *LOGOS* (1:14)

Having reached the meeting point of the chiasm, we begin to descend through the parallel lines in the Prologue's stylistic arrangement. John 1:14, among other things, offers the positive response to the *logos* that contrasts with the negative response by "his own" who rejected him in 1:9–11. By describing the positive reception in terms of the *logos* becoming flesh, the author further unpacks three concepts subtly introduced earlier; the personified *logos* came into the world (1:9), he was in the

---

90. Moloney, *John*, 38.
91. Dunn, "Christology (NT)," 987.
92. E.g., Brant, *John*, 26, 34, mistakenly describes John 1:14 as the climax of the prologue after she admits that 1:12–13 is the center point of the passage's chiasm.

world (1:10), and he came to his own (1:11). The embodiment of the personified word of God, often called the "incarnation" of the *logos*, presents a key christological theme in the presentation of Jesus within the Gospel of John. The flesh that the *logos* became describes Jesus in his human capacity, a genuine humanity that is repeatedly emphasized throughout the narrative of John.[93] The personified *logos* that preexisted with God is embodied in the human Jesus, probably at the moment of his birth due to the following designation that Jesus is the unique son of the Father.[94]

While it is true that there are no parallels in pre-Christian Jewish literature to the embodiment of the word of God in human beings, we have already observed several key instances where personified wisdom is portrayed as becoming flesh.[95] The earliest reference is located in the book of Proverbs, where Jewish women during the Persian period embody the very traits and characteristics of Lady Wisdom from chapters 1–9 (Prov 31:10–31). The incarnation of personified wisdom in Proverbs influenced Ben Sira, who similarly illustrated Lady Wisdom with several details and features that were also employed in the description of the historical high priest Simon ben Onias (Sir 50:1–24). Similarly, the author of the Aramaic text Genesis Apocryphon applies several characteristics of personified wisdom from Proverbs to Sarah, Abraham's wife, resulting in Sarah appearing as Wisdom become flesh (1Q20 19–20). We may observe the impact of the incarnation of personified wisdom within Proverbs upon the first-century writings of Philo. On several occasions, Philo Judaeus identifies multiple remarkable women (Sarah, Rebekah, Leah. Zipporah) as Wisdom herself. Contrary to the claim that several scholars promote suggesting that personified wisdom texts from Judaism offer no parallel or precedent, the Prologue's portrayal of Jesus as the human incarnation of the personified word of God is thoroughly biblical, deeply Jewish, and in direct continuity with many strands of wisdom traditions.[96] Culpepper

---

93. McGrath, *John's Apologetic Christology*, 94; Dunn, *First Christians*, 124; King, "Wisdom Became Flesh," 183; Kuschel, *Born before All Time?*, 382.

94. Some interpreters have suggested that the *logos* became flesh at Jesus' baptism, rather than his birth, but this conclusion overlooks the Jewish context of Wisdom becoming flesh in Proverbs, Sirach, Genesis Apocryphon, and Philo, where no baptism is ever in view. Coloe, *John 1–10*, 17, cites BDAG, 197, which has as its first meaning of *ginomai*, "To come into being through process of birth or natural production, *be born, be produced*" (emphasis original to BDAG).

95. See Dunn, "Incarnation," 47.

96. E.g., Scott, *Sophia*, 105, is typical of this sort of conclusion when he mistakenly suggests that the phrase "the word became flesh" is a step "beyond anything said directly

recognizes the traditions of God's wisdom behind the imagery in John 1:14 when he explanations that the preexistent wisdom of God "came in human form in the person of Jesus."[97] Furthermore, the depiction of the *logos* as a personification of the preexisting creative and powerful speech of God shows influence from these former wisdom texts in which God's wisdom is a personification that preexists.[98] Since the personified word of God closely resembled Lady Wisdom, readers of John 1:14 familiar with these wisdom texts could very well understand Jesus as "Wisdom become flesh."[99]

As the embodiment of God's personified *logos*, the human Jesus dwelt among us—presumably a self-reference to those who accepted the *logos* and believed in his name. The Greek verb "to dwell" (*skenoo*) expresses the act of pitching a tent, echoing images of the tabernacle from Israelite history. It also echoes images of Lady Wisdom coming down from heaven to dwell among the children of Israel from various Jewish texts. Most remarkable among the parallels is the portrayal of personified wisdom's journey within Sirach 24.[100] Wisdom speaks in the first person, telling of her desire to find a resting place—a territory in which she may abide (Sir 24:7). The Creator chose a location for Lady Wisdom's tent (*skene*), commanding her, "Make your dwelling [*kataskenoo*] in Jacob" (Sir 24:8).[101] Therefore, she ministered in the holy tent (*skene*) in Zion

---

of Sophia in the tradition." Several other commentators are equally guilty of overlooking the motif of Lady Wisdom's incarnation in pre-Christian Judaism: Haenchen, *John 1*, 119; Lincoln, *John*, 104; Lindars, *Gospel of John*, 79; Ringe, *Wisdom's Friends*, 51; Harris, *Prologue and Gospel*, 198; Phillips, *Prologue*, 197; Fuller, *New Testament Christology*, 226; Burnett, "Wisdom," 876.

97. Culpepper, *Gospel*, 16–17.

98. Wilson, *Proverbs*, 126, discusses this crucial point in her commentary: "Jesus fulfills and embodies OT wisdom . . . but the personified figure of Proverbs 8:22–31 is not a description of the pre-incarnate Christ."

99. Clifford, *Proverbs*, 31–32, comes to the same conclusion: "Early Christians saw Jesus as a wisdom teacher and employed traditions about personified wisdom to express his incarnation . . . John draws most explicitly on Proverbs to present Jesus as incarnate wisdom." McHugh, *John 1–4*, 95: "The sense of Jn 1.14 is that all that had previously been true of the Word and Wisdom of God in the OT is from a particular moment in time, the moment of the incarnation, embodied in Jesus of Nazareth, Jesus the Christ." Borg, *Meeting Jesus Again*, 108: "Sophia became flesh and dwelt among us." Richardson, *Theology*, 163: "Wisdom, i.e., God himself in action, became flesh-and blood, became a piece of human history." See also Cullmann, *Johannine Circle*, 92.

100. Haenchen, *John 1*, 119. Oh, "John 1:14," 212, remarks that this interpretation is "the most popular scholarly view" as of the year 2022.

101. Schnackenburg, *Gospel*, 1:269; Scott, *Sophia*, 106; Dillon, "Wisdom Tradition,"

(Sir 24:10). Similarly, Baruch tells how personified wisdom appeared on earth among the children of Israel, taking the form of the book of God's commandments (Bar 3:37—4:1). Incarnate Wisdom, not the law, has come to find acceptance among the followers of Jesus.[102] 1 Enoch 42:1-2 also describes how wisdom came down out of heaven in order to dwell among the people, only to return to heaven after finding no suitable dwelling place.[103] Mary Coloe brilliantly draws attention to how the episode in John 2:13-22 where Jesus cleanses the temple is best viewed as Sophia claiming her temple dwelling, particularly because 1:14 indicates that Wisdom became flesh and tabernacled among us.[104] The Prologue's depiction of the incarnate *logos* dwelling among the children of God, therefore, draws considerable influence from Jewish texts detailing personified wisdom's descent from heaven to dwell among the children of Israel.[105]

The Johannine community—the original intended readers of the Fourth Gospel—beheld the glory (*doxa*) of the *logos* made flesh, a glory that is naturally associated with the tabernacle imagery of the verb "to dwell." Although the linkage between the word of God and "glory" is notably absent from Second Temple Jewish texts, it is rather abundant when we consider the passages describing God's personified wisdom. Within the book of Proverbs, Lady Wisdom openly declares that "riches and glory [Hebrew: *kavod*; LXX: *doxa*] are with me" (Prov 8:18). Ben Sira assures his readers that whoever holds fast Lady Wisdom inherits glory (Sir 4:13). Those who find wisdom and take upon her yoke will wear her like a robe of glory (Sir 6:29-31). We can observe similar imagery in Wisdom of Solomon. For example, personified wisdom is a pure emanation of the glory of the Almighty (Wis 7:25).[106] Solomon's prayer beseeches God to send forth wisdom so that she can guard him with her glory (Wis 9:10-11).[107] Despite his youth, Solomon believes that he will possess

276; Brown, *John I-XII*, 32; Charlesworth, "Lady Wisdom," 117–18; Witherington, *Jesus the Sage*, 288; Von Wahlde, *John*, 2:11; Lincoln, *John*, 96, 104.

102. Talbert, *Reading John*, 72.

103. Haenchen, *John 1*, 124–25; Barrett, *Gospel*, 166.

104. Coloe, *John 1–10*, 65–69.

105. Brown, *John I-XII*, 33, is helpful here: "In making his dwelling among men, the Word is acting in the manner of Wisdom." See also Talbert, *Reading John*, 69; Carter, *John and Empire*, 116; Coloe, *John 1–10*, 15; Tobin, "Logos," 354; Achtemeier et al., *New Testament*, 182; Manns, "Jewish Approach," 267.

106. Brown, *John I-XII*, cxxiii.

107. Scott, *Sophia*, 106.

glory because of Lady Wisdom (Wis 8:10). The author of the Enochic *Book of Parables* illustrates the wisdom of God flowing like water, and in doing so he notes how glory is measureless before God (1 En. 49:1). The conclusions of Evans are decisive at this point: "God's wisdom, has, in a manner not unlike the very glory of God descending and occupying the leather tent of Exod 40, entered into the human realm as a human being."[108] Therefore when personified wisdom became flesh and dwelt among the Johannine community, they beheld the glory that Jewish texts frequently associated with God's wisdom.[109]

John 1:14 continues by further defining this glory as the glory of the unique one (*monogenes*).[110] Since the one-of-a-kind, unique one is from the Father, it is self-evident that he is the Father's son.[111] The Greek adjective *monogenes*—an extremely rare word in pre-Christian Judaism—is a direct quote from Wis 7:22, where the author paints Lady Wisdom as "unique" among several other characteristics. It is important to observe the fact that the Prologue's depiction of the Johannine Jesus with the adjective *monogenes* directly draws upon imagery describing Lady Wisdom, while there are no parallels to the *logos* with this adjective in pre-Christian Jewish texts.[112]

As the incarnation of the word and wisdom of God, Jesus is full of the Father's grace (*charis*) and truth (*aletheia*). These two attributes distinctively belong to YHWH, according to several passages in the Hebrew Bible.[113] However, both of these traits also characterize Jewish portrayals

---

108. Evans, "Evidence of Conflict," 151–52.

109. Ringe, *Wisdom's Friends*, 51; Carter, *John and Empire*, 116; Witherington, *Jesus the Sage*, 288; *John's Wisdom*, 55.

110. While it used to be favorable to interpret the adjective *monogenes* as "only-begotten," Greek grammarians have almost universally shifted, based upon sound etymology, to the understanding of "unique, one of a kind, one and only." See the examples in BDAG, 658; Keener, *Gospel of John*, 1:412–16. Coutsoumpos, "ΜΟΝΟΓΕΝΗΣ ΘΕΟΣ," 436–37, offers examples from the LXX, Hellenistic authors, and writings of Clement of Rome, Clement of Alexandria, and Eusebius demonstrating that they understood *monogenes* to mean "only"/"unique." Collins and Collins, *King and Messiah*, 176–77, observe that the adjective is attested with the meaning "only-begotten" in the later patristic Christian texts. In the Greek texts contemporary with the Gospel of John, however, *monogenes* means "the only member of a kin or kind."

111. Barrett, *Gospel*, 166. The implication here should not be overlooked; while God has *many* children (*tekna*, 1:13), he only has *one* son—the only son (1:14).

112. Talbert, *Reading John*, 69; Scott, *Sophia*, 107; Von Wahlde, *John*, 2:12; Ringe, *Wisdom's Friends*, 51; Sidebottom, *Fourth Gospel*, 203; Carter, *John and Empire*, 116.

113. 2 Sam 15:20; Pss 25:10; 40:11; 57:10; 89:1, 2, 14, 24, 33, 49. I credit Epp, "Wisdom, Torah, Word," 139, for these references.

of Lady Wisdom.[114] In the book of Proverbs, personified wisdom will place a garland of grace (LXX: *charis*) upon the head of those who prize her and embrace her (Prov 4:7–9). Those who keep sound wisdom and understanding will find life for their soul and adornment to their neck (LXX: "grace around your neck" [Prov 3:21–22]). After Lady Wisdom descends from heaven to make her dwelling among the children of Israel, she takes root as a terebinth. This tree spreads forth its branches as branches of grace (Sir 24:16). As a vine, wisdom sprouts forth grace (Sir 24:17). Ben Sira also describes the lack of God's grace as direct evidence of the lack of Wisdom herself (Sir 37:21). Similarly, truth is a frequent property of personified wisdom within Jewish texts. Out of the mouth of Lady Wisdom comes truth (Prov 8:7), and Proverbs later places the acquisition of truth and wisdom in synonymous parallelism (Prov 23:23).[115] In a similar fashion, Ben Sira states that wisdom becomes known through speech, and then exhorts the reader to never speak against the truth (Sir 4:24–25). Wisdom of Solomon reports that those who trust in the Lord will understand truth, while those who despise wisdom are miserable (Wis 3:9–11). Later, the author claims, "I will tell you what wisdom is . . . and I will not pass by truth" (Wis 6:22). The Prologue of John can definitively claim that Jesus is full of grace and truth because he is the incarnation of God's wisdom—the wisdom that reveals the grace and truth of Israel's God.[116]

(D') JOHN THE BAPTIST'S TESTIMONY (1:15)

The prose witness of John the Baptist is the next parallel line we encounter in the Prologue's chiastic arrangement. The Baptist's role is twofold: he wants to lessen the significance readers might perceive of him in order to not rival the importance of Jesus Christ and he wants to act as an authorized prophet who testifies about the true messianic status of Jesus. John accomplishes this with his testimony, saying that Jesus, who was born after John, has a higher rank than John. As the Jewish Messiah and the unique one from the Father, Jesus would certainly rank higher than even a premier, heaven-sent prophet like John, despite John being chronologically older than Jesus. However, John offers an additional reason as

---

114. Ringe, *Wisdom's Friends*, 51.
115. Scott, *Sophia*, 110.
116. Von Wahlde, *John*, 1:413.

to why Jesus ranks higher than him: "for he was before me." The Baptist points to the preexistence of the *logos* in order to answer how Jesus outranks John. Since Jesus is the embodiment of the personified word and wisdom of God—both of which preexisted all things—John concludes that Jesus was before him.[117] The personified *logos* that was with God in the beginning has become flesh, and John the Baptist continues to see the activity and work of the *logos* operating in the person of the human Jesus. From the perspective of the Baptist's present, he recognizes the *logos* incarnate and speaks of preexistence because Jesus embodies the preexistent personified *logos*. Therefore, Jesus outranks John the Baptist because of his messianic status and because of the preeminent origins of the word and wisdom of God.

(C') RECEIVED GRACE (1:16)

The unique son who is full of grace and truth exudes grace upon grace. Those who received the *logos* (1:12) are now spoken of as having received an abundance of grace out of the son's fullness. While, admittedly, the noun for "fullness" (*pleroma*) does not appear in the relevant Jewish wisdom texts in relation to the wisdom of God, the corresponding verb "to fill" (*pleroo*) does yield some interesting results. The Greek translation of Ps 104:24 uses the verb to illustrate how the earth that YHWH created with wisdom as his agent is filled with creatures (Ps 103:24 LXX). The wisdom theologian who authored Wisdom of Solomon offers a similar portrayal. In Wis 1:6–7, personified wisdom is likened to the activity of the Spirit of the Lord, who has "filled" the inhabited earth. So, there are good reasons to situate the interpretation of the fullness of the incarnate *logos* within the context of God's wisdom.[118] The Prologue's chiasm sets John 1:16 in parallel with 1:4–5, where humanity receives life and the light that illuminates the darkness. The characteristics of grace, life, and light amid darkness all belong to God's personified wisdom within the Jewish sapiential texts. As the embodiment of the wisdom of God, the unique son blesses those who receive him with the fullness of his grace.

---

117. Some have tried to argue that the last phrase of 1:15 should be rendered "for he was my superior," but this fails to take seriously how the preposition "for" functions as an elaboration of how the preceding statement in 1:15 is true. To say that Jesus ranks higher than John because Jesus is superior is needlessly redundant.

118. Scott, *Sophia*, 112.

(B') GRACE AND TRUTH THROUGH JESUS (1:17)

Just as all things were made through the personified *logos* (1:3), grace and truth are realized through the *logos* incarnate, Jesus Christ. This is the first time the son's name appears in the Johannine Prologue, even though initiated readers would not be unfamiliar with him or his messianic role. John 1:17 sets Moses and Jesus in parallel lines, and the relationship between these lines is likely synthetical. The law that came through Moses contained grace and truth, but readers can experience grace and truth in an exceedingly superior way through Jesus Christ.

Personified wisdom is identified with the Mosaic law in Sirach (Sir 24:8–12), Baruch (Bar 3:37—4:1), and throughout the Tannaitic and Amoraic literature.[119] In fact, several of the characteristics of the *logos* illustrated in the Prologue appeared in contemporary Jewish descriptions of the Torah.[120] More to the point, the wisdom of God—in the form of the law—came through Moses, but now wisdom is available and embodied in a person, Jesus Christ. With this parallel line, the Prologue accomplishes the portrayal of the Mosaic law as a positive thing through which wisdom was commonly thought to be found, while at the same time pointing to the flesh that Wisdom became as the definitive and final locus of God's wise and self-expressive activity.[121] By striking this balance, the author of the Prologue does not place the law and Christ in an either/or relationship; he instead transfers the wisdom-empowered characteristics from the holy law to the man Jesus.[122]

---

119. m. 'Abot. 3:14; Gen. Rab. 1:1, 4; 8:2; 54:1. Epp, "Wisdom, Torah, Word," 136, helpfully observes: "Torah comes naturally to mind in a Wisdom hymn context."

120. Epp, "Wisdom, Torah, Word," 133–35, offers a detailed list demonstrating that Torah preexisted; was with God in the beginning; played an instrumental role in creation; was related to light, life, salvation, and truth; made an appearance in the world; and was characterized by glory.

121. Culpepper, *Gospel*, 58, argues that the Johannine community, by taking the high claims made for Wisdom and using them to describe Jesus, gives credence to their claim that the revelation Jesus offers is higher than what Moses offered. See also McGrath, *Apologetic*, 152–53, 176–77; Lincoln, *John*, 108; Ringe, *Wisdom's Friends*, 52. The emphasis on Jesus as the embodiment of Wisdom, rather than the law of Moses, will frequently reappear throughout the narrative of the Gospel of John.

122. Epp, "Wisdom, Torah, Word," 141, fleshed out this point by arguing that the Johannine Jesus, by fulfilling the role that the holy law anticipated in such passages as John 1:45; 5:39, 45–46; 7:19–23, 42, 49–51; 8:17; 10:34; 12:34; 15:25; 18:31–32, has displaced the law without casting the law in a negative light.

(A') THE UNIQUE SON IS WITH GOD (1:18)

The final verse of the Prologue concludes in a similar fashion to the way it began. The personified *logos* was with the God of Israel (1:1-2), and now the unique son—the *logos* made flesh—is in the bosom of the Father. The former speaks about the past and the latter speaks about the present. The parallelism clarifies that "the God" in the opening lines (1:1-2) is none other than the Father—the unseen God. While the Prologue contends that no one has ever seen God, the unique "son" (arguably the most likely textual variant) has made the unseen God known to the world.[123] John 1:18 draws influence from three characteristics of personified wisdom. First, the son who reveals the unseen God is called the unique one (*monogenes*), an adjective that, as we observed in John 1:14, deliberately cites one of the traits describing Lady Wisdom in Wis 7:22.

Second, the unique son is in the bosom of the Father, a location that indicates an intimate relationship between God and his son.[124] The first-person speech of Lady Wisdom in Proverbs 8 offers a remarkably similar illustration of her measure of intimacy with YHWH. "I was daily his delight," says Wisdom, "rejoicing always before him, rejoicing in the world, his earth" (Prov 8:30-31). As the embodiment of wisdom, the man Jesus continues the close-knit relationship with God that personified wisdom maintained with YHWH at creation.

Third, the unique son functions as the definitive revealer of God, the one who "exegetes" (*exegeomai*) the Father to the world. The wisdom poem in Job 28 uses the same verb to illustrate how the Creator God saw wisdom, declared her (*exegeomai*), established her, and searched her

---

123. See the arguments in Schnackenburg, *Gospel*, 1:279-80; Haenchen, *John 1*, 121; McGrath, *Only True God*, 64-67; Moloney, *John*, 46-47; Harris, *Prologue and Gospel*, 103; Coloe, *John 1-10*, 17. McHugh, *John 1-4*, 69, admits that while the two major variant readings ("*monogenes* God" and "*monogenes* son") are delicately balanced, the latter is more widely attested when the manuscripts, ancient versions, and the early church fathers are looked at together. The critical versions of the Greek New Testament (UBS5 and NA28) favor *monogenes theos* on the argument that the least likely variant is to be preferred, but it is difficult to grasp why a scribe would change "God" to "son" in the manuscripts, thus effectively demoting their own view of Christ. Von Wahlde, *John*, 2:16, follows Ehrman, *Orthodox Corruption of Scripture*, 78-82, in favoring the reading "son" over "God" by pointing out that the latter reading is isolated to Alexandrian manuscripts and that it is so difficult as to be meaningless.

124. If the idea that "Torah lies on God's bosom" ('Abot R. Nat. 31 [8b]) preserves a sentiment contemporary to the late first century CE, then the Prologue would here continue to display the idea from 1:17—Wisdom incarnate has fulfilled the role of Torah.

out (Job 28:27 LXX).[125] Ben Sira also presupposes that no one has ever seen God and asks, "Who has seen him and who can describe him?" (Sir 43:31). In this verse, the verb "to describe" is semantically related to *exegeomai*: *ekdiegeomai* ("to provide detailed information when telling something").[126] In other words, Ben Sira wants to know who has seen God and who can reveal him. The answer comes shortly after: "For the Lord has made all things, and to the godly he has given wisdom" (Sir 43:33). It is Lady Wisdom, the personification of God's wise interactions and self-expression, who is able to make God known. Since Sirach portrays wisdom as the revealer of God, those who serve her are, in effect, ministering to the Holy One, God (Sir 4:14). According to Wisdom of Solomon, it is personified wisdom who has been initiated into God's knowledge, exclusively qualifying her to reveal that knowledge to others (8:4).[127] Since Jesus—the unique son—is wisdom made flesh, he is exceptionally qualified to function as the human revealer of God.[128] This particular emphasis will reappear later in the narrative when Jesus declares, "He who has seen me has seen the Father" (John 14:9).

CONCLUSION

As we bring this chapter to a close, it is crucial that we take stock of the overwhelming influence that Jewish texts and traditions concerning God's personified wisdom had upon the Johannine Prologue. This chapter sought to demonstrate how the origins and activity of God's personified *logos* overlap with Jewish descriptions of Lady Wisdom, which ultimately serve to characterize the main subject of the Gospel of John—Jesus Christ—in terms of wisdom.[129] Hans Weder summarizes the data by insisting that the Prologue "cannot be understood without reference to the wisdom theology of Hellenistic Judaism."[130] Marianne

---

125. McHugh, *John 1–4*, 74.

126. BDAG, 300; Manns, "Jewish Approach," 267.

127. Dillon, "Wisdom Tradition," 277; Talbert, *Reading John*, 70; Carter, *John and Empire*, 116.

128. Gaston, *Dynamic Monarchianism*, 15.

129. Several scholars draw the same conclusion: Kovalishyn, "Wisdom in the New Testament," 177; Dunn, *First Christians*, 145; Ashton, "Transformation of Wisdom," 174; Devillers, "Prologue," 328; Meyers et al., *Women in Scripture*, 554; Kee, *Jesus in History*, 243–47.

130. Weder, "Deus Incarnatus," 328–29. Köstenberger, *John*, 26–31, seems desperate

Meye Thompson draws a similar conclusion at the close of her exegesis on the Johannine Prologue: "Wisdom and word, coordinated with John's presentation of Jesus as the Son, advance such a Christology."[131] The Johannine Jesus takes on the functions and role of Lady Wisdom.[132] Here is a summary of the data demonstrating the impact of the wisdom of God upon the Johannine Prologue:

1. The opening phrase "In the beginning" recalls similar language that was widely used of God's wisdom (Proverbs, Aristobulus, Sirach, Wisdom of Solomon, Tannaitic and Amoraic literature).
2. The personified *logos* was "with" God in the beginning, just as the personified wisdom was with God (Proverbs, Sirach, Wisdom of Solomon).
3. God's *logos* fully expresses God, like how personified wisdom expresses God's wise interactions (Sirach, Wisdom).
4. The *logos* in the Prologue is a personification, not a conscious person, exactly as wisdom was a personification and not a person in contemporary Jewish literature (Job, Proverbs, Aristobulus, Sirach, Wisdom of Solomon, "Hymn to the Creator," Philo, 1 Enoch).
5. God created all things through his *logos*, which parallels how God created all things through his wisdom (Psalms, Proverbs, Wisdom of Solomon, "Hymn to the Creator," Philo, Tannaitic and Amoraic literature).
6. Life is found in the *logos*, just as life is found in personified wisdom (Proverbs, Sirach, Baruch, Wisdom of Solomon, Genesis Apocryphon).
7. The *logos* of God brings light to darkness, and personified wisdom brings light to darkness (Proverbs, Aristobulus Sirach, Baruch, Wisdom of Solomon).

---

in his attempt to affirm his understanding that the *logos* is the second member of a triune God so that he downplays the influence of personified wisdom texts on the Prologue, despite his acknowledging of the strength of such influence. Köstenberger's move to divorce John from his Jewish context while at the same time importing an anachronistic fifth-century understanding of God into the Prologue is wholly unconvincing.

131. Thompson, *John*, 39. See also the helpful comments in Scott, *Sophia*, 113.
132. Achtemeier et al., *New Testament*, 182.

8. The *logos* was in the world and rejected by the world, remarkably similar to how God's wisdom suffered rejection by the world (Proverbs, Sirach, Baruch, Wisdom of Solomon, 1 Enoch).

9. Those who received the *logos* become children of God, just like those who receive personified wisdom (Proverbs, Sirach, Wisdom of Solomon, Philo).

10. "Belief" is the appropriate response to encountering the *logos*, and the same behavior is expected from one who appropriately responds to the wisdom of God (Sirach).

11. The personified *logos* becomes incarnate in Jesus, which shows influence from former depictions of personified wisdom becoming incarnate in various human beings (Proverbs, Sirach, Genesis Apocryphon, Philo).

12. The embodied *logos* dwelt/tabernacled among us, echoing back to images of personified wisdom dwelling among Israel (Sirach, Baruch, 1 Enoch).

13. The incarnate *logos* reveals the Father's glory, just as the wisdom of God reveals God's glory (Proverbs, Sirach, Wisdom of Solomon, 1 Enoch).

14. The *logos* that is made flesh is the "unique one" (*monogenes*), which quotes from an earlier list of descriptions of Lady Wisdom (Wisdom of Solomon).

15. The incarnate *logos* is full of grace, and grace is a trait belonging to wisdom (Proverbs, Sirach).

16. The incarnate *logos* is also full of truth, and personified wisdom is a regular synonym for truth (Proverbs, Sirach, Wisdom of Solomon).

17. The readers have benefited from the fullness of the incarnate *logos*, and the Jewish wisdom texts used the related verb to portray the activity of God's wisdom (Psalms, Wisdom of Solomon).

18. The law came through Moses, and grace and truth came through Jesus; all three of these are strongly associated with the wisdom of God (Sirach, Baruch, Tannaitic literature).

19. The unique son is in the bosom of the Father, just as Lady Wisdom was in an intimate relationship with YHWH (Proverbs, Wisdom of Solomon).

20. The unique son authoritatively reveals the unseen God, just as wisdom reveals God (Job, Sirach, 1 Enoch).

The argument that the Johannine Prologue is dependent upon the portrayals of the wisdom of God in Jewish wisdom literature does not rest on accepting all twenty of these conclusion points. Discerning readers will likely find some of these points stronger and more well represented in the wisdom literature than others. I was careful to document the specific Jewish sources that could conceivably impact the various descriptions of the *logos* in the Prologue, while also citing scholars who have come to observe similar connections. The conclusion would still stand if only ten of the points were deemed as persuasively demonstrating the legitimacy of the wisdom parallels from Jewish literature. In other words, this argument rests on the weight of the entire argument taken generally, not by accepting all twenty of these connections.

In any case, I will argue that these twenty points will remain important as we continue our examination of Wisdom Christology in the Gospel of John, particularly because the Prologue functions as the introduction for the rest of the narrative.[133] Ben Witherington's insights are helpful here: "The *whole of the Fourth Gospel* is dependent on the Wisdom hymn in the first chapter."[134] This means that we can expect the images of Jesus in terms of the wisdom of God to reappear as the narrative unfolds and tells its story.[135] James D. G. Dunn offers similar guidance by arguing that the Gospel of John was intended to be read through the lens of the Prologue.[136] As it will soon become apparent, the narrative of the Gospel of John is heavily saturated with images of Jesus that show influence from Jewish traditions of the wisdom of God, and many of these have been introduced in the Prologue.

I have chosen to organize the various characterizations of the Johannine Jesus in terms of wisdom in five distinct categories. In chapter 4, we will explore how the relationship between the preexisting wisdom and God the Father continues in the life and ministry of Jesus Christ. In

---

133. O'Boyle, *Wisdom Christology*, 160–61, observes that much of what is presented in the Prologue would not have sounded foreign to anyone familiar with the Jewish wisdom traditions.

134. Witherington, *John's Wisdom*, 54, emphasis added.

135. Scott, *Sophia*, 114–15, indicates that the Prologue "in some way anticipates the Gospel as a whole" is a conclusion generally shared by scholars. See also Carter, *John and Empire*, 115.

136. Dunn, "Let John Be John," 334; "New Testament Christology," 24.

the fifth chapter, we will examine precisely how Jesus, the incarnation of personified wisdom, continues in wisdom's mission to wisely interact with God's creation. Chapter 6 will focus on Christology, with titles, images, and metaphors of Jesus that draw influence from Jewish wisdom texts. In chapter 7 we will investigate how embodied wisdom continues to suffer rejection from Jesus' opponents. Finally, chapter 8 will delve into the various ways in which wisdom interacts with the disciples in order to transform them into the children of God. In this approach, we will be exploring the Wisdom Christology within the Gospel of John *thematically*, rather than chronologically.

Let us now turn to the rest of the Fourth Gospel so that we may begin to study the various ways the author embedded the wisdom of God within the wider narrative.

4

Wisdom and God in the Narrative of John

IN THE PREVIOUS CHAPTER, we observed that the Johannine Prologue—which serves as the introduction to the contents of the Gospel of John—begins with the assertion that the word was with Israel's God. With a view to the author's present day, the Prologue concludes with a parallel statement: the unique son embodying the word is currently in the bosom of the Father. We noted that readers familiar with Jewish texts pertaining to wisdom would have inferred several points of influence upon the *logos* by earlier depictions of Lady Wisdom. Since the personified word of God effectively overlapped in meaning and function with the personified wisdom of God, we are fully within our rights as interpreters to regard the opening and closing lines of the Prologue (1:1, 18) as speaking about *personified wisdom* that was with the God of Israel in the beginning, as well the unique son—*the incarnation of personified wisdom*—in the bosom of the Father.

In this chapter, I will sketch the various ways in which this close connection between God and his wisdom continues to be expressed in the narrative of the Gospel of John.[1] Since the opening line of the Prologue speaks to the preexistence in ways that echo Lady Wisdom's preexistence, our first task will be to discuss what preexistence means and how passages in the Fourth Gospel draw on Wisdom traditions to speak about Jesus' preexistence. Since wisdom was in the beginning with God, discussing the sending of wisdom into the world to perform the works of

---

1. Schüssler Fiorenza, *Jesus*, 167, points out that the narrative characterization of Jesus within the Gospel of John is that of Wisdom incarnate.

God will be our second point of focus. Jesus frequently acknowledges his sent status, so our third task will be to examine how he acts in obedience to the God who sent him. I will also demonstrate the close ties between sending the obedient son and the love that God has for the son. Therefore, exploring the ways in which the Father loves the son will be our fourth task. Our chapter will conclude with a look at the united purpose and oneness shared by God and the obedient son. I will begin each of these five points by surveying how the Gospel of John sets them forth in its plot, and then I will discern in what ways these portrayals exhibit influence from the Jewish wisdom texts, thereby assessing the many ways in which the Johannine Jesus is deliberately portrayed in terms of God's wisdom.

THE PREEXISTENCE OF LADY WISDOM

Jewish preexistence is a fascinating concept. Jews and early Christians speculated about how a person, thing, or attribute could exist alongside God from the beginning. However, it would be a fool's errand to assume that the concept of preexistence contains within it only a single meaning. For more than one hundred years, biblical scholarship has noticed at least two distinct ways in which speculations about preexistence found their meaning.[2] The first way in which the concept of preexistence is discussed in Jewish and early Christian literature is what we might label as literal preexistence: something that physically existed in the beginning with God. The existence of the subject in this sort of preexistence is real and actual. The second way in which Jewish and early Christian texts explored preexistence is what we might call notional preexistence; a person or thing exists notionally—that is, in God's mind. This manner of preexistence is not the actual existence of the thing or person in question. Notional preexistence pertains to the existence of a subject strictly in the plans and purposes of God. Sometimes interpreters assume these two different ways in which the concept of preexistence was understood are one and the same, but this would be a mistake, as the two definitions are incompatible with each other.[3] David Capes distinguishes the

2. Barton, "Jewish-Christian Doctrine," 78–79, notes several scholars who distinguish between ideal preexistence and real preexistence. See especially Irons et al., *Son of God*, 165–66; Keener, *John*, 1:367.

3. See the extensive documentation in Strack et al., *Commentary on the New Testament*, 2:388–400.

two meanings as "ideal (existence in the mind or plan of God) or actual (existence alongside and distinct from God)."[4] Robert Hamerton-Kelly also acknowledges the distinction between the two types of preexistence, labeling them as "either in the mind of God or in heaven."[5] Larry Hurtado admits that sometimes it is difficult to discern if a text is describing "an independent, heavenly existence to some other kind of prior reality in the mind or plan of God."[6] In short, the concept of Jewish preexistence is not a monolithic idea.

What sort of Jewish preexistence fits with the claim that Jesus is the incarnation of God's personified wisdom? By following Larry Hurtado's wise caution, I conclude that the Johannine Jesus is the embodiment of the wisdom of God—Wisdom who is a personification, not a conscious, preexisting person.[7] This careful distinction suggests that while it is accurate to speak about Jesus Christ possessing a preexistence within the Gospel of John, the nature of his preexistence must be interpreted following the definition of Lady Wisdom. To say that "Jesus preexisted as wisdom" is, therefore, not to suggest a literal, conscious preexistence of Jesus.[8] Rather, it is to both identify the preexistent wisdom as the personification of God's wise intentions and to interpret Jesus as the present locus of the wise interactions and self-expression of the Father. Since the author of the Prologue has labored to portray Jesus as preexistent Wisdom's embodiment, we must carefully observe the important personified quality of this wisdom when we encounter references to preexistence within the Gospel of John.[9]

In chapter 3 we examined the testimony of John the Baptist that concerns his relationship to Jesus, both in rank and in chronology (1:15). The Baptist acknowledges that Jesus came after John, while paradoxically also indicating that Jesus was before John. As a prophet authorized by God (1:6), John the Baptist would have insight into the person, purposes,

---

4. Capes, "Preexistence," 956. See also Dunn, *Theology of Paul*, 273; Richardson, *Theology*, 155.

5. Hamerton-Kelly, *Pre-Existence*, 11, 21.

6. Hurtado, "Pre-Existence," 744.

7. It may be more precise to observe a differentiation between preexistence in God's mind and preexistence as a personification (wisdom or word). Both constitute a category that is distinct from literal, conscious preexistence.

8. See the discussion of the preexistence of the Jewish Messiah as ideal in Klausner, *Messianic Idea in Israel*, 460.

9. On the portrayal of Wisdom as preexisting in the heavenly abode, see the helpful discussion in Gammie, "Spatial and Ethical Dualism," 365–66.

and origins of Jesus Christ. Since the Prologue indicates that Wisdom was in the beginning with God and that this Wisdom became flesh in the man Jesus, John's testimony that Jesus was before John should be understood in light of Jesus' preexistence as personified wisdom. In John 1:30, we find an almost identical confession from John about Jesus, their relationship, rank, and origins: "This is he on behalf of whom I said, 'After me comes a man who has a higher rank, for he was before me.'" Like the Baptist's testimony in 1:15, Jesus is presented paradoxically as coming after John in addition to being before John. The reaffirmation in 1:30 confirms the birth of Jesus chronologically after John while simultaneously explaining Jesus' high rank in light of his preexistence. Again, we should interpret the nature of Jesus' preexistence based on the clear affirmations from the Prologue—Jesus preexisted in the form of the personified wisdom of God.

The Baptist's restatement carries with it the additional christological feature that Jesus is a man, a human being. While the Fourth Gospel presents Jesus as the embodiment of Lady Wisdom, who was with God in the beginning, this Jesus is still a genuine member of the human race, without any sort of qualification from John that would suggest that Jesus' humanity is anything less than authentic or real. As James D. G. Dunn astutely observes, "Jesus was not himself pre-existent; he was the man that pre-existent Wisdom became."[10] Personified wisdom has come down out of heaven and become incarnate in the human Jesus—a man who outranks the prophet John despite being younger than him.

The motif of Jesus' preexistence in terms of the wisdom of God occurs in two further instances during the course of Jesus' prayer to the only true God (17:1–26). The first occurrence is in 17:5, where Jesus beseeches the Father to "glorify me with yourself with the glory that I had before the world was." This petition combines two characteristics of Lady Wisdom from Jewish literature: wisdom's *glory* and her *preexistence* alongside the Father.[11] The prayerful Jesus, conscious of the fact that he is the embodiment of the wisdom of God, speaks about wisdom's preexistent glory as he draws a line backward from his life to a time before the world was. In uttering this request, Jesus acknowledges the authority of the Father as the one able to glorify Jesus and answer this petition. While the outcome of this process of glorification will become apparent in the

---

10. Dunn, *Unity and Diversity*, 238.
11. Shafer, "Wisdom Christology," 56.

upcoming crucifixion of Jesus, the glory is something that Lady Wisdom possessed from the beginning. According to the book of Proverbs, personified wisdom, who possesses glory (Prov 8:18), was "with" YHWH (Prov 8:30). The same preposition (*para*) used here is the same one that appears in John 17:5 to describe the glory Jesus had "with" (*para*) God. The prayer in Wisdom of Solomon reaffirms that wisdom was "with" God and that she was present when God created the world (Wis 9:9–10).[12] These lines of influence from Jewish wisdom literature confirm our use of Wisdom Christology to interpret the statement of Jesus' preexistence in John 17:5.[13]

The second instance of preexistence theology in Jesus' prayer occurs in John 17:24. Jesus shifts to praying for the disciples, their unity, and for them to experience his glory. In his explanation for this request, Jesus states to the Father that "you loved me before the foundation of the world." Since we are already alerted to the characteristics of wisdom in depictions of the Johannine Jesus' preexistence, we can consider what elements of this passage show influence from the Jewish wisdom traditions. Jesus' petition mentions the intimate love between him and God as well as the concept of preexistence before the world's foundation. Both concepts appear in the sapiential literature portraying the wisdom of God as well as within the Prologue of John. One such passage is Proverbs 8, which details the intimacy between personified wisdom and YHWH (Prov 8:30–31). The same chapter also illustrates Lady Wisdom's preexistence before the time when YHWH created the world (Prov 8:22–30). The poem in Job 28 further demonstrates the close and deep knowledge that God had of his wisdom at the time of creation (Job 28:23–27). As the wisdom of God made flesh, Jesus is able to speak in terms of his own preexistence by drawing upon the language and imagery describing God's personified wisdom. In doing so, Jesus demonstrates his commitment to Wisdom Christology, and he prays that his followers would share in the oneness of purpose that God shares with his wisdom.[14]

---

12. Schnackenburg, *John*, 3:174.

13. Witherington, *John's Wisdom*, 269, rightly observes that Wisdom Christology lies behind the discussion of "glory" in 17:5 but incorrectly regards Wisdom as something more than a personification. Witherington seems to have conveniently forgotten his own conclusions expressed in *Jesus the Sage*, 115–16, where he plainly stated that Wisdom is not a person or goddess, but is instead a personification.

14. O'Boyle, *Wisdom Christology*, 173–75.

GOD LOVES HIS WISDOM

We are observing a close association between the preexistence of God's wisdom and the loving, intimate relationship between wisdom and God the Father. This is remarkable at the level of Hebrew poetry, as it indicates that Lady Wisdom was daily the delight of YHWH and that the feeling was mutual (Prov 8:30–31). The Johannine Prologue demonstrates significant influence of this close, loving connection between God and his personified wise attribute by bookending the opening hymn with references to the *logos* that was with God in the beginning (John 1:1) as well as the present indicator that the unique son currently resides in the Father's bosom (1:18). The theme of God's love for Lady Wisdom flows forth from the Prologue's bookends into the wider narrative of the Gospel of John with several instances of the Father loving the son—the incarnation of wisdom.

In the final speech of John the Baptist, we can observe a notable occurrence of this loving relationship between God and Jesus within the Fourth Gospel. In John 3:35, the Baptist declares, "The Father loves the son, and he has given all things into his hand." The focus in this passage on the subject—the Father—is twofold. First, it demonstrates that God continues to exercise a loving relationship with the son with a love that extends back to the beginning, when God delighted in wisdom personified. Second, it reveals how the Father's love is manifest, namely, with the Father sharing all things with the son. The Baptist, therefore, testifies again concerning the high-ranking status of Jesus by declaring that the son is the authorized bearer of the Father's own prerogatives and unique privileges.[15] Furthermore, the perfect tense of the verb "has given" (*dedoken*) indicates that the son still possesses all things that the Father has given to him. Just as Lady Wisdom functions as a personified extension of YHWH's wise attribute and concern for an ordered world, the Father empowers the son—Wisdom's embodiment—to continue to act as an extension of the Father's influence.

The theme of the Father's intimate love for the son continues in Jesus' speech in John 5, which acts as a controversy discourse. After the Jews accuse Jesus of profaning the Sabbath and making himself equal with God (5:18), Jesus issues an apologetic defense of his words, deeds, and relationship with God. "The Father," Jesus insists, "loves the son and he shows him all things that he is doing, and he will show him even greater

---

15. Bauckham, *Jesus*, 138; Thompson, "John, Gospel of," 377.

works than these in order that you may marvel" (5:20). Jesus answers the misunderstood claim that he was "making himself" God's equal by declaring that the Father not only loves the son but also reveals to the son all that the Father is doing. Jesus is not some messianic pretender claiming a relationship with God that he does not legitimately possess.[16] On the contrary, as Wisdom's embodiment, Jesus truly has the Father's love, and as the one whom the Father loves, Jesus is the chosen revealer of the Father's works, with even more revealed works to come.[17] Thompson's insights are appropriate at this juncture of our study: "John addresses the charge by asserting that the Son does indeed exercise the unique and life-giving prerogatives of the Father because the Father has granted him this power (5:25–27)."[18] In sum, as a response to the accusation that Jesus is making himself equal to the Father, Jesus asserts that the Father loves him and he now functions as the Father's authorized revealer.

The next reference to the Father's love of the son also occurs in close proximity to a story involving a controversy between Jesus and the Jews. Prior to the accusation that misunderstands Jesus making himself out to be God (10:33),[19] Jesus reiterates the claim of being in an intimate relationship with the Father: "For this reason, the Father loves me because I lay down my life in order that I may take it up again" (10:17). This declaration by Jesus of the Father's ongoing love for the son, in addition to exhibiting influence from the Jewish wisdom texts portraying YHWH's love for Lady Wisdom, is also the first connection of the Father's love with the death of his son. This is not to say that the son earns the Father's love by laying down his life; the love that the Father has for the son is well established in the narrative of the Gospel of John by this point.[20] Jesus expresses himself as an obedient son who willingly lays down his life on his own accord. God loves the world (3:16), so it naturally follows that God's love for the son is expressed in the death of the obedient son on behalf of the world. Additionally, the son continues to function as the one whom the Father empowers with all things by stating that he possesses the authority to take up his life again (10:18). God's intimate relationship with personified wisdom is not limited to creation; it extends

---

16. McGrath, *Apologetic*, 89.
17. Keener, *John*, 1:648–50.
18. Thompson, *God of the Gospel of John*, 47.
19. McGrath, *Apologetic*, 118–19.
20. O'Day, "Gospel of John," 671.

to the redemptive works made possible through the death of Wisdom's embodiment—the Father's obedient son.

Within the Farewell Discourse, Jesus reemphasizes the Father's intimate relationship with the son, while also expanding this love in a new and important way. Jesus announces to his disciples, "Just as the Father loved me, I also loved you; abide in my love" (15:9). God's love for his wisdom, which is as ancient as creation itself, has now created a new relationship of affection, this time between wisdom's incarnation—Jesus—and the disciples. The followers of Jesus, who have the responsibility to remain in this newfound love, are to demonstrate obedience to the son, just as the son was obedient to his loving Father (15:10). Jesus' community, therefore, defines itself by imitating a loving intimacy that preexisted the creation of all things. These disciples of Jesus have effectively become the children of Lady Wisdom—those who imitate and learn from her as a child learns from its mother.[21]

The final farewell prayer of Jesus to the only true God (17:3) offers the concluding occurrences of the Father's intimate love of the son. In total, Jesus' prayer refers to this love of the Father three times, while at the same time indicating that the Father also loves the world. In praying for his disciples that they reach a perfection in unity, Jesus states his desired outcome: "In order that the world may know that you sent me and you loved them, just as you loved me" (17:23). The love that the Father expresses toward the son is the very same love that the Father also has for the world. The second reference to the Father's love for the son in Jesus' prayer involves the desire to reveal Wisdom's glory to the faithful, "in order that they may see the glory that you have given to me because you loved me before the foundation of the world" (17:24).[22] In such, Jesus recognizes that he is the incarnation of the very same personified wisdom that preexisted creation in a loving relationship with the Father. Last, Jesus concludes the prayer by interceding for the world by confessing his intimate knowledge of the Father, his mission to reveal the Father, and his hope that the Father's love of the son may expand to a wider intimacy with the world: "In order that the love with which you have loved me may be in them, and I also may be in them" (17:25–26). The Father does not reserve his intimacy for his wisdom alone, for Wisdom's embodiment

---

21. Schüssler Fiorenza, *Jesus*, 167.

22. Witherington, *John's Wisdom*, 271, points to the parallels between God giving his glory to Jesus and to Lady Wisdom possessing God's glory in Wis 7:25; 9:10.

strongly desires that this love may be among the world, resulting in further intimacy with Wisdom and creation.

The various portrayals of the Father who loves the son show dependence upon and influence from Jewish wisdom texts. Beginning with the book of Proverbs, YHWH delights in his wisdom, personified as a female figure (Prov 8:30–31). Lady wisdom creates a loving relationship with her children—those who learn from her—according to Ben Sirach: "Wisdom teaches her children and gives help to those who seek her. Whoever loves her loves life . . . the Lord loves those who love her" (Sir 4:11–14). Wisdom's love for her disciples creates a oneness of love that ultimately includes the love from the Lord God. Additionally, Wisdom of Solomon reflects on God's love for his wisdom: "The Lord of all loves her" (Wis 8:3). The intimacy between God and Lady Wisdom is then given meaning: "For she is an initiate in the knowledge of God and an associate of his works" (Wis 8:4). The passage concludes with the author determining to take personified wisdom "to live with me" (Wis 8:9). We can take special note of the way God gave (*edoken*) Wisdom incarnate authority over "all things"[23] and the depiction of Wisdom who gave (*edoken*) the first human being strength to rule "all things" (Wis 10:2).[24] In sum, we have noticed several wisdom themes that provide remarkable parallels to the Fourth Gospel's depiction of the Father's love for the son.[25] God loves the son, and the son shares in the Father's works, knowledge, and authority. The son also loves the disciples, who respond by abiding/living with him, and desires that the Father's love comes to positively influence the world.

GOD SENDS HIS WISDOM

The Gospel of John repeatedly qualifies the authenticity of Jesus' messiahship by insisting both that God has sent Jesus and that Jesus is the son who has been sent by God. "Sending" language is so prominent in the Fourth Gospel's portrayal of Jesus' relationship with God that the narrative employs two different Greek verbs (*apostello* and *pempo*), which combine for more than forty instances.[26] In Jewish wisdom literature, the God of Israel sends forth his wisdom, suggesting parallel themes

---

23. John 5:26–27; 13:3; 16:33; 17:2.
24. Sidebottom, *Fourth Gospel*, 207.
25. O'Boyle, *Wisdom Christology*, 176–77; Schroer, *Wisdom*, 119.
26. Charlesworth, "Lady Wisdom," 107.

intended by the Fourth Gospel. If the Gospel of John presents Jesus as Wisdom incarnate, then this raises the question whether the depiction of God sending Jesus owes at least some of its inspiration to earlier Jewish passages in which God sends forth Lady Wisdom.

The relationship between the one who sends (God) and the one whom God sends (Jesus) requires a closer look at both parties. On the part of the son, the narrative of the Fourth Gospel regularly emphasizes the sent nature of Jesus, the agent of God.[27] John the Baptist testifies that "he whom God has sent speaks the words of God" (3:34). Jesus rebukes the unbelieving Jews as those who "do not believe him whom [the Father] sent" (5:38). When the crowds inquire what to do in order that they may work the works of God, Jesus responds by defining the premiere work: "This is the work of God, that you believe in him whom [God] has sent" (6:29). In a reply to those Jews who accuse Jesus of blasphemy, he describes himself as him "whom the Father sanctified and sent into the world" (10:36). While praying to the Father, Jesus defines the life of the age to come in terms of knowing God and knowing Jesus as he whom God has sent: "This is eternal life, that they may know you, the only true God, and Jesus Christ whom you have sent" (17:3).[28] John Ashton points out what appears to be rather self-evident in the Fourth Gospel: the Father "is simply an alternative name for God."[29] Towards the conclusion of the same prayer, Jesus petitions the Father to unite believers in purpose "so that the world may believe that you sent me" (17:21). Understanding Jesus as the commissioned agent of the Father is vitally important to the Fourth Gospel's christological portrayal of the son.[30]

As the agent whom the Father authorizes, Jesus regularly directs his audience toward God as the authority figure who authorizes and legitimizes his messianic mission.[31] John 3:17 portrays God commissioning

---

27. Jonge, *Jesus*, 147, notes that the Johannine Christology of the agent acting "in the name of the one who has sent him" is the most frequently occurring expression in John.

28. For further discussion on the Father as the only true God in the Fourth Gospel, see Anderson, "Having-Sent-Me Father," 34; Lee, "Beyond Suspicion," 145–46; McGrath, *Only True God*, 55–70.

29. Ashton, *Understanding the Fourth Gospel*, 82.

30. Lincoln, *Gospel*, 60, stresses the same point: "Jesus, then, is viewed as God's authorized agent, who fully and reliably represents the intentions and cause of the one who has sent him . . . Jesus as the sent one fully represents God the sender." See also Friend, "Like Father, Like Son," 22; Loader, *Christology*, 155; Anderson, "Having-Sent-Me Father," 34–36; Thompson, "John, Gospel of," 377.

31. Perkins, "John," 944.

the son as the agent while simultaneously offering a purpose statement for this task: "For God did not send the son into the world *in order to* judge the world, but *in order that* the world might be saved through him."[32] In announcing that the Father has shared his prerogative to judge with the son, Jesus warns that "he who does not honor the son does not honor the Father who sent him" (5:23). Craig Keener helpfully acknowledges that while the Jewish concept of agency implies the subordination of Jesus to the Father, it also stresses Jesus' *functional equality* with the Father, since he must be honored in the same way as the Father whose representative he is.[33] The Father, by sending the son, commissions the son to enact the will of the Father (5:30).[34] When Jesus performs the works of the Father as his obedient agent, these works testify that the Father has truly sent Jesus (5:36). God conveys his teaching, words, judgments, and commandment through the son whom he sends (7:16; 8:26; 12:49–50).

The Fourth Gospel's consistent portrayal of God having sent and commissioned Jesus presupposes the Jewish principle of agency.[35] Peder Borgen famously argued that the "idea of agency plays a central role in the Johannine idea of Jesus as the Son of God."[36] The principle of agency, which the Jewish rabbis traced all the way back to the Torah,[37] consists of several key features. First, when the sender commissions forth an agent, that agent is as the sender himself.[38] The agent represents the one who sent him to the degree that the rabbis argued that the agent is identical to the sender.[39] The agent's ability to represent the sender covered the effects and functions of judicial issues.[40] The Jewish principle of agency recognized the authority of the sender in relation to the agent, namely, that the one who sends is greater than he who is sent.[41] The subordinate agent, therefore, obeys the commissioning, will, and mission of his

32. Emphasis added.

33. Keener, *Gospel of John*, 1:316. See also Thompson, "John, Gospel of," 377–78.

34. Thomas Aquinas, *John 1–5*, 272–73, observes the Wisdom Christology in this passage by drawing attention to Sir 24:5.

35. I am indebted to the article by McIlhone, "Jesus as God's Agent," 295–315.

36. Borgen, "God's Agent," 137; *Bread from Heaven*, 158–64.

37. b. Ned. 72b.

38. b. Ber. 5.5.

39. b. Qidd. 43a.

40. Borgen, "God's Agent," 139.

41. Gen Rab. 78.1; see Borgen, "God's Agent," 140. Borgen cites b. B. Qam. 113b as also demonstrating this point: "The agent of the ruler is like the ruler himself."

sender.⁴² As such, the agent is to act in accordance with his mission, refusing to disrupt or misuse the authority with which he has been empowered to perform in the name of his sender.⁴³ Any will or agenda belonging to the agent must naturally be set aside in order to accomplish the work of the sender. In legal contexts, the agent functions as a partner of the sender to the point that ownership is transferred from the sender to the agent. In this case, if the agent acquires a piece of property on behalf of the sender, it is the sender who is receiving ownership.⁴⁴ Last, when the agent has completed his mission, he returns to the sender. Raymond Brown argues that the Gospel of John functions within the cultural sphere of the Jewish principle of agency by depicting God as the sender and Jesus as the subordinate agent.⁴⁵ These rules that govern the principle of agency also appear as common conventions for the diplomacy of an envoy in the first-century Greco-Roman world.⁴⁶

Within the Jewish wisdom literature, the God of Israel sends forth his wisdom as a personified agent of his wise interactions with creation.⁴⁷ In Sirach 24, the Creator of all things commands Lady Wisdom to go and make her dwelling among the children of Israel (Sir 24:8). The prayer of Solomon in the Wisdom of Solomon contains some remarkable parallels with the Gospel of John. Solomon petitions the God of his ancestors to "give me the wisdom that sits by your throne" (Wis 9:4).⁴⁸ The prayer continues with the urgent request to "send her forth from the holy heavens, and from the throne of your glory send her in order that she may labor at my side" (Wis 9:10).⁴⁹ In this passage, the author of Wisdom of Solomon uses two Greek verbs to illustrate the sending of Lady Wisdom (*apostello*

---

42. Borgen, "God's Agent," 144; Thompson, "John, Gospel of," 378.

43. m. Ter. 4:4; m. Qidd. 3:1; b. Qidd. 42a; b. ʿErub. 31b–32a; Anderson, "Having-Sent-Me Father," 34.

44. Borgen, *Bread from Heaven*, 160–61, who points to b. B. Qam. 70a and its parallel in John 6:39, 44; 12:32.

45. Brown, *John XIII–XXI*, 655.

46. Borgen, "John and Hellenism," 101–2. Borgen helpfully points to Philo's *Legat*. 369 ("the sufferings of envoys recoil on those who have sent him").

47. Thompson, "John, Gospel of," 377.

48. Dillon, "Wisdom Tradition," 276, draws attention to Wis 9:1–4 and its influence on the portrayal of Jesus in the Gospel of John. Dillon also suggests that Wis 9:1–4 has probably borrowed from Daniel 7. This is an attractive proposal since Dan 7:9 indicates that multiple "thrones" were set up.

49. Keener, *Gospel of John*, 1:316, points to the parallel between Wis 9:10 and God sending Wisdom incarnate as his agent.

and *pempo*), the same two verbs in the Fourth Gospel that describe God's sending of his agent, the son. Moreover, the passage supplies the Greek conjunction "in order that" (*ina*) to explain the reason for the petition for God to send his wisdom. We observed a remarkably similar passage in John 3:17, where God's act of sending the son is not in order that (*ina*) he may judge the world, but in order that (*ina*) the world would be saved through him. Solomon's prayer concludes by acknowledging that when God sends his wisdom, the "people were taught what pleases you and they were saved by wisdom" (Wis 9:17–18). James D. G. Dunn has pointed to the portrayal of personified wisdom in Wis 9:17–18 as having likely shaped the language and theology of John 3:16–17.[50] The combination of God sending the son with an express purpose to save (John 3:17) suggests the impact of Wisdom of Solomon 9 and its request for God to send his wisdom in order to bring about a positive outcome, resulting in the salvation of the people. Ben Witherington has drawn attention to Jesus' admission to being God's "apostle"/agent in John 13:16: "The slave is not greater than his master, nor is the one sent [*apostolos*] greater than the one who sent him."[51] In short, the Jewish wisdom texts wherein Israel's God sends forth his personified wisdom to accomplish the saving tasks seem to exhibit influence in the Fourth Gospel's portrayal of God commissioning his son as the agent of his salvific purposes.[52]

WISDOM OBEYS GOD

When the Gospel of John depicts God sending forth his son as an agent, the son willingly responds with obedience, submission, and respect for the sender.[53] John A. T. Robinson characterizes this relationship as the son living "in *absolutely intimate dependence* upon God as his Father."[54] The obedience of the sent son is another aspect of the relationship

---

50. Dunn, *Jesus according to the New Testament*, 65.

51. Witherington, *John's Wisdom*, 141. See also John 13:20; Keener, *Gospel of John*, 2:912; McIlhone, "Jesus as God's Agent," 312; Borgen, *Bread from Heaven*, 159; "John and Hellenism," 101.

52. Evans, *Word and Glory*, 145; Ringe, *Wisdom's Friends*, 58–59; Lincoln, *Gospel*, 60; McGrath, *John's Apologetic Christology*, 92–93; *Only True God*, 58–59; Schüssler Fiorenza, *Jesus*, 167. Fuller, "Incarnation," 65, points to the parallel between the Father's call/response of the son and the eternal relationship between God and his heavenly wisdom.

53. Ladd, *Theology*, 251, observes that the son who is dependent upon the Father is pictured in thoroughly human terms.

54. Robinson, "Christology Today," 68, emphasis original.

between God and Jesus where we may find evidence of influence from the Jewish wisdom texts. Throughout the Fourth Gospel, Jesus speaks about his unwavering willingness to conduct the mission and purposes of God the sender. When asked about food that he may possess, Jesus responds by claiming that "My food is to do the will of him who sent me and to accomplish his work" (4:34).[55] Jesus constantly reoriented his will around the actions and initiative of the Father: "The son can do nothing of himself unless it is something that he sees the Father doing; for whatever the Father does, these things the son also does in like manner" (5:19).[56] In commenting on this passage and its context, Brant offers a refreshingly honest take on the relationship between God and Jesus in 5:19: "John does not offer a full-blown trinitarian doctrine . . . The language of persons, being, and essence found in the fourth-century creeds used to define the relationships of Jesus and God is not in sight."[57] Similarly, Jesus confesses that "I can do nothing on my own initiative . . . I do not seek my own will, but the will of him who sent me" (5:30; cf. 6:38).[58] Upon being questioned about his messianic identity, he again stresses his subordination to God: "I do nothing on my own initiative, but I speak these things just as the Father taught me" (8:28).[59] As the agent of the Father, Jesus speaks of the sender's authority that he possesses—an authority to lay down his life and to take it up again (10:18). Even the works that the son performs belong to the sender: "I showed you many good works from the Father" (10:32). At the conclusion of his mission, the agent plans to report back to the sender: "I go to the Father, for the Father is greater than I" (14:28).[60] Francis Moloney aptly summarizes the relationship between the agent and the Father as "the Johannine Jesus' complete subordination of his mission to the will and design of the Father."[61]

55. Borgen, *Bread from Heaven*, 155.
56. See Gaston, "High Christology," 133.
57. Brant, *John*, 110.
58. Lincoln, *John*, 229.
59. Anderson, "Having-Sent-Me Father," 41, convincingly argues that Jesus "can do nothing without the Father, and the Father is greater than he."
60. Barrett, "Father Is Greater than I," 28, insists that John 14:28, along with other subordinationist passages, "cannot be interpreted in terms of the eternal relations between the Persons of the Trinity; it belongs within the setting which John himself is careful to provide for it, namely that of the historic ministry."
61. Moloney, *Gospel*, 414. Cowan, "Father and Son," 117–34, while trying to maintain a high christological reading, nevertheless argues that Jesus is subordinate to God based on his being sent as an agent, his dependence on and obedience to the Father, and

While the obedient son of the Father within the Fourth Gospel closely resembles the Jewish principle of agency, the portrayal likewise suggests the impact of wisdom texts wherein personified wisdom obeys the God of Israel.[62] We observe in the lengthy prayer within Wisdom of Solomon the royal petitioner asking God to send forth Wisdom from the holy heavens—a commissioning she obeys. Having submitted to God's sending, Wisdom is able to impart to the petitioner God's will (Wis 9:9-11). The Johannine Jesus similarly obeys God, demonstrates awareness of the will of God, and accomplishes the task to which he was entrusted (John 4:34; 5:30; 6:38-40).[63] Ben Sira's first-person poem of personified wisdom (Sirach 24) is indicative of the idea that when the Jewish sages personified the wise intentions of God, this wisdom would naturally be lesser than and obedient to God himself. Lady Wisdom refers to Israel's God as the Creator of all things, who "gave me a command" and "choose the place for my tent" (Sir 24:8). God's command to wisdom is that she is to make her dwelling in Jacob and receive her inheritance in Israel. Lady Wisdom obeys the command of her Creator, establishes herself in Zion, and ministers before God in the holy dwelling (Sir 24:10). She acknowledges that it was God who gave her a resting place—Jerusalem as her domain (Sir 24:11). In obedience, wisdom took root in an honored people, in the portion of the Lord (Sir 24:12). When Ben Sira paints the high priest Simon ben Onias as the incarnation of Lady Wisdom, Simon exemplifies the faithful practice of the priesthood within the temple (Sir 50:1-21). It is clear that Simon—personified wisdom's embodiment—carried out the obedient acts of wisdom within the temple that she was sent to perform.[64] Marianne M. Thompson, in her related study, sums up her findings in a fitting manner for our inquiry: "Wisdom is a *category of agency* that allows for the closest possible unity between the agent and God."[65] The obedience of Lady Wisdom to the Creator God within the sapiential literature and the obedient son acting as the agent of the Father in the Gosple of John both offer analogous features worthy of consideration for our study.[66]

---

the usage of Father-son language to define God and Jesus.

62. Witherington, *Jesus the Sage*, 372.
63. Von Wahlde, *John*, 1:413.
64. Kealy, *Wisdom Books*, 247-48.
65. Thompson, "Thinking about God," 231, emphasis added.
66. Witherington, *John's Wisdom*, 140, convincingly argues that the Fourth Gospel combines Wisdom language with agency language in describing the relationship

WISDOM IS UNITED WITH GOD IN MISSION AND PURPOSE

All these themes coalesce into a united portrayal of the Father and the son. The Father authorizes the son's messianic mission to reveal the life-giving purposes of God, and the son obediently submits to this mission without hesitation, wavering, or doubt. The intimacy between the unique son, characterized by his resting in the bosom of the Father, further reflects this common bond shared between the two. The Father's love for the son, which the son in turn shares with believers, adds an additional characteristic describing this joint venture. When Jesus intercedes for those who will come to believe, he requests that they may be made complete and united in purpose: "That they may be perfected in unity, in order that the world may know that you sent me and you loved them, just as you loved me" (17:23).

The foundational statement for this united front is John 10:30, where the obedient son declares, "I and the Father are one." The cardinal number one in this passage and in all subsequent passages that discuss the united mission of the Father and the son is grammatically neuter (see 17:21, 22). The neuter number one indicates a single thing, a common purpose, a united objective that we would come to expect from the agent who fulfills the will and mission of his sender.[67] The context of John 10:30 sheds further light on the meaning of this unified pact between God and Jesus.[68] The Jews present at the Feast of Dedication[69] press Jesus to speak plainly about his messianic status. Jesus answers them by claiming his status as the agent of the Father's deeds: "The works that I do in my Father's name, these testify about me" (10:25). Those who belong to Jesus' sheep listen to Jesus, are known by Jesus, and follow Jesus. To these, Jesus offers eternal life and promises that no one will snatch them out of his hand (10:27–28). Jesus then turns to speak of the Father: "What the Father has given to me is greater than all, and no one is able to snatch them out of his

---

between Jesus and the Father.

67. Haenchen, *John 2*, 50, notes that by acknowledging the oneness that God and the son share, "John is a representative of an expressly subordinationist Christology."

68. Witherington, *John's Wisdom*, 191.

69. When the narrator sets the scene for the Feast of Dedication, he makes it a point to draw attention to Jesus as he was walking in the portico of Solomon—the famous king endowed with the wisdom of God. This may have alerted readers to the fact that Jesus, the incarnation of the same wisdom King Solomon possessed, is about to display the wise attributes and characteristics of wisdom.

hand" (10:29). The sheep, therefore, find security in the hands of both the Father and the son precisely because the son functions as the agent of the Father's redemptive works. Loader arrives at the same conclusion: "The oneness lies in the fact that the Son does as the Father does, speaks what he has heard, tells what he has seen . . . Jesus and God are two distinct beings, with the Son subordinate."[70] What is true of the sender is true of the sent agent.[71] Sharing this common mission to offer life to the believing sheep, the son and the Father are one—united in purpose.

The oneness of the Father and the son is expressed in several other ways within the Fourth Gospel. When Jesus asks that his opponents consider the works of the Father that he performs as the Father's agent, he claims, "Believe the works, in order that you may know and understand that the Father is in me and I am in the Father" (10:38).[72] This claim to a mutual indwelling is indicative of the strongest sense of intimacy between Jesus and his Father. In the Farewell Discourse, Jesus continues to stress his role as the authorized agent of the Father, to the point that those who see Jesus have seen the Father (14:9). He then repeats his assertion of mutual abiding: "Do you not believe that I am in the Father and the Father is in me? The words that I say to you I do not speak on my own initiative, but the Father abiding in me performs his works" (14:10). Moreover, Jesus prays to the Father that he would keep those believers who are in the world "so that they may be one, just as we are" (17:11). In other words, Jesus petitions that believers would come to share in the united purpose and task that he and his Father experience.[73]

The Gospel of John's portrayal of the oneness in mission that the Father and son share is comparable to the unity of Israel's God and his wisdom within the Jewish sapiential texts.[74] In the book of Proverbs, personified wisdom shouts in the streets in order to persuade her audience to repent and listen to her words (Prov 1:20–23). However, her words are a synonym for the fear of YHWH (Prov 1:29), since the fear of YHWH is the beginning of wisdom (Prov 9:10). Readers of Proverbs can enact

---

70. Loader, "Central Structure," 202.

71. Robinson, "Christology Today," 74; O'Day, "Gospel of John," 676–77.

72. Witherington, *John's Wisdom*, 191, observes five parallels between Lady Wisdom's portrayal in Wisdom of Solomon 7–9 and Jesus' response to the Jews.

73. Keener, *John*, 2:1061.

74. Thompson, *God of the Gospel of John*, 238, emphasizes how the categories of personified wisdom and word are "pressed into service to speak not only of Jesus as God's agent but of the unity of Jesus with God."

the fear of YHWH by following God's wise teachings that personified wisdom teaches by extension. Wisdom of Solomon likewise portrays the oneness of God and Lady Wisdom. For example, Solomon can call upon God in prayer, and the spirit of wisdom comes to him (Wis 7:7). Similarly, those who acquire wisdom "obtain friendship with God" (Wis 7:14). In each generation, Lady Wisdom indwells holy souls and transforms them into friends of God (Wis 7:27). The author closely connects personified wisdom with knowing God and his deeds: "She is an initiate in the knowledge of God, she is an associate in his works" (Wis 8:4). Regarding acts of creation, God has formed humankind with the agency of his wisdom (Wis 9:1–2), and the close connection between the Creator God and his wisdom is sometimes expressed with Lady Wisdom being the fashioner (7:22; 8:6). Finally, Wisdom of Solomon details the history of Israel, beginning with God's interaction with Adam all the way through the events surrounding the exodus from Egypt, and substitutes Lady Wisdom in all the places where the Hebrew Bible records God's deeds and acts (Wis 10:1–21). In sum, the close workings of God and his personified wisdom within Jewish wisdom literature offer exceptional parallels to the Fourth Gospel's description of the Father and the son as united in purpose and mission.[75]

CONCLUSION

This chapter set out to explore how the Gospel of John expresses the close ties between God and his wisdom within its wider narrative. In doing so, we discovered five specific emphases that exhibited discernable evidence of influence from the Jewish wisdom texts. The preexistence of the Johannine Jesus fits most appropriately in the category of notional preexistence (rather than literal preexistence) since the wisdom of God was a preexisting personification. The motif of loving intimacy between God and Jesus recalls the closeness shared by YHWH and his wisdom. Furthermore, the sending of Jesus by the only true God evokes the sending of Wisdom, in addition to the widespread Jewish understanding that a commissioned agent fully represents his sender. Moreover, Jesus' obedient and subordinate behavior to the Father conjures up several images of the Lady Wisdom obeying the Creator. We also observed the oneness of mission shared by the Father and the son as continuing in the Jewish tradition of

---

75. Dunn, "Let John Be John," 331.

God's wisdom functioning as a personification of his wise interactions with his people. The Fourth Gospel appears to have deliberately framed the relationship between Jesus—Wisdom incarnate—and the God of Israel in terms of former Jewish depictions of personified wisdom and YHWH. Readers of the Gospel of John who are familiar with these Jewish sapiential books would feel quite at home with this christological illustration of the Johannine Jesus.

Having identified Jesus as the commissioned and authorized agent of the only true God, what sort of insights would an examination into Jesus' ministry reveal? Does the Fourth Gospel frame the public ministry of Jesus in light of its Wisdom Christology? Our next chapter will focus on finding answers to these questions.

5

Wisdom and the Mission of Jesus

THE WISDOM OF GOD became flesh and dwelt among us, the Prologue insists. This chapter will explore the various ways in which the Fourth Gospel illustrates its depiction of Jesus Christ's public ministry in terms of the wisdom of God. Our investigation will commence with a survey of various public arenas in which Jesus—Wisdom incarnate—encounters those with whom he ministers, teaches, and even fiercely debates. Within his public ministry, Jesus distinguishes himself as a rabbi, an authoritative teacher of the children of Israel. Consequently, our next exploration will be into the portrayal of Jesus as a teacher of wisdom. The primary function of the teaching activity of the Johannine Jesus is to unveil the heavenly things of the Father, so I will investigate the different ways in which the ascent and descent of Jesus plays this crucial role. As the one who authoritatively reveals the unseen God, we must give space to explore the christological emphasis on Jesus as the revelation of the knowledge of God. As Jesus functions as the Father's sent agent, he summons the crowds to follow him, often with noteworthy "I am" statements followed by a metaphor from Judaism's history. These invitations regularly point to Jesus as the gift of God, which offers an additional opportunity for study. Those who accept Jesus and believe come to receive the life of the age to come (eternal life). However, the meaning of this life is given an interesting twist in that it is regularly presented in the present tense without suggesting that its fullest realization in the future is diminished. Herein lies yet another window into the ministry of Jesus worthy of study. The concept of eternal life is closely linked with the kingdom of God, suggesting that we should explore this notion of the rule of God. In addition to offering the life of the age to come and entrance into the kingdom, Jesus gives water, food, and drink. Last, the Gospel of John frames the narrative of Jesus' ministry in terms of seven signs, not unlike the seven signs in Wisdom of Solomon. Needless to say, the ministry of the Johannine Jesus offers several points of contact with Jewish wisdom literature that are worthy of study and exploration.

WISDOM IN THE PUBLIC ARENA

As the agent of the Father's life-giving purposes, Jesus endeavors to make himself available and accessible. Throughout the narrative of the Gospel of John, we notice that the ministry of Jesus takes place in the public arena, out in the open. This tendency is the norm for Jesus, although there are some exceptions worth noting. Nicodemus approaches Jesus at night (3:2), but this was at the initiative of Nicodemus, not Jesus.[1] Additionally, chapter 13 marks a shift in the narrative from public interactions to an intimate, private supper with his disciples. Still, most of Jesus' signs, teachings, and speeches occur in locations where he is accessible to the world.

When the narrative begins with the baptizing acts of John, the narrator sets the location of John and Jesus in Bethany, beyond the Jordan (1:28). After interacting with a few of John's disciples, Jesus purposes to travel to Galilee for the wedding (1:43), and along the way he encounters Philip and Nathaniel. The wedding at Cana in Galilee positions Jesus with his mother and his disciples at such a crowded venue that the wine runs out, resulting in the transformation of at least 120 gallons of water into good wine (2:1–11). When the Passover was near, Jesus went to Jerusalem and enacted a prophetic sign of judgment in the sight of the money changers, the Jews, and those who came to believe in his name (2:13–25). In Judea, Jesus and his disciples were baptizing more disciples than John was. These public baptisms eventually caught the attention of the Pharisees, resulting in Jesus leaving for Galilee (4:1–3). On his journey to Galilee, Jesus stops at Jacob's Well outside of Sychar, encounters a Samaritan woman, and eventually stays with the Samaritan community for an additional two days (4:4–42). In the portico of the temple, Jesus heals a man who was unable to walk (5:1–15), which results in a controversy

---

1. Witherington, *John's Wisdom*, 94, notices that while Nicodemus begins the story in the *dark of night*, he comes to encounter Wisdom incarnate, of whom Wis 7:26 describes as a reflection of eternal *light*.

and Jesus' apologetic speech within the temple (5:16–47). Jesus feeds five thousand with loaves and fish while on the mountainside in Galilee (6:1–14). When he is beside the sea, he preaches to the crowds (6:25–71). Returning to Jerusalem, Jesus offers an extended dialogue with the Jews in the temple that lasts for a few days (7:14—8:59). Leaving the temple, Jesus encounters a blind man, heals him, and defends his miraculous sign (9:1—10:21). Another story involving controversy takes place during the Feast of Hanukkah, between Jesus and the Jews (10:22–42). Jesus travels to Bethany in order to visit Mary, Martha, and Lazarus (11:14–37). Finally, Jesus enters Jerusalem one last time for the Feast of Passover, where the Greeks visit him, and he preaches openly to the crowds (12:14–36, 44–50). After Jesus is arrested, he speaks to the high priest by reminding him that he has spoken openly to the world, teaching in the synagogues and in the temple (18:19–20).[2] During these public encounters, many heard the preaching of Jesus, experienced his signs, and came to believe in him. The Johannine Jesus presents himself as a very accessible figure.

One of the most notable features of personified wisdom in the various Jewish sapiential texts is her deliberate positioning in the public arena in order to minister to the people of God.[3] The open accessibility of Lady Wisdom is quite prominent in the book of Proverbs. Wisdom is in the streets shouting, in the public square, at the head of the streets, and at the entrance of the gates within the city (Prov 1:20–21). Proverbs situates personified wisdom in an open, urban center, within the midst of society in order that her voice may be more readily heard.[4] The same portrayal of wisdom appears in Prov 8:1–3, where the sage depicts her standing in outdoor locations where she may call forth to whoever would listen. In particular, Lady Wisdom lifts her voice on the top of the heights, beside the road, at the meeting of the pathways, beside the gates, at the opening of the city, and at the entrance of the doors. It seems very possible that when Jesus raises his voice in public (John 12:44), he is imitating the behavior of Lady Wisdom in Prov 1:21 and 8:1.[5] The constant refrain of Wisdom's public addresses serves to highlight her accessibility to those who would give an ear to her instruction as well as contrasting the seclusive nature of Lady Folly, who resides in the privacy of her home (Prov

---

2. Brown, *John XIII–XXI*, 825, finds parallels between this confession of Jesus speaking openly and with Prov 8:2–3; 9:3; Wis 6:14, 16; Bar 3:37.

3. Schüssler Fiorenza, *Jesus*, 167.

4. Schipper, *Proverbs 1–15*, 88.

5. Witherington, *John's Wisdom*, 227; Coloe, *John 11–21*, 352.

7:7-9).⁶ As the embodiment of wisdom, the Johannine Jesus exercises his ministry in the open, public arena in a manner that demonstrates the influence of the portrayal of personified wisdom's accessibility within the book of Proverbs.⁷

WISDOM THE TEACHER

In the Synoptic Gospels, the most common title that the crowds attribute to Jesus is that of a teacher. It seems clear that Jesus made an impact on others through his ability to communicate, instruct, and make disciples. The Gospel of John similarly portrays Jesus as a dominant teaching figure, both according to Jesus' self-assessment and the assessment of others. Two of John the Baptist's disciples address Jesus as "Rabbi," the Aramaic word for "teacher." They conclude that he would possess a location where he customarily taught his students just like other Jewish rabbis, and ask him, "Where are you staying?" (1:38).⁸ Jesus demonstrates his agreement with this role and invites John's disciples to follow him (1:39). Nicodemus endorses Jesus as a God-given teacher: "Rabbi, we know that you have come from God as a teacher, for no one can perform these signs that you do unless God is with him" (3:2).⁹ Jesus describes the content of his instruction as "teaching" that he receives from the Father: "My teaching is not mine, but his who sent me. If anyone is willing to perform his will, he will know about the teaching, whether it is of God or whether I speak from myself" (7:16-17). The narrator even illustrates Jesus' speech in the temple as an act of "teaching" (7:28; 8:20). Martha, in announcing the arrival of Jesus to her sister Mary, calls him "the Teacher" (11:28). Jesus demonstrates his agreement with all these descriptions as he informs his disciples, "You call me Teacher and Lord, and you say well, for so I am" (13:13, author's translation). He then repeats this affirmation by pointing to himself as the teacher who washes the feet of the disciples (13:14). Jesus' reputation as a teacher was so prominent that the high priest specifically questioned him about his teaching at his trial (18:19). After Jesus'

---

6. Clifford, *Proverbs*, 94.

7. Johnson, "Jesus, the Wisdom of God," 284; Ringe, *Wisdom's Friends*, 57; Ceresko, *Old Testament Wisdom*, 178. See also the comments connecting the public ministry of Jesus with Wisdom in Prov 1:20-28 by Brown, *John I-XII*, 79.

8. Moloney, *John*, 54.

9. Witherington, *John's Wisdom*, 94, notes that the particular role of teacher or sage that Jesus takes here is that of Wisdom, based upon the influence of Wis 10:9-10.

resurrection from the dead, Mary Magdalene, upon recognizing him, addresses him as "Rabboni" (20:16). The Fourth Gospel's portrayal of Jesus as a Jewish rabbi creates an inclusio in which the title is both stated and translated at the beginning and end of the narrative, indicating that the contents in between contain the instruction of Rabbi Jesus. In chapter 21, the story ends with an editorial note indicating that there are many other things Jesus did that would fill numerous books (21:25). It is not unreasonable to assume that these traditions of Jesus included further teachings and sermons.

Within the Jewish wisdom literature, the wisdom of God frequently plays the role of a teacher. In the book of Proverbs, Lady Wisdom calls for the naïve to turn at her reproof, for "I will make my words known to you" (Prov 1:23). The Greek translation of this phrase stresses the role of wisdom as a teacher: "I will teach you with my word." The sage father instructs his son with teaching that is closely associated with the acquisition of wisdom: "He taught me . . . 'Let your heart hold fast my words; keep my commandments and live; get wisdom!'" (Prov 4:4–5). The father describes his own teaching in terms of directing the sons "in the path of wisdom" (4:11). Again, the Greek translator emphasizes the role of a teacher in his rendering of the Hebrew: "I will teach you wisdom's paths" (Prov 4:11 LXX). Toward the end of the collection of proverbs, the words of Agur indicate that he has not learned wisdom, but the Greek translation renders this in a much more positive tone: "God has taught me wisdom" (Prov 30:3 LXX). In Ben Sira, personified wisdom is likened to an ever-flowing river that pours out teaching for all future generations (Sir 24:30–34).[10] The portrayal of Lady Wisdom in the role of a teacher continues in Wisdom of Solomon. The great monarchs are summoned to learn wisdom, thereby transforming them into holy disciples who have been instructed (Wis 6:9–10). The author attributes his own instruction of what is secret and what is manifest to Lady Wisdom, the one who "taught me" (Wis 7:21). The prayer of Solomon finds its conclusion by ascribing to personified wisdom acts of teaching and saving (Wis 9:18). It is no surprise, therefore, that the Johannine Jesus resembles the figure of Wisdom, especially in her role as the teacher of God's wise instructions and ways.[11] Those interested in learning the teaching of Israel's God

---

10. Witherington, *John's Wisdom*, 357–58, regards Sirach's portrayal of Wisdom as a river of instruction teaching future generation as the influence behind the concluding verse of John 21.

11. Schroer, *Wisdom*, 119; Johnson, "Jesus, the Wisdom of God," 284–85; Ringe,

should look to the Johannine Jesus, Wisdom's incarnation, rather than looking to Moses.¹²

THE DESCENT AND ASCENT OF WISDOM

As Wisdom incarnate, Jesus authoritatively teaches the words of God, and in doing so he functions as the revealer of God. The son's role as the definitive revealer of God combines with his role as the agent—one who is commissioned from the sender, performs the specific mission parameters, and then returns to the sender once the task is complete. The Gospel of John paints the ministry of Jesus in terms of "descending" and "ascending," and these verbs are given various synonyms to help in this christological portrayal. As the embodiment of the word of God, the Johannine Jesus follows the pattern that we find in Isa 55:11 where YHWH declares, "So will my word be that goes forth from my mouth; it will not return to me empty, without accomplishing what I desire, and without succeeding in the matter for which I sent it." Just as God sends his personified word out to accomplish his will and to return once the mission is accomplished, the incarnate word descends to perform the tasks as God's agent, only to ascend when the tasks come to completion.

Jesus offers explicit testimony regarding his descent from heaven in the Discourse on the Bread of Life. In John 6:32, Jesus asserts that it is not Moses who has given the Jews the bread of heaven, but it is his Father who currently gives the true bread of heaven. When the crowds request this new bread, Jesus responds by claiming to be this bread that the Father is offering: "I am the bread of life" (6:34–35). While maintaining the metaphor of the bread of life, Jesus portrays himself in terms of the obedient agent who has descended from God: "I have come down from heaven, not to do my own will, but the will of him who sent me" (6:38, 51). During Jesus' private supper with his disciples, the narrator informs the readers that Jesus "had come forth from God and was going to God" (13:3), thereby combining both the motifs of descending and ascending.¹³ The same emphasis reappears in John 16:28, where Jesus speaks of himself in terms of Isaiah's descending and ascending word: "I

Wisdom's Friends, 59–60; Witherington, *John's Wisdom*, 245; Shafer, "Wisdom Christology," 56.

12. Lee, *Symbolic Narratives*, 148.

13. Fuller, "Incarnation," 64, explains this passage as dealing with the entry of Wisdom into the world and her subsequent return to heaven.

came forth from the Father and have come into the world; I am leaving the world again and going to the Father."

We have observed that the Johannine Jesus views himself as the commissioned agent of the Father who must descend in order to perform the appointed tasks of his ministry and then ascend to his Father upon completing these tasks. While Jesus frequently speaks of himself as the sent agent of God, he also demonstrates awareness of his mission that requires him to ascend to God at the conclusion of his ministry. We can find statements of his intent to go to God on the lips of Jesus: "For a little while longer I am with you, then I go to him who sent me" (7:33); "I go to the Father" (14:12). Jesus encourages his disciples to celebrate at the notion that after completing his mission, the agent would ascend to the Father: "If you loved me, you would have rejoiced that I go to the Father, for the Father is greater than I" (14:28). Indeed, it is to the advantage of the disciples that Jesus goes away because then the Spirit of truth can come (16:7, 10). When Mary Magdalene encounters the risen Jesus, he informs her, "I have not yet ascended to the Father, but go to my brethren and say to them, 'I ascend to my Father and your Father, and my God and your God'" (20:17).[14] As the authorized agent of God, Jesus was conscious of his mission to descend and ascend to God.

In addition to drawing on the imagery of God's personified word from Isa 55:11 to illustrate the motifs of descending and ascending, the Gospel of John is also indebted to the Jewish wisdom literature and its frequent depiction of personified wisdom's descent and ascent.[15] Within the book of Proverbs, Lady Wisdom originated in heaven at God's side (Prov 8:22, 27, 30). At some point, she descends from heaven to take upon the role of a prophet and teacher in the public arena (Prov 1:20-21; 8:1-3), only to uproot and leave when fools refuse her counsel (Prov 1:24-28). In fact, personified wisdom's warning in which "they will seek me but they will not find me" (Prov 1:28) sounds remarkably like Jesus' cautioning in John 7:34: "You will seek me and you will not find me."[16] The Jews even respond to this warning and discuss it among themselves, repeating Jesus' words in the process, which serves to call the reader's attention to them (John 7:35-36). Ben Sira describes the descent of Lady Wisdom in terms of God pouring her out as a gift: "He saw her and took her measure; he poured her out upon all his works, according to his gift

---

14. See esp. Thompson, *God of the Gospel of John*, 235.

15. Brown, *Introduction to the Gospel of John*, 258-59; Culpepper, *Gospel*, 86.

16. See the extended discussion of this motif in Culpepper, *Gospel*, 167-68.

he poured her upon all the living, he lavished her upon those who love him" (Sir 1:9–10). Personified wisdom's acknowledgment that "I came forth from the mouth of the Most High and covered the earth like a mist" (Sir 24:3) parallels Jesus' statement that he came forth from the Father and has come into the world (John 16:28). However, Sirach does offer a similar caution to what personified wisdom stated in Prov 1:28, "If they go astray, Wisdom will forsake them, and she will hand them over to their ruin" (Sir 4:19). In forsaking the disobedient, the personified wisdom of God presumably ascends to heaven. The prayer of Solomon beseeches the God of Israel to have wisdom descend from heaven: "Give me the wisdom who sits by your throne . . . send her forth from the holy heavens" (Wis 9:4, 10).[17] The theologian who authored the *Book of Parables* in 1 Enoch illustrates both the descent and ascent of the wisdom of God. According to 1 En. 42:1, Wisdom came down from heaven so that she may dwell among humanity. Having found no suitable place for her dwelling, she ascended to heaven (42:2). These themes are also present in the Gospel of John, as the *logos* was with God in the beginning, became flesh, dwelt among the people, suffered rejection, and subsequently ascended to heaven. To summarize, the Johannine Jesus details his mission as the agent of God in terms of descending and ascending, resulting in a christological portrayal wherein the personified wisdom of God comes down from heaven, takes on flesh, fulfills its ministry, and returns to God afterward.[18]

WISDOM REVEALS THE KNOWLEDGE OF GOD

One of the primary functions that we have observed of personified wisdom within the sapiential literature is that when she descends from heaven, she reveals the wise knowledge of Israel's God. As the human incarnation of Lady Wisdom, the son is the definitive revealer of the unseen God (John 1:18). Jesus' role as the revealer of God's knowledge reemerges within the wider narrative of the Fourth Gospel, particularly in defining the purpose of Jesus' ministry. When Jesus encounters Nathanael for the first time, he indicates that he possesses knowledge about

---

17. Scott, *Sophia*, 175.

18. O'Boyle, *Wisdom Christology*, 175–76; Brown, *Introduction to the Gospel of John*, 261.

Nathanael's character (1:47).[19] After causing the controversy in the Jerusalem temple, the narrator explains why Jesus was not entrusting himself to those who believed in him: "For he knew all people, and because he did not need anyone to testify concerning people, for he himself knew what was in everyone" (2:24–25). The Samaritan woman attributes the special knowledge that Jesus possesses concerning her former husbands to him being a prophet, an agent who speaks forth the words of God (4:17–19).[20] As the dialogue progresses, she comes to learn that Jesus is more than a prophet; he is the Messiah. She indicates that her understanding of the coming Messiah is that he would be a revelatory figure: "I know that Messiah is coming . . . when that one comes, he will declare all things to us" (4:25). Jesus immediately affirms this christological understanding: "I who speak with you am he" (4:26).[21] Catrin Williams confirms that Jesus is here self-identifying as the Messiah in his response to the Samaritan woman.[22] When she returns to her city, she testifies about Jesus as the revealer of the knowledge of God, resulting in many coming to believe in him: "He told me all the things that I have done" (4:39). As the anointed agent of God, Jesus functions as the one who reveals all things from the Father.

When Jesus' status as the messianic son of God is controversially called into question in John 5, Jesus answers his critics by restating his role as the rightfully commissioned revealer. To justify why he felt it was lawful to heal on the Sabbath, Jesus reveals that "my Father is working until now, and I myself am working" (5:17). As the obedient son, Jesus sees what the Father is doing and then performs these works in like manner (5:19). By confessing that the Father "shows him all things that he himself is doing, and he will show him greater works than these" (5:20), Jesus indicates that the messianic son of God is the authorized revealer

---

19. Keener, *John*, 1:486–87, rightly observes that the sort of insight expressed by Jesus is typical of prophets, magicians, and God, but then Keener unconvincingly collapses Jesus and God.

20. Thomas Aquinas, *John 1–5*, 220, sees in the reference to Jesus being a prophet a Wisdom Christology influenced by Wis 7:27.

21. Thomas Aquinas, *John 1–5*, 227, detects the Wisdom influences of Wis 6:14; 14:21 behind Jesus' claim to be the Christ. Robinson, *Priority of John*, 385, rightly notes that Jesus' use of *ego eimi* here reaffirms the Messiah of whom the woman spoke in the previous verse. More recently, see Nemes, *Trinity and Incarnation*, 166.

22. Williams, *I Am He*, 259, affirms that the self-declaration of the identity of the Messiah is the "most obvious . . . interpretation" of the Greek *ego eimi*.

of God.²³ The son is even able to speak forth judgments because God has given all judgment to the son, effectively sharing with Jesus God's prerogative as the cosmic judge (5:22–24, 30).²⁴ As the empowered and authorized judge, Jesus declares to his critics that "I know you, that you do not possess the love of God in yourselves" (5:42).

The Gospel of John continues to depict Jesus as the one who makes the unseen God known, to his disciples, the crowds, and his enemies. When Jesus asks Philip where he intends to purchase bread to feed the large crowd, the narrator informs the readers that Jesus knows what Philip was intending to do (6:5–6). After the well-fed crowds identify Jesus as the prophet foretold in Deut 18:15–19 (a title bearing several indicators of Wisdom Christology),²⁵ Jesus implicitly accepts this title by withdrawing to the mountains due to his prophetic knowledge of their intentions to forcefully make him their king (6:14–15). In the aftermath of Jesus' lengthy Discourse on the Bread of Life from heaven, he demonstrates his conscious awareness of what his disciples were saying in response to his difficult words (6:61). Sometime later, when Jesus was teaching in the temple, he cries out and confesses that he has been sent as God's agent: "You both know me and know where I am from, and I have not come of myself, but he who sent me is true, whom you do not know. I know him because I am from him, and he sent me" (7:28–29). Jesus' claim to be the one who knows God and reveals God appears again later in the same discourse (8:28–29, 55) as well as in his discussion of the role of the good shepherd (10:15). Functioning as the definitive revealer of the Father's knowledge involves Jesus maintaining the Father's commandments—an obedient act that Jesus summons his disciples to emulate (15:10). It is only after Jesus once again proves his awareness of the internal deliberations of his disciples (16:19) that they come to confess him as the authorized revealer whom God has sent: "Now we know that you know all things,

---

23. Thomas Aquinas, *John 1–5*, 276, discusses the influence of Wisdom in this christological portrayal.

24. Fuller, "Incarnation," 61; Anderson, "Having-Sent-Me Father," 42; Thompson, "John, Gospel of," 377.

25. Dillon, "Wisdom Tradition," 278–79, astutely points out that the shift from the feeding miracle to the identification of Jesus as the prophet from Deut 18:18 makes sense once we recognize that Wisdom invites men to eat the bread of understanding (Sir 24:19–21). Since it is Wisdom who gives the understanding of God, this fits the role of the prophet, who speaks the words of God. For an extensive treatment of Deut 18:15–22 as motivation for the portrayal of Jesus as the agent of God, see Anderson, "Having-Sent-Me Father," 36–40.

and we have no need for anyone to question you; by this we believe that you came from God" (16:30; see 18:4). Even after the resurrection, Jesus is able to reveal his prophetic insight to Peter regarding his past and his future (21:18–19).

Jesus' lengthy prayer to the Father in John 17 acts as a further window into the son's unique position as the revealer of the unseen God. At the beginning of this prayer, Jesus identifies the person to whom he is praying as the only true God, the Father.[26] Jesus then defines the present reality of eternal life as both knowing the only true God and knowing the one whom this God has sent as his agent—Jesus Christ (17:3).[27] In other words, Jesus prays that people would come to intimately know the true God and the one who has been commissioned as the true God's revealer.[28] As the Father's agent, Jesus confesses that he has shared the Father's words with the disciples in a manner that proves his God-given ministry: "The words that you gave me I have given to them; and they received them and truly recognized that I have come forth from you, and they believed that you sent me" (17:8). The prayer draws to a close with Jesus repeating the declaration that his disciples recognize Jesus as the agent of the true God's knowledge (17:25). In order to fully grasp the Johannine Jesus, the reader must also understand the relationship between God and Jesus, the sent revealer of the Father.[29]

---

26. Thompson, *God of the Gospel of John*, 239, is on point with her concluding remarks: "John's fundamental assumption about God is that there is one God, and that this God is the 'only true God,' the living Father, the one who alone is God and has 'life in himself.' As the living God, God is also the source of all life, the creator of all that is."

27. Witherington, *John's Wisdom*, 269, describes the role of Jesus here as "God's agent, his apostle, his sent one." Thompson, *God of the Gospel of John*, 51, defines what it means to know God as knowing "God as the Father of the Son."

28. Robinson, *Twelve More*, 175, judges that "John is as undeviating a witness as any in the New Testament to the fundamental tenet of Judaism, of unitary monotheism."

29. Carter, *John and Empire*, 196, in discussing the attribution of "God" to Jesus in John 20:28, stresses the importance of Wisdom Christology and the nuance necessary when interpreting this passage, "This identification as God is functional and not ontological, as posed in later christological formulations. Appropriate to John's pervasive wisdom paradigm and Jesus' revelatory role as the agent sent by God, Jesus is God in God's knowability (14:7), visibility (14:9), and audibility (14:10, 24), in manifesting God's power and beneficence." Similarly, Thompson, *God of the Gospel of John*, 98, concludes that speaking of God as Father "is not some 'ontological' predication in and of itself that can be separated from speaking of the Father's relationship to the Son." Meyer, "Father," 256, interprets 20:28 as a fulfilment of 14:9, rather than the elimination of the regular distinction between God and Jesus.

As the personification of God's wise activity and intention, Lady Wisdom frequently acts as the agent of God's revelatory knowledge within the Jewish sapiential literature.[30] The poem in Job 28 not only defines wisdom in synonymous parallelism as God's understanding (Job 28:20, 28), but it also argues that God alone understands her ways and knows her place (28:23). Wisdom is a declaration of God—the one who established her and searched her out (28:27). This theme of personified wisdom functioning as the understanding of God is picked up by the sages in the book of Proverbs. When fools reject Lady Wisdom, they scoff at knowledge (Prov 1:22). When God wants to pour out his Spirit—that is, make his words known to the people—he does so through the agency of personified wisdom (Prov 1:23). The fear of YHWH is poetically given meaning as Lady Wisdom's counsel and reproof (Prov 1:29–30). When YHWH gives forth his wisdom, this is the same as knowledge and understanding coming forth from his mouth (Prov 2:6). Furthermore, God's gift of wisdom is later illustrated as wisdom actively entering the heart of the upright, resulting in pleasant knowledge for the soul (Prov 2:10). The sages of wisdom could confidently assert that the acceptance of God's wise words is closely related to his knowledge because creation itself came into existence through God's wisdom, understanding, and knowledge: "YHWH by wisdom founded the earth, by understanding he established the heavens, by his knowledge the deeps were broken up and the skies drip with dew" (Prov 3:19–20). In other words, the wisdom that God used to wisely order creation itself is the same wisdom offered to those who submit to the fear of the Lord. When Lady Wisdom speaks, she utters forth words of the knowledge of YHWH (Prov 8:8–9). This is true because personified wisdom dwells with and finds similar personifications to herself: prudence, knowledge, and discretion (8:12). The wisdom literature in the Hebrew Bible portrays Lady Wisdom as the personified revelation of God's wise knowledge.

The depiction of Wisdom within Sirach and Baruch likewise expresses the way the God of Israel reveals himself to creation. Lady Wisdom rains down the knowledge of God and his discerning comprehension, and in the process she heightens the glory of those holding her fast (Sir 1:19). After coming down and making her dwelling in the form of the law of the commandments, Wisdom overflows with understanding like many noteworthy rivers (Sir 24:25–26). Furthermore, this wisdom-embodied

---

30. Shafer, "Wisdom Christology," 56; Brown, *Introduction to the Gospel of John*, 262.

law is likened to the Nile as it pours forth God's instruction (Sir 24:27). The image of God revealing himself by pouring forth his wisdom like water is picked up by the author of Baruch as he offers his explanation as to why Israel is in exile:

> Why is it, O Israel, why is it that you are in the land of your enemies,
> that you are growing old in a foreign country,
> that you are defiled with the dead,
> that you are counted among those in Hades?
> You have forsaken the fountain of wisdom. (Bar 3:10–12)

In order to learn the way of the knowledge of God, one must lay hold of wisdom and understand her paths (Bar 3:20). Those whom God did reveal the way of knowledge perished because they did not possess wisdom (Bar 3:27–28). However, God gave his wisdom to his servant Jacob, and in doing so he found the whole way of his knowledge (Bar 3:36; 4:1–2).

Wisdom of Solomon comparably offers several examples of God revealing his knowledge through his wisdom. In Wis 7:15–22, the author credits God with giving him "unerring knowledge of what exists, to know the structure of the world and the activity of the elements." This understanding includes the span of times, the ways in which the solstices and seasons change, the year's cycle, the stars' constellations, the temperament of animals, and other noteworthy things. Then, the author details how he came to receive all this God-given knowledge: "For Wisdom, the fashioner of all things, taught me" (Wis 7:22). Lady Wisdom is an initiate in God's knowledge, a personified associate of his works (Wis 8:4). Considering her privileged role as the revealer of the knowledge of God, the author can direct those who "long for experience" toward her since she knows the things of old and is able to discern the things to come (Wis 8:8). We can discern the influence of this passage upon several texts where Jesus, Wisdom incarnate, possesses knowledge of things both in the past and to come (e.g., John 2:24–25; 4:1; 6:15, 70–71; 21:17).[31] Wisdom also understands speech and riddles; she possesses foreknowledge; and she knows the outcome of the times. Within Solomon's prayer to God, he acknowledges that Lady Wisdom is with him: "She who knows your works . . . she understands what is pleasing in your sight and what is right according to your commandments" (Wis 9:9). A. T. Hanson has convincingly drawn attention to the influence of Wis 9:10 ("Send her forth . . . that I may learn what is pleasing to you") upon Jesus' acknowledgment that he

---

31. Witherington, *John's Wisdom*, 160.

always does what is pleasing to the one who sent him (John 8:29).[32] The author of Wisdom of Solomon confesses personified wisdom's revelatory role in no uncertain terms: "She knows and understands all things and she will wisely guide me in my works" (9:11). Personified wisdom's role as God's agent in conveying his revelatory knowledge continues within the ministry of Jesus Christ—the incarnation of wisdom. Raymond Brown draws the same conclusion:

> The function of Wisdom among men is to teach them of the things that are above (Job 11:6-7; Wis 9:16-18), to utter truth (Prov 8:7; Wis 6:22), to give instructions as to what pleases God and how to do His will (Wis 8:4; 9:9-10), and thus to lead men to life (Prov 4:13; 8:32-35; Sir 4:12; Bar 4:1) and immortality (Wis 6:18-19). This is precisely the function of Jesus as revealer, as portrayed in numerous passages in John.[33]

WISDOM'S FIRST-PERSON INVITATIONS

As the Johannine Jesus carries out his mission to reveal and explain the unseen God to the world, he offers invitations to his audience to come forth and believe. Jesus regularly offers these invitations in the first person, using the "I am + metaphor" formula, followed by a statement summoning a crucial response from his hearers. This distinctive speech only appears in the Fourth Gospel, being completely absent from the three Synoptic counterparts. As a unique christological feature within the Gospel of John that also shows influence from the Jewish wisdom literature, it is a worthy topic of exploration in the ministry of the Johannine Jesus.

Within the Bread of Life Discourse, we observe the initial occurrence of Jesus' first-person invitations. Having emphasized that the Father currently offers true, life-giving bread out of heaven, which resulted in the crowds eagerly expressing their interest in what he was saying, Jesus reveals himself as the true bread: "I am the bread of life; he who comes to me will not hunger, and he who believes in me will never thirst" (6:35).[34] The gift of God's life-giving bread culminates in the person and work of the Johannine Jesus, whose self-referential metaphor is accompanied by the invitation to come to him and to believe in him. These

---

32. Hanson, *New Testament Interpretation*, 172.

33. Brown, *John I–XII*, cxxiii. See the similar statements in Sidebottom, *Fourth Gospel*, 203; Kümmel, *Introduction*, 227.

34. Feuillet, *Johannine Studies*, 86; Brown, *Introduction to the Gospel of John*, 262.

two responses are synonymous phrases, for whoever comes to Jesus must believe in him as the agent of God's life-giving purposes. Later in the discourse, Jesus repeats the first-person metaphor and follows it with an invitation to participate in the eating of this bread from heaven: "I am the living bread that came down out of heaven; if anyone eats of this bread, he will live forever; and the bread also that I will give for the life of the world is my flesh" (6:51).[35] In other words, Jesus invites the crowds to come and participate in a sacramental meal resulting in life forever in light of Jesus' fleshly sacrifice. The second invitation that the author pairs with a first-person metaphor is in John 8:12: "I am the light of the world; he who follows me will not walk in darkness but will have the light of life."[36] By drawing on creation themes from the Prologue, the author paints Jesus as the light of humanity that shines in the darkness (see 1:4–5). Jesus' invitation encourages his hearers to follow him as disciples who are to possess the light of life. The third instance of this motif occurs in John 10:7–9, where Jesus claims to be the door of the sheep: "I am the door; if anyone enters through me, he will be saved and will go in and out and find pasture." This offer positions Jesus as the means through which those who believe find salvation and pasture as his sheep. Upon hearing of the death of Lazarus, Jesus tells Martha, "I am the resurrection and the life; he who believes in me will live even if he dies, and everyone who lives and believes in me will never die" (11:25–26). This invitation serves to emphasize the life that Jesus offers both in the present and in the future. Within the Farewell Discourse, many of these themes reappear in Jesus' claim to be the way, the truth, and the life (14:6). These three metaphors accompany the clarifying invitation regarding how to access the Father: "No one comes to the Father but through me." Finally, Jesus utilizes the first-person formula with the image of the vine in chapter 15: "I am the vine, you are the branches; he who abides in me and I in him, he bears much fruit, for apart from me you can do nothing" (15:5). The summons to abide/remain in Jesus in order that one may bear fruit indicates the seriousness of the disciple's commitment. In short, Jesus frequently utilizes first-person metaphors as a self-reference and follows these claims with invitations to discipleship.

35. Borgen, *Bread from Heaven*, 156, gives attention to similar "I"-style self-predications of personified wisdom in Proverbs 8 to what appears in the Bread of Life Discourse (i.e., John 6:35, 41, 48, 51).

36. Robert and Feuillet, *Introduction*, 875, draw attention to the parallels between Wisdom and Jesus' ability to offer the light of life to humanity.

The portrayal of the Johannine Jesus speaking in the first person and issuing summons to follow him draws upon various depictions of Lady Wisdom offering similar first-person invitations within the Jewish sapiential literature.[37] The book of Proverbs contains some of the longest first-person speeches of personified wisdom, and most of these speeches contain personal invitations to those who are willing to accept her words. Proverbs 8, for example, records several instances where Lady Wisdom invites her listeners to heed her: "Take my instruction and not silver, and knowledge rather than choicest gold" (Prov 8:10); "listen to me, for blessed are they who keep my ways" (8:32); "blessed is the person who listened to me, watching daily at my gates, waiting at my doorposts" (8:34). Those who accept personified wisdom's invitations find life and favor from YHWH (8:35). Another first-person speech of Wisdom appears in Proverbs 9, where she builds a house and prepares a meal for those who would come to her and partake.[38] Her summons includes, "Come, eat of my bread and drink of the wine I have mixed . . . forsake folly and live, and proceed in the way of understanding" (9:5–6).[39] Peder Borgen has shown that Wisdom's invitation to "come" in Prov 9:5 and Sir 24:19 accompany several of Jesus' first-person summons (John 5:40; 6:37, 44–45, 65; 7:37), demonstrating what Borgen describes as a certain dependence upon the Jewish wisdom traditions.[40] It is not an accident, therefore, that the motifs of bread, life, door, and the way reemerge in the first-person metaphors of the Johannine Jesus.[41]

Ben Sira offers a similar portrayal of Lady Wisdom inviting her listeners to take hold of her within the context of an extended first-person speech (Sir 24:1–34). Her summons encourages those who desire her to "come to me . . . eat your fill of my fruits" (24:19).[42] She then expresses her worth as greater than honey and the honeycomb (24:20). Those who

---

37. Brown, *John I–XII*, 537–38, connects the first-person discourses in John with the wisdom passages in Proverbs and Sirach. See also the discussion in O'Boyle, *Wisdom Christology*, 162–63; Dunn, "Let John Be John," 331; Schroer, *Wisdom*, 119.

38. Brown, *John I–XII*, 328, draws attention to the parallels in Prov 9:3–6 and Wisdom incarnate's invitations in John 7:37–39.

39. Schnackenburg, *John*, 2:44–45, argues: "When we recall that wisdom too came down from heaven in order to live among the sons of men . . . it becomes even more probable that John has these wisdom texts in mind."

40. Borgen, *Bread from Heaven*, 154–55; followed by Sandelin, *Wisdom as Nourisher*, 177–78.

41. Kobel, *Dining with John*, 191–92; Ceresko, *Old Testament Wisdom*, 178.

42. Coloe, *John 1–10*, 168.

partake of wisdom's meal will be forever fed: "Those who eat of me will hunger for more, and those who drink of me will thirst for more" (24:21). Her invitation concludes with a promise that those who obey her will never be put to shame, and the parallel promise assures those who work with her will not sin (24:22). The Johannine Jesus embodies the invitation of Wisdom in Sirach 24, where she invites interested persons to eat and drink of her in an ongoing, intimate relationship involving obedience and good works.[43] The author of the Fourth Gospel appears to be indebted to the Jewish wisdom traditions in his characterization of Jesus as summoning disciples in first-person invitations.[44]

THE GIFT OF WISDOM

The Johannine Jesus ministers as the authorized agent of the unseen God. The author of the Gospel of John illustrates Jesus' God-endorsed ministry by using "gift" terminology—vocabulary that also appears within the Jewish wisdom literature. The Father "gives" the son, indicating that God commissions the son as the Father's empowered agent to minister the life-giving purposes of salvation to the world.[45] God loves the world in this way, namely that "he gave his unique son," so that whoever believes in him will possess the life of the age to come (3:16). The unique son is a gift of the Father for the salvation of those in the world who choose to believe. When Jesus speaks with the Samaritan woman, he seems to refer to himself (or the results of his ministry) as God's gift: "If you knew the gift of God and he who it is who says to you, 'Give me a drink,' you would have asked him, and he would have given you living water" (4:10).[46] In the Bread of Life Discourse, Jesus introduces himself by contrasting the manna that God gave in the past with the gift that God is currently giving to Jesus' audience (6:32). While the motif is not widespread, the Gospel of John is distinctive in its portrayal of Jesus as the gift from God.[47]

---

43. Coloe, *John 1–10*, 180.

44. Dunn, *Neither Jew nor Greek*, 643; Scott, *Sophia*, 117; Brown, *John I–XII*, cxxiii; Johnson, "Jesus, the Wisdom of God," 284; Witherington, *Jesus the Sage*, 375; Schüssler Fiorenza, *Jesus*, 167; Charlesworth, "Lady Wisdom," 109; Manns, "Jewish Approach," 268.

45. Anderson, "Having-Sent-Me Father," 34.

46. Lee, *Symbolic Narratives*, 76, points to the strong overtones of personified wisdom in Jesus' offer of the gift.

47. Keener, *John*, 1:567, notes, however, that the verb "give" occurs sixty-three times,

Within the Jewish sapiential literature, God gives his wisdom as a gift to humankind. In Baruch, the God of Israel gave wisdom to Israel, whom he loved (Bar 3:36). The theme of God loving Israel so that he gave his wisdom is strikingly similar to what is expressed in John 3:16.[48] The parallel becomes stronger as Baruch continues; "Afterward she appeared on earth and she lived among humankind" (Bar 3:37). Baruch goes on to identify wisdom as the book of the commandments of God (4:1), thereby equating wisdom's presence on earth in terms of the law of Moses. The Gospel of John contrasts God's gift to the generation of the wilderness with God's present gift of Jesus—Wisdom's embodiment. So, while Baruch portrays God loving and gifting wisdom in the form of the law of Moses, the Fourth Gospel portrays God loving and giving Wisdom incarnate in the man Jesus Christ. The author of Wisdom of Solomon also paints wisdom as the gift of God. In particular, Solomon connects the various threads in Wis 8:21: "I perceived that I would not possess wisdom unless God gave her to me—and it was a mark of insight to know whose gift she was." This passage combines both the noun and the verb as the actions of God's offering of Lady Wisdom. Solomon continues with his extended prayer, where he explicitly petitions God to "give me the wisdom that sits by your throne" (9:4). In fact, Solomon admits that unless God gives wisdom, one cannot discern his counsel (9:17). The distinctive christological emphasis within the Fourth Gospel where God gives wisdom in the person of the human Jesus is indebted to the Jewish sapiential literature wherein the sages portray wisdom as the gift of Israel's God.[49]

ETERNAL LIFE, STILL TO COME

As the agent of God's life-giving purposes, Jesus offers eternal life, the life of the age to come. The life of the age to come is the resurrection life that many Jews anticipated would accompany the arrival of the Messiah of Israel and the day of judgment. Scholars have for a long time noticed that while the Synoptic Gospels portray the kingdom of God as primarily future but also breaking into the present, the Gospel of John uses the

---

making its action a common motif.

48. Schweizer, "Zum religionsgeschichtlichen Hintergrund," 208–10, notes particularly how the Wisdom themes present in the Prologue give meaning to John 3:16.

49. McHugh, *John 1–4*, 314; Johnson, "Jesus, the Wisdom of God," 285; Talbert, "Descending-Ascending Redeemer," 109.

concept of *eternal life* in the same way. Since God has empowered the son with the prerogative to give life (John 5:20, 26–27), Jesus anticipates a coming hour in which he will raise the dead and offer resurrection life to those who commit good deeds: "An hour is coming, in which all who are in the tombs will hear his voice and come forth; those who did good works to a resurrection of life, those who did evil works to a resurrection of judgment" (5:28–29). The language of "coming forth" appears again in John 11 when Jesus raises the deceased Lazarus from the dead: "Lazarus, come forth" (11:43).[50] Martha confesses that she knows that her brother Lazarus will rise again in the resurrection on the last day (11:24), to which Jesus responds by claiming to be "the resurrection and the life" (11:25). Jesus makes several references to the future resurrection on the last day in the Bread of Life Discourse.[51] As the agent authorized by God to give life, Jesus repeats the promise that he will raise up anyone who comes to him on the last day (6:39, 40, 44, 54). The ministry of Jesus characterizes the son as the one who will confer resurrection life to the faithful.

The author of Wisdom of Solomon speaks about immortality and positions it as a gift from Lady Wisdom. As the author sets forth to define the beginning of wisdom, he arrives at the conclusion that "giving heed to her laws is an assurance of immortality, and immortality makes one near to God" (Wis 6:18–19). Those who follow the ways of personified wisdom are guaranteed a never-ending life. Later in the work, Solomon reflects on the benefits of possessing the wisdom from God. He credits wisdom with the promise of eternal life: "Because of her I will possess immortality and I will leave an everlasting remembrance to those who come after me" (Wis 8:13).[52] If God possesses the power over life and death, and if he leads mortals down to the gates of Hades and back again (Wis 16:13), then Wisdom incarnate, whom God has empowered with the prerogative to give life, can resurrect the dead to eternal life (John 5:20–29).[53] The Wisdom Christology within the Gospel of John portrays Jesus as the giver of immortal, resurrection life on the last day, just as we can observe in Wisdom of Solomon.[54]

50. Keener, *John*, 2:850.

51. Borgen, *Bread from Heaven*, 166, observes the coalescence of the themes of Torah, wisdom, and agency in the offer of eternal life within the Bread of Life Discourse.

52. Dillon, "Wisdom Tradition," 277; O'Boyle, *Wisdom Christology*, 169.

53. Witherington, *John's Wisdom*, 143.

54. Witherington, *Jesus the Sage*, 377; Von Wahlde, *John*, 1:414; Ceresko, *Old Testament Wisdom*, 178–79.

ETERNAL LIFE, EXPERIENCED NOW

The Gospel of John presents eternal life as something yet to be realized in addition to a present reality for those who believe in Jesus.[55] The future immortality of bodily resurrection is offered in the present as a metaphor for conversion. Jesus describes the current experience of life for those who hear his word and trust in the God who commissioned Jesus: "Truly, truly, I say to you, he who hears my word and believes him who sent me, has eternal life and does not come into judgment, but has passed out of death into life" (5:24). For believers, eternal life is a current reality involving the death and resurrection of conversion. Jesus quite frequently speaks of eternal life as a present possession of those who demonstrate belief and obedience (3:36; 6:37, 54; 10:28; 17:3).[56] As the authorized and empowered agent of the Father, Jesus "gives life to whomever he desires" (5:21). As the bread of life, Jesus gives life to the world (6:33). Peter acknowledges Jesus' God-given authority and confesses that "you have words of eternal life" (6:68). While the thief comes to destroy, Jesus has come in order that the sheep might have life in the present—abundant life in the present (10:10). The Johannine Jesus anticipates the future bodily resurrection with the present offering of life as a metaphor for converting and believing in him.[57]

Just as personified wisdom promised immortality to those who take hold of her, she also offers a present experience of life.[58] In Wisdom of Solomon, while portraying eternal life as a future reward that Lady Wisdom will confer, the righteous are said to possess a sense of "living" already in the present. While contrasting the former way of living that is full of wickedness wherein the ungodly "cease to be" (Wis 5:13–14), the author defines the status of the righteous as "living into the age" (5:15), using the present tense of the verb "to live" in the process.[59] This experience of life

---

55. Coloe, *John 11–21*, 318–19, observes that out of the seventeen references to "eternal life" within the Fourth Gospel, fifteen deal with a present reality and only two refer to a future life.

56. Dillon, "Wisdom Tradition," 277, argues that John 17:3 is itself a "short summary of the Johannine Wisdom-life theme."

57. Keener, *John*, 1:329.

58. Coloe, *John 1–10*, 103, aptly summarizes this point: "The Johannine Jesus speaks as divine Sophia, whose children . . . participate in the life of God *now*, sharing God's own eternity life, which is this Gospel's understanding of what salvation mean" (emphasis original).

59. O'Boyle, *Wisdom Christology*, 168; Coloe, *John 11–21*, 319.

in the present fits into the theology of Wisdom of Solomon, considering the promised assurance of immortality that belongs to those who love personified wisdom and keep her laws (6:17–18). Furthermore, Solomon argues that in this life, Wisdom is the greatest of desirable riches (8:5), further enhancing the connection between the two. In fact, nothing in this life is greater than that which Lady Wisdom teaches (8:7). Life with Wisdom, Solomon argues, "has no pain, but gladness and joy" (8:16). Of course, Wisdom is able to provide eternal life in the present because she, rather than the serpent, is "the savior of all" (16:5–7). This statement creates an outstanding parallel with John 3:14–16, where the themes of the serpent, salvation, and eternal life coalesce with Wisdom's incarnation, Jesus.[60] Just as personified wisdom offers life in the present that continues to life immortal, the Johannine Jesus, who himself embodies wisdom, similarly offers an available experience of resurrection life that anticipates the raising of bodies from the dead on the last day.[61]

THE KINGDOM OF GOD

Although the Fourth Gospel stresses the experience of eternal life far more frequently than the concept of the kingdom of God, the kingdom is not wholly absent from Jesus' teachings. In fact, the metaphor of eternal life realized in the present closely resembles the New Testament's teaching of the kingdom's realized eschatology.[62] The Johannine Jesus does discuss the kingdom of God on a few occasions, notably in his dialogues with Nicodemus and Pontius Pilate. To the former, Jesus announces that one must be born from above in order to see the kingdom of God (John 3:3). Nicodemus responds with one of the typical Johannine misunderstandings, where he interprets Jesus' words concerning birth literally, resulting in an inappropriate question. Jesus clarifies his statement for the confused Nicodemus: "Unless one is born of water and the Spirit, he cannot enter into the kingdom of God" (3:5).[63] With this clarification,

60. Coloe, *John 1–10*, 101; Charlesworth, "Lady Wisdom," 110.

61. Borgen, *Bread from Heaven*, 168–72; Johnson, "Jesus, the Wisdom of God," 285; O'Boyle, *Wisdom Christology*, 169; Carter, *John and Empire*, 340–41.

62. Keener, *John*, 1:328.

63. Sidebottom, *Fourth Gospel*, 206, points to the parallel between Wis 9:17 ("Who has learned your counsel, unless you have given Wisdom and sent your holy spirit from on high?") and Jesus telling Nicodemus that one must be born from above, that is, born of water and of the Holy Spirit.

we observe two important points. First, the new birth from above is a birth defined by water and spirit, likely drawing upon the promises of renewal in Ezek 36:25–27. Second, the concept of seeing the kingdom of God gains further clarity; "seeing" is entering into the kingdom. Discussion on the topic of the kingdom fizzles out because Nicodemus fails to comprehend Jesus' words regarding the new birth (John 3:9).

When Jesus talks about the kingdom of God with Pilate, Pilate does not fare much better than Nicodemus. The actions of Jesus lead to Pilate directly asking him, "Are you the King of the Jews?" (18:33). This notion of kingship eventually leads the conversation to Jesus defining the kingdom of God's origins: "My kingdom is of not of this world. If my kingdom were of this world, then my servants would be fighting so that I would not be handed over to the Jews, but as it is, my kingdom is not from here" (18:36). The Johannine term "world" is often indicative of the created realm in need of redemption, so Jesus defines his kingdom as one that does not derive from this unredeemed realm. Pilate sees in Jesus' response about his kingdom an implicit affirmation to kingship, resulting in the question, "So you are a king?" (18:37). Jesus unambiguously answers in the affirmative, claiming that for this purpose he was born and came into this world. He then defines his kingdom ministry as coming to testify to the truth, noting that everyone who belongs to the truth listens to his voice. In other words, Jesus' kingdom is closely associated with the speaking of truth and creating a community defined both by this truth and by obeying Jesus' leading. In another example of the Johannine theme of misunderstanding, Pilate asks an inappropriate question in response to Jesus' statement: "What is truth?" (18:38). Although Jesus does not offer a clarifying remark to help Pilate out of his confusion, his discussion confirms the connection with the kingdom of God and Jesus' role as the messianic king.

By highlighting Jesus as the king, the Gospel of John identifies Jesus as the royal ruler of the kingdom of God. As such, the various royal titles further emphasize the extent of the kingdom of God's pervasiveness within the wider narrative. The only two occurrences of the Greek noun *messias* ("messiah") within the New Testament appear in the Gospel of John, indicating Jesus' anointed position of kingship (1:41; 4:25). The equivalent to *messias*, "Christ," appears some nineteen times in the Gospel of John in order to further define Jesus as the anointed king of the kingdom. Additionally, the Johannine Jesus is affirmed as the "King of Israel" on several occasions (1:49; 12:13, 15; 19:3, 14, 19, 21). Lastly, the title "son of God" frequently associates Jesus as the anointed Israelite king within John's Gospel (1:49; 11:27; 19:3–7; 20:31).[64] The concept of the kingdom of God is expressed in both the redemptive realm of God as well as in the role of Jesus as the king of the Jews.

The sages who composed the Jewish sapiential literature associated the role of kingship as one that Lady Wisdom empowers and blesses. In the book of Proverbs, Wisdom declares that a cluster of important traits belongs to her (counsel, sound wisdom, understanding, power), reflecting the empowerment of King Solomon, who prayed for wise discernment (Prov 8:14; see 1 Kgs 3:9). Personified wisdom then declares that the ability to rule is closely bound together with her active involvements: "By me kings reign, and rulers decree justice. By me princes rule, even nobles, all who judge rightly" (Prov 8:15–16). In effect, the wisdom that God used to wisely order creation is the same wisdom that human rulers should utilize in order that they may enact a wise reign.

The author of Wisdom of Solomon adopts these themes from Proverbs and significantly elaborates on them. The threat of swift and terrible judgment is issued against the servants of God's kingdom for failing to rule rightly, keep the law, and walk according to his purposes (Wis 6:4–5). It is to these monarchs specifically that the author directs his rebuke, encouraging them to "learn wisdom and not transgress" (6:9). The implication is that the kings of the kingdom of God can only rule correctly and live in accordance with the purposes of God by learning wisdom. Without wisdom, the kings and their kingdom fail to function appropriately. In fact, the desire for Lady Wisdom—to listen to her instruction and laws—leads precisely to a kingdom (6:17–20).[65] We can observe the influence of this motif in Jesus' discussion with Pilate, where he claims to be the king of a kingdom involving a community defined by those who listen to his voice. Solomon's prayer largely focuses on the involvement of wisdom in his capacity to rule as the king of Israel's kingdom. Solomon first acknowledges God as the one who used wisdom as his agent to create humankind in order that they may have dominion over the creatures, to rule the world in holiness (9:1–3). If God's wisdom was instrumental in the creation of humanity, whose purpose is to rule and reign, then wisdom can certainly help rulers bring about these ordered

---

64. For the royal overtones of the Jewish title "son of God," see Ps 2:7; 2 Sam 7:14.

65. Several scholars have come to regard this text as impacting the interaction between Jesus and Nicodemus that pertains to the kingdom of God. See e.g., Coloe, *John 1–10*, 92.

results. This leads Solomon to pray and request that God would give to him this wisdom (9:4, 10) so that she may guide him wisely in his actions (9:11). Only after Solomon possesses personified wisdom will he be able to judge the people justly and be worthy of the throne of his father David (9:12). Lady Wisdom also shows up in the retelling of the life of the patriarch Jacob. Wisdom showed the kingdom of God to Jacob as she guided him on straight paths (10:10). Scholars have often drawn comparisons between Wis 10:10 and Jesus' conversation with Nicodemus about the kingdom of God.[66] It is also by the hand of Wisdom that Jacob eventually received authority and rulership over the kingdom of Egypt (10:14). In short, the accounts of personified wisdom working closely with individuals in order that they may rule well and possess a kingdom have made an impact on the christological portrayal of Jesus in the Fourth Gospel, who promises participation and entrance into God's kingdom to those belonging to his obedient community of truth.

WISDOM AS WATER

On a few occasions, Jesus expresses the work of his ministry in terms of water and various bodies of water, such as a spring and a river, resulting in the outpouring of eternal life. Since the imagery of water is a characteristic of God's wisdom, it would be prudent to explore the potential connection of themes within the life and teachings of the Johannine Jesus. The image of water first appears in Jesus' dialogue with the Samaritan woman as they discuss the relevance of Jacob's Well. Jesus begins by requesting a drink from the woman, resulting in her questioning how a Jew could conceivably ask to receive water from a Samaritan (John 4:7–9). Jesus' response shifts the topic from well water to "living water" as he invites the woman to pursue deeper the identity of this Jew who is speaking with her: "If you knew the gift of God and who it is who says to you, 'Give me a drink,' you would have asked him, and he would have given you living water" (4:10). After the Samaritan woman expresses confusion about the origins and location of this living water, Jesus offers some much-needed clarification: "The water that I will give will become in them a spring of water gushing up to eternal life" (4:14). The woman, albeit confused about the true nature of this water, expresses her desire to possess it nonetheless

---

66. Keener, *Gospel of John*, 1:537; Morris, *John*, 212; Coloe, *John 1–10*, 93, 96; Witherington, *John's Wisdom*, 94, who explicitly identifies the Wisdom Christology, "I would suggest that [Jesus] is portrayed as Wisdom here."

(4:15). Jesus' water is "living" because it is the means of life everlasting, not because it comes from a natural source or even from Jacob's Well,[67] which some Jewish traditions interpreted as having overflowed with water for a limited period of time.[68]

Jesus reintroduces the topic of water leading to eternal life during the last day of the Festival of Tabernacles. According to the Mishnah, it was customary for the Jewish priests to poor water onto the altar on each day of the celebration.[69] This gives the appropriate context for Jesus' invitation to those present to come to him in belief and partake of the water he offers: "If anyone thirsts, let him come to me and drink. He who believes in me, as the Scripture said, 'From his innermost being will flow rivers of living water.'" (7:37–38).[70] The narrator immediately clarifies the meaning of this metaphor, identifying the water as the Holy Spirit that believers were to receive (7:39). Within the Farewell Discourse, Jesus indicates that it will be after his departure that the Paraclete will come, thus giving fulfillment to the promise of the Spirit (14:26; 15:26; 16:13–15). By making this statement, Jesus encourages those present to look to him—the tabernacling presence of Wisdom—for living water, rather than to the waters poured out from within the Jerusalem temple during the festival.

Within the Jewish wisdom literature, it was quite commonplace to associate water imagery with God's wisdom.[71] Lady Wisdom speaks about making her words known to those who respond appropriately to her reproof, and the way in which she conveys her words is that she "pours out" her spirit as if it was water (Prov 1:23). Later on, Proverbs indicates that those who are thirsty are to come to Wisdom (9:5), not unlike Jesus' invitation to those who thirst in John 7:37-38.[72] The sages

67. Thompson, *John*, 100.

68. Tg. Neof. 28:10; Tg. Ps-J. 28:10; Gen Rab. 70:19. I credit these references to Thompson, *John*, 101.

69. m. Sukkah 4:9–10.

70. Witherington, *John's Wisdom*, 173–74, suggests that the passage to which Jesus is alluding is the same that Sirach discusses during his exposition of Lady Wisdom as the source of a noteworthy river (Sir 24:30–32). Sandelin, *Wisdom as Nourisher*, 175, in addition to Sirach 24, observes the similarity to Wisdom's call in Prov 9:5. Coloe, *John 1–10*, 211, notes that in the absence of the Jerusalem temple during the time of the writing of the Fourth Gospel, Wisdom incarnate is the provider of water and light that the temple formerly supplied during Tabernacles.

71. Thompson, *John*, 101. Schnackenburg, *John*, 2:154, concludes: "The invitation to come to Jesus and drink (from him) finds its strongest parallels in the Wisdom literature."

72. Keener, *Gospel of John*, 1:729; Ringe, *Wisdom's Friends*, 60; Schroer, *Wisdom*, 119.

later depict the sayings that come forth from a man's mouth in terms of a fountain of wisdom—a bubbling brook (Prov 18:4). John McHugh perceptively points out that the Greek phrase for "well of water" (*pygy zoys*) appears in eight other places, all wisdom texts.[73] Ben Sira continues to expound these themes with even greater poetic freedom. For example, he portrays personified wisdom as a nourisher who feeds with the bread of learning and offers her own water as a drink (Sir 15:3).[74] The extended first-person monologue of Wisdom in chapter 24 offers several illustrations in terms of various bodies of water, with six rivers in total from Israel's history.[75] After coming down to earth and taking shape as the law of the commandments, Wisdom causes it to overflow like the Pishon and Tigris Rivers (Sir 24:25). Additionally, the Wisdom-embodied law is compared to Euphrates when it runs over, and to the Jordan at harvest time (24:26).[76] As the Nile River pours forth water, so too does the law pour forth instruction. The same is true for the Gihon River (24:27). Even the thoughts of Lady Wisdom are compared with bodies of water; they are more abundant than the sea, and her counsel is deeper than the abyss (24:29).[77] The chapter comes to a close with Sirach characterizing himself as a sage whose instruction and teaching further extends the water imagery from Wisdom. He is a canal from a river that waters his garden and drenches his flowerbeds. His canal expands to a river and then further into a sea as he seeks wisdom (24:30–34). Readers of the Gospel of John who are familiar with these images of God's wisdom overflowing like water would naturally identify Jesus as Lady Wisdom.[78]

The illustration of wisdom as water continued in the Jewish literature that preceded the Fourth Gospel.[79] The author of Baruch criticizes the nation of Israel's disobedience in terms of "forsaking the fountain of

---

73. McHugh, *John 1–4*, 274, citing Prov 10:11; 13:14; 14:27; 16:22; 18:4; Sir 21:13; Ps 36:9; Song 4:15.

74. Sandelin, *Wisdom as Nourisher*, 174–75.

75. Skehan and Di Lella, *Wisdom of Ben Sira*, 337. Charlesworth, "Lady Wisdom," 105, argues that the Fourth Evangelist has inherited these thoughts concerning Wisdom and advances them by applying them to Jesus.

76. Coloe, *John 1–10*, 126, compares this passage to Jesus, Sophia's embodiment, in his offer of life-giving water to the Samaritan woman.

77. Thomas Aquinas, *John 1–5*, 217, see this passage as directly influencing the Wisdom Christology in Jesus' interaction with the Samaritan woman.

78. Beasley-Murray, *John*, 60; Koester, *Symbolism*, 193; Brown, *John I–XII*, 178, 322; Witherington, *John's Wisdom*, 119, 174; Lincoln, *John*, 174.

79. Dunn, *Jesus according to the New Testament*, 66.

wisdom" (Bar 3:12), which eventually led to their exile and defilement. In the retelling of the history of Israel in Wisdom of Solomon, the account of the Israelites receiving water from the rock in the wilderness is interpreted in light of Wisdom's involvement. The children of Israel called upon Lady Wisdom, and she gave to them water from the rock, a remedy for their thirst (Wis 11:4). First Enoch envisages multiple springs of wisdom located in the heavenly throne room, from which the thirsty did drink. Those who partook of these springs were "filled with wisdom" (1 En. 48:1). The author of the *Parables* has already located personified wisdom in heaven after her descent to earth and her subsequent return (42:1–3), so it is natural that her springs of water are also found there. Even Wisdom herself is said to be "poured out like water" (1 En. 49:1).[80] Additionally, Philo shows evidence of the interpretation of God's wisdom with water metaphors: as a deep well and as a constantly changing stream.[81] To sum up, the wisdom of God was widely portrayed in Jewish wisdom sources in terms of water and various bodies of water. This wisdom overflows in its influence and encourages the thirsty to partake of her stream. As the wisdom of God made flesh, the Johannine Jesus continues to offer the life-giving purposes of God in terms of water for those who thirst after him.[82]

WISDOM AS THE GIVER OF FOOD AND DRINK

Along similar lines to wisdom's water imagery, the Gospel of John presents Jesus offering food and drink throughout his ministry. The Jewish portrayal of Lady Wisdom as the giver of food and drink allows for another opportunity to explore potential parallels and areas of influence on the Johannine Jesus. Jesus' first sign occurs at the wedding in Cana of Galilee (2:1–11), where Mary looks to Jesus when the wine is exhausted. Jesus commands the servants to fill the empty waterpots with water and draw from them, resulting in the water turning into wine. Jesus not only provides drink for the thirsty, but he also transforms the water into a superabundance of good wine as a manifestation of his glory, resulting in

---

80. Nickelsburg and VanderKam, *1 Enoch 2*, observe the association of the water imagery as a thirst-quencher in 1 En. 48:1; Sir 24:25–31; and John 7:37–39.

81. *Ebr.* 112–13; *Somn.* 2:270–271; *Det.* 117.

82. McHugh, *John 1–4*, 275, offers a similar conclusion: "This living water is, quite simply, the knowledge of the word and wisdom of God as contained in the tradition of Israel." See also Schroer, *Wisdom*, 119; Schüssler Fiorenza, *Jesus*, 167.

many coming to believe. On the mountainside by the Sea of Galilee, Jesus performs another sign, this time multiplying the five loaves of bread and the two fish in order to feed five thousand hungry persons (6:1–14).[83] The multiplication of the food even resulted in an excess of twelve baskets. This feeding miracle eventually leads into the Bread of Life Discourse, where Jesus encourages the crowds to work "for the food that endures to life eternal" (6:27). Eventually, the conversation shifts to Jesus revealing himself as the bread of life, and in doing so he promises that those who come to him will no longer hunger and those who believe in him will no longer thirst (6:35). Scholars have detected Eucharistic symbolism within this discourse, especially with the imagery of mutual indwelling between the Son of Man and those who eat of his flesh and drink of his blood (6:53–58).[84] Finally, the Appendix of the Gospel of John includes an account where several disciples attempt to fish on the Sea of Tiberias (21:1–11). Jesus asks those on the boat if they have any fish, to which they reply, "No." Jesus encourages them to cast their net on the right side of the boat, which results in such a large haul that they are unable to lift it back onto the boat. The story concludes with a note about the overabundance of fish caught—153 large fish. The ministry of Jesus contains stories of providing food for the hungry and drink for the thirsty, and each of these feeding miracles delivers far more food and wine than is needed for the occasion.

The Jewish sages offer multiple examples of the personified wisdom of God feeding the hungry and offering drink to the thirsty.[85] Beginning in the book of Proverbs, we find Wisdom playing the role of the host within her home (Prov 9:1–6). After slaughtering the animals, mixing the wine, and preparing the table, she offers her invitation: "Come, eat of my bread and drink of the wine that I have mixed" (9:5).[86] The request to dine with Lady Wisdom is clarified in terms of living according to her ways—by laying aside folly and walking upon the way of insight (9:6). Ben Sira, who demonstrates the influence of Proverbs, offers a similar illustration of personified wisdom: "She will feed him with the bread of

---

83. Ringe, *Wisdom's Friends*, 60.

84. See e.g., Coloe, *John 1–10*, 187; Charlesworth, "Lady Wisdom," 104–5.

85. Dunn, "Let John Be John," 331; Shafer, "Wisdom Christology," 56.

86. Witherington, *John's Wisdom*, 233, observes a remarkable parallel between Wisdom's invitation to the naïve to eat (Prov 9:4–6) and the supper of Jesus where he reveals the identity of his betrayer, to which the remaining disciples respond in a typical naïve fashion (John 13:28–29).

learning, and she will give him the water of wisdom to drink" (Sir 15:3).[87] The first-person speech of Wisdom in Sirach 24 includes a personal summons to those who desire her to eat of her fruits (24:18–21).[88] Those who partake of Wisdom are given the promise that they will hunger for more; those who drink of Wisdom will thirst for more (24:21). The wording of Lady Wisdom's promise in Sir 24:21 ("Those who eat me") probably lies behind a similar statement of the Johannine Jesus in John 6:57 ("he who eats me").[89] Many scholars have identified a remarkable parallel to this invitation with Jesus' statement in John 6:35, where he identifies himself as the bread of life and states that those who come to him will hunger no longer and those who believe in him will no longer thirst.[90] The life-giving ministry of Jesus includes the continuation of Wisdom's gift of food and drink to those who take hold of her and her ways.[91]

WISDOM'S SEVEN SIGNS

We noticed that most of the stories involving Jesus providing an abundance of food and drink are framed by the narrator of the Gospel of John as "signs" (2:11; 6:14, 26). Although six signs are explicitly mentioned during the ministry of the Johannine Jesus, there are good reasons to view the death (and subsequent resurrection) of Jesus as the seventh and final sign.[92] The author of Wisdom of Solomon dedicates a lengthy section (chapters 11–19) that elaborates on seven of its own signs. The seven signs in Wisdom of Solomon involve antitheses wherein the children of Israel find benefit from the very things with which Egypt is punished during the story of the book of Exodus.[93] Since these seven signs are each

---

87. Dunn, *Jesus according to the New Testament*, 66; Ringe, *Wisdom's Friends*, 60.

88. Manns, "Jewish Approach," 268; Lincoln, *John*, 174; Charlesworth, "Lady Wisdom," 105; Feuillet, *Johannine Studies*, 86.

89. Beasley-Murray, *John*, 92; Borgen, *Bread from Heaven*, 155.

90. Bachmann, "Jesus Ben Sira 24," 96–97; Brown, *John I-XII*, 269; Von Wahlde, *John*, 1:414–15; Morris, *John*, 366; Sidebottom, *Fourth Gospel*, 204; Borgen, *Bread from Heaven*, 154–55; Feuillet, *Johannine Studies*, 87; Manns, "Jewish Approach," 268.

91. Johnson, "Jesus, the Wisdom of God," 284; Culpepper, *Gospel*, 97; Dunn, "Aspect of Theology," 384.

92. Most recently, this has been argued by Crowe, "Seven Signs," 66, who builds upon the earlier study of Girard, "Composition structurelle," 315–24. Clark, "Signs in Wisdom and John," 205–6, concludes from the parallels that the Gospel of John is dependent upon Wisdom of Solomon in the form of a causal relationship.

93. Kolaricik, "Book of Wisdom," 528.

prefaced by Lady Wisdom's personal involvement in the affairs of the children of Israel through the prophet Moses, this allows us yet another opportunity to explore possible connections between Jewish wisdom literature and the Gospel of John's presentation of Jesus.

Beginning with the miraculous signs within the Gospel of John, we have Jesus transforming water into wine at the wedding in Cana of Galilee. The narrator informs us that this is the first of his signs (2:11). After Jesus leaves Samaria, he encounters a royal official whose son has fallen ill. Jesus restores the sick child without having to physically be present with him, healing the official's son from a distance.[94] This is the second of Jesus' signs (4:54). The following chapter provides the third sign, where Jesus heals the paralyzed man on the Sabbath so that he is able to walk and participate in the temple (5:1-15).[95] Jesus feeds the five thousand with loaves of bread and a few fish, leading to an extended interaction about the true bread from heaven that contrasts the manna that Moses provided. This miracle is the fourth sign that Jesus performs (6:1-14, 26, 30). Some among the crowds identify Jesus' restoration of the blind man's sight as a sign, although there is a dispute about its legitimacy because it takes place on the Sabbath (9:16). The healing of the blind man, therefore, functions as the fifth sign. The resurrection of Lazarus marks a turning point in the story, resulting in the Pharisees and chief priests gathering and admitting that "this man is performing many signs" (11:47). The death and resurrection of Lazarus marks Jesus' sixth sign. In what is without a doubt the most significant miracle in the Gospel of John, Jesus suffers a glorious death, followed by being raised from the dead. The reference to the seventh sign of the Fourth Gospel follows Jesus' resurrection appearances (20:30). It is highly probable that the author of the Gospel of John regarded the death and resurrection of Jesus as the seventh and final sign.

The seven signs in Wisdom of Solomon pertain to the plagues that God sent upon the Egyptians by the hand of Moses, whom the text designates as the prophet empowered by Lady Wisdom herself (Wis 10:15-16;

---

94. Before agreeing to heal the royal official's son, Jesus appears to lament the fact that people will not believe unless they see "signs and wonders" (*semeia kai terata*) in 4:48. Sidebottom, *Fourth Gospel*, 207, has persuasively demonstrated that this passage parallels Wis 8:8, where Lady Wisdom possesses foreknowledge of "signs and wonders" (*semeia kai terata*).

95. Thomas Aquinas, *John 1-5*, 266, suggests that Jesus' actions involving the healing of the paralyzed man and the subsequent effort to go find him in the temple exhibit Wisdom Christology, drawing on Wis 6:14.

11:1). The first sign details how the water was turned into blood in a manner that both hurt the Egyptians and offered benefit to the Israelites (Wis 11:5–14). In the second sign, God sends forth frogs and lice, while also sending quail to the righteous (11:15–20; 16:1–4). God healed those who suffered from the bites of serpents through his powerful and curing word, according to the third sign (16:5–14). Although the fiery hail punished Israel's enemies, Israel received the food of angels from heaven—manna—in the fourth sign (16:15–29). The following antithesis offers the details of the plague of darkness that fell upon the Egyptians while the rest of the world was illumined with brilliant light (17:1—18:4). The sixth sign features the death of the Egyptian firstborn children (18:5–25). The drowning of the Egyptians in the sea while the children of Israel were delivered from death accounts for the seventh and final sign (19:1–9).

When we compare the seven signs from the Gospel of John with the seven signs in Wisdom of Solomon, we find some remarkable similarities. The first signs share the characteristics involving the transformation of water, one into blood and the other into wine. The second pair of signs describe acts of sending, one of frogs and quail and the other of healing power to an ailing child. Acts of healing are the common denominator in the third set of signs: healing from the plague of locusts and healing the lame man. The fourth group of signs both deal with manna from heaven. The themes of darkness and light characterize the fifth sign. A plague of darkness covered Egypt while light shone on the rest of the world, and Jesus gives sight to a blind man while describing his enemies as blind. The sixth pair of signs pertain to the topic of death—the death of the firstborn Egyptians and the death of Lazarus. Last, the seventh signs detail moments of climactic death and the deliverance from the death of the righteous. The pursuing Egyptians die in the waters of the Red Sea while God rescues the Israelites from their demise. In the Gospel of John, Jesus is the one who dies, and God delivers the righteous Jesus from the dead by raising him back to life. The seven signs in the Gospel of John appear to directly draw upon the seven antitheses in Wisdom of Solomon, both in number and in the order in which they are presented. The signs within Wisdom of Solomon—which are prefaced by the guiding hand of personified wisdom—have come to influence the miraculous signs within the ministry of the Johannine Jesus, who is personified wisdom made flesh.[96]

96. The literary dependance of Wisdom of Solomon upon the Gospel of John has long been recognized. See e.g., Ziener, "Weisheitsbuch und Johannesevangelium," esp.

CONCLUSION

This chapter's aim was to explore the various ways in which Jewish portrayals of Lady Wisdom shaped and impacted the ministry of Jesus within the Fourth Gospel. We observed several ways in which the Johannine Jesus recalls the behavior, characteristics, and interactions of personified wisdom in the sapiential literature. The Johannine Jesus repeatedly ministers in the public arena, which continues the motif of Wisdom's accessibility. Similarly, Jesus takes upon himself the role of a wise teacher that formerly belonged to Wisdom. The various Jewish passages characterizing the descent and ascent of God's wisdom have influenced the accounts of Jesus' mission to the world. Like Wisdom, Jesus functions as the definitive revealer of the true God. The invitations offered by Jesus draw considerable influence from the Jewish wisdom literature. Moreover, we observed noteworthy parallels between YHWH's gift of Wisdom and the Father's gift of the Johannine Jesus. Just as the wisdom of God offers life in the future and in the present, Wisdom incarnate issues forth the same two promises. We also took note of the ways in which the concepts of kingship and kingdom relate to both God's wisdom and the Johannine Jesus. The frequent portrayal of Wisdom in terms of water in the sapiential literature has made a substantial impact on the water imagery surrounding Jesus. He is commonly depicted as the giver of food and drink in a manner that exhibits an indebtedness to the Jewish literature where Lady Wisdom offers food and drink to her audience. Last, we saw that there were some interesting similarities between the seven signs in Wisdom of Solomon and the seven signs in the Gospel of John. In sum. the Gospel of John has deliberately framed the ministry of Jesus to demonstrate the extensiveness of Wisdom's influence, particularly in the teachings, works, and signs that Jesus performed.[97]

In many of the passages surveyed, we frequently observed that Jesus' efforts to minister to others were accompanied by a summons to believe in him, thereby pointing to the person of Jesus. To come to Jesus is to understand and accept the Wisdom Christology within the Fourth Gospel. Therefore, our investigation will now turn toward studying the

---

399–415. Keener, *John*, 1:276, rightly discerns that the signs within the Gospel of John serve a christological function, but he fails to explore the possible parallels with Jewish wisdom literature.

97. Contra Kovalishyn, "Wisdom in the New Testament," 177, who downplays the presentation of the Johannine Jesus as a wisdom teacher and the identification of him as personified wisdom.

intersection between the Christology of the Gospel of John and how the wisdom of God has shaped it.

6

Wisdom and Christology

THE EXPRESSLY STATED PURPOSE of the Gospel of John is to summon its readers to believe that the Johannine Jesus is the Christ, the son of God (20:31). While the concept of belief is vitally important to the author of the Fourth Gospel, readers are called to exercise that belief in a manner that characterizes Jesus in a very specific light. The Prologue, by introducing the human Jesus as the incarnation of personified wisdom, sets the expectation that the Johannine Jesus will consistently embody the identity, function, and purposes of God's wisdom. This chapter aims to explore the wisdom-molded christological portrayal of Jesus within the Gospel of John. To begin, I will look at the intersection between the title "Son of Man" and the theme of wisdom that occurred among apocalyptic-minded Jews. The Gospel of John closely connects the activity of the Father and the son in terms of Jesus revealing the Father, so the way the person of Jesus acts as the definitive revealer of the unseen God will be our next area of study. Since the Fourth Gospel's purpose statement is intended to persuade readers to believe that Jesus is the Christ, I will give attention to the messianism present within the Gospel of John and the ways that Jewish wisdom literature helped shaped the role of Israel's Messiah. A study of the Christology of John would be incomplete without a close look at the seven metaphors used in the formulaic "I am" statements (the bread of life; the light of the world; the door; the good shepherd; the resurrection and the life; the way, the truth, and the life; and the true vine), so these seven titles deserve due consideration. I will also give attention to a rare title that scholars often overlook in their assessment of Johannine Christology, "the Holy One of God." Last, the Gospel of John stands alone among the four New Testament gospels in illustrating Jesus as the "unique" son, using the adjective *monogenes*, which formerly described personified wisdom in Wisdom of Solomon. It is imperative, therefore, that I examine how this rare adjective is used to portray Jesus, in whom Wisdom became flesh within the wider narrative of the gospel. These important characteristics of the Johannine Jesus will allow us to grasp a more accurate portrayal of the Wisdom Christology within the Fourth Gospel.

THE SON OF MAN

The Gospel of John frequently ascribes the title "Son of Man" to Jesus Christ, totaling thirteen occurrences. The title finds its origins in Daniel 7, where a vision reveals a human mortal who becomes the recipient of God's prerogatives—dominion, glory, kingship—as well as functioning as a representative figure for the suffering people of God destined for vindication and kingship (Dan 7:13–27). The book of Daniel, however, does not paint the Son of Man figure with the characteristics of the wisdom of God. We do find this noteworthy intersection of wisdom themes with the Son of Man in 1 Enoch, particularly within the Enochic *Book of Parables* (chapters 37–71). Before looking closely at this data, I must first survey how the Johannine Jesus is depicted in terms of the Son of Man. Only then can we reasonably conclude if the Gospel of John owes its depiction of Jesus as the Son of Man to the visions in Daniel 7 or if John shares the wisdom-infused understanding of the Son of Man with the *Parables* of 1 Enoch.

Almost all the occurrences of the title "Son of Man" within the Gospel of John come from the mouth of Jesus, who uses the title as a self-reference. The two places in which persons other than Jesus use the title appear as a response to Jesus' claim to be the Son of Man (12:23, 34). This leaves eleven passages in which Jesus describes himself with the title, suggesting that this is crucial christological understanding that the author of the Gospel of John wanted to impress upon his readers. The first time Jesus uses the title is in response to Nathaniel acknowledging Jesus as "Rabbi," "Son of God," and "King of Israel" (1:49). Jesus answers him by promising that he will experience even greater things. In particular, Jesus claims with the emphatic double "Amen" that "you will see heaven opened and the angels of God ascending and descending upon the Son of Man" (1:51).[1] This illustration draws upon the patriarch Jacob's dream of a ladder connecting heaven and earth, upon which the angels were ascending and descending (Gen 28:12). In effect, the Johannine Jesus is claiming to be the ladder whose role is to connect heaven and earth. The imagery surrounding the open heavens indicates a revelatory purpose in which the things of God are going to be unveiled to earth, and Jesus, the Son of Man, is to act as the authorized revealer of heavenly things. It is noteworthy that the role of the definitive revealer of the heavens belongs to a truly human figure—the Son of Man. The Johannine Jesus seems to be well aware of his role as the authorized human figure who unveils the heavenly words of God to the world.

The next time Jesus speaks of himself as the Son of Man occurs in his exchange with Nicodemus. Jesus informs the Jewish teacher that he must be born from above, and later he clarifies this new birth as being born of water and of the Spirit (3:3–7). When Nicodemus fails to grasp the concept of new birth that Jesus offers, Jesus responds by asking how it is that the heavenly things can be understood if one is unable to comprehend the earthly things (3:12).[2] This suggests that Jesus regards "earthly things" as that which he attempted to convey to Nicodemus thus far in the exchange, while the "heavenly things" are of greater complexity and value. In the following verse, Jesus clarifies his role as the revealer of heavenly things: "No one has ascended into heaven except the one who has descended from heaven, the Son of Man" (3:13). Not only is Jesus using the title "Son of Man" self-referentially to explain how he is able to authoritatively communicate the things of heaven, but he also claims exclusivity in that role.[3] From the perspective of the Gospel of John, the Son of Man is the only person who can truly claim to have attained heavenly knowledge, a claim that is probably intentional in its exclusion of other competing revelatory figures in Judaism.[4] What is striking is that

---

1. The pronoun "you" to whom Jesus responds is second-person plural, indicating that Jesus is speaking to more than simply Nathaniel. This is likely a saying that is directed to the intended audience of the Fourth Gospel.

2. Sidebottom, *Fourth Gospel*, 206, draws attention to the parallel between Wis 9:16–17 ("We can hardly guess at what is on earth, and what is at hand we find with labor; but who has traced out what is in the heavens? Who has learned your counsel unless you have given Wisdom") and John 3:12.

3. Keener, *Gospel of John*, 1:562, discerns Wis 9:17 ("Who has learned your counsel, unless you have given Wisdom . . . from on high") behind the statement in John 3:13.

4. Carter, *John and Empire*, 151; Dunn, "Let John Be John," 323. Borgen, "John and Hellenism," 103.

Jesus describes the role of the authorized revealer of heavenly things in distinctly human terms—as the Son of Man. This undoubtedly recalls the Prologue's insistence that Jesus is the incarnation of God's word and wisdom,[5] thus giving an explanation to how the Son of Man both possesses heavenly knowledge and came to be depicted as a descending human being. Additionally, there is evidence from the Jewish wisdom literature describing attempts to ascend into heaven to acquire the wisdom of God, indicating an assumption that heaven was the precise location where wisdom resides.[6]

The manner in which this revelatory activity takes place is offered in the following verse (3:14). Just as Moses lifted up the serpent in the wilderness, so too must the Son of Man be lifted up. This passage plays on the double meaning of the verb "to lift up" by incorporating both the act of Jesus being hoisted upon the cross and his glorious exaltation. It is by the death of this highly authorized Son of Man that the heavenly things are to be unveiled to the world. As the Son of Man is to be lifted on the cross, so too is he glorified. The intended result, like those who gazed upon Moses' serpent, is to bring salvation and deliverance, namely eternal life to those who respond with belief (3:15). We can discern the theme of rejection of God's chosen revealer with the imagery of being lifted up on the cross, suggesting that this Son of Man is to experience suffering as a crucial part of his vocation.[7] In total, Jesus' dialogue with Nicodemus offers a multifaceted portrayal of the Son of Man—the highly qualified human revealer of God's heavenly secrets who is to experience suffering, rejection, and a death that doubles as a glorious exaltation.

The portrayal of the descending Son of Man continues in John 6:62, where Jesus offers a response to those disciples of his who grumbled at his Discourse on the Bread of Life. "What then," he asks, "if you see the Son of Man ascending to where he was before?" As the embodiment of the wisdom of God that came down out of heaven, Jesus demonstrates awareness that once the mission is accomplished, Wisdom must return to God, the sender.[8] In other words, once the bread from heaven carries

---

5. Shafer, "Wisdom Christology," 56.

6. See McHugh, *John 1–4*, 234, who cites Prov 30:4 (see 30:3 for context); Bar 3:29; and Wis 9:16–17. See also the discussion in Brown, *John I–XII*, 145.

7. Coloe, *John 1–10*, 101, gives attention to Wis 16:7 (Lady Wisdom is the savior of all, not the serpent) as very likely influencing John 3:14–16.

8. Keener, *Gospel of John*, 1:694, points to the wisdom traditions in which Wisdom departs from the earth in light of her rejection.

forth the life-giving ministry of God, the bread must ascend to God. Ascending would place the wisdom of God where it was previously.[9] Again, Jesus speaks of himself in terms of the Son of Man—the qualified and authorized human agent of the revelatory purposes of God.

Other references to the Son of Man within the Fourth Gospel offer supporting evidence to the depiction of the human revealer who embodies the word and wisdom of God. Jesus possesses the shared prerogative of God to enact judgment precisely because of his role as the qualified human agent—the Son of Man (5:27). Furthermore, the Son of Man explains his role as the giver of the life of the age to come in terms of God having set his seal of approval upon him (6:27).[10] This life is to be experienced in the sacrament of the Eucharist with the human Son of Man in the center of the ritual (6:53). When the Jews lift up the Son of Man onto the cross, they will know that he is the revelatory agent of God who speaks that which the Father has taught him (8:28).[11] This human agent gives sight, offers illumination in truth, and is the object of belief (9:35). The act of lifting up the Son of Man is the moment of his glorification (12:23; 13:31), something the narrator makes clear to the readers, but the crowds misunderstand it (12:32–34).[12] In the glorious death of the Son of Man, God's revelatory purposes are made complete.

The *Parables* of 1 Enoch offer several passages in which wisdom motifs accompany portrayals of the Son of Man. By examining these crucial texts, we can observe how at least some apocalyptically minded Jews understood the intersection between the wisdom of God and the Son of Man during a period contemporary with the formation of the Gospel of John.[13] We have already seen that the portrayal of the wisdom of God within the *Parables* is one of inaccessibility. Personified wisdom sought a dwelling place on earth, leaving her abode in heaven to do so. After failing to find a place to dwell among humanity, she returned to heaven (1 En. 42:1–2). However, it is the Son of Man who makes the wisdom

---

9. McGrath, *John's Apologetic Christology*, 178–79; Gaston, "High Christology," 138.

10. Witherington, *John's Wisdom*, 155, emphasizes the agency language in this passage.

11. Williams, *I Am He*, 274.

12. Borgen, *Bread from Heaven*, 161, points to the convincing parallel between the Jesus, the legal agent, taking possession of the belongings of the sender (John 12:32), and the principle of Jewish agency in b. B. Qam. 70a.

13. McGrath, *John's Apologetic Christology*, 22, notes that the Son of Man and the imagery associated with Wisdom suggest that the depicting of Jesus in John is "a more developed form of what earlier Christians said and believed."

of God available through his revelatory activities: "He has revealed the wisdom of the Lord of the Spirits to the righteous and the holy ones" (48:7). In other words, the righteous must turn to the Son of Man in order to have access to the elusive wisdom of God. Not only does the Enochic Son of Man reveal God's wisdom to the righteous; he is also the embodiment of that very wisdom: "In him dwells the spirit of wisdom" (49:3). As the bearer of the wisdom of God, the Son of Man possesses the divine prerogative to judge the secret things (49:4). He accomplishes this task because he possesses the good pleasure of God—the Lord of the Spirit. The *Parables* of 1 Enoch provide a fascinating parallel image of the Son of Man to what we see in the Gospel of John.[14] Both works depict the Son of Man as a revelatory figure who unveils the God of heaven. Both illustrate the Son of Man together with the personified wisdom of God that descends from and ascends to heaven. Both works also portray the Son of Man as embodying this wisdom of God in some capacity. Moreover, the Son of Man functions as the agent of God[15] who, according to God's good pleasure, enacts God's judgment in both 1 Enoch and the Fourth Gospel. In short, the Gospel of John presents Jesus as the authorized Son of Man whose ministry closely resembles the Enochic Son of Man in whom the wisdom of God dwells. While it is unlikely that the author of John had direct access to the *Parables* of 1 Enoch, he nevertheless demonstrates his indebtedness to the book of Daniel as well as later apocalyptic traditions that helped solidify his presentation of the wisdom-steeped Son of Man. As such, the Johannine Jesus defines himself in terms of the Son of Man in whom personified wisdom from heaven has become incarnate.[16]

REVEALER OF GOD THE FATHER

Within the Gospel of John, the agent Jesus not only unveils the life-giving purposes of God to the world; he also reveals God himself. The conclusion of the Prologue sets the expectation that the wider narrative of the Fourth Gospel will detail how exactly the unique son reveals and

---

14. Witherington, *Jesus the Sage*, 371–72.
15. Anderson, "Having-Sent-Me Father," 42.
16. Dillon, "Wisdom Tradition," 284, draws a similar conclusion: "There seems to be little doubt that, in John's perspective, the Son of Man title bears the eschatological, heavenly coloring which it received in its usage by the apocalyptic books and its *adaptation by the Wisdom traditions*" (emphasis added). See also Dunn, "Let John Be John," 330.

exegetes the unseen God to his people (1:18).[17] Since we have observed the influence of personified wisdom's role as the revealer of the God of Israel upon the Prologue, it is reasonable to expect a similar portrayal within the ministry of Jesus. We may begin to find confirmation of this hypothesis in 3:11–12, where Jesus offers the revelation of the things of heaven—namely the things of God that he knows and has seen. John the Baptist similarly portrays Jesus as the one who testifies to what he has seen and knows (3:32), which includes the very words of God that Jesus speaks as God's agent (3:34). In an attempt to validate the authenticity of his ministry, Jesus describes his sender as the true God, who authorizes him to speak and to judge (8:26). God has taught the son what to say, and the empowered son refuses to speak on his own initiative (8:28; 12:49–50).[18] In addition to the words that he learned from God, Jesus performs the works of God in an obedient fashion (9:3). When the Jews question and criticize Jesus, he continually reaffirms that he is doing the Father's good works (10:32). As the revelation of the Father, the Johannine Jesus continually speaks forth the words of God and works the deeds of God.

After Jesus invites his disciples to come to the Father through him as the "way" (14:6), he indicates that those who know him have come to know the Father by extension. In fact, those who know Jesus have already experienced and seen the Father because Jesus reveals the unseen Father (14:7). Philip, declaring his ignorance, requests that Jesus show the disciples the Father, resulting in Jesus definitively claiming that "He who has seen me has seen the Father" (14:9).[19] As an obedient son, Jesus has made known to his disciples (newly designated as friends) everything that the Father said to him (15:15). This includes manifesting the Father's name to humanity (17:6), which is a revelation of the Father's intimate love (17:26). As the authorized agent, the son fully represents and unveils the Father to the role of one who is commissioned.

The Fourth Gospel's depiction of Jesus as the ultimate revealer of the unseen God exhibits signs of influence from Jewish wisdom literature and its portrayal of personified wisdom. When YHWH gives his wisdom,

---

17. Thompson, *God of the Gospel of John*, 50, concludes from her study of the Fourth Gospel that God is most typically the Father or "the Father who sent [Jesus]."

18. Keener, *Gospel of John*, 2:887, stresses the pivotal concept of Jesus as the agent of God.

19. Witherington, *John's Wisdom*, 250, rightly notes that Jesus is the "the perfect likeness and exegesis of the Father as his unique Son, as God's Wisdom, the expression of the very mind and character of God."

his knowledge and understanding flow forth from his mouth (Prov 2:6). This revelatory wisdom is set in parallel with the insight and knowledge that come from God (Prov 2:10–11). The beginning of wisdom, Proverbs defines, is the fear of YHWH; thereby closely associating God with his personified wisdom (Prov 9:10). Later, the fear of YHWH is portrayed in slightly different terms as "instruction in wisdom" (15:33). Ben Sira picks up these themes regarding personified wisdom as the starting point for attaining the fear of the Lord and reproduces them several times in the introductory chapter (Sir 1:14, 16, 18, 20). One must find and attain wisdom in order to possess the fear of the Lord (Sir 1:27; 19:20). Sometimes, Sirach positions wisdom as the one who reveals Israel's God. On one hand, the Lord God reveals secrets (1:30), but on the other, the secrets are revealed through the agency of God's wisdom (4:18). Furthermore, those who serve Lady Wisdom by obeying her ordinances find themselves ministering to God—the Holy One. Those who love Wisdom will experience the love of God because Wisdom functions as the revealer of God's love (4:14). Similarly, Wisdom of Solomon describes the ways in which God interacts with the righteous in terms of personified wisdom clarifying God's interactions. God makes himself known through the agency of wisdom making herself known (Wis 6:13). As a teacher, Wisdom instructs by making manifest the things of God (7:21). She reveals God's breath and God's power as an emanation of the Almighty's glory (7:25). Furthermore, she acts as a mirror that reflects God's light, a spotless mirror of God's interactions. Finally, the goodness of God is expressed in Wisdom's role as an image (7:26). By acting as the definitive revealer of the Father, the Johannine Jesus continues to carry out the role of Lady Wisdom in her work of manifesting the true God to creation.[20]

JESUS AS THE ROYAL MESSIAH

At the most fundamental level of New Testament Christology, the messianic status of Jesus identifies him as Israel's anointed king, God's Christ. The Johannine portrayal of Jesus in terms of Israel's Messiah is nevertheless worth investigating, especially since the sages who composed the Jewish wisdom literature often associated a king's ability to rule well with the possession of or interaction with God's personified wisdom.

---

20. Dunn, *Neither Jew nor Greek*, 768, is helpful here: "It is true of course that Jesus as the incarnate Word and Wisdom fulfils the role previously filled in Second Temple reflection on Word and Wisdom—not least their role as revealers."

The Gospel of John emphasizes the messiahship of Jesus in some unique ways. For example, the only two biblical occurrences of the Greek noun *messias* ("messiah") appear in the Fourth Gospel. Andrew announces to his brother Peter that they have found the Messiah, and this term is immediately defined by the narrator as meaning "Christ" (1:41).[21] Nathaniel confesses that Jesus is the rightful bearer of two synonymous titles: he is "Son of God" and "King of Israel" (1:49).[22] In Jesus' dialogue with the Samaritan woman, we observe confirmation of this messianic title's legitimacy in the response that Jesus offered. The woman confesses to Jesus that she knows that the Messiah is coming and that he will declare all things upon his arrival (4:25). Jesus responds by declaring that he is this long-awaited Messiah: "I who speak with you am he" (4:26).[23] After he performs the miracle with the loaves and fish, the crowds rush by force in an attempt to make Jesus king (6:15). Those who confessed Jesus to be the Christ were to be excommunicated from the synagogue (9:22). Martha makes this confession to Jesus, claiming that he is "the Christ, the Son of God" (11:27), and this declaration matches the purpose statement of the Gospel of John (20:31). When Jesus enters Jerusalem, he is greeting with palm branches and shouts claiming that he is the King of Israel (12:13). The narrator follows up this claim by citing Zech 9:9, which in effect labels Jesus as "your king" (12:15). Jesus himself prayed that people would come to know the only true God and Jesus Christ as God's sent agent, defining this as "eternal life" (17:3). For the author of the Gospel of John, believing that Jesus is truly the Jewish Messiah is an intentional literary goal that readers were to grasp.[24]

When we examine the chapters surrounding Jesus' betrayal and crucifixion, we find a deliberate emphasis placed on his messianic vocation, suggesting a conscious effort to define the role of the Messiah in terms of suffering and a glorious death. At Jesus' trial, Pontius Pilate directly confronts him with the question, "Are you the King of the Jews?" (18:33).

21. Thomas Aquinas, *John 1–5*, 120, observes the influence of Prov 3:13 here ("Happy is the man who finds wisdom").

22. Beasley-Murray, *John*, 27, suggests that there may be here a deliberate attempt at framing Jesus as the royal possessor of God's wisdom: "It is possible that we may have here a reflection of the Wisdom tradition wherein the 'Son of God' is marked as having wisdom from God; the Son has received from God his Father knowledge and revelation, of which Solomon, the Son of David, the supremely wise man, was the model, he who knows the hearts possesses wisdom."

23. Freed, "John 1:20 and 4:25," 291; Witherington, *John's Wisdom*, 121.

24. Bekken, *Lawsuit Motif*, 236–37.

After Jesus makes an inquiry into the motivation prompting Pilate's question, he acknowledges that his kingdom is not of this world, and if it were, his followers would be fighting for his release (18:36–37). In doing so, Jesus associates his role as the messianic king with a kingdom that is not defined by the unredeemed realm. Pilate takes this opportunity to press the question further: "So you are a king?" To which Jesus offers an affirmative answer and supplements his response by pointing to his birth and his entrance into the world (18:37). Although Pilate does not see Jesus as a legitimate political threat, Jesus nevertheless lays claim to the role of the Jewish messianic king. Throughout the crucifixion process, Jesus is variously mocked as "King of the Jews," beginning with the soldiers (19:3), the Jews (19:12), and with Pilate's inscription on the cross (19:19). The political nature of the role of Messiah is confirmed when the Jews argue that "everyone who makes himself out to be a king opposes Caesar" (19:12) and "we have no king but Caesar" (19:15). The chief priests quibble about the wording on the inscription on the cross, suggesting that it should reflect the assertion that Jesus was making himself out to be the Messiah: "Do not write, 'The King of the Jews' but that he said, 'I am King of the Jews'" (19:21). For the author of the Gospel of John, the royal messiahship of Jesus is highlighted and confirmed in his glorious death.

The sages who composed the Jewish wisdom literature often associated the image of Lady Wisdom with royal, kingly themes.[25] In personified wisdom's speech within Proverbs 8, we note the close association of these motifs. By Wisdom kings reign and rulers decree justice; by Wisdom even princes and nobles rule (Prov 8:15–16). The capacity to govern well and reign is directly tied to Lady Wisdom's involvement with those in positions of leadership. The author of Wisdom of Solomon bears influence from the eighth chapter of Proverbs and seeks to magnify the royal themes even further. In chapter 7, King Solomon attributes the success of his reign to his prayerful petition to God, resulting in reciting the spirit of wisdom (Wis 7:7). Although he prefers her more than scepters, thrones, and a king's wealth, health, and beauty, he acknowledges that all good things came to him because of her (7:8–11). In fact, Solomon portrays Wisdom as the mother of all these things (7:12). He prays that God would

---

25. Schroer, *Wisdom*, 34–35, helpfully points out that God's wisdom empowered the Israelite monarchy (e.g., 1 Kgs 3:28; 4:29–34; Isa 11:2; Ecc 1:13), but the book of Proverbs presents personified wisdom as accessible to the wise who seek after the fear of YHWH. Within the Gospel of John, the wisdom-endowed king and personified wisdom from Proverbs are combined.

grant to him the ability to speak with judgment, and Solomon explains his reasoning in terms of God being the guide of Lady Wisdom and the corrector of wise persons (7:15). Having already portrayed Wisdom as a mother figure, Solomon also sees her as a bride for whom he desires. His determination to take her to live with him brings about good counsel, encouragement, glory, honor, keen judgment, and the propensity to govern the people (8:2–16). In Solomon's prayer, he requests that God send forth Wisdom so that she may labor at his side and wisely guide him in his actions, which include justly judging the people and being worthy of the throne (9:10–12). It is no surprise, then, that we find a close connection between Jesus and royal, messianic themes in the Gospel of John, since the book bears considerable influence from the wisdom sages who formerly associated personified wisdom and the ability to rule well.

THE BREAD OF LIFE

The Johannine Jesus is presented in terms of seven metaphors that draw upon the religion of Israelite piety. As we will see, all seven of these titles depict the Johannine Jesus as the wisdom of God by drawing upon the traditions contained within the Jewish wisdom books.[26] The first of such metaphors is the image of the bread from heaven, which recalls the exodus from Egypt event when God provided manna to the children of Israel in their trek across the desert. John 6 begins with Jesus performing the miracle of the loaves of bread, dividing them in order to feed five thousand hungry persons while also having leftovers remaining after everyone was filled. While crossing in a boat to Capernaum, the disciples witness another miracle—Jesus walks upon the water (6:19–20).[27] The crowds followed Jesus to Capernaum, where he instructed them to seek the food that endures to eternal life, rather than perishable food (6:26). As the

---

26. Kümmel, *Theology*, 284, observes the influence of self-presentations and self-commendations in Jewish wisdom literature upon the "I am" statements made by the Johannine Jesus.

27. Meier, *Marginal Jew*, 909, observes that Jesus' appearance on the water is a part of John's theology that depicts Jesus in the terms and metaphors of the personified wisdom of God described in the Old Testament. Lincoln, *John*, 218, compares Jesus' walking on the sea with a remarkable parallel statement in Sir 24:5–6, where Lady Wisdom walks on the sea. Coloe, *John 1–10*, 166–67, connects the story of the disciples encountering Jesus on the rough sea with Wis 14:5, which states that the deeds of Wisdom are apparent in those persons who have faith while on a small piece of wood that they may arrive to land safely.

conversation continues, Jesus reveals that he himself is the bread of life, the true bread from heaven that the Father is giving in the present, which deliberately contrasts the bread that Moses gave in the past (6:32).[28] Jesus makes this claim boldly and definitively: "I am the bread of life" (6:35). In doing so, Jesus speaks of preexistence by using the metaphor of bread; he is the bread of life that has come down from heaven—a claim repeated, emphasized, and discussed in the discourse (6:38, 41–42, 50–51). Of no insignificant importance is Jesus' claim that the bread that he will give for the life of the world is his own "flesh" (6:51–56). In fact, Jesus summons his hearers to participate in the eating of his flesh and the drinking of his blood, which bears unmistakable eucharistic implications. The result of this discourse is that many Jews argued with one another and even many of Jesus' disciples found it difficult to understand.

The Bread of Life Discourse shows signs of considerable influence from the Jewish wisdom traditions that portrayed Lady Wisdom as the giver of bread.[29] The earliest evidence of this connection is in Proverbs 9, where Wisdom invites participants into her house for a meal (Prov 9:1–6). This meal that Wisdom prepares is accompanied by a summons to "come, eat of my bread and drink of the wine I have mixed" (9:5).[30] Wisdom's encouragement here no doubt served as the direct influence on the eucharistic summons by Jesus in John 6:51–56.[31] Readers of the Gospel of John who are familiar with the portrayal of Wisdom offering bread in Prov 9:1–6 would naturally regard Jesus as Lady Wisdom's embodiment.

In the first century CE, Philo often discussed the meaning of the manna from heaven in ways that also shed light on the Johannine discourse. For example, Philo quotes Exod 16:4 and offers his interpretation through the lens of personified wisdom in the tractate *On the Change of Names*:

---

28. Lee, *Symbolic Narratives*, 127, helpfully draws attention to the fact that Jesus, as Lady Wisdom, "both gives and is the gift offered."

29. Beasley-Murray, *John*, 98; Coloe, *John 1–10*, 180; Dillon, "Wisdom Tradition," 275; McGrath, *John's Apologetic Christology*, 177–79; Dunn, *Jesus according to the New Testament*, 66; Johnson, "Jesus, the Wisdom of God," 284; Schroer, *Wisdom*, 119; Davies, *Rhetoric and Reference*, 198; Schüssler Fiorenza, *Jesus*, 167. O'Day and Hylen, *John*, 76–78, helpfully point out that "Jesus is manna . . . He is wisdom given by God."

30. O'Boyle, *Wisdom Christology*, 163; Brown, *John I-XII*, 273; Thompson, *John*, 151; Witherington, *John's Wisdom*, 149–50; Lincoln, *John*, 229.

31. Lincoln, *John*, 234; Feuillet, *Johannine Studies*, 86; Dunn, "Aspect of Theology," 384.

> And men occupied in agriculture cooperate to produce the food from the earth, but God, the only cause and giver, rains down the food from heaven without the cooperation of any other being. And, indeed, we read in the Scriptures, "Behold, I rain upon you bread from heaven." Now what nourishment can the Scriptures properly say is rained down, except heavenly wisdom?[32]

Philo, like the Johannine Jesus, contrasts ordinary food with the bread from heaven offered by God. In doing so, Philo recalls the period of the exodus when God rained down bread from above. This heavenly nourishment is then interpreted by Philo to be "heavenly wisdom."[33] In other words, Philo regards the activity of God in terms of "raining" in the present tense precisely as raining wisdom from heaven. Wisdom in Philo, as we have observed, is a personification, so it is unlikely that Philo intended that God's wisdom that comes down from heaven would be understood as referring to a preexisting, conscious female. Rather, it descends as the nourishment of God's wise instructions and interactions, particularly located in the law of Moses.[34]

Philo continues his description of the nourishing food that God offers in the tractate *On the Preliminary Studies*. In verses 170–74, he seeks to understand how God afflicted the Israelites in the wilderness, interpreting this affliction from hunger in ways that do not involve actual food. Then Philo contrasts the food of the earth with the manna from heaven, which he clarifies as "the all-nourishing food of wisdom."[35] Here again, we observe Philo interpreting the manna from heaven precisely as God's own wisdom—a wisdom that offers nourishment exceeding what ordinary food can accomplish.

Finally, Philo's understanding of wisdom in terms of the manna from the exodus narrative appears in his tractate *Allegorical Interpretation*. The third book of this tractate contains his discussion about the nourishment that the body requires as distinguished from the nourishment the soul requires.[36] Drawing on Gen 2:7, Philo views it as quite consistent with reason to say that the body, which was formed from the dust of the earth, requires earthly nourishment, such as meat and drink. The soul,

---

32. *Mut.* 259.

33. Brown, *John I–XII*, 266; Borgen, *Bread from Heaven*, 122–23; Koester, *Symbolism*, 101.

34. Borgen, *Bread from Heaven*, 2.

35. *Congr.* 174.

36. *Leg.* 3.161–62.

according to Philo, is ethereal, and it is thus nourished by knowledge—by the heavenly food. In order to justify this point, Philo again cites Exod 16:4: "Behold, I will rain upon you bread from heaven." Since this is the same passage Philo quoted earlier where he directly interpreted the bread from heaven as God's wisdom, we can reasonably conclude that this is in Philo's mind in our present passage. The food from heaven that is contrasted with ordinary nourishment for the body is knowledge—particularly the wise knowledge of God that personified wisdom offers.

While it is extremely unlikely that the Gospel of John contains demonstrable influence from the writings of Philo,[37] it is apparent that the idea of interpreting the manna from heaven in terms of the wisdom of God was a viable reading in the first century CE. Both John and Philo regard heavenly wisdom as superior to perishable bread. Both authors draw upon the Israelite story from the book of Exodus in order to make their points. Both writers locate the wisdom of God in heaven prior to coming down to earth. This suggests that the Johannine Jesus' claim to have "come down from heaven" is looking backward to the personified wisdom of God that became flesh, not to a preexisting person in heaven. For Jesus is Wisdom's embodiment, and those who partake of Wisdom's bread of life will certainly live forever.[38]

THE LIGHT OF THE WORLD

The second significant title of the Johannine Jesus drawn from Israelite religion is introduced in John 8:12. In what appears to be a continuation of the discourse that began in John 7, Jesus makes the first-person claim to be "the light of the world." This title is accompanied by the summons to his listeners to follow him out of darkness and promises them the light of life. Jesus repeats this self-referential title in John 9:5 in his discussion of the man born blind. Having claimed this title again, the themes of seeing and blindness pervade the entirety of Blind Man Discourse (9:1–41). When Jesus informs his disciples that he desires to return to Judea, he states that those who walk during the day will not stumble because they see "the light of the world" (11:9–10). During his final public discourse,

---

37. Harris, *Prologue and Gospel*, 199. Borgen, *Bread from Heaven*, 3, articulates the similarities between Philo and the Gospel of John as a parallel phenomenon.

38. Fuller, "Incarnation," 63–64; Ringe, *Wisdom's Friends*, 61; Witherington, *Jesus the Sage*, 375; Koester, *Symbolism*, 101. Thompson, *John*, 153, observes, "the bread is God's word, instruction, or wisdom both brought by and embodied in Jesus."

Jesus encourages the crowds to walk while they have the light and to believe in the light. Those who respond appropriately are, according to Jesus, children of light (12:35-36). This discourse concludes with one final claim to the title "light of the world" in John 12:46. The dualistic language of light and darkness serves to distinguish Jesus and those who believe in him as God's commissioned Messiah from those who do not believe.

The themes of light and darkness first appear in the Johannine Prologue, which set the anticipatory tone for the "light of the world" title that Jesus repeatedly claims. As we have observed, the preexisting word/wisdom of God possesses life, and this life is the light of humanity (1:4). The Prologue forecasts Jesus' light-bringing role by declaring that the light shines in the darkness, and the darkness is unable to overcome it (1:5). We noted in our study of the Prologue that its portrayal of light bears the influence of Jewish wisdom traditions wherein God's personified wisdom brings light to darkness. Just as Lady Wisdom rescues the righteous from paths of darkness (Prov 2:10-13), the Johannine Jesus promises that those who follow him will not walk in darkness. Sirach characterizes the instruction that Lady Wisdom teaches in terms of light that shines brighter and brighter (Sir 24:25-27, 32). Similarly, Jesus summons the crowds to "believe" in him and "walk" in his light, actions that transform them into disciples who obey his instructions. Baruch offers a comparable invitation to Israel: "Take hold of Wisdom and walk to the shining of her light" (Bar 4:2). Baruch's emphasis on those who find Wisdom possessing light for their eyes parallels the Blind Man Discourse involving the blind man who believes in Jesus, while the Pharisees are designated as blind for their failure to believe (see Bar 3:14). We can also recall the characteristic of Lady Wisdom that illustrates her as a reflection of eternal light (Wis 7:26), which serves as a parallel to the title "light of the world."[39] Mary Coloe helpfully sums up the christological significance of this title: "When Jesus says, 'I am the light of the world' (8:12), he affirms the glory of Sophia."[40] As the embodiment of God's wisdom, the

---

39. Charlesworth, "Lady Wisdom," 106; Brown, *John I-XII*, 344; O'Boyle, *Wisdom Christology*, 163; Witherington, *John's Wisdom*, 174-75; Lincoln, *John*, 265; Shafer, "Wisdom Christology," 56; Dunn, "Let John Be John," 331.

40. Coloe, *John 1-10*, 217. Davies, *Rhetoric and Reference*, 236, helpfully remarks, "No doubt the Gospel is interpreting Jesus' teaching in terms of wisdom which brings light . . . and Jesus speaks as personified wisdom."

Johannine Jesus continues the mission of shining light into darkness and illuminating the lives of those who accept him and follow him.[41]

THE DOOR OF THE SHEEP

The third of the seven titles that the Johannine Jesus claims is that of "the door of the sheep" (10:7), a designation contrasting Jesus from thieves and robbers who attempt to access the sheep in unauthorized ways. The image of Jesus as the door of the sheep naturally relates to the role of the good shepherd, but the two titles deserve individual attention. As the metaphorical door, Jesus has access to the sheep, which is a common designation for the people of God. Jesus' claim to the title is accompanied by an invitation: "If anyone enters through me, he will be saved, he will go in and out, and he will find pasture" (10:9). This summons not only places him at the focal point for the sheep's salvation but also distinguishes Jesus from other contenders, the false shepherds. If this discourse is a continuation of Jesus' dispute with the Pharisees from the Blind Man Discourse in John 9, then the strangers are identified with the Pharisees. While the Pharisees claimed the de facto role of the leaders of the Jews after the destruction of the Jerusalem temple in the year 70 CE, the Johannine Jesus claimed with the emphatic use of the first-person Greek pronoun that "*I* am the door of the sheep." By asserting this title, Jesus stresses that he is the locus of God's salvific purposes for the flock.

Lady Wisdom also famously appears in the role of the door in Proverbs 8. At the conclusion of her lengthy appeal to the naïve, she summons them to listen to her, calling them "blessed" if they keep her ways and heed her instruction. Specifically, Wisdom locates these wise hearers at her gates and at her doorposts (Prov 8:32–34). The Greek translation of this passage renders the noun for "doorpost" as a "door" (Greek: *thura*), which is the same word adopted in the Gospel of John for the title "door of the sheep." Lady Wisdom continues by promising life to whoever finds her (Prov 8:35), not unlike the Johannine Jesus promising salvific life to whoever enters through him, even abundant life in the present (John 10:10).[42] The connection between Proverbs and John's Gospel is

---

41. Ringe, *Wisdom's Friends*, 61; Schüssler Fiorenza, *Jesus*, 167; McGrath, *John's Apologetic Christology*, 204; Keener, *Gospel of John*, 1:740; Johnson, "Jesus, the Wisdom of God," 285; Witherington, *Jesus the Sage*, 375; Morris, *John*, 437, who follows Barrett, *Gospel*, 336–37.

42. O'Boyle, *Wisdom Christology*, 166–67.

strengthened upon noticing how Jesus' claim to the title is followed with a description of the sheep as those who "listen to my voice" (John 10:16). Martin Scott's insights are helpful here: "At this point we may discern a real overlap in meaning between the Johannine idea and that expressed in the text of Prov 8.34-35, for it is precisely by sitting at Sophia's door and listening that her disciple comes to have life."[43] By claiming to be the door of the sheep, Jesus exhibits characteristics that further define him as the incarnation of personified wisdom.[44]

THE GOOD SHEPHERD

Immediately after Jesus makes his claim to be the door of the sheep, we find the fourth of the seven titles drawn from Israelite religion: "the good shepherd" (John 10:11-18). Jesus contrasts this title with others who are unqualified to watch over the sheep, namely the hired hand who flees at the appearance of an approaching wolf, demonstrating his lack of concern over the sheep. As the good shepherd, Jesus stresses his intimate relationship involving the sheep: "I know my own and my own know me even as the Father knows me" (10:14-15). As the shepherd who deeply cares for the sheep, Jesus continually stresses the corresponding role of one who lays down his life for them (10:10, 15, 17-18). The offering of the life of the shepherd is surely related to the salvific life of abundance that is accessible to the sheep. Jesus also speaks of other sheep that he will bring into the fold to create a single flock under one shepherd. These sheep will listen to the voice of Jesus, resulting in an obedient orientation (10:16). Lastly, he openly acknowledges that the shepherd's intimate role of laying down his life for the sheep is directly based upon authority that Jesus has received from the loving Father (10:17-18).

The intimacy between Jesus and the sheep displays influence from Jewish portrayals of personified wisdom.[45] Wisdom of Solomon describes the closeness that she shares with humanity by characterizing her as passing into holy souls in each generation, making them friends of God and prophets in the process (Wis 7:27). Solomon expresses his love for Wisdom in terms of his resolve to have her as his wife and his intimate love for her beauty (Wis 8:2). Wisdom herself offers her good counsel

---

43. Scott, *Sophia*, 122.
44. Witherington, *Jesus the Sage*, 375; Ringe, *Wisdom's Friends*, 61.
45. Dunn, "Aspect of Theology," 384.

and encouragement in times of grief and care (8:9). Furthermore, companionship and life with her is portrayed in a positive light, possessing gladness and joy (8:16). Ultimately, Solomon depicts immortality as the outcome of having a loving kinship with Lady Wisdom, pure delight from her friendship, and understanding as a result of her company (8:17–18). In Wisdom of Solomon, the strongest possible language has been employed to express the deep intimacy between personified wisdom and those who accept her.

The wise listen to and heed Lady Wisdom, just as the sheep hear the voice of the good shepherd. We already noted this connection in our survey of the title "the door of the sheep," but the way in which this behavior displays the shepherd's intimacy suggests a deeper examination. The book of Proverbs is replete with references indicating the actions of the wise as those who actively hear and obey personified wisdom (Prov 1:23, 33; 8:1–11, 33–35; 9:3–6). Ben Sirach picks up on this theme and expands it. Lady Wisdom characterizes her intimate relationship with those who desire her in terms of coming to her and eating her fruits (Sir 24:19). The memory of Wisdom is sweeter than honey, and possessing her is sweeter than the honeycomb. She provides for those who eat and drink from her, for they will long for more of what she has to offer (24:20–21).[46] These metaphors of eating and drinking are revealed as obeying and working with Wisdom (24:22). The loving relationship that the good shepherd shares with his sheep closely resembles the close bonds that Lady Wisdom shares with the wise.[47]

THE RESURRECTION AND THE LIFE

The fifth title that Jesus claims for himself is "the resurrection and the life" (John 11:25). This self-designation comes during the Lazarus Discourse, where "resurrection" indicates both the new life that Jesus offers in the present as well as the act of bodies being raised from the dead on the last day. Within the Hebrew Scriptures, the concept of resurrection appears primarily in Dan 12:2, where it is said that those who sleep in the dust of the ground will one day awaken to the life of the age to come. By the first century CE, it was widely accepted that the resurrection of the dead would accompany the appearance of the Jewish Messiah, thus initiating

---

46. O'Boyle, *Wisdom Christology*, 167.
47. Dunn, "Let John Be John," 331.

the age to come and the kingdom of God. For early Christians, including the author of the Gospel of John, the arrival of Jesus inaugurated this kingdom and shifted the events of the coming age into the present, resulting in the insistence that the promised resurrection life is available now by believing in the Messiah while the consummation of the resurrection is yet future. This can be observed in the summons that Jesus offers after his claim to be the resurrection and the life: "He who believes in me, even though he dies, will live, and everyone who lives and believes in me will never die" (11:25–26). According to Jesus, eternal life—the life of the age to come—can be experienced in the present by anyone who expresses loyalty to him, the locus of God's life-giving purposes.

We have already observed in the Johannine Prologue the theme of life and the way its appearance in the Prologue anticipates the ministry of Jesus, especially his title "the resurrection and the life." John 1:4 indicates that life was in the personified *logos* and this life was the light of humanity. We noted that the association of the concept of life with the creative speech of God is evident in Genesis 1 and that the parallels are far more voluminous in the Jewish wisdom texts. In Proverbs, for example, it is personified wisdom who brings life (Prov 3:16; 8:35).[48] Proverbs 9 contrasts the invitations to share a meal offered by Lady Wisdom on the one hand (9:1–12) and Lady Folly on the other (9:13–18). The summons uttered by Wisdom includes the promise of life (9:11), and this assurance juxtaposes the death that awaits those who dine with Folly (9:18). The author of Wisdom of Solomon is much more specific with the type of life that personified wisdom offers; she presents immortality, resulting in a remembrance that is everlasting (8:13). In the first century CE, Philo demonstrated the influence of the depiction of Wisdom as the giver of life (Prov 3:16) in his explanation of Eve's appearance in Gen 3:20. In doing so, Philo interpreted Eve's name ("the mother of all living") and then described Wisdom as the mother of all living.[49] Elsewhere, Philo allegorized the tree of life from the Genesis narrative as "the tree of wisdom."[50] It is no surprise, therefore, that we observe the impact of the Jewish traditions that portrayed God's personified wisdom as the giver of life to those who seek her upon the portrayal of Jesus within the Gospel of John.[51] As the incarnation of Lady Wisdom, the Johannine Jesus continues the mission

48. Witherington, *John's Wisdom*, 158.
49. *Her.* 52–53.
50. *Leg.* 3:52.
51. O'Boyle, *Wisdom Christology*, 167–69; Ceresko, *Old Testament Wisdom*, 178.

to offer to those who demonstrate belief in the life defined by resurrection promises, especially in his claim to the title "the resurrection and the life."[52]

THE WAY, THE TRUTH, AND THE LIFE

In John 14:6, Jesus claims his sixth "I am" title, this time illustrating himself with three overlapping labels. While it is not altogether clear what the relationship is between these three substantives, the immediate context sheds some helpful light. The chapter begins with Jesus declaring to his disciples that he is departing in order to prepare a place for them, concluding with the assurance that they know the way that he is going (14:2–4). Thomas responds to Jesus by objecting to his claim, stating the collective misunderstanding of the disciples pertaining to where Jesus is going and how to discern the way (14:5). In typical Johannine fashion, Jesus clarifies the misunderstanding held by his interlocutors, this time by drawing attention to his own self with the emphatic use of the Greek pronoun "*I* am." He is "the way." The summons Jesus offers that immediately follows his titular claim further clarifies the meaning of the way: it is only through Jesus that one may obtain access to the Father. This stress upon Jesus as the way to God strongly suggests that the two other metaphors that Jesus claims—the truth and the life—further elaborate the way Jesus functions as the way to God.[53] As the agent who bridges the gap between the Father and the world, the Johannine Jesus is the bearer of God's truth and life-giving purposes.

Having established that the threefold metaphor that Jesus claims primarily focuses on the predicate "the way," we are now in a good position to look for parallels in Jewish literature for Wisdom functioning as the way. The book of Proverbs rather frequently illustrates God's personified wisdom as the righteous path/way, and the Greek translator of Proverbs used the same Greek noun (*odos*) that appears in John 14:6. For example, the description of Lady Wisdom in Proverbs 3 assures the reader that "her ways are pleasant ways, and all her paths are peace" because they lead the righteous to God (3:17).[54] Those who keep sound wisdom will

---

52. Witherington, *Jesus the Sage*, 375; Coloe, *John 11–21*, 326.

53. Potterie, "Je suis la Voie," 928–29; Davies, *Rhetoric and Reference*, 206; Scott, *Sophia*, 126; Brown, *John I–XII*, 621.

54. Ringe, *Wisdom's Friends*, 61.

find that she becomes life for the soul and a secure way upon which to walk (3:21-23). Speaking to his son, the sage declares: "I have directed you in the way of wisdom; I have led you in upright paths" (4:11). When Wisdom herself speaks, she not only highlights the way of righteousness and offers a blessing to those who keep her ways (8:20, 32), she also contrasts the evil paths (8:13). In fact, Lady Wisdom's invitation to share a meal with her in her house is deliberately set alongside the similar invitation offered by Lady Folly, who calls out to those who are trying to make their ways straight (9:15). Needless to say, the link between God's personified wisdom and the way of righteousness is a constant reoccurrence in the book of Proverbs.

Several other Jewish authors associated "the way" with God's wisdom.[55] The poem in Job 28, which seeks to locate personified wisdom, insists that her "way" (Greek: *odos*) is unknown to everyone except for God. He understands Wisdom's way and he knows her place (28:23). Similarly, Ben Sirach beseeched his readers to come to Wisdom with all their soul and keep her ways with all their might (6:26). Those who seek out her ways will find rest and joy (6:27-28). Raymond Brown calls attention to the Latin translation of Sir 24:25, where an interpolator seems to have incorporated Wisdom Christology into the new reading: "In [Wisdom] is the gift of every way and truth; in me is every hope of life and virtue."[56] Wisdom of Solomon portrays "the way" along a comparable vein. Lady Wisdom guided the Israelites along a marvelous way during the exodus from Egypt narrative (Wis 10:17).[57] Those who have chosen a different path from obeying the righteous commands of God are portrayed as those "who strayed from the way of truth" (Wis 5:6), which combines "way" and "truth" similar to what we observe in Jesus' title in John 14:6. Last, we may observe Philo's description of God's wisdom as the personified guide of the Israelites, just as we observed in Wisdom of Solomon:

> But perhaps, Moses does not mean here to speak of the flesh alone as corrupting his way upon the earth, so that he deserves to be considered to have erred in the expression which he has used, but rather to speak of the things of the flesh, which is corrupted, and of that other being whose way the flesh endeavors to

---

55. O'Day and Hylen, *John*, 145, draw attention to passages where God's law and God's wisdom are associated with "the way." The Fourth Gospel, therefore, is insisting that Wisdom incarnate is now the exclusive way to Israel's God.

56. Brown, *John XIII-XXI*, 630.

57. Brown, *Introduction to the Gospel of John*, 262.

injure and to corrupt. So that we should explain this expression thus: all flesh corrupted the perfect way of the everlasting and incorruptible being which conducts to God. And know that this way is Wisdom. For the mind being guided by Wisdom, while the way is straight and level and easy, proceeds along it to the end; and the end of this way is the knowledge and understanding of God.[58]

It seems clear to Philo that the function of Wisdom is to be the means through which one can confidently find God and his knowledge and understanding. It is no surprise, then, that Philo's first-century contemporary, the author of the Gospel of John, portrays Jesus as the Wisdom-become-flesh who acts as the decisive way to God and to the truth and life that God offers. In short, the title "the way, the truth, and the life" exhibits strong lines of influence from the Jewish wisdom texts, further defining the Johannine Jesus in terms of God's personified wisdom.[59]

THE TRUE VINE

The seventh and final "I am" metaphoric title that Jesus claims (John 15:1) draws upon the imagery of the vine that frequents the prophets of the Hebrew Bible. The primary referent is Isa 5:1–7, where the people of Israel are likened to a choice vine that was expected to produce good grapes, but it produced worthless grapes instead. The prophet Isaiah insists that this vine will not be pruned or hoed, and it will no longer receive any rain. Jeremiah also characterizes Israel as a vine that possesses branches, able to be gleaned for its grapes (Jer 6:9). The imagery of the vine appears quite extensively in Ezekiel's prophecies (15:1–6; 17:5–10; 19:10–14), who also defines the vine in terms of Israel—the inhabitants of Jerusalem (15:6). Ezekiel prophesies that God will use fire in order to judge Jerusalem's disobedience (15:4–6; 19:12, 14), which is characterized as disobedient behavior. These prophetic analogies reappear in Jesus' declaration to be the vine in John 15:1–11. The explanation of these themes that Jesus offers indicates that the Father is the vinedresser and that Jesus himself is "the true vine"—formerly an image for the people of Israel. The branches of the vine are the disciples (15:4–5), who, like Israel before them, are expected to bear fruit or suffer the judgment of fire (15:6). Like

---

58. *Deus* 142–43.

59. O'Boyle, *Wisdom Christology*, 171–72; Ringe, *Wisdom's Friends*, 60–61; Ceresko, *Old Testament Wisdom*, 178.

the other "I am" metaphoric titles that the Johannine Jesus claims, this one is accompanied by a summons. Jesus invites his followers to abide in him (15:4) and to obediently keep his words (15:7), thereby functioning as branches to the vine. It is crucial, therefore, to consider the roles of the vine and the branches together in our inquiry.

As we survey the Jewish literature for parallels to Lady Wisdom, the most striking data comes from the intertestamental period. In what scholars are describing as clear evidence that the author of the Gospel of John knew and read the book of Sirach,[60] personified wisdom is extensively portrayed as the vine in Sir 24:17–22.[61] In this passage, Wisdom, after having descended from God to be among Israel, speaks in the first person:

> Like the vine, I bud forth delights, and my blossoms become glorious and abundant fruit. Come to me, you who desire me, and eat your fill of my fruits. For the memory of me is sweeter than honey, and the possession of me sweeter than the honeycomb. Those who eat of me will hunger for more, and those who drink of me will thirst for more. Whoever obeys me will not be put to shame, and those who work with me will not sin.

Personified wisdom here likens herself to the vine and invites those who come to her to share in her fruits, which is explained in terms of obeying her. These four points (identifying as the vine, invitation, fruit, and obedience) reappear in Johannine Jesus' claim to be the true vine.[62] Throughout Sirach, Lady Wisdom functions in the role of the vine. For example, Sir 1:16 characterizes Wisdom as intoxicating mortals with her fruits. A few verses later, we observe wisdom possessing branches that offer long life (1:20). Happy are those who position their children under the shelter of Wisdom, particularly under the shelter of her branches (14:26). She offers protection to those who lodge in her glory (14:27). Sometimes, Wisdom is likened to a terebinth tree, no doubt influenced by Wisdom's portrayal as the tree of life in Prov 3:18, and as a terebinth, she spreads out her branches of glory and grace (Sir 24:16).[63] The image of Wisdom's branches continues in the following verse, where she describes herself

---

60. O'Day, "Gospel of John," 756.

61. For a recent study on the influence of Sirach 24 upon John 15, see Uusimaki, "Tree of Wisdom," 203–17.

62. Schnackenburg, *John*, 3:107.

63. Coloe, *John 11–21*, 418–19.

as the vine, as we observed above (24:17).[64] When the author of Sirach recounts how his heart delighted in Wisdom, he describes the process from the first blossom to the ripening of a grape, again utilizing the imagery of fruit to portray his obedience to her (51:15). In striking contrast, a disobedient woman is illustrated as possessing branches that will not bear any fruit (23:25)—almost certainly a deliberate point that anticipates the following chapter in Sirach, where Lady Wisdom depicts herself as a vine with fruit-bearing branches. Last, we note that Philo Judaeus also interprets God's wisdom as a vine that bears branches of fruit, particularly grapes.[65] It seems clear that the christological portrayal of Jesus contained within his claim to be the true vine is indebted to Sirach and his illustration of personified wisdom as the vine.[66] By claiming to be the "true" vine, Jesus emphasizes himself as the locus of Wisdom's fruit-bearing and life-giving activity in contrast to alternatives that do not yield fruit. The image of Wisdom as a vine in Philo's writings demonstrates that this connection of themes was an active interpretation in the first century CE. The Christology of the Gospel of John uniquely positions Jesus in terms of Lady Wisdom, whose branches offer fruit to those who come to her and obey her words.[67]

THE HOLY ONE OF GOD

At the conclusion of the Bread of Life Discourse, we observe the unfortunate fallout of Jesus' preaching that began with the dividing of the loaves and the fish. Several of Jesus' followers departed, no longer desiring to be his disciples (6:66). As a result of this departure, Jesus poses the question to the Twelve regarding whether they too want to leave. At this point, Peter speaks on behalf of the group, declaring that they have nowhere else to turn since Jesus possesses the words that offer the life of the age

---

64. Sidebottom, *Fourth Gospel*, 204, connects Wisdom's descent from heaven to abide with Jacob in the form of a vine (Sir 24:8, 17) with the Prologue's claim that Wisdom became flesh and tabernacled among us (John 1:14).

65. *Somn.* 2:170–171. Philo also contrasts this positive image of Wisdom as a vine with personified folly functioning as a false vine in *Somn.* 2:190–192.

66. Von Wahlde, *John*, 1:414; Witherington, *John's Wisdom*, 255; Charlesworth, "Lady Wisdom," 104.

67. Ringe, *Wisdom's Friends*, 61; O'Boyle, *Wisdom Christology*, 163, 172; Witherington, *Jesus the Sage*, 375; Lincoln, *John*, 403; Achtemeier et al., *New Testament*, 182.

to come.⁶⁸ He then confesses that the Twelve "have come to know that you are the Holy One of God" (6:69). Peter's confession functions as a climactic summation of the christological emphases expressed in the chapter. As the provider of abundant provisions, the prophet likened to Moses, the bread of life from heaven who functions as the revealer of God's life-giving purposes, and the one who satisfies hunger and thirst, the Johannine Jesus is now regarded by his followers as "the Holy One of God." This title appears only here within the Fourth Gospel, but its position at the conclusion of the episode's unfolding christological look into the significance of Jesus serves to underscore the title's importance. In the Synoptic gospel accounts, only the demonic unclean spirit acknowledges Jesus as the Holy One of God, a confession to which Jesus issues forth a rebuke and a command to remain silent.⁶⁹ Since holiness pertains to being set apart from the profane, the most likely explanation of the Synoptic designation is that Jesus is God's Holy One because he received the Spirit at his baptism. The fact that the earlier Synoptic accounts of Jesus material record an unclean spirit identifying Jesus as God's Holy One only serves to make Peter's confession in the Gospel of John all the more striking.

Although the role of God's Holy One was sometimes applied to angelic messengers, the priest Aaron, and the prophet Elisha,⁷⁰ the writers of the Jewish sapiential literature frequently ascribed the trait of holiness to Lady Wisdom.⁷¹ We find the emphasis on the holiness of personified wisdom in several passages within Wisdom of Solomon. It is precisely because Wisdom is holy and disciplined that she will not dwell in a sinful person (Wis 1:4–5). Rather, she inhabits those persons who are holy, making them friends and prophets (7:27). Among the twenty-one characteristics of Lady Wisdom is the clear description of her holiness (7:22). Before coming to earth, Wisdom's habitation was located in the holy heavens (9:9–10). The author of Wisdom of Solomon sets the Holy Spirit in close parallel to the wisdom that God sends from the heavens (9:17). When Lady Wisdom interacted with notable persons in Israel's history, she gave knowledge of holy things, she opened the mouths of the mute to

---

68. The portrayal of Wisdom in Prov 8:35 may lie behind the claim that Jesus possesses the words of eternal life.

69. Mark 1:24 and its parallel in Luke 4:34.

70. For angels, see Deut 33:2–3; Ps 89:5, 7; Dan 4:17. For Aaron, see Ps 106:16; cf. Num 16:3–5; Sir 45:6. For Elisha, see 2 Kgs 4:9; cf. Sir 45:2–6.

71. I am drawing upon the work of Domeris, "Confession of Peter," 155–67.

sing to God's holy name, and helped others succeed by the hand of a holy prophet (10:10, 20; 11:1). It is not surprising that after Peter confesses the belief of the Twelve in Jesus as the Holy One of God, Jesus divides the disciples by separating the one among them who was to betray Jesus (John 6:70–71). Having observed the influence of wisdom themes in the dividing of the loaves and fish, in the role of the prophet likened to Moses, in the title "bread of life," in the promises to satisfy both hunger and thirst, and in the motif of the descending and ascending Son of Man, it is not surprising that we also find evidence of the impact of wisdom themes in the climactic title of John 6.[72] As God's Holy One, the Johannine Jesus embodies the trait of holiness formerly ascribed to personified wisdom.[73]

THE UNIQUE SON

Among the four New Testament gospels, the Gospel of John stands alone in portraying Jesus as the "unique" (Greek: *monogenes*) son. The adjective appears twice in the Johannine Prologue, and these occurrences anticipate two further appearances in John 3. In our examination of the Prologue, we found that after the personified word of God became flesh, it is then characterized as the unique one from the Father (1:14). The Prologue concludes by indicating that the unique "son" (if that is the correct textual variant) expounds and reveals the unseen God (1:18). In the Prologue, the adjective *monogenes* illustrates the Johannine Jesus as a one-of-a-kind revelatory agent of God who continues the role and mission of the personified *logos*. When we move into the body of the Gospel of John, the two further descriptions of Jesus as the *monogenes* continue the expectations that the Prologue has set for the reader. At the closing of the dialogue between Nicodemus and Jesus, the narrator steps in to shift the emphasis from the role of the Son of Man to the role of God the Father. The narrator carefully announces that God loved the world in this way, namely that he *gave* the unique son (3:16). At this point, it is certain that Jesus as the unique one is the son of God, which indicates that God is the Father of the *monogenes* Jesus. The following verse (3:17) indicates that the *commissioning* of the son as the agent of God parallels the act of God

---

72. Sandelin, *Wisdom as Nourisher*, 179, stresses the plethora of links between the texts describing Wisdom and the portrayal of Jesus in John 6.

73. Witherington, *John's Wisdom*, 160–61; Domeris, "Confession of Peter," 167.

giving the unique son in 3:16.⁷⁴ In other words, the unique son functions as both the gift of God and the agent of God. The final appearance of the adjective *monogenes* occurs in 3:18, where the name of the unique son of God functions as the intended object of belief. As the agent of God, Jesus is the locus of God's world-saving purposes and thereby operates as a suitable object of trust, loyalty, and obedience. The adjective *monogenes* helps emphasize these crucial christological concepts in the narrative of the Gospel of John.

These four occurrences of the adjective "unique" come into greater clarity once we are reminded that the word was formerly used to illustrate the characteristics of personified wisdom. In Wisdom of Solomon 7:22–24, the author attributes to Lady Wisdom twenty-one characteristics, three times the number of completion (seven). Among these qualities is the adjective *monogenes*, indicating that the personified wisdom of God is, as David Winston translates, "unique of its kind."⁷⁵ The author of the Gospel of John drew upon this rare quality in order to further shape the christological portrayal of the son of God in terms of Wisdom. As the embodiment of the preexisting word—a synonym for Wisdom—the Johannine Jesus continues to bear the unique characteristic of Wisdom as a human being. As the unique agent of the unseen God, Jesus can exclusively unveil, expound, and fully represent the Father's salvific purposes. These purposes include the giving of the unique son and the necessity for the world to believe in the name of the unique son. As the incarnation of Wisdom, the Johannine Jesus carries on the uniquely wise interactions of God, resulting in belief and the life of the age to come.

CONCLUSION

Even though the noun "wisdom" does not appear anywhere in the Gospel of John, the presentation of Jesus therein overwhelmingly indicates a christological portrayal in which the subject embodies the wise personification present within Jewish wisdom literature. We observed that the title Son of Man bears resemblance to the Enochic Son of Man in whom God's wisdom dwells. By examining the Johannine passages in which the Son of Man is expressed, we come to discern that the inaccessible wisdom of God is now made available in Jesus precisely as the apocalyptic

---

74. McIlhone, "Jesus as God's Agent," 301.
75. Winston, *Wisdom of Solomon*, 180.

Son of Man. In the same vein, we noted that the Johannine Jesus shares in Wisdom's role as the wise means of revealing, unveiling, and manifesting God and his purposes to the world. We also saw how the messianic status of Jesus within the Gospel of John has been shaped by the Jewish traditions in which acts of ruling and kingship directly involved Wisdom herself. Since Lady Wisdom directs those in positions of royalty within Israel's history to rule well, she is the most qualified to become flesh and act as the christological agent of God's dawning kingdom. Furthermore, the seven titles that Jesus claims exhibit considerable influence from the Jewish texts depicting Wisdom with the same metaphors. Witherington has reached a similar conclusion: "it is hard to doubt that in these 'I am' sayings Jesus is presented as God's divine Wisdom . . . he is the expression of the one true God, God's Word and wisdom."[76] These metaphoric self-designations represent the Johannine Jesus as the wise bearer of Israel's history, traditions, and purposes.[77] Reginald Fuller's summary of the influence of Wisdom upon the seven "I am" titles is worth some reflection at this juncture: "The 'I am' sayings are properly self-predicates of wisdom, whose spokesman and embodiment however is Jesus. They involve a kind of *communication idiomatum*. What is predictable of wisdom is predicable of Jesus and vice versa."[78]

We also drew comparisons to the characteristic of Lady Wisdom's holiness in the title that Jesus and the Twelve confess of Jesus—the Holy One of God. Last, we explored the ways in which the author characterized Jesus as the unique son of God by adopting a rare adjective formerly used to express the unique, one-of-a-kind wisdom of God, especially in his role as the agent of the unseen God and the object of believing faith. What we find, in light of all this data, is a robust Wisdom Christology in the Gospel of John that resonates with Jesus' mission, words, actions, and salvific death at the hands of his enemies.

This raises yet another important point in the Gospel of John in that Jesus, as the wisdom of God, is ultimately rejected, handed over, and killed. These enemies of Jesus repeatedly misunderstand him and his messianic claims, often creating schisms among the crowds. Jesus responds to his opponents by remaining hidden from them until the climactic moment of his glory—his death at the hands of his enemies. It is reasonable to pursue the topic of how Jesus interacts with his opponents

76. Witherington, *John's Wisdom*, 154.
77. Shafer, "Wisdom Christology," 62.
78. Fuller, "Incarnation," 65.

in the context of Jewish portrayals of the wisdom of God to see if there are any meaningful parallels that might shed light on the Fourth Gospel's plot. Therefore, it is prudent that we turn our attention to examining the conflicts between Wisdom's embodiment and the opponents within the Gospel of John.

7

Wisdom and Her Opponents

IN THE FOURTH CENTURY BCE, Aristotle famously wrote that the goal of literary tragedies consists of a combination of events and plot.[1] The Prologue of the Gospel of John sets the stage for Wisdom in that the world did not receive her, nor did they know her. Readers encountering the plot of the Fourth Gospel for the first time will come to better understand who it was that did not receive or know Jesus. These opponents are an essential part of the plot that creates the tragedy of the rejection of personified wisdom. This chapter will explore the way the conflicts between the Johannine Jesus and his opponents have been shaped by the author under the influence of Jewish wisdom texts. Our first area of focus for this study will involve the various schisms in which Jesus finds himself. What are the causes of these conflicts, and who acts as the instigators? Second, I will look closely at the theme of rejection in the Gospel of John, noting carefully *who* rejects Jesus and discerning *why* they have chosen to do so. Closely related to the rejection of Jesus is the attitude held by the opponents who seek to kill Jesus. Those who seek Jesus, however, are often characterized as not being able to find him. How might this motif of brutally seeking but not finding Jesus exhibit influence from Jewish wisdom texts? This chapter will examine the available data in order to give an answer to this question. Next, I will consider the response of Jesus toward these enemies and opponents, namely in his curious behavior of hiding himself from them. Why does Jesus act in this manner, and how might it be shaped by the traditions of Wisdom's hiddenness

1. Aristotle, *Poetics*, 6.

and inaccessibility? Last, I will examine how Jesus functions within the God-given prerogative of the judge who enacts judgment upon those who reject his message. The goal of these lines of inquiry is to better understand the extent to which Jewish texts illustrating the wisdom of God have influenced, organized, and fashioned the tragedy of the Johannine Jesus and his opponents.

SCHISMS INVOLVING WISDOM

The Prologue sets the stage for the divisions involving Jesus and his opponents. Although the world was made through the agency of personified wisdom, the world did not know her. Wisdom came to her own people, but those people refused to accept her God-given message (1:11–12). During the ministry of Wisdom's embodiment, we can observe how these introductory themes come to fruition. The narrator recalls these motifs through the dualism of light and darkness—light has come into the world, and humanity loved the darkness rather than the light. The reason the author gives as to why humanity preferred the darkness over the light that Wisdom offered is that the deeds of humanity were evil (3:19). The schism formed due to this conflict between light and darkness is illustrated in terms of evildoers hating the light and refusing to come to the light for fear that their evil deeds will be exposed (3:20; 7:7).

In addition to acts of hate directed toward Jesus, we may discern grumbling among those with whom he came into contact. At the Feast of Booths, the crowds grumbled greatly, but their grumbling led to a difference of opinion regarding Jesus' identity and motive. Some among the crowds thought that Jesus was a good man, while others were convinced that Jesus was a messianic pretender who was leading people astray (7:12). The heart of the breach concerns the validity of Jesus' mission as the messianic agent of the God of Israel. This provokes a response from Jesus wherein he cries out, "You both know me and know where I am from, and I have not come of myself, but he who sent me is true, whom you do not know" (7:28). This leads, inevitably, to another division among the crowds, with many responding with belief and speculation about the number of signs that the Christ is supposed to perform (7:31). The Pharisees, however, are unconvinced, and after they witness the positive response to Jesus exhibited by the crowds, they convene with the chief priests to send officers to seize Jesus (7:32).

At three key points in the narrative, the author of the Gospel of John uses the noun "schism" (Greek: *schisma*) to explicitly indicate the rift that Jesus and his message created among his listeners. The noun first appears in 7:40–43 as a conclusion to the deliberation that took place among the crowds.[2] While some among the crowds exclaim that Jesus certainly is the Prophet—a true but incomplete assessment of Jesus' messianic status—others are saying that he is the Christ.[3] A third group announce their skepticism considering Jesus' Galilean upbringing, noting that Scripture says the Messiah was to be a descendant of King David and come from David's village, Bethlehem. From the perspective of this third group, if Jesus was a resident of Galilee and not of Bethlehem, this would disqualify any claims to messiahship. The narrator specifies that a "schism" occurred within the crowd because of Jesus (7:33), resulting in some desiring to apprehend him (7:44). A similar instance occurs in the Blind Man Discourse (John 9) immediately following the miracle that took place on the Sabbath. The man who was formerly blind is brought before the Pharisees and an interrogation ensues (9:13–15). After the man confesses to the miracle and explains how it took place, the narrator notes that a schism developed among the Pharisees (9:16). While some of the Pharisees remain unconvinced that Jesus is truly God's authorized human agent due to the fact that the miracle took place on the Sabbath, other Pharisees question how it is that Jesus, if he truly is a sinner, could perform such miraculous signs. This division, like the schism in 7:33, rests on the person of Jesus and the legitimacy of his God-given ministry. The third story in which the narrator characterizes the divided response to Jesus as a "schism" appears in John 10. After claiming to be the good shepherd, Jesus speaks about the authority he possesses to lay down his life and take it up again. As to where he received this authority, Jesus emphatically declares that the Father bestowed it upon him and loves him, thus further legitimizing his messianic claims (10:15, 18). The narrator then indicates that a division took place because of these sayings of Jesus, proceeding to illustrate the different ways in which the Jews understood these claims. Many among the Jews regarded Jesus as demon-possessed, asking those present why they listen to him (10:20). Others, noting the legitimacy of the recent miracle where Jesus gave sight to the man born

---

2. Painter, *Quest*, 297.

3. Lincoln, *John*, 258, suggests that the messianic understanding present here might be influenced by the association of Lady Wisdom's springs of water from which all may come and partake, based on 1 En. 48:1, 10; 49:1.

blind, question how he could, in fact, have a demon (10:21). In all three instances where the narrator illustrates the division as a schism, some believe in the messianic claims that Jesus makes, while others—his opponents—regard him as a dangerous fraud, a pretender that is not truly commissioned by God. The enemies of Jesus within the Gospel of John appear to be, at least primarily, Jewish opponents who are unconvinced by the book's overarching claim that Jesus is the Christ, the son of God (20:31).

When we examine the characterization of Lady Wisdom in the book of Proverbs, it soon becomes clear that her speeches and interactions with people cause division. In other words, not everyone is thrilled to hear what the wisdom of God has to say. In Wisdom's first speech, she offers life, security, and ease to whoever listens to her and turns at her reproof (Prov 1:23, 33). To the scoffers who refuse when she calls, their destiny lies in calamity, death, and destruction (1:24–32). The behavior of those who choose to not listen to Lady Wisdom's summons is characterized by hostility; they "hate" knowledge (1:22, 28) and they "spurn" reproof (1:30). The longer speech of Wisdom in Proverbs 8 further reinforces the diverse ways in which her hearers will respond. She offers a blessing to those who listen to her, keep her ways, and act wisely. In addition to calling them blessed, she promises life and the favor of YHWH to them (8:32–35). Those who refuse to heed Wisdom and walk in her way of righteousness will injure themselves in the process (8:20). We can again observe the hostile nature of those who oppose Wisdom; they sin against her and hate her. In fact, by hating Wisdom, they reveal their true motives—they love death (8:36). The division between those who respond appropriately to Wisdom and those who prefer Folly is more evident in Proverbs 9, where Lady Wisdom's house is set alongside Lady Folly's house (9:1–6, 13–18). While Wisdom offers life to those who eat of her bread and drink of her wine, Folly's guests—those who partake of her stolen water and bread—are poised to accompany the dead into the depths of Sheol. Folly's path, the way of the wicked (4:19), claims the lives of many victims (7:25–26). The descriptions of the two competing invitations highlight the responses of those who listen to and accept Wisdom's instructions on one hand while contrasting those who reject her straight pathways on the other.

The motif of the division of pathways expressed in Proverbs was picked up by other Jewish wisdom texts. Wisdom of Solomon, for example, foresees how the unrighteous will admit to straying from the "way of truth" (Wis 5:6), namely the way of the Lord (5:7). Later, the book explains how Lady Wisdom guided the Israelites on the way of marvel (10:17). Along the same vein, Sirach assures his readers that the faithful will inherit and obtain Wisdom (Sir 4:16). The process of evaluating these potential heirs involves Wisdom walking with them upon tortuous paths, disciplining them and testing them until she trusts them. If they earn her trust, she will gladden them and reveal her secrets to them; if they stray from her then she will abandon them to their ruin (4:17–19). Sirach later comments on the tough love that Wisdom enacts, identifying in the process those who are fools and undisciplined (6:20). However, after being evaluated, it is the fools who are said to cast Wisdom aside, not the other way around (6:21). In other words, it is those who oppose Wisdom and her wise teachings who reject her. For those who search her out and refuse to let her go, she will reward them with rest, joy, and the adornment fit for royalty (6:26–31). In short, the Jewish sages who composed Proverbs, Sirach, and Wisdom of Solomon expressed the wise instructions of Israel's God in terms of a female personification that caused a schism among the people. This division is indicated by the righteous—those who actively take hold of Wisdom and walk along her path—and the unrighteous—those who voluntarily refuse to listen to Wisdom and, in turn, walk upon the path that leads to ruin and death. This characterization of positive and negative (and often hostile) ways in which those who interact with the wisdom of God seems to reappear in the Gospel of John, especially in the way that it illustrates the enemies of the Johannine Jesus in their refusal to recognize and listen to him.

REJECTING WISDOM

The earliest readers of the Gospel of John identified with the rejection that Jesus suffered in light of their own ostracization from Jewish communities of faith. This sense of finding solidarity with the negative experiences of Jesus by the reader seems to be a deliberate literary intention by the author of the Fourth Gospel. The Prologue, which sets the stage for the narrative of Jesus' life, indicates that God's personified *logos*—Wisdom's synonym—was not known by the very world through which it came into being (1:10). Furthermore, the *logos*—embodied as the Johannine Jesus—came to the Jewish people, but they did not receive him (1:11). The theme of rejection, which is introduced in the Prologue with the rejection of God's word/wisdom, becomes a substantial part of the story of Jesus within the Gospel of John. The world's rejection of the *logos* and the refusal of the people to receive him creates a sense of irony, as the reader would expect quite a different reception on the part of the Jewish people. If the readers, however, identified their own experiences of rejection and banishment by their kinsmen with the Johannine Jesus, then the irony could function, at least in part, as a source of comfort. For while his own people rejected Jesus, those who did receive him—namely the ideal readers—came to possess the authority to become children of God (1:12–13).

The narrative of the Gospel of John offers several examples pertaining to the ironic rejection of Jesus by his enemies. In John 5:43, after a lengthy apologetic treatment concerning his authorized position vis-a-vis the Father, Jesus calls out those Jews who do not receive him. In doing so, Jesus points to the irony that if someone else comes in his own name, the Jews will receive him. Jesus, however, declares himself as the agent of God: "I have come in my Father's name." The Jews refused to accept Jesus because they remained unconvinced of the validity of his claims to be the one authorized by the Father.[4] By Jesus healing on the Sabbath and boldly claiming that God was his own Father, he appeared to those present in Jerusalem to be a messianic pretender who deliberately scorned the ritual of the seventh day. According to the Jews, Jesus was twice guilty—once for breaking the Sabbath and once again for claiming a prerogative of God as his own.[5] Therefore, they reject Jesus' claim to be God's empowered and authorized agent.

John 7 again locates Jesus in Jerusalem, this time teaching in the temple (7:28). After he identifies himself as the commissioned agent of God,[6] the people of Jerusalem seek to seize him (7:30). While the narrator informs the reader that many among the crowd put their faith in Jesus at that time, the Pharisees and the chief priests send forth officers to seize Jesus (7:31–32). In response to this rejection by Jerusalem's authorities, Jesus declares his intent to go to the one who commissioned him, again underscoring his role as God's agent (7:33). Then, Jesus announces, "You will seek me, and you will not find me," which quotes the remarkably similar statement uttered by Lady Wisdom in Prov 1:28. The rejection of

---

4. Meyer, "Father," 257–58, 265.

5. Bekken, *Lawsuit Motif*, 69–70.

6. Jesus here characterizes God as he who "is true" (7:28). Later in Jesus' lengthy prayer, he explicitly identifies the Father as "the only true God" (17:3).

Jesus by those in Jerusalem again centers on his claim to be the authorized agent of God, a claim with which his opponents strongly disagree.

The rejection Jesus experiences in the Gospel of John extends to his followers in the form of expulsion from the synagogue. This punishment by excommunication first appears in the account where Jesus gives sight to the blind man (9:1-41). The Jews summon the blind man's parents to interrogate them about their son and the legitimacy of his former blindness. While they acknowledge that the man whom Jesus healed is indeed their son and that he was born blind, they fearfully claim to be ignorant to the circumstances that led to his newfound ability to see, suggesting to their interrogators that they ask him concerning the details (9:18-21). The narrator then informs the readers in 9:22 that the reason the parents made this reluctant claim was in fear of the agreement made by the Jews that anyone who confessed Jesus to be the Christ is to be "put out of the synagogue" (Greek: *aposynagogos*). This rare adjective, appearing three times in the New Testament, is found only in the Gospel of John. The second occurrence of rejection from the synagogue community appears in conjunction with Jesus' final public speech (12:35-50). Again, the narrator points out to the reader that many of the rulers feared openly confessing their belief in Jesus because the Pharisees would put them out of the synagogue (12:42). The third occurrence of this form of excommunication is found on the lips of Jesus during the Farewell Discourse. He warns them that "the world" will put them out of the synagogue, which may even lead to the deaths of the disciples (16:1-2). Jesus attributes this behavior on the part of the world to their failure to know him and the Father (16:3). The rejection of the disciples from the Jewish community—an experience that was almost certainly shared by the original readers of the Gospel of John—stems from the rejection that Jesus suffered at the hand of the Jerusalem authorities.[7]

We can detect another example of Jesus' ironic rejection during the exchange between Pilate and the Jews on the day of the crucifixion. After Pilate declares Jesus' innocence and attempts to give him back to the Jews, they inform Pilate that they are required by the law of Moses to put Jesus to death because he, in their view, made himself the son of God (19:6-7). Paul N. Anderson has put forth a compelling study that observes numerous points of influence of the prophet likened to Moses (Deut 18:15-22) on the Fourth Gospel's portrayal of the Father sending

---

7. Dunn, "Let John Be John," 318-21.

Jesus as his authorized agent.[8] Anderson points to this Jewish response given to Pilate and sees Deut 18:20 ("the prophet who speaks a word presumptuously in My name which I have not commanded him to speak ... that prophet shall die.") as the specific law underlying the complaint. By observing Deut 18:20 as the law bound up in the Jewish complaint recorded in John 19:7, it sets the stage for a rather striking occurrence of irony and rejection.[9] The Jews claim that Jesus is guilty of blasphemy for making false and presumptuous claims to be the son of God, the messianic king of the Jews. However, at the conclusion of the exchange with Pilate, the Jews declare that they have no king but Caesar (19:15), which itself is a blasphemous claim. Ignorant of their own wrongdoing, they accuse Jesus of doing that of which they are guilty.[10] This reading also has the benefit of framing the rejected Jesus in terms of the prophet from Deut 18:15–18, which bears several recognizable similarities to aspects of Wisdom Christology that we have already discussed. The prophet likened to Moses speaks the words of YHWH, obeys YHWH, and acts as YHWH's authorized agent, and those who refuse to listen to the prophet will suffer judgment. As God's wisdom and *logos* made flesh, Jesus speaks the words of God, Lady Wisdom obeys God, God has sent his wisdom as his agent, and those who refuse to listen to the son have already been judged because the Father has given all judgment to the son. Not only is Jesus rejected as king, but he is rejected as the prophet and as the locus of Wisdom's embodying influence.

The Jewish sages frequently characterized the wisdom of God as suffering rejection from the unrighteous, namely those who refuse to listen to and obey her.[11] Proverbs 1 illustrates Lady Wisdom as a prophetess who urges the naïve, the simple, the scoffers, and the fools to repent at her words of reproof (1:20–23). However, instead of heeding her call, many reject her wise instructions. The nature of this rejection is detailed by the author: refusing Wisdom's call and paying no attention to the counsel that she offers (1:24–25). As a direct result of this behavior, Wisdom announces the specifics of the judgment that is to fall upon the unrighteous. Calamity, dread, distress, and anguish will come upon those who refused her (1:26–27). The conclusion of this judgment is death and destruction, while those who choose to listen to Wisdom's instructions will dwell

---

8. Anderson, "Having-Sent-Me Father," 33–57.
9. Dunn, "Let John Be John," 321–22.
10. Keener, *John*, 2:1132.
11. Brown, *Introduction to the Gospel of John*, 262.

securely and be at ease from evil's dread (1:32–33). The passage spends most of its attention on those who reject Wisdom while offering only a few lines of positive comments pertaining to the faithful listeners. This stress upon those foolish enough to reject the wisdom of God in Proverbs 1 is also apparent in the Johannine portrayal of Jesus, the rejected Messiah, who acts as the climactic embodiment of Wisdom.

The portrayal of personified wisdom as primarily rejected by the people of God that we observe in Proverbs 1 made an impact on the author of Baruch. The passage pertaining to Israel's interactions with the wisdom of God similarly characterizes that relationship in terms of the rejection of Wisdom (Bar 3:9—4:4). The author, speaking on behalf of the prophet Baruch, invites Israel to listen to the commandments of life, which are further defined as wisdom (3:9). However, Israel has "forsaken the fountain of wisdom" (3:12), and this rejection of God's wise commandments has resulted in the punishment of exile, living in a foreign country, defilement, and being counted among those in Hades. After reflecting on the events of the Babylonian exile, the author encourages Israel to learn where there is wisdom in order to discern life and peace (3:14). The author proceeds to rhetorically ask about personified wisdom's location (3:15, 29–30), revealing that only one person knows where she resides, the God of Israel (3:35). God gave Wisdom to Jacob, appearing on earth and now located in the book of the commandments of God (3:36—4:1). After the author locates personified wisdom in the law, he offers a promise of life to those who hold her fast and the threat of death to those who forsake her. Baruch, therefore, highlights Wisdom's value by reminding its readers of the former consequences that fell upon those Israelites who rejected her in the past, resulting in the encouragement to seek her out or suffer the same mortal judgment. The Gospel of John, importantly, pinpoints personified wisdom residing in the person of the human Jesus rather than in the law of commandments, which Baruch insists is the case. In both instances, Wisdom is primarily a rejected figure.

It is also important to recall our observation that the author of 1 Enoch 42, who also described the rejection of God's wisdom by Israel, was a first-century contemporary of the author of the Gospel of John. This indicates that the idea of rejected wisdom was held by at least one non-Christian Jewish source composed around the same time as the Fourth Gospel. The author of 1 Enoch 42 briefly illustrates the career of personified wisdom by first positioning her in the heavens where a place was found for her, presumably by God himself (42:1). Afterward, she descended to earth in order that she might live among humanity, but unfortunately, she was unable to find a suitable dwelling place with them. Having suffered rejection from the people, she returned upward to the heavens (42:2). This short-lived career of personified wisdom emphasizes her desire to live among humanity, only to find that humanity does not want her to dwell with them. The parallels between the portrayal of Wisdom in 1 Enoch 42 and in the Gospel of John are remarkable.[12] The Johannine Prologue locates the personified word—wisdom's functional synonym—with God in the beginning. This wisdom descends from heaven, becomes flesh in the human Jesus, and dwells among the people. However, his own people did not receive him, resulting in his death. After being raised from the dead, Jesus—the embodiment of Wisdom—ascended to heaven, the place where personified wisdom began her journey. The Gospel of John, in short, offers an account of how the people of God rejected his wisdom in continuity with former Jewish wisdom sources that told the same story.[13]

SEEKING BUT NOT FINDING

Having just discussed the themes of Wisdom's rejection within the Gospel of John, it is appropriate to now turn to explore a closely related element, namely the way those who rejected Jesus seek to put him to death, but strangely cannot find him. These dual traits of a wicked person seeking but not finding are often linked within the Gospel of John, but the former appears far more frequently. Catherine Cory points out that a significant concentration of these motifs appears in the Tabernacles Discourse (John 7:1—8:59), noticing that the author attributes these behaviors to the enemies of Jesus, not to those who are earnestly seeking Jesus in order to believe in him.[14] The discourse begins with the author informing the reader that Jesus was unwilling to walk in Judea because the Jews were seeking to kill him (7:1), a remark that recalls the account where Jesus healed the lame man on the Sabbath that resulted in the Jews

---

12. See e.g., Coloe, *John 1–10*, 280: "Jesus's experience parallels the experience of Sophia as recorded in 1 Enoch 42."

13. Johnson, "Jesus, the Wisdom of God," 285; Witherington, *Jesus the Sage*, 377; Schüssler Fiorenza, *Jesus*, 167. Brown, *John I-XII*, 301, observes the rejection of personified wisdom in the Bread of Life Discourse.

14. Cory, "Wisdom's Rescue," 101. I am indebted to Cory's insights for this portion of my argument.

"all the more seeking to kill him" (5:18). After his brothers went to the feast, Jesus went up in secret, as the Jews present were seeking him there (7:10–11). Both references to the Jews seeking Jesus at the Feast of Tabernacles involve their inability to find and locate him. When Jesus presents himself in the temple in order to teach, an act that prompts the Jews to question how it is that Jesus appears to be well educated, he replies by describing himself as the authorized agent of God's teaching (7:14–18).[15] However, instead of rightly regarding Jesus as the legitimate agent of the true God, Jesus points out that they are seeking to put him to death, a claim that provokes a few different responses from the crowds that each repeat the seeking motif (7:19–20, 25).[16] As the discourse continues, the narrator explains that none of Jesus' enemies seized him because his hour had not yet come, and this statement purposefully sets up Jesus repeating the motif of seeking but not finding: "I go away, and you will seek me . . . where I am going, you cannot come" (8:20–21). Jesus ties the behavior of those who seek to kill him to their rejection of his word (8:37), an act that does not fit the children of Abraham (8:40).[17] At the conclusion of the discourse, the Jews seek to stone Jesus, but they are unable to find him as he leaves the temple (8:59).[18] The Tabernacles Discourse begins and concludes with references to the enemies of Jesus seeking to put him to death but find that they are unable to locate him.

The motif of seeking but not finding appears in subsequent stories involving controversies between Jesus and his enemies who reject his claim to be the messianic agent of God. During the Feast of Dedication, Jesus makes a claim to possess a oneness in mind and purpose with the Father, a claim that the Jews label as blasphemous and consider worthy of putting Jesus to death (10:28–31). While the Jews regard Jesus as illegitimately making himself out to be God, Jesus disagrees with their conclusion, defending his actions as one whom the Father has sanctified

---

15. Keener, *John*, 1:712, notes that Jesus is probably stressing his subordinate status to God.

16. Brown, *John I-XII*, 317, also sees evidence here to the portrayal of Jesus as "Wisdom incarnate."

17. Robinson, "Use of the Fourth Gospel," 72, observes that the Hebraic use of sonship designates a functional relationship marked by character: "To be a son is to show the character, to reproduce the thought and action, of another, whether it be Abraham, or the Devil, or God."

18. Keener, *John*, 1:774, connects Jesus' withdraw with Jewish accounts of Wisdom's rejection on earth.

and commissioned as an agent (10:33-36).[19] The episode comes to a close with another instance of the Jews seeking to seize him, and the author notes that Jesus "eluded their grasp" (10:39). Shortly after this story, Jesus learns that his friend Lazarus has fallen gravely ill. Jesus announces to his disciples his intent to return to Judea, and the disciples, keenly aware that Jesus' enemies reside there, respond, "Rabbi, the Jews were just now seeking to stone you, and you are going there again?" (11:8). The disciples here repeat the recurring motif: the enemies of Jesus in Jerusalem seek to put him to death, but while he is not present in Jerusalem, the enemies are unable to find him. Despite the correct understanding that the disciples possess of the situation, Jesus visits Mary and Martha in Bethany and proceeds to raise their brother Lazarus from the dead. The resurrection of Lazarus proves to be a pivotal miracle in the narrative of the Gospel of John, forcing the Pharisees and the chief priests to gather in order to assess the implications of Jesus' actions if left unchecked from their control. After some discussion involving the high priest, Caiaphas, the narrator concludes this council by indicating that from that day they plan to kill Jesus (11:47-53).[20] In light of this agreement among the Jerusalem authorities, Jesus "therefore no longer continued to walk publicly among the Jews" (11:54), a statement that reinforces the motif of seeking but not finding in the Gospel of John. The narrator has emphasized this motif as the conclusion of three significant episodes involving controversy: the Tabernacles Discourse, the Feast of Dedication, and the resurrection of Lazarus.

This important motif of seeking but not finding owes its origins to the portrayal of personified wisdom in the book of Proverbs. The first wisdom passage in Proverbs (1:20-33) emphasizes the consequences of those who reject Wisdom's instruction as well as offering the reasons for their refusing her. As Wisdom makes herself unavailable to those who rejected her and begin to suffer various acts of judgment, we observe the foundational line for the Johannine seeking-but-not-finding motif. Lady Wisdom states: "Then they will call on me, but I will not answer;

---

19. Robinson, *Twelve More*, 175, points out that Jesus refuses the claim to be God in 10:33.

20. Coloe, *John 11–21*, 329-30, points to the prophecy uttered by Caiaphas that looks to the gathering of the children of God as a result of Jesus' rejection and death (11:51-52), which recalls the reference to the children of God in the Prologue (1:12). In Wis 5:5, Coloe observes, Lady Wisdom enables the righteous to become "numbered among the children of God."

they will seek me diligently, but they will not find me" (1:28).²¹ The Greek translation of this verse utilizes the verb *zyteo* ("to seek"), and this is the same verb that the author of the Gospel of John adopts fifteen times in describing the actions of the Jews who seek to put Jesus to death in chapters 5–11.²² We have already observed that the Johannine Jesus speaks the words of personified wisdom in John 7:34, a statement that appears to be a deliberate attempt to carry forth the seeking-but-not-finding motif from Prov 1:28 into the conflict involving Jesus and those who oppose him.²³ The sages are careful to illustrate what the enemies of Wisdom will find instead of her: their own death and demise (Prov 1:31–32). Later in the collection of proverbs, the motif reappears: a scoffer seeks wisdom and finds none (14:6). The Greek translation again employs the verb *zyteo* ("to seek") in its reworking of the Hebrew: "You will seek wisdom with evil people, but you will not find it" (Prov 14:6 LXX). This reference reinforces the key point that those who seek Wisdom but are unable to find her are wicked people who rejected her initial invitation, not well-meaning persons interested in obeying her wise instructions. To sum up, the Gospel of John has shaped the hostile interactions between Jesus and his Jewish enemies under the direct influence of the seeking-but-not-finding motif that the Jewish sages who composed the book of Proverbs utilized in portraying how the wicked interact with God's personified wisdom.²⁴

THE HIDDENNESS OF WISDOM

Having demonstrated the links between the behavior of Jesus' enemies and the seeking-but-not-finding motif present in the book of Proverbs, we can now explore an important and closely related theme: the hiddenness of Jesus as he escapes his enemies. Throughout the narrative of the Gospel of John, Jesus actively hides from others. Many times, those from

21. Brown, *John I–XII*, 318; Sidebottom, *Fourth Gospel*, 206.

22. John 5:18; 7:1, 11, 19, 20, 25, 30, 34, 36; 8:21, 37, 40; 10:39; 11:8, 56.

23. Witherington, *Jesus the Sage*, 377; McGrath, *John's Apologetic Christology*, 200; Brown, *Introduction to the Gospel of John*, 263; Keener, *John*, 1:720. The connection between the motif in Prov 1:28 and the Gospel of John appears more frequently than simply Jesus' quote in John 7:34 if we further consider 7:36 and the loose allusions in 8:21; 10:39; 13:33; 16:19.

24. Brown, *John I–XII*, cxxiv, 318; Johnson, "Jesus, the Wisdom of God," 285; Von Wahlde, *John*, 1:415.

whom Jesus hides are seeking to do him harm, although this is not always the case. The narrator regularly informs the readers that harm will not befall Jesus until the climactic hour of his glorious death (7:30; 8:20; 12:27; 13:1; 16:21; 17:1).[25] We first observe this motif of hiddenness at the wedding at Cana. After Jesus instructs the servants to fill the waterpots, the head waiter discovers that the water had been transformed into good wine. The story unfolds with an editorial note indicating that the head waiter did not know from whence the wine came (2:9). In fact, Jesus, the one who performed this miraculous sign, plays no further role in the episode. He has manifested his glory while remaining inaccessible. A similar emphasis appears in Jesus' discussion with Nicodemus. In the context of discussing the new birth from above, entrance into the kingdom of God, and the importance of believing in the unique son, Jesus describes how the wind blows, stating, "You do not know where it comes from and where it is going" (3:8). The motif of hiddenness involves, as we can observe, the Spirit-enabled new birth from above. The interaction involving Jesus and the Samaritan woman further elaborates this theme—Jesus possesses living water while having nothing with which to draw from the well (4:11), and he has food to eat about which the disciples do not know (4:32–33).[26] The water and food that Jesus offers are, at least initially, hidden from the perception of those who inquire. The Bread of Life Discourse builds upon these points by depicting Jesus testing Philip by asking him, "Where are we to purchase bread, so that these people may eat?" (6:5–6). Philip answers by indicating that the funds they have at their disposal are only sufficient to provide a small portion of bread to all of those present (6:7), proving to be unaware of Jesus' hidden intent to perform another miraculous sign not unlike what took place at the wedding at Cana. After Jesus multiplies the loaves of bread and the fish, he perceives that the people are about to take him by force, choosing then to withdraw from their presence (6:14). The next day, the crowd crosses the sea in their attempt to locate Jesus, who remains inaccessible to them until they arrive at Capernaum (6:24–25).

The hiddenness theme appears alongside the seeking-but-not-findin'" motif beginning in the Tabernacles Discourse.[27] Following Jesus'

---

25. The author alerts the reader to the nature of the coming climactic hour as early in the narrative as the wedding at Cana (2:4).

26. Thomas Aquinas, *John 1–5*, 231, suggests that this statement by Jesus is another reference to Wisdom Christology by pointing to Sir 15:3.

27. Painter, *Quest*, 290.

claim to be the agent whom the true God has commissioned, the narrator declares that the Jews sought to seize him, noting that because his hour had not yet arrived, no one laid a hand on him (7:28-30). Shortly after, Jesus informs those attempting to apprehend him of his intent to become inaccessible: "For a little while longer I am with you, then I go to him who sent me. You will seek me, and you will not find me, and where I am, you cannot come" (7:33-34). This provocative statement leads to another example of the Johannine theme of misunderstanding, as the Jews interpret him literally and discuss whether Jesus will depart to teach the Greeks in the Diaspora. In doing so, they focus specifically on the exact wording of Jesus' claim to go to a place where they cannot come (7:35-36).[28] The narrator here expresses the motif of hiddenness as Jesus' enemies attempt to pursue him. The motif reappears later in the discourse as Jesus, in condemning the Pharisees' failure to follow him, says that he knows where he came from and where he is going, but they do not know (8:14). The inaccessibility of Jesus is bound together with the refusal of the enemies of Jesus to accept his messianic claims. As the conversation continues to contrast Jesus from the unbelieving Jews, Jesus reaffirms his claim to be the Jewish Messiah ("I am he"), resulting in the Jews picking up stones in order to execute this perceived messianic pretender.[29] Jesus, however, "was hidden" and went out of the temple (8:58-59).[30] The author of the Gospel of John employs the verb *krupto* ("to conceal") and in doing so deliberately stresses the hiddenness of Jesus as a result of Jesus' enemies failing to believe his messianic aspirations.

The following three episodes in the Gospel of John (the Blind Man Discourse, the Feast of Dedication, and the Lazarus Discourse) each

---

28. The narrator intends to stress the specific wording of the misunderstood Jews by repeating Jesus' statement from 7:34 in 7:36 word-for-word in Greek.

29. Robinson, *Twelve More*, 176-77, argues that readers should reject the interpretation that *ego eimi* means "I (Jesus) am God." For a similar denial of the interpretation where Jesus claims divinity, see Davies, *Rhetoric and Reference*, 82-87; Nemes, *Trinity and Incarnation*, 166-67.

30. Witherington, *John's Wisdom*, 169, argues unpersuasively that Jesus' claim—as Wisdom—to preexist and possess divine origins would naturally solicit the accusation of blasphemy. This implausible reconstruction fails to account for the meaning of *ego eimi* ("I am he [the Messiah]") that has been evident since John 4:26. Freed, "John VIII. 24," 163, provides evidence demonstrating that the messianic understanding of *ego eimi* in John 4:25-26 is the clue for understanding all other passages in John where Jesus uses the expression. Painter, *Quest*, 303, is also helpful here: "The Messiah remained hidden because the Jews regarded his interpretation of and claim to messiahship as blasphemy."

elaborate on the motif of Jesus' hiddenness. Following the encounter with the man born blind in which Jesus restores his sight, the neighbors interrogate the man to ascertain whether he was the former beggar and how he is able to see. He answers their questions by describing Jesus as the man who "made clay and anointed my eyes," to which the neighbors request to know where Jesus is currently. The former beggar indicates that he does not know where Jesus is, a reply that highlights the fact that Jesus has removed himself from the scene in order to be inaccessible (9:10–12).[31] At the conclusion of the discourse, Jesus describes the goal of his messianic mission as coming into the world for judgment so that those who do not see may see and those who see may become blind (9:39). The Pharisees who were present ask Jesus if they too are blind, to which Jesus responds by revealing the sin of their position that claims to see while refusing to believe in him (9:40–41). The rejection of Jesus and his messianic claims results in a blindness that, naturally, makes Jesus hidden. The following episode involves a controversy over Jesus' assertion that he shares a oneness of purpose with the Father, a claim with which the Jews strongly disagree and consider worthy of death by stoning (10:27–31). Jesus' attempt to apologetically defend his statement as not blasphemous inevitably does not persuade the Jews, who attempt again to seize him. However, Jesus eludes their grasp (10:39), effectively hiding himself from their attempts to take him. During the subsequent episode involving the resurrection of Lazarus, the Johannine Jesus declares himself to be "the resurrection and the life," claims that provoke Martha to confess her belief in Jesus as "the Christ, the Son of God" (11:25–27). The raising of Lazarus is the sign that leads to the chief priest and the Pharisees convening a council in which they decide to kill Jesus (11:53). As a direct result of this decision by the Jerusalem leadership, the narrator reports that Jesus no longer walked publicly among the Jews (11:54).[32] Jesus hides precisely because his enemies fail to believe in him as the Jewish Messiah whom the God of Israel has commissioned.

Jesus' final public speech before the Farewell Discourse combines the motif of hiddenness, the theme of misunderstanding, and the wisdom images of light and the way/path. He announces judgment upon

---

31. Although Jesus makes himself inaccessible to his opponents in this discourse, he nevertheless seeks out and finds the blind man (9:35). Brown, *John I-XII*, 375, astutely points out that this reference is analogous with Wis 6:16, where Lady Wisdom searches for those by finding them on their paths.

32. Coloe, *John 11-21*, 330.

the world and the verdict that the world's ruler will be cast out from it. Jesus' claim to be lifted from the earth is in close proximity to these statements concerning judgment, which uses the typical Johannine double entendre "lifting up," which refers to exaltation and the act of being propped up onto the cross in order to die (12:31–32). Jesus' use of the double entendre serves as the first step for the misunderstanding that follows. The narrator inserts an editorial comment in order to make sure the reader identifies Jesus' statement with his crucifixion, which looms on the horizon. The crowds respond with a typical misunderstanding of Jesus by being unable to square their tradition of the Son of Man, who is to remain forever, with the claim that Jesus will be lifted up to die.[33] The third step of the theme of misunderstanding, wherein Jesus clarifies his misconstrued comments, consists of him speaking of himself as the light that is among his audience "for a little while longer" (12:35). During this brief period that the light is present, Jesus calls them to walk in order that darkness will not overtake them. Furthermore, he summons them to place their faith in the light, resulting in a change of identity: becoming children of light (12:36). The narrator concludes Jesus' explanation of the misunderstanding by informing the reader that Jesus "was hidden from them" (again using the Greek verb *krupto*, "to hide").

The Farewell Discourse, in which Jesus offers private and intimate exhortations to his disciples, contains several references to Jesus' hiddenness. Of noteworthy attention is Jesus' reminder that he previously informed the Jews, "You will seek me . . . where I am going, you cannot come" (John 13:33; cf. Prov 1:28). Jesus accompanies this remembrance with his intent to become inaccessible, as he is with them for a little while longer. Shortly after this announcement, he speaks of his intent to leave the disciples in order that he may prepare a place for them (14:2–3). At the conclusion of this declaration, Jesus assures his disciples that they already know "the way" to where he is going—a statement that sets up another misunderstanding. Thomas responds with a confused question regarding what Jesus means by "the way" and the manner in which it relates to Jesus' destination. Jesus offers a clarifying answer to Thomas, and, in doing so, he points to himself as the way and identifies the Father as the destination (14:4–6). In claiming this Wisdom-infused christological title, Jesus explains his desire to depart to be with the Father and, in doing so, become inaccessible to the disciples until he returns. Jesus' intent to

---

33. Keener, *Gospel of John*, 2:881.

depart is cause for his followers to have sorrow in their hearts (16:5–6), and Jesus attempts to offer comfort by promising that he will send the Spirit of truth to function in his place. In a final reference to the hiddenness of Jesus, he informs the disciples that they will not see him for "a little while" (16:16). This prompts yet another misunderstanding among some of his followers, who focus on the duration "a little while" in private deliberation among themselves (16:17–18). Jesus offers forth an explanatory answer that indicates that his death will bring temporary lamentation among his followers, only to be followed with joy when, as he assures them, "I will see you again" (16:22). His death will give opportunity for his enemies—the world—to rejoice, as they will have succeeded in seizing him and putting him to death (16:20). As such, Jesus combines the motif of hiddenness with his glorious death and with a reference to his enemies who seek to do him harm.

We have observed that the hiddenness of personified wisdom is one of her signature characteristics, according to the Jewish sages. The wisdom poem in the book of Job (Job 28:12–28) explicitly conveys the inaccessibility of the wisdom of God. In fact, this is the poem's primary purpose. The poem begins by rhetorically asking where Wisdom can be found and asserting that humanity does not know her value. Wisdom is not among the land of the living because she is "hidden" and "concealed," and the passive voice in these two verbs is almost certainly a divine passive (28:21). Only God knows Wisdom's whereabouts since he is the Creator who established her (28:23–27). If humanity desires to acquire God's wisdom, then she can be found in the fear of YHWH. Personified wisdom's speech in Proverbs 8 suggests that while she makes herself available in public places (8:2–3), she occasionally is reclusive. By announcing to her listeners that "those who seek me will find me," she indicates that she is not always present out in the open since she is in a location that requires one to locate and seek her out (8:17). The portrayal of Wisdom in the book of Proverbs holds the accessibility and the hiddenness characteristics in tension.

The intertestamental Jewish literature demonstrates influence from the book of Job and Proverbs in illustrating personified wisdom as aloof and hidden. Ben Sira describes how Wisdom interacts with the undisciplined and the foolish (6:20–22). For these persons, Wisdom is not readily perceived due to her inaccessibility (6:22). Those who are disciplined—who take upon the yoke of Wisdom—will search and seek her out (6:24–27). To these, Wisdom will make herself known, and they will discover the rest that she offers (6:27–28). The book of Sirach, like Proverbs, portrays the figure of Wisdom as hidden from the unrighteous but able to be found by those who diligently seek to obey her wise instructions. Baruch draws upon Job's wisdom poem in an attempt to encourage its readers to acquire wisdom. The author issues a summons to learn *where* there is wisdom in order to find life and peace (3:14). Like Job, Baruch asks, "Who has found her place? And who has entered her storehouses?" (3:15). The prophet, while describing those generations of the past, notes that they failed to learn her way of knowledge, understand her paths, and take possession of her (3:20). Wisdom is inaccessible in Canaan and Teman; even Hagar's descendants do not know the way to her. In fact, no one knows the way to her, except the Creator God himself (3:22–35). The formerly inaccessible wisdom has come down to earth and is now located in the Torah, the law of the commandments (3:37—4:1). Baruch, therefore, paints the figure of Wisdom as primarily inaccessible and hidden unless she is sought out in obedience to the law of Moses. The author of Wisdom of Solomon offers a similar treatment of the subject of Lady Wisdom's aloofness. Although she is not entirely a public figure, those who love her will discern her location; those who seek her will find her (6:12). In fact, those who desire her will find that she will quickly reveal herself to them, having no difficulty. However, the "love" that one must have in order to find Lady Wisdom is defined by the author of Wisdom of Solomon as "the keeping of her laws" (6:18). The motif of Wisdom's hiddenness that appears in the Hebrew Bible and in the intertestamental wisdom texts has made a sizable impact on the author of the Gospel of John, who characterizes the Johannine Jesus as deliberately hiding from the hostile and unbelieving enemies. To those who earnestly seek him, he makes himself available, thus depicting Jesus as both accessible and hidden, depending on the motives of those who seek him. In this manner, Jesus clearly embodies the motif of Lady Wisdom's hiddenness in the Fourth Gospel.

THE ENACTOR OF WISE JUDGMENTS

The true God loved the world in this way: he gave his unique son, in order that whoever believes in him will not perish but come to possess the life of the age to come (3:16). This famous text indicates that the mission of the Johannine Jesus was to offer life to those who responded with faith and allegiance. It is reasonable to ask, then, what about those who refused the Messiah, whom the God of Israel authorized and commissioned? To reject an agent is to also reject the one who sends the agent. In the case of the Gospel of John, refusing Christ's message is ultimately refusing the only true God who appointed Christ, resulting in a verdict of judgment. The Johannine Jesus declares himself the enactor of God's judgments, particularly on those who refuse his message and mission. Following the inability of Jesus to convince the Jews in Jerusalem of his prerogative to heal the lame man on the Sabbath, he defends his actions by expressing that the Father gave all judgment to the son (5:22), a claim that strengthens Jesus' apology as the obedient son with whom God has shared his unique prerogatives.[34] As the agent of God's judgment, Jesus promises the life of the age to come as a present experience to anyone who listens to his message and believes God who commissioned him—a life that follows death and ignores judgment (5:23).[35] In doing so, Jesus demonstrates that he bears the authority to enact judgment and offer life. To this second point, Jesus also announces that the Father has bestowed upon the son the prerogative to bestow life (5:26).[36] The Father shares these two divine privileges with Jesus precisely because he is the Son of Man—the human figure from Daniel 7 with whom the Ancient of Days shares the prerogatives of dominion, glory, and kingship (Dan 7:13-14). The life that Jesus offers to those who both believe that God has truly commissioned him and also believe in his message is not only life in the present; it includes resurrection life in the future. For those who did good works, the Son of Man will bestow a resurrection of life, but to those who committed evil, he will issue forth a resurrection of judgment (John 5:28-29). Jesus offers these verdicts of just judgment as an obedient son who listens to the Father in order to accomplish his will, rather than Jesus' own will (5:30). In other words, the Johannine Jesus is the enactor of God's judgment in the role of a subordinate son who seeks to listen to and obey his Father.[37]

The Gospel of John similarly paints Jesus as the authorized agent of judgment on several other occasions. John 3:19 offers a definition of "the judgment" as the light coming into the world, only to encounter people

34. See the discussion in Fuller, "Incarnation," 61-62; Bauckham, *Jesus*, 138.

35. Thomas Aquinas, *John 1-5*, 282-83, draws attention to the influence of Prov 8:35 in this portrayal of Wisdom Christology.

36. Borgen, *Bread from Heaven*, 162: "The life of the Father as the sender is transferred to the agent, the Son." Borgen points to b. Qidd. 43a; b. Sanh. 111b; b. Git. 32 as evidence of this concept in the Jewish principle of agency.

37. Keener, *John*, 1:655, seems confused when suggests that Jesus is both claiming to be deity and functions as a perfect agent who obeys the Father's will.

who commit evil deeds and prefer darkness instead. This characterization draws on the imagery set forth in the Prologue, where the personified *logos* of God possesses life, which was the light of humanity, shining in the darkness (1:4–5). The theme reappears after Jesus claims to be the light of the world (8:12), wherein Jesus responds to the Pharisees, who note that his testimony by itself is not enough to be valid (8:13). In answering this objection, Jesus confesses that he, in his capacity to function as judge, is not alone. The Father, who authorizes Jesus as the agent of God, testifies on Jesus' behalf (8:16–18). The cluster of themes pertaining to judgment and light shows up again in Jesus' speech concerning the man who was born blind. After the recently healed man responds to Jesus with a confession of faith and a display of worship, Jesus announces that his mission relates to judgment, namely that those who are blind may come to see and those who see will become blind (9:39). This statement combines physical blindness with the inability to accept Jesus as God's messianic agent. To this point, Jesus issues a stark warning to those Pharisees who claim the ability to see, despite their unbelief: "Your sin remains" (9:40–41). Finally, Jesus issues a verdict on the ruler of this world, rendering him one who will be cast out (12:31) and judged (16:11). By functioning in his role as the enactor of God's judgment, Jesus pronounces those who reject his God-ordained mission and the world's ruler as guilty.

This portrayal of Jesus as the agent of God who decrees judgment shows unmistakable indicators of influence from the Jewish wisdom tradition, particularly the book of Proverbs. In the first speech of personified wisdom in Proverbs 1, we observe a scene involving the prophetess Wisdom and her audience (Prov 1:20–33). She issues forth her summons within her role as the agent of God who speaks forth wise commands, and to those who reject her, she declares God's judgments. The scoffers and fools who do not listen to Wisdom will suffer calamity, dread, distress, and anguish (1:24–27). Wisdom herself speaks forth these punishments and even goes on to clarify the guilty as those who are bringing forth death (1:32). To the obedient who listen to and obey Wisdom's prophetic instructions, she promises security and life without disaster or dread (1:33). The portrayal of Wisdom in Proverbs 8 underscores her prophetic roles even further. Kings and rulers decree justice due to the direct influence ("by me") of the wisdom of God (8:15). Even rulers and nobles owe their ability to rightly govern to Lady Wisdom (8:16). This wisdom poem ends with another summons for the reader to listen to her, keep her ways, and not refuse her instruction (8:32–34). Wisdom judges those who obey her wise teachings as worthy of life and of YHWH's favor, while she harshly criticizes those who hate her as lovers of death (8:35–36). Last, we should draw special attention to the parallel between the way in which God works through the agency of Wisdom to empower human beings to "pronounce judgment" (Wis 9:2–3) and the portrayal of God empowering the Son of Man—Wisdom incarnate—to pronounce judgment (John 5:26–27).[38] Just as Lady Wisdom functions as the agent of YHWH's prophetic judgments in the Jewish wisdom tradition, the Johannine Jesus acts as the Father's agent of judgment, and in doing so, Jesus exercises the divine prerogatives of judge and giver of life.[39]

CONCLUSION

Although the Johannine Jesus functions as the authorized and empowered messenger of the only true God, he nevertheless suffers rejection at the hands of his opponents. We demonstrated that the Fourth Gospel draws upon the portrayals of rejected Wisdom from Jewish literature in order to further illustrate both the protagonist and the antagonists of the story. The various schisms between Jesus and his opponents exhibit parallels to earlier Jewish texts in which fools and scoffers show hostility toward personified wisdom and the righteous persons who accept her instructions. We noted the influence of the Jewish sages who illustrated the rejection of the wisdom of God at several points in the narrative of the Fourth Gospel. Furthermore, we detected noticeably clear lines of inspiration from Proverbs' seeking-but-not-finding motif in Jesus' own words, wherein he practically quotes the words of personified wisdom on this topic. Similarly, we were able to discern the impact of the hiddenness of wisdom upon the actions of Jesus when he regularly encounters mortal threats from his opponents. Last, the christological portrayal of Jesus sharing in the Father's prerogative echoes back to Lady Wisdom functioning as the personified agent of YHWH's judgments and life-giving acts.

The Johannine Prologue set the expectations for readers of the gospel concerning the rejection of the incarnate wisdom of God (1:10–11). In doing so, the Prologue juxtaposes the opponents of Jesus with the disciples—those who place their trust in and offer obedience to him

38. Sidebottom, *Fourth Gospel*, 206.
39. Thompson, *God of the Gospel of John*, 230–31.

(1:12–13). If the Fourth Gospel shows influence from the Jewish sages who portrayed Wisdom's hostile opponents, how might it frame those who accept and follow Wisdom as disciples? Does the Gospel of John portray the relationship between Jesus and his followers in ways that exhibit influences from Jewish wisdom literature? We will attempt to offer answers to these important questions in our next chapter.

8

Wisdom and Her Disciples

THE GOSPEL OF MATTHEW records an important saying of Jesus where he summons his disciples to come to him, take his yoke, learn from him, and experience the rest that he offers: "Come to me, all who are weary and heavy-laden, and I will give you rest. Take my yoke upon you and learn from me, for I am gentle and humble in heart, and you will find rest for your souls. For My yoke is easy and My burden is light" (Matt 11:28–30). Specialists of Matthew's Gospel regularly point out that this saying bears a remarkable similarity to a passage describing Lady Wisdom in the book of Sirach.[1] In Sir 51:19–28 we observe the sage personifying the wisdom of God and describing his pursuit of her. In doing so, he records the summons to draw near to her and learn from her: "Come near to me, you who are not instructed, and lodge in the house of instruction" (Sir 51:23). The one who acquires Lady Wisdom places their neck under her instructive yoke and accepts her teaching, resulting in the promise of much rest (51:25–27). The passage brings the book of Sirach to a close by issuing forth an invitation to its readers to become disciples of personified wisdom. Matthew picks up this motif and incorporates it into his biography of Jesus, specifically by illustrating Jesus as wisdom's incarnation who invites disciples to come, learn from him, take upon his yoke, and find rest.

If early Christians remembered Jesus as embodying Wisdom's invitation to disciples, is it possible that the Fourth Gospel portrays a similar

---

1. See further in Suggs, *Wisdom, Christology, and Law*, 77–83; Deutsch, *Lady Wisdom*, 57–60; Wainwright, *Shall We Look*, 79–83.

relationship between Jesus and his followers? This chapter will explore the bond and its dynamics between Jesus and the disciples within the Gospel of John. Our aim is to ascertain to what degree, if any, the relationship Jesus has with his followers is influenced by earlier descriptions of the wisdom of God by the Jewish sages. Our search will begin with an exploration of the manner in which Jesus gathers his disciples into a community. Next, I will look closely at the individual stories of several noteworthy women in the Fourth Gospel to see if they exhibit inspiration from Jewish wisdom literature. The act of love characterizes and defines the close connection between disciple and teacher in the Gospel of John, so this offers another avenue of exploration for our study. Once the disciples of the Johannine Jesus are initiated, they become "friends" in a manner that echoes back to similar portrayals of Lady Wisdom and her wise followers. This close-knit connection gains a further factor of intimacy with the verb "abide," which often appears in the Fourth Gospel, offering another opportunity to study possible wisdom influences. Last, Jesus explains to his disciples that he is going away and the Spirit will come to empower, guide, and convict. Since we have observed a close connection between the wisdom of God and the Spirit in Jewish wisdom literature,[2] I will take advantage of this opportunity to explore potential lines of impact. Since the Gospel of John provides a lot of data pertaining to the relationship between Jesus and his disciples, this chapter's aim has the capacity to unearth noteworthy developments in our overall study of Wisdom Christology.

WISDOM INVITES DISCIPLES INTO A COMMUNITY

Of the four New Testament gospel accounts, the Gospel of John dedicates the most attention to private discourses between Jesus and his disciples. Five chapters (13–17) reflect the nonpublic exchanges during a period shortly before the Feast of Passover. As I have demonstrated with many of the key motifs in the Fourth Gospel, the Prologue sets forth the expectation for what is elaborated in the larger narrative. John 1:12–13 indicates that Jesus bestowed the privileges to be children of God upon those disciples who received him. The passage clarifies the nature of Jesus' followers as those who believe in his name, resulting in a new birth from God. These believers demonstrate their ongoing commitment and

---

2. See chapter 2.

fidelity to Jesus, as the present participle "believe" indicates. Since the concluding remark and purpose statement of the Fourth Gospel similarly portrays the ideal readers as those who believe, resulting in life in Jesus' name (20:31), we can confidently assume that the relationship between the Johannine Jesus and the disciples is to be of noteworthy significance within the wider narrative.

Our hypothesis begins to find fruit in the episode that immediately follows the Prologue, where Jesus' first actions involve the issuing forth of invitations for several to join him as disciples. Andrew and an unnamed disciple of the Baptist are the first to "follow" Jesus (1:37), a move that both transitions them to the instruction of a new teacher as well as begins the journey of a follower.[3] After addressing Jesus as "Rabbi" (a term that the narrator clarifies for the reader as meaning "Teacher"), they request to know where Jesus is staying. Jesus responds with a summons to come and see, an invitation that the two disciples immediately obey (1:38–39).[4] On the following day, Jesus finds Philip and subsequently invites him to become a follower. After accepting Jesus' call, Philip recruits Nathaniel with the words "Come and see." Eventually, Nathaniel too begins to address Jesus with a trio of titles, the first of which is "Rabbi," underscoring his role as a disciple of Jesus the teacher (1:43–49).[5] The passage concludes when Jesus indicates to both Nathaniel and the readers that they will indeed see him function as the revelatory Son of Man, who bridges heaven and earth (1:51). As the narrative of the Fourth Gospel begins, Jesus wastes no time gathering disciples into a community of lifelong learners.

The Parable of the Good Shepherd offers further insight into the community of disciples that the Johannine Jesus is forming. Jesus positions himself in the parable as the leading shepherd while illustrating the disciples as his sheep (10:1–3). As the shepherding guide of the sheep, he calls them by name (10:3); leads them in word and actions (10:4); and promises salvation, pasture (10:9), and abundant life (10:10). By promising to lay down his life for the disciples, Jesus demonstrates his full-fledged commitment to their well-being (10:15). The behavior exhibited

---

3. Brown, *John I-XII*, 78; Keener, *Gospel of John*, 1:467–68; Schnackenburg, *John*, 1:308.

4. Witherington, *John's Wisdom*, 70, observes here a parallel between Jesus' invitation to "Come and see" and Lady Wisdom's invitation in Prov 8; Wis 6; Sir 51:23, 25–27.

5. Coloe, *John 1-10*, 44, probes the text to see if the disciples are overlooking the identity of Wisdom who has taken the initiative to reveal herself.

by the sheep accentuates their attitude of discipleship; they listen to and obey Jesus' voice (10:3, 16), they follow to where he leads (10:3-4), and they recognize him (10:4). The relationship between Jesus and disciples articulated in the Good Shepherd Parable is deeply intimate, bearing the marks of self-sacrificial love on the part of the teacher of the sheep.[6]

The most intimate interaction between the community of disciples and Jesus occurs in the Farewell Discourse (13:31—17:26). This is the most heavily concentrated area of Jesus' private communication with his followers among all the New Testament gospels. This discourse is highlighted by several markers of personal instruction to the disciples that are not present in the public discourses in the Book of Signs (John 1-12). As the teaching rabbi, the Johannine Jesus begins to address his students as little children (13:33; see 1:12). He redefines his community in terms of possessing and enacting love for one another—a love that he models for them (13:33-35; 15:12-13). His followers are to demonstrate their loving fidelity to him by keeping his instructions (14:15, 23; 15:14). Jesus promises to reciprocate their love by loving and disclosing himself further to them (14:21-23). Furthermore, he offers his community peace (14:27), friendship (15:13-15), and the promise of joy to comfort grief (16:20-22).[7] As the authorized revealer of the Father, Jesus repeatedly discloses heavenly instructions to his disciples. He manifests to them the true God's name; the God-given authority given to Jesus; and God's commands, protection, and gospel (17:6-14). Jesus prays that the Father would set apart the community of disciples in holiness—a sanctifying act defined by Jesus' evangelistic word (17:17, 19). Finally, Jesus bestows his God-given glory to his followers in order that they might experience the same oneness of purpose that Jesus and God possess (17:22; cf. 10:30). Those who accept the summons to follow the Johannine Jesus enter into a close-knit community and come to encounter the benefits of the Jewish teacher in whom Wisdom has made her abode.[8]

The representation of Jesus creating a community of disciples within the Gospel of John shows several marks of impact from Jewish texts where Lady Wisdom gathers to herself a group of followers who are

---

6. Keener, *John*, 1:805-6.

7. Charlesworth, "Lady Wisdom," 111, demonstrates that the Johannine Jesus brings joy because its Christology has been shaped by the wisdom traditions.

8. Jesus also addresses his disciples as "children" in 21:5. On the possible influences of Jewish wisdom texts on the reference to children in John 21:5, see Coloe, *John 11-21*, 540-41.

eager to learn from her wise instruction. In the book of Proverbs, personified wisdom enters the public arena, offers an invitation to potential disciples, makes known her instructions, and promises a life of security (Prov 1:20-28). Raymond Brown and Richard Dillon have argued that this passage served as the inspiration for the public interaction of Jesus and the disciples in John 1:35-43.[9] A similar account of Lady Wisdom issuing her summons to potential followers occurs in Prov 9:1-6. This passage describes Wisdom's invitation to the uninstructed to come into her house, share an intimate meal, and become discipled in the path of understanding. The narrative's description of the disciples requesting to know where Jesus is staying contains two features of the portrayal of Wisdom in Prov 9:1-6: the recognition that Wisdom has a place of dwelling and that she desires disciples to join her in her abode.[10] Aiden O'Boyle suggests that the illustration of Wisdom seeking those worthy of her by appearing to them on their paths (Wis 6:16) functions as a direct parallel to Jesus seeing Nathaniel and praising him for his virtuous behavior (John 1:47).[11] The author of Sirach further develops on the theme of personified wisdom inviting disciples into the community. The sage describes his followers as children during the offering of education (Sir 2:1; 3:1-2, 17; 4:1; cf. John 13:33).[12] Similarly, personified wisdom takes the role as the teacher who instructs and helps her children: "Wisdom teaches her children and gives help to those who are seeking after her" (Sir 4:11). The child who chooses a disciple's training will surely find Wisdom, whether they are of old age or are a youth (6:18).[13] Although she has won the favor of every people and nation (24:6), Lady Wisdom makes her dwelling in Israel among the honored people (24:8-12). In doing so, she offers her invitation to potential disciples: "Come to me..." (Sir 24:19; cf. John 1:39, 46). We already drew attention to the conclusion of Sirach (51:19-28), where the sage invites the uneducated to come, enter her house, take upon her yoke, hear and learn instruction, and ultimately find rest.[14] While the Gospel of Matthew drew on Sirach's portrayal of

---

9. Brown, *John I-XII*, 79; Dillon, "Wisdom Tradition," 281-82.

10. See especially McHugh, *John 1-4*, 151-53.

11. O'Boyle, *Wisdom Christology*, 178.

12. Brown, *Introduction to the Gospel of John*, 262.

13. Witherington, *Jesus the Sage*, 378-79.

14. Witherington, *John's Wisdom*, 64, draws attention to Sir 51:23 as directly influencing John 1:19-34: "The Fourth Evangelist is also interested in portraying Jesus as a sage and Wisdom, and by definition potential disciples of Jewish sages were expected

Wisdom in order to illustrate Jesus as Wisdom inviting disciples to come and learn, we have observed that the Johannine Jesus embodies this motif far more extensively.

Baruch provides a comparable connection between the wisdom of God and the invitation to heed her instruction. The poet bids Israel to listen to the commandments leading to life and to learn wisdom/prudence[15] (Bar 3:9). By rebuking the generation of the Babylonian exile, the author implicitly indicates the sort of behavior the readers should adopt. Rather than forsaking the fountain of wisdom, Israel should drink from her wise instructions (3:12–13). If one functions as a disciple and "learns" the place of wisdom, then they will be able to "discern" where there is life, light, and peace (3:14)—all of which the Johannine Jesus promised to his followers. Without wisdom, the people do not possess life and subsequently perish (3:28). The Creator God has bestowed his wisdom upon the people of Israel, but they must choose to come to her and hold her fast (3:32—4:4). By describing the appropriate response to the life that personified wisdom offers in terms of learning, discerning, and coming to her, the poetic author of Baruch contributes to the motif of the community of disciples that significantly impacted the depiction of Jesus in the Gospel of John.

This motif finds additional support in the portrayal of wise disciples within Wisdom of Solomon. The sage encourages potential followers of Lady Wisdom by indicating that they can easily discern and find her. Those who seek her show the intensity of their pursuit by loving her. In fact, she rushes to present herself to those who desire to learn from her. She meets those who seek after her as they are walking along their paths (6:12–16). It seems likely that this way of thinking about Wisdom and those who are interested in learning from her is the foundation for the story of Jesus meeting his first disciples in John 1:35–51.[16] The two disciples of John the Baptist quite easily recognize Jesus and follow him. To some, Jesus meets them where they are, like Philip. Personified wisdom takes the role of a teacher and intimately interacts with holy persons in every generation, resulting in a newfound relationship with God (Wis

---

to seek the sage and seek out Wisdom."

15. Saldarini, "Book of Baruch," 961, suggests that while Baruch uses four different words for wisdom in Greek, they effectively possess overlapping meanings. The NRSV helpfully translates all four of these words as "wisdom."

16. Brown, *John I–XII*, 79, also draws attention to the parallels between the disciples and Wis 6:12–13, 16.

7:22, 27; cf. John 15:13–15). God responds to this close-knit community of disciples of Wisdom by expressing his love for such a relationship: "God loves nothing so much as the person who lives with Wisdom" (Wis 7:28). Since the Creator God formed humanity through the creative agency of personified wisdom (9:2), it is not surprising that she seeks to establish a loving community with those who desire to learn from her. The author offers several instances within the history of Israel where Wisdom has deeply pursued human beings. She protected, delivered, and strengthened Adam (10:1–2), directed Noah to the wood needed to build the ark, resulting in the earth's salvation (10:4), and preserved Abraham's blamelessness (10:5). Lady Wisdom additionally pursued loving and protective relationships with Lot, Jacob, Joseph, and the generation of the exodus from Egypt by working through the hand of Moses (10:6—11:1).[17] The Fourth Gospel demonstrates its dependence on the motif of Wisdom seeking a community of followers by repeatedly characterizing Jesus as Lady Wisdom's incarnation who gathers and tutors a close-knit group of disciples eagerly desiring to learn from Wisdom's instruction.[18]

WISDOM MINISTERS TO WOMEN

A unique feature of the Fourth Gospel is the lengthy discourses between Jesus and several women. Women play a key role within the narrative of the Gospel of John as they each help further the book's aim of presenting Jesus as the Christ, the unique son of God.[19] Mary, the mother of Jesus, plays a pivotal role at the wedding in Cana. The Samaritan woman openly confesses Jesus to be the promised Messiah before she shares this good news with her kinfolk. The sisters Mary and Martha play a dominant role in Jesus' journey to resurrect their brother Lazarus. This same Mary later anoints Jesus with a costly perfume during a dinner meal. At the cross, several women, including Jesus' mother, remain while most of the disciples have fled. Finally, Mary Magdalene is the first to witness the resurrected Jesus, even before Peter and the Beloved Disciple. We have already observed that personified wisdom in Proverbs associates with

---

17. Coloe, *John 1–10*, 46–47, detects the influence of Lady Wisdom revealing heavenly secrets to Jacob (Wis 10:10) in Jesus' response to Nathaniel wherein he would see greater things from the Son of Man (John 1:51).

18. Johnson, "Jesus, the Wisdom of God," 285; Witherington, *Jesus the Sage*, 374.

19. Schüssler Fiorenza, *In Memory of Her*, 333, describes these women as "paradigms of women's apostolic discipleship."

female servants in her attempt to interact with God's creation (Prov 9:1–6; 31:10–31). It would be prudent for our study to examine the various discourses that focus on how these women interact with Jesus to ascertain in what way, if any, they exhibit influences of the Jewish wisdom texts.[20]

The Mother of Jesus in Cana

The first of Jesus' seven signs within the Gospel of John occurs at the wedding in Cana (2:1–11). In this story, the main characters are Jesus and his mother. Jesus' disciples and the wedding participants are minor background characters, while Mary takes the dominant role opposite Jesus.[21] As soon as the supply of wine runs out, her first action is to bring the matter to Jesus' attention. Jesus responds by asking her why the lack of wine should involve the two of them, asserting in the process that his climactic hour has not yet come. This short interaction between Mary and Jesus strongly suggests that she anticipated a particular response from him, resulting in the answer with which Jesus replied.[22] In turn, Mary commands the wedding servants to obey anything that Jesus tells them to do. The story continues with Jesus giving specific instructions, leading to the miracle of the water turning into an abundance of good wine, the first of Jesus' signs. The narrator indicates that the disciples expressed belief in him after the miraculous sign took place, but the mother of Jesus seems to indicate her belief in Jesus' ability to intervene and supply the wine prior to the act occurring.[23]

Within Jesus' interaction with his mother, we detect some noteworthy influences of personified wisdom's activity from Jewish wisdom literature.[24] We have observed that Wisdom is characterized as having female disciples in the context of a proverb where Wisdom prepares her own wine (Prov 9:2–3). Lady Wisdom sends forth her maidens, and it is fair to assume that they function as delegated agents carrying forth her agenda. Wisdom offers a hospitable invitation that specifically includes

---

20. I am deeply indebted to the insights of Martin Scott in this section of my argument. See his *Sophia*, ch. 4.

21. The narrator makes sure to note the presence of Jesus in the opening sentence of the discourse: "The mother of Jesus was there" (2:1).

22. O'Day, "Gospel of John," 536; Coloe, *John 1–10*, 55.

23. Keener, *John*, 1:509.

24. Dillon, "Wisdom Tradition," 286–95; Brown, *John I–XII*, 106–7.

a summons to drink of the wine that she has mixed.²⁵ The author of the Fourth Gospel carefully notes that it is precisely when the wine ran out that Mary spoke of the incident to Jesus. Since the Johannine Jesus is the embodiment of Lady Wisdom—the mixer of wine—Jesus would certainly be able to produce more.²⁶ The overwhelming amount of wine Jesus produces further reflects the impact of traditions surrounding Lady Wisdom's lavish provision.²⁷ Mary knew exactly who Jesus was, joining the likes of John the Baptist and Nathaniel, who recognized Jesus prior to him personally interacting or speaking with them. Since the ideal disciple is one who believes in Jesus *before* witnessing miraculous signs (John 20:29), Mary distinguishes herself from the disciples present at the wedding, who only express their belief *after* the sign takes place. Mary effectively functions as a disciple/maiden of Wisdom who expresses her faith in Jesus as incarnate Wisdom, the mixer and provider of wine. By recognizing the impact of personified wisdom traditions upon the story of the wedding at Cana, we can grasp the key role that the author gives to Mary, an ideal Johannine disciple.²⁸

The Woman at the Well

The second notable story involving Jesus and women is the Samaritan Woman Discourse (4:1–42). Although other characters are present at various times during this story (the disciples and the Samaritans living in Sychar), the woman takes center stage alongside the Johannine Jesus. Upon arriving at Jacob's Well, Jesus requests a drink of water from the unnamed woman. As the two discuss the topic of Jewish-Samaritan relations, Jesus shifts the conversation to talk about "living water" that leads to the life of the age to come. Eventually, the Samaritan woman comes to realize that Jesus is no ordinary Jewish traveler but he is the promised Messiah, the Christ. She returns to the city and shares her experience

---

25. Prov 9:5; cf. Sir 24:21; Lee, *Symbolic Narratives*, 36. Witherington, *John's Wisdom*, 76, brilliantly notes that Jesus provides a better wine than what appears in Prov 9:5 because Jesus' wine is not mixed with water. The superior wine that Wisdom incarnate provides is indicative of the superabundance that Wisdom regularly offers in the Fourth Gospel.

26. McHugh, *John 1–4*, 196; Dillon, "Wisdom Tradition," 287–88; Schüssler Fiorenza, *Jesus*, 167; Johnson, "Jesus, the Wisdom of God," 284; Ringe, *Wisdom's Friends*, 60.

27. Sir 1:16; 6:19; 24:19–21; Wis 7:11, 14. McHugh, *John 1–4*, 192–96, offers evidence from the OT, Sirach, and Philo that associates wisdom with wine.

28. Schüssler Fiorenza, *In Memory of Her*, 327.

about Jesus with the locals, effectively becoming the first female Christian preacher.[29] While she is away, Jesus' disciples enter the scene, resulting in a brief conversation about food and the fields that are ripe for harvest. The story concludes with the woman's testimony leading many Samaritans to place their faith in Jesus and invite him to stay a few days with them. The Samaritan woman's encounter with Jesus is the catalyst to salvation coming to members of her community.[30]

The exchange between the Johannine Jesus and the Samaritan woman exhibits several points of impact from the Jewish wisdom sources. First, the emphasis on Jesus deliberately choosing to sit by the well belonging to the famous patriarch Jacob suggests an allusion to Sir 24:7–9, where personified wisdom seeks a resting place for herself, resulting in the Creator commanding her to make her dwelling in Jacob. The author of Baruch paints a similar picture with Wisdom appearing on earth to live among humanity—specifically among Jacob (3:36–37). Moreover, God commands Jacob to take hold of Wisdom and walk toward her light (4:2). Wisdom of Solomon retells various stories of Jacob by interweaving the steadfast influence of the wisdom of God (10:10–12). Readers of the Gospel of John familiar with these traditions that associate Lady Wisdom with Jacob would expect the narrative to display similar behavior from Jesus—Wisdom's embodiment—as he approaches Jacob's well. Jesus' offer to the Samaritan woman to grant her living water recalls the portrayal of God's wisdom as the giver of water.[31] We observed in chapter 4 several examples within the Jewish wisdom literature where the sages characterize the wisdom of God in terms of water, fountains, springs, rivers, and streams.[32] Philo offers some allegorical readings of encounters at a well within the Hebrew Bible that may illuminate the Samaritan Woman Discourse. For example, when Rebecca, Jacob's mother, fills her ewer from a well, Philo interprets the water as "divine Wisdom from whom all the particular sciences are irrigated."[33] He repeats this characterization of the water that Jacob's mother retrieves from the well as Lady Wisdom.[34]

---

29. Bailey, *Middle Eastern Eyes*, 212; Meyers et al., *Women in Scripture*, 454.

30. Keener, *John*, 1:626.

31. Sanford, *Mystical Christianity*, 108–10; Von Wahlde, *John*, 1:414.

32. McHugh, *John 1–4*, 272, draws attention specifically to Sir 24:21 ("the wise person's ever-increasing thirst for more wisdom") when interpreting Jesus' offer of water that leads to eternal life.

33. *Fug.* 195; *Post.* 136.

34. *QG* 4.98, 101, 107; Scott, *Sophia*, 188.

When Philo offers forth an allegorical interpretation of the well in Num 21:18, he argues that the well symbolizes none other than Wisdom.[35] The discussion over the water that leads to the life of the age to come brings the Samaritan woman to a place where she acknowledges Jesus as the Messiah. Her confession and realization that this traveling Jew is the promised Christ leads her back to the city in order to share the news with the locals. Those readers who were familiar with Sir 24:30–34, where the sage depicts Wisdom as a growing body of water who pours out her teaching for all future generations who seek after her, would recognize the passage's influence upon the Samaritan woman's behavior. She recognizes Jesus as the embodiment of wisdom, she accepts his invitation to take of wisdom's living water, and she shares this knowledge with others, many of whom come to faith in Jesus.[36] His discussion with the disciples about the ready harvest finds fulfillment in the woman's act of bringing salvation to her fellow Samaritans.[37] Not surprisingly, the actions of Jesus and the Samaritan woman evoke Sir 24:26, where Wisdom runs over like the Euphrates and like the Jordan at harvest time.[38] The Samaritan city is the harvest that came as a result of Wisdom incarnate's actions that overflowed from the encounter at the well. The behavior of the unnamed woman within the story is exemplary, befitting a maiden of Lady Wisdom who goes forth and summons others to partake of the life that Wisdom has prepared (Prov 9:3–6).[39] James McGrath has persuasively argued that the popular conception that the Samaritan woman is a sinful and shady person[40] is a misreading of the story, and that her background is circumstantially tragic but not immoral.[41] In fact, the Johannine Jesus, in whom the Wisdom of God has become incarnate, breaks down multiple cultural barriers with this encounter, since some traditions portray Wisdom in terms of the law of Moses, which acts harshly toward women (Sir 42:14) and toward the Samaritan people (Sir 50:25–26). Within the narrative of the Fourth Gospel, the Samaritan woman contributes to the positive

---

35. *Ebr.* 112–13; McHugh, *John 1–4*, 277.
36. Scott, *Sophia*, 189.
37. O'Day, "Gospel of John," 570; Coloe, *John 1–10*, 123.
38. Coloe, *John 1–10*, 126.
39. Thomas Aquinas, *John 1–5*, 230; Witherington, *John's Wisdom*, 119.
40. Scott, *Sophia*, 191–92.
41. McGrath, *What Jesus Learned*, 70–86. McGrath rightly comments that it is "extremely irresponsible as well as profoundly unkind to take a woman's tragic life experiences and recast them as instead hinting at immoral actions on her part" (76).

portrayal of women by accepting the gift of God's wisdom and sharing that wisdom with others, resulting in many coming to faith.[42]

Martha, the Sister of Lazarus

The third story involving Jesus and women occurs in John 11:1–44. This discourse details how Jesus interacts with Martha and Mary of Bethany as he travels to resurrect their brother Lazarus from the dead. The story begins with Martha and Mary taking the initiative to send word to Jesus, letting him know that their brother is sick. The narrator impresses upon the reader that Jesus loved the three siblings (11:3, 5, 36), suggesting that Jesus possessed a deeper, more close-knit relationship with them than with others. These are the first times that the Fourth Gospel portrays Jesus as the subject showing love, a feat that does not occur anywhere else in the Book of Signs. After hearing that Lazarus has fallen asleep in death, Jesus travels to Bethany and Martha meets him along the way. He reassures her that Lazarus will rise again, to which she confesses her belief that he will rise on the last day, at the resurrection. In response to this confession, Jesus claims to personally be the locus of God's life-giving purposes: "I am the resurrection and the life" (11:25). When Jesus questions Martha as to whether she believes he can function in this role, she responds with an affirmation and a climactic confession of faith that mirrors the intended purpose of the entire book (11:27; see 20:31).[43] Eventually, Mary finds Jesus and expresses her faith that her brother would still be alive if Jesus had been present. After acknowledging her belief in Jesus as the agent of God's life-giving functions, she is moved to tears. The story concludes with Jesus raising Lazarus back to life, resulting in several witnesses coming to faith as well as demonstrating that Jesus authoritatively bears God's prerogative of life-giver. Although the sisters Mary and Martha stand out in this discourse as prominent disciples exhibiting faith in the Johannine Jesus, Martha plays the larger of the two roles. Mary will reappear shortly in the narrative (12:1–8) and take the position of the leading protagonist there.

Having been alerted to Wisdom motifs in the two previous encounters between Jesus and women within the Gospel of John, it would be

---

42. Ringe, *Wisdom's Friends*, 60.

43. Schneiders, *That You May Believe*, 179; Schüssler Fiorenza, *In Memory of Her*, 329; O'Day, "Gospel of John," 688–89.

prudent for us to examine the possibility of similar themes in the Lazarus Discourse, especially considering the presence of multiple noteworthy women. Within the Lazarus Discourse, two notable emphases appear to exhibit the influence of Jewish wisdom texts: the prominence of Jesus' love toward the three and the life-giving prerogative that Jesus exercises.[44] Since Mary, Martha, and Lazarus are the first to function as objects of explicit statements where Jesus shows love within the Fourth Gospel, it seems that the author wished to portray them as prominent members of the disciples. The Jewish sages also emphasized the love that Wisdom shows to her disciples. In the book of Proverbs, personified wisdom speaks in the first person to convey her feelings toward her followers: "I love those who love me" (8:17). The Greek translator of Prov 8:17 utilized two different verbs for "love" (*agapao* and *phileo*), and it is striking that the author of the Fourth Gospel uses these same two verbs when illustrating Jesus' love for the three siblings. According to Sirach, God loves those who love Wisdom (Sir 4:14), a sentiment that also appears in Wisdom of Solomon 7:28. When Sirach describes Lady Wisdom's descent to earth in order to live among humanity, he is careful to note how she resides in a city that she loves (24:11). Furthermore, the disciples of Wisdom who reciprocate her love also love life (Sir 4:12), a statement that connects the two themes that we find in the Lazarus Discourse: love and life.[45] We have already observed that the claim to be "the resurrection and the life" borrows from several texts in the Jewish wisdom literature that associate personified wisdom with the motif of life. In particular, Prov 8:35 promises that one who finds Lady Wisdom finds life, and the key detail that both Martha (John 11:20) and Mary (John 11:29) took the initiative to come out to meet Jesus as he approached to raise Lazarus back to life suggests an intentional echo. Proverbs 9:1–6 illustrates Wisdom's invitation to follow her path, which results in life, and she sends forth her disciples (maidens) to assist in this summons. Martha plays the role of Wisdom's maiden by informing Mary of Jesus' invitation. After Jesus gives life to the deceased Lazarus, many witnesses of the miracle put their faith in Jesus. In a sense, the scholarly description of this story as the "Lazarus Discourse" leaves out the two leading women, whose interaction with Jesus presents some noticeably obvious signs of impact from the Jewish portrayals of personified wisdom. Jesus, as the embodiment of Wisdom,

---

44. Scott, *Sophia*, 199–202.

45. Thomas Aquinas, *John 1–5*, 303, argues that Sir 4:14 directly influences the Wisdom Christology of the Johannine Jesus—the giver of life.

shares his love with Martha, Mary, and Lazarus by functioning as the empowered agent of God's life-giving purposes.

Mary, the Sister of Lazarus

The fourth key encounter between Jesus and women in the Fourth Gospel appears in John 12:1–8, where Mary of Bethany, Martha's sister, anoints his feet. Coincidently, the narrator anticipates this story before it takes place by illustrating Mary at the beginning of the Lazarus Discourse as the one who anointed the Lord with ointment and wiped his feet with her hair (11:1–2). No other woman within the Gospel of John gets this heightened treatment, and it serves to draw attention to the significance of her service to the Johannine Jesus. Within the story itself, the three siblings are present at their home six days prior to the Passover. They make supper for Jesus, and they each participate in their own way. Martha serves during the meal, Lazarus reclines at the table with Jesus, but Mary initiates an intimate act of foot-washing. By letting her hair down and anointing Jesus' feet with expensive perfume—an act resulting in the smell of the perfume permeating the entire house—she demonstrates her commitment as a disciple.[46] In fact, the initiative that Mary takes to wash Jesus' feet prior to Jesus commanding his disciples that they should perform foot-washing (13:14–15) further highlights her status as an outstanding disciple.[47]

Having taken note of the impact of several texts describing Lady Wisdom upon the portrayals of Martha and Mary in the Lazarus Discourse, it seems reasonable to hypothesize a similar influence in the story of Mary's foot-washing. The biggest detail in Mary's encounter with Jesus is the attention the narrator gives to the perfume and its value. After describing the perfume of pure nard as costly (12:3), the narrator gives even more attention to how its cost provoked greed in Judas Iscariot (12:4–6). Mary did not simply perform a loving deed of foot-washing for Jesus; she served him with a luxurious perfume with a value that those present openly recognized and discussed (12:7–8). This emphasis on the costly commitment on the part of Mary's discipleship recalls images of those who wholeheartedly pursue personified wisdom, particularly due to her worth. For example, in Prov 3:13–15 the sage pronounces a blessing on

---

46. O'Day, "Gospel of John," 702.

47. Culpepper, *Gospel*, 202–3; Coloe, *John 11–21*, 338.

the person who finds Wisdom because her value is greater than silver, gold, and jewels. In fact, nothing can compare to her immeasurable worth, a sentiment that reappears frequently in Proverbs (8:10–11; 16:16; 23:23). The disciple of Wisdom is to love, acquire, and prize her because of her importance (4:6–8). Those who long for her and her oracles express their commitment by watching at her gates every day (8:34). When personified wisdom becomes incarnate in the Woman of Substance, the sage illustrates her first characteristic as more costly than jewels (31:10). Mary demonstrates no hesitancy in expending a perfume worth nearly a year's wages as she serves at the feet of Jesus because Jesus—the embodiment of Wisdom—possesses immeasurable worth. The contrast between, on one hand, Mary's discipleship and acknowledgment of Wisdom's worth, and, on the other, Judas's compromised discipleship and failure to comprehend Jesus as Wisdom further underscores the value that the Gospel of John places upon the maidens of Wisdom (Prov 9:3).

The Mother of Jesus at the Cross

We may observe the fifth exchange between the Johannine Jesus and women at a scene of his crucifixion (19:25–27). After the soldiers divide Jesus' outer garments, we witness his interaction with several women and the Beloved Disciple. The women who are present at the cross are Jesus' mother, his mother's sister, Mary the wife of Clopas, and Mary Magdalene. Although there is some uncertainty concerning how we should number these women, particularly in whether the sister of Jesus' mother is distinguished from or identified as the wife of Clopas, we observe a noticeable absence of male disciples from this scene.[48] However we count the number of women present, the narrator seems to highlight one in particular—the mother of Jesus. When Jesus notices his mother and the Beloved Disciple nearby, he informs her of her new familial relationship: "Behold, your son."[49] Similarly, Jesus speaks to the disciple whom he loves and announces his role in this new relationship with Jesus' mother: "Behold, your mother."[50] As the eldest son, Jesus would bear the primary responsibility of caring for and attending to his mother (on the assumption

---

48. John 16:32 indicates that the disciples would be scattered, and this seems to be the case at the cross, with the noticeable exception of the Beloved Disciple.

49. O'Day, "Gospel of John," 832. Brown, *Death of the Messiah*, 2:1020–21, draws attention to Jesus' role as the revealer as he announces the new relationship with "Behold."

50. Coloe, *John 11–21*, 489.

that her husband Joseph is no longer alive). Aware of his looming death, Jesus entrusts his responsibility of looking after his mother to the Beloved Disciple, since Jesus' brothers were not believers (7:5).[51] In doing so, he demonstrates his faithful commitment to her, likely reciprocating the faithfulness that she exhibits toward him by remaining close to the cross while most of the other disciples have fled. The rejected Jesus nevertheless remains faithful toward his followers, tending to their needs in lieu of his impending departure.

We have already taken note of Mary the mother of Jesus at the wedding in Cana, where we discerned key themes in the story indicating her awareness of Jesus as the incarnation of personified wisdom. Are there any additional influences from the Jewish wisdom literature that we may detect in the encounter at the cross? Two particular elements of this story emerge as presenting ties to former descriptions of Lady Wisdom. The first theme is the family language that the Johannine Jesus uses to define the Beloved Disciple and Mary. The sages who composed the wisdom books quite regularly employed familial terms to characterize those who either learn or impart to others the instructions of wisdom.[52] The father's instruction to his son that is faithfully carried out is likened to wisdom and discretion (Prov 1:8-9; 3:21-22). Disciples of Wisdom's teachings are identified more than a dozen times in the book of Proverbs with the reference "my son,"[53] and more generally as "child" or "children" in more than twenty instances within the book of Sirach.[54] Furthermore, it is a mother or father who passes along these wise teachings (Prov 1:8; 6:20). Lady Wisdom herself even takes the familial role of a mother and parent in several Jewish texts, suggesting that her disciples are children.[55] Since Mary has already distinguished herself as a maiden of Wisdom at the wedding at Cana, and since the Beloved Disciple contributed to the Fourth Gospel's Christology, it makes sense that these two disciples are worthy of participating in the family defined around personified wisdom and her teachings.[56]

---

51. Keener, *John*, 2:1145.

52. Scott, *Sophia*, 221-22.

53. E.g., Prov 1:8, 10, 15; 2:1; 3:1, 11, 21; 4:10, 20; 5:1, 20; 6:1, 3; 7:1.

54. Sir 2:1; 3:1, 12, 17; 4:1; 6:18, 23, 32; 10:28; 11:10; 14:11; 16:24; 18:15; 21:1; 23:7; 31:22; 37:27; 38:9, 16; 40:28; 41:6, 14.

55. Sir 15:2; Wis 7:12; *Fug.* 109; *Det.* 54; *Ebr.* 30-31.

56. Witherington, *John's Wisdom*, 238, detects a subtle clue at the first appearance of the Beloved Disciple, who reclines on the bosom of Jesus (13:23). This reference,

The second connection between the women at the cross and wisdom themes is the sheer faithfulness and commitment they demonstrate by remaining with Jesus during the last moments of his life. While most of the disciples have fled, these women exhibit the loyalty that characterizes disciples of Wisdom. Those who acquire the Wisdom of God are encouraged not to forsake her and to show her love. To these, Wisdom promises to guard and watch over them (Prov 4:5-6). Ben Sira shows his dependence upon Proverbs in offering a similar promise: "If they remain faithful, they will inherit her, and their descendants will obtain her" (Sir 4:12-16). Sirach reiterates this assurance later by guaranteeing that the one who leans on Wisdom and relies on her will not fall and will not be put to shame (15:4). The reciprocating faithfulness that Lady Wisdom shows to those who are faithful to her is precisely what we see at the foot of the cross, particularly with Jesus' mother and implicitly with Mary Magdalene, whose personal story we will give attention to shortly. The appearance of the loyal women at the scene of Jesus' crucifixion in addition to the ensuing bestowal of a new family status further highlight the Fourth Gospel's Wisdom Christology.

Mary Magdalene, Witness of the Resurrection

The sixth and final scene in which the narrative focuses on women occurs after the resurrection (John 20:1-18). Mary Magdalene, who was present at the foot of the cross along with Jesus' mother, takes center stage in this story. Mary arrives at the tomb incredibly early on Sunday morning, and after noticing that the stone has been moved, she hastily departs to inform Peter and the Beloved Disciple that the tomb is empty. After these two examine the tomb for themselves and depart for their own homes, Mary remains at the tomb, quite saddened. When she peers into the tomb, she discovers two angels, who ask her, "Why are you weeping?"[57] Mary soon turns to encounter the risen Jesus behind her, thinking that he is a gardener. Jesus repeats the question posed by the two angels and follows

---

Witherington suggests, alludes to John 1:18 where Jesus as Wisdom is in the bosom of the Father and is the one who makes the Father known. The Beloved Disciple similarly makes Wisdom incarnate known in the Fourth Gospel.

57. Coloe, *John 11-21*, 512, offers a rich interpretation where the position of the two angels would recall the two cherubim on top of the ark of the covenant that was placed in the holy of holies. This suggests, Coloe argues, that Mary, who entered the tomb, is functioning as the high priest who enters the holy of holies, thereby allowing Mary to assume a priestly role.

up with an additional question: "Whom are you seeking?" (20:15). Upon hearing Jesus address Mary by name, she immediately recognizes him and addresses him as "Rabboni," an endearing way to address the teacher (20:16).[58] Jesus requests from her that she refrain from touching him. Instead, she should go to Jesus' brethren and announce his resurrection to them (20:17). With Mary arriving first to the tomb and being the first to see the risen Jesus, she underscores her status as a premier disciple, even among the likes of Peter and the Beloved Disciple.

Mary Magdalene's interaction with the Johannine Jesus offers some clear echoes of ways in which the sages characterized Lady Wisdom. The most notable indication is the motif of seeking Wisdom that Mary illustrates in this account. She takes the initiative to arrive early at the tomb before any of the other disciples, who only come to know about the empty tomb because Mary runs to inform them. She remains alone at the tomb when Peter and the Beloved Disciple leave. The additional question that Jesus asks makes clear what Mary has been doing—*seeking*. Personified wisdom has promised that "those who diligently seek me will find me" (Prov 8:17), and this is precisely what takes place with Mary.[59] We have already observed the theme of Wisdom's inaccessibility for those who refuse to believe,[60] but Mary was one of the few of the faithful who stayed with Jesus during his last moments of life on the cross. While the Johannine Jesus embodies the hiddenness of Wisdom to many, he reveals himself to Mary first because she is seeking Wisdom, just as Ben Sirach illustrates (Sir 6:24–28). The title with which Mary addresses the risen Jesus upon recognizing him stresses his role as a teacher, one of the most important roles that Lady Wisdom takes in Jewish sapiential literature. We have already taken notice of this prevalent theme that characterizes both Lady Wisdom as a teacher and her followers as the teacher's disciples within Proverbs and the Wisdom of Solomon.[61] Mary's declaration that the risen Jesus is a gardener in addition to the theme of new creation inaugurated with Jesus' resurrection may be part of the author's attempt at framing this story as a restoration of Eden. If that is the case, then Jesus' words spoken to Mary, "Stop touching me" (20:17), would recall the

---

58. O'Day, "Gospel of John," 842.

59. Schüssler Fiorenza, *In Memory of Her*, 333, regards Mary's faithfulness to seek the Lord-Sophia as what transforms her into the primary apostolic witness to the resurrection.

60. See chapter 7.

61. See chapter 5.

warning given to Eve that she must not "touch" the tree (Gen 3:5 LXX).[62] This would, in turn, liken Jesus to a tree, and Lady Wisdom is illustrated as a tree of life in Prov 3:18. Mary thus demonstrates her faithfulness in a manner that contrasts Eve's disobedience. In addition to the themes of seeking God's wisdom and Wisdom's roles as a teacher and tree of life, we detect a subtle allusion to one of Jesus' self-declared titles in this story. At the Feast of Dedication, Jesus claims to be the good shepherd and he elaborates on his role as the shepherd as one who knows his own and calls them by name (10:3, 14). When Jesus interacts with Mary, he exhibits his role as the good shepherd by calling her by name (20:16). We noted earlier that the title "good shepherd" exhibited strong influences of personified wisdom's intimacy and care for her followers,[63] and these themes reappear in Mary's dialogue with the risen Jesus. Mary Magdalene, like the notable female disciples before her, sets herself apart as one of Lady Wisdom's maidens (Prov 9:3) by seeking after Wisdom, acknowledging Wisdom as "Teacher," and sharing in Wisdom's intimate care.[64]

WISDOM FORMS A COMMUNITY DEFINED BY LOVE

There can be no doubt that love is one of the defining traits of the community of the Johannine Jesus' disciples. Throughout the Farewell Discourse, we find several instances where Jesus instructs his followers on the importance of loving one another. The "new commandment" that Jesus offers seeks to set himself as the example of demonstrating love for the disciples: "even as I have loved you" (13:34-35; 15:12). The love that the disciples have for Jesus is not merely heartfelt, for it involves obedience to his instructions (14:15; 15:14). Jesus promises to reciprocate this love to his loyal followers, and he assures them that the Father will likewise share his love with them (14:21; 15:10). As the example to his disciples, Jesus models the obedient posture: "so that the world may know that I love the Father, I do exactly as the Father commanded me" (14:31). We find further expressions of the motif of the community's love in the Fourth Gospel's Appendix, particularly when Jesus seeks to convey his commitment to Peter after Peter denies him. The three times Jesus

---

62. Coloe, *John 11-21*, 517, notes that the same verb "to touch" (*apto*) appears in Gen 3:5 LXX and John 20:17, suggesting intentionality.

63. See chapter 6.

64. Schüssler Fiorenza, *In Memory of Her*, 332-33.

asks Peter to express his love are followed by three responses by Peter acknowledging his love for Jesus. In each instance, Jesus shares with Peter the prerogative of the good shepherd: "Tend to my lambs"; "Shepherd my sheep"; "Tend to my sheep" (21:15–17). In doing so, Jesus ensures that after he has ascended into heaven, his community will continue to function as a society that reciprocates the love that the Johannine Jesus expresses.

We have already noticed some hints that the shared love between Lady Wisdom and her followers has made its impact upon the Gospel of John, so the emphasis on Jesus creating a community of disciples defined by love grants us an opportunity to explore the wisdom influences more closely.[65] Beginning with the book of Proverbs, we find several passages with remarkable similarities to the emphasis on the community's love in the Fourth Gospel. For example, Prov 4:5–6 summons the student of Wisdom to acquire her, not to forsake her, and to love her. For those who obey these instructions, the sage promises that Wisdom will watch over and guard them. When Lady Wisdom speaks in the first person, she plainly articulates the reciprocity of her love: "I love those who love me" (Prov 8:17). Paul Himes has recently shown that the Greek translation of this passage employs two different verbs for "love" (*agapao* and *phileo*), and Himes has argued that this passage serves as the motivation for the exchange between Peter and the risen Jesus in John 21:15–17, where the same two Greek verbs appear.[66] This observation would confirm the existence of Wisdom Christology in the Fourth Gospel's Appendix by portraying Jesus as incarnate Wisdom, who desires a community of love so strongly that he is willing to reconcile with a disciple who rejected him. The book of Proverbs also depicts Lady Wisdom endowing those who express love toward her with wealth (8:21). These images from the book of Proverbs persuaded Ben Sira and the author of Wisdom of Solomon to offer comparable portrayals of Wisdom's love. Those who love Wisdom love life, and God shares his love with those who love Wisdom (Sir 4:12, 14).[67] Sirach's insistence that those who desire Wisdom must keep the commandments (Sir 1:26) is probably the influence behind Jesus' statement that those who love him must keep his commandments

---

65. Charlesworth, "Lady Wisdom," 110–11, remarks that the Jewish wisdom traditions "are evident in the Fourth Gospel since Lady Wisdom and Jesus are depicted as bringing love and joy."

66. Himes, "Loving Wisdom," 387–402. In Prov 8:17 LXX, personified wisdom loves (*phileo*) those who love (*agapao*) her.

67. Sidebottom, *Fourth Gospel*, 204.

(John 14:15). Within Wisdom of Solomon, we observe further occurrences of this loving reciprocity. To those who love Lady Wisdom, she will quickly make herself known to them (Wis 6:12–13). We detect yet another parallel to John 14:15 in Wis 6:17–18, which states that those who love her will keep her laws.[68] Those who live with Wisdom (and, by extension, her teachings) will experience the greatest expression of God's love (Wis 7:28). It seems that the sages who composed Proverbs, Sirach, and Wisdom of Solomon made a lasting impact on the shape of the Johannine Jesus in his efforts to form a group of disciples who exhibit love for Wisdom and for one another.

WISDOM MAKES FRIENDS

Jesus' community of disciples is not only enacting reciprocal love but also experiences a close-knit friendship. The connection between the themes of love and friendship can be observed within the Farewell Discourse: "Greater love has no one than this, that one lays down his life for his friends. You are my friends if you do what I command you" (15:13–14).[69] Having accepted the summons of Jesus the teacher to keep his instructions, the disciples find themselves with a new status: friends of Jesus. He follows up this statement by indicating that he no longer regards his followers as slaves, which might seem at odds with the emphasis that Jesus places on the need for the disciples to obey his commands.[70] He clarifies the shift from slave to friend by reminding them that he has shared with them all things from the Father as the Father's revelatory agent (15:15). In effect, the new role of friendship indicates an inclusion into the knowledge of the Father's will that the disciples now experience, without indicating that they should no longer view Jesus as their teacher and master (13:13).

The various themes surrounding the disciples' status as friends of the Johannine Jesus also appear in Ben Sirach, who dedicates a lengthy passage to the importance of friendship. Sirach advises that when you gain

---

68. Dillon, "Wisdom Tradition," 277; Sidebottom, *Fourth Gospel*, 204.

69. The theme of friendship was already introduced when Jesus describes Lazarus as "our friend" (11:11), but the concept was undefined until the Farewell Discourse. Coloe, *John 11–21*, 328, is typical among those scholars who draw attention to the relevance of Lazarus and the theme of Wisdom's friends: "As the embodiment of Sophia, Jesus calls his friend Lazarus by name."

70. Thompson, *John*, 329.

friends, they should be tested and not trusted too quickly (6:7). This appears to be a position that Jesus adopts by granting to his disciples the status of friends once they have demonstrated obedience to his commands. Sirach warns of certain friends who are not true and faithful: those who do not remain with you in troubling times and those who quickly change into your enemies. Some of these so-called friends will even sit at your table, only to abandon you in times of trouble (6:8–10).[71] Jesus, however, set the standard for his community of friends by illustrating their great love for one another—a love that shows itself by laying down one's life for another friend.[72] What makes Sirach's exposition on friendship relevant for our study is that it is expanding the earlier teaching of Lady Wisdom, who "tests" her followers to see if they are loyal (4:11–17).[73] Wisdom refers to these disciples as "friends" (4:12).[74] As such, both Lady Wisdom and the Johannine Jesus put their disciples through a test that results in friendship for those who prove utterly faithful.[75] We find an additional text in Wisdom of Solomon that contributes to the friendship motif in the Gospel of John. In Wis 7:27, the author depicts personified wisdom passing into holy persons, thereby making them "friends of God" as well as "prophets."[76] Both of these themes (friends and prophets) appear in John 15:13–15, particularly in the reason Jesus gives for why the disciples are friends—because he has shared with them the heavenly knowledge of God.[77] Raymond Brown helpfully concludes: "Wisdom tests these disciples and forms them . . . until they love her . . . and they become friends of God."[78] The formation of faithful disciples as true friends within the Fourth Gospel offers another glimpse into its Wisdom Christology.[79]

---

71. Sir 6:7-10 is part of a major unit (4:11—6:17) that Jeremy Corley describes as "Applying Wisdom Personally." See his *Ben Sira's Teaching*, 42–43.

72. Coloe, *John 11-21*, 426.

73. Dillon, "Wisdom Tradition," 277, who sees in the motif of testing direct influence upon the Fourth Gospel's Wisdom Christology.

74. The Hebrew text of Sir 4:12 calls them "her friends" (*ohabeyah*), but the Greek translation rendered "her friends" into the singular "the one who loves her."

75. O'Boyle, *Wisdom Christology*, 178.

76. Thompson, *John*, 328; Coloe, *John 11-21*, 426; Brown, *Introduction to the Gospel of John*, 262; Ringe, *Wisdom's Friends*, 67; Schnackenburg, *John*, 3:111.

77. Sidebottom, *Fourth Gospel*, 206.

78. Brown, *John I-XII*, cxxiii.

79. Dillon, "Wisdom Tradition," 277; Charlesworth, "Lady Wisdom," 111; O'Boyle, *Wisdom Christology*, 177–78; Schüssler Fiorenza, *Jesus*, 167; Manns, "Jewish Approach," 268.

THE DISCIPLES ABIDE WITH WISDOM

In addition to creating a community of disciples that exhibits the traits of love and faithful obedience, Jesus summons them to persevere by abiding in him. After announcing that he is the true vine and expressing the ideal that branches should bring forth fruit, he summons his followers to play the role of these branches by remaining in him (15:1–17). Within this relationship, Jesus also plays an active role by abiding in the members of his community of disciples. This mutual abiding allows the disciples to faithfully remain in Jesus' teachings because they attach themselves to the True Vine. Within this passage, we find eleven references to the pivotal act of abiding/remaining, suggesting that this steadfast experience is crucial to the community's disposition.[80] Those disciples who continually abide as branches upon the True Vine are to be rewarded with answered requests, Jesus' love, joy, and lasting fruit.[81] However, those who commit apostasy by refusing to abide in the True Vine will undergo a fiery end. Jesus traces the origins of the mutually abiding community back to God, for it is the Father who loved Jesus, resulting in Jesus showing love to his followers (15:9). In the same vein, Jesus obeyed the Father, giving the disciples an example to follow as they carry out acts of obedience to Jesus. Within this description, Jesus elaborates on what abiding in love looks like, for it entails loyally following his instructions (15:10). Abiding in the Johannine Jesus, therefore, is crucial to the role of discipleship that the author expects of his readers.

Within this multifaceted invitation to abide in Jesus, we can detect the unmistakable influence of Lady Wisdom from several sapiential Jewish passages. Beginning with the book of Sirach, we can trace similar images of Wisdom inviting her students to participate in close-knit experiences akin to mutual indwelling. Ben Sira encourages those interested in pursuing Wisdom to come to her like a farmer who sows and plows, waiting for the harvest belonging to her (Sir 6:19). As he unpacks this analogy, he illustrates the farming disciple as one who cultivates Wisdom to share in her produce. The passage continues by inviting the farmer to take upon her yoke: "Put your feet into her fetters and your neck into her collar. Bend your shoulders and carry her, and do not fret

---

80. John 15:4 (thrice), 5, 6, 7 (twice), 9, 10 (twice), 16. Feuillet, *Johannine Studies*, 87, draws attention to the way in which the imagery of Jesus as the vine and the summons to abide in him recalls the eucharistic themes from the Bread of Life Discourse.

81. Charlesworth, "Lady Wisdom," 104.

under her bonds" (6:24–25). This illustration of the disciple of Wisdom closely abiding in her instruction as a farmer resurfaces at the conclusion of Sirach's treatise, where Ben Sira summons the reader to again place one's neck under the yoke of her instruction (51:26). In addition to the portrayal of a farmer who abides in her wise commands, we find an additional metaphor involving camping. The student of Lady Wisdom is one who camps near her home, fastens his tent peg to her walls, pitches his tent according to her hands, and inhabits a good place of lodging (14:24–25). Followers will also bring their children to shelter and stay the night under her branches when Wisdom takes the role of a tree. To these, she shelters from the heat as they lodge in her glory (14:26–27). This image of Wisdom's disciples lodging in her glory under her branches may act as a plausible influence of Jesus as the True Vine who summons his followers (branches) to abide in him. Sirach offers one final metaphor describing the close association of Wisdom and her followers in terms of a school for the uninstructed. These prospective students are encouraged to draw near to Wisdom and lodge in the house of instruction (51:23).[82] Within Wisdom of Solomon, we can take notice of a rather explicit parallel: "for God loves nothing as much as the person who lives with Wisdom" (7:28).[83] Similarly, the author portrays Solomon as desiring to take personified wisdom to be his bride, indicating a joining of the themes of love for Wisdom with the desire to abide (8:2). While maintaining the role of the personified bride, Solomon determines "to take her and live with me" (8:9). Wisdom also takes an active role in abiding in those not enslaved to sin (1:4; 6:13, 16).[84] The portrayal of ideal readers of Sirach and Wisdom of Solomon longing to abide with Lady Wisdom presents a likely parallel to the Johannine Jesus inviting his disciples to abide in him. Readers of the Gospel of John familiar with these images would conclude that Jesus is the wisdom of God.[85]

WISDOM AND THE HOLY SPIRIT

It is important to give attention to the role of God's Spirit within the Fourth Gospel, especially as it pertains to our inquiry into the extent the

---

82. Witherington, *Jesus the Sage*, 379.
83. Dillon, "Wisdom Tradition," 278.
84. O'Boyle, *Wisdom Christology*, 178; Dillon, "Wisdom Tradition," 278.
85. Witherington, *John's Wisdom*, 255; O'Boyle, *Wisdom Christology*, 178.

depiction of the Johannine Jesus has been shaped by the Jewish wisdom texts. The Spirit plays a vital role within the Gospel of John, especially as it pertains to continuing the ministry of Jesus after his glorification (7:39). While the Spirit makes sporadic appearances within the narrative, such as at the baptism of Jesus in the form of a dove (1:32–33), in the discussion with Nicodemus concerning the new birth from above (3:5–8), and briefly in the Bread of Life Discourse (6:63), discussion of the Spirit is concentrated in the Farewell Discourse. The Spirit of truth is that which the world is unable to receive,[86] but Jesus assures the disciples that it will be with them (14:17). We can observe an important correlation between the Johannine Jesus and the Spirit in several passages—an extraordinary emphasis within the Fourth Gospel but utterly absent from Matthew, Mark, and Luke.[87] Just as the Father sent Jesus as his agent, the Father will also send the Spirit in Jesus' name, and it will take over Jesus' role as the one that teaches all that Jesus spoke (14:26).[88] When the Spirit comes, it will testify about Jesus (15:26), convict those who refuse to believe in Jesus (16:8–9), and it will take what belongs to Jesus and declare it to the disciples (16:14). The characterization of the Spirit as that which does not speak on its own initiative but rather speaks on what it hears (16:13) seems to be an intentional move to replicate the self-described behavior of the Johannine Jesus.[89] Just as Jesus functions as the obedient agent of God who only speaks what he is told, the Spirit is to function as the agent of Jesus after his departure.[90] Additionally, the Spirit takes the role of a guide to the community of disciples that reveals and discloses truth (16:13). In the Fourth Gospel's version of the Great Commission, the risen Jesus breathes on his disciples and states, "Receive the Holy Spirit" (20:21–23).[91] This interaction serves to empower the disciples to continue Jesus' life-giving mission by offering forgiveness

---

86. This line recalls the Prologue where the world did not receive Wisdom, but the disciples did receive her (1:10–12).

87. Witherington, *John's Wisdom*, 251.

88. Keener, *Gospel of John*, 2:961; Anderson, "Having-Sent-Me Father," 43.

89. John 5:30; 7:17, 28; 8:28, 42; 12:49; 14:10.

90. Brant, *John*, 229, draws a similar conclusion: "the Paraclete is Jesus's agent, or even a reference to Jesus himself, rather than the third person of the Trinity." See also McIlhone, "Jesus as God's Agent," 309.

91. Just as God empowered Jesus with the Spirit at the beginning of his ministry (1:31–34), Jesus now empowers his followers with the very same Spirit at the start of their ministry. See the discussion in Keener, *Gospel of John*, 2:1204.

to others as well as to characterize the disciples as the new creation.[92] The author of the Gospel of John has placed great emphasis on closely associating Jesus and the Spirit, especially as they pertain to the community of faithful disciples.[93] Richard Dillon concludes with his helpful commentary: "Jesus sends the Spirit, and His activity and the Spirit's are joined and complementary."[94]

Within the Jewish sapiential literature, we observe a common tendency among the sages to connect the Spirit with the wisdom of God. When Lady Wisdom takes the role of a prophetess in the book of Proverbs, we can observe that she pours forth the Spirit of YHWH: "I will pour out my spirit on you; I will make my words known to you" (1:23).[95] Ben Witherington also calls attention to this trait of Wisdom as he draws a comparison to the Johannine Jesus pouring out the Spirit upon his followers in John 20:22.[96] The author of Wisdom of Solomon opens by closely identifying Wisdom as a kindly spirit—the Spirit of the Lord (1:6–7).[97] One of the primary functions of this wise Spirit is to convict the ungodly of their lawless works (1:9), not unlike the Spirit that Jesus gives to convict the world of sin.[98] When Solomon prays to God for understanding, his petition receives this answer: "the Spirit of Wisdom came to me" (7:7). At the head of the list of the twenty-one traits of Lady Wisdom is the assertion that within her is a Spirit that is intelligent (7:22). Similarly, when God gives his wisdom, he sends his Holy Spirit from on high—a statement that closely identifies the two (9:17).[99] Since personi-

---

92. John 20:22 employs a rare verb "to breathe upon" (*emfusao*) in what appears to be an intentional echo to Gen 2:7 LXX, where God breathes the breath of life into Adam, humanity's first creation. John 20:22 is the only occurrence of this verb in the New Testament.

93. Dunn, *Unity and Diversity*, 246; Witherington, *John's Wisdom*, 342; Keener, *Gospel of John*, 2:961–62.

94. Dillon, "Wisdom Tradition," 278.

95. Corley, "Proverbs and Ben Sira," 161, draws attention to how Ben Sira takes up Wisdom's promise to her followers to pour out the Spirit in Prov 1:23 by drawing on Job 28:25; "I will pour out by measure my spirit" (Sir 16:25). Ben Sira essentially speaks what Wisdom said, just as the Johannine Jesus speaks what Wisdom said.

96. Witherington, *John's Wisdom*, 343; Robert and Feuillet, *Introduction*, 875, who argue that Prov 1:23 directly influences the Fourth Gospel's portrayal of Jesus in terms of Wisdom.

97. Witherington, *Jesus the Sage*, 378; Keener, *Gospel of John*, 2:964.

98. Sidebottom, *Fourth Gospel*, 206, argues for a parallel between Wisdom's behavior that convicts (Wis 1:3; 4:27) and the Spirit that Wisdom incarnate sends in John 16:8.

99. Dillon, "Wisdom Tradition," 278; Keener, *Gospel of John*, 2:964.

fied wisdom is so closely tied with the Spirit of God, she can inhabit holy people and transform them into Spirit-enabled prophets (7:27). Solomon's boast that God's wisdom understands all things and acts as a guide may lie behind the statement in John 16:13, where both points reemerge in Jesus' discussion of the Spirit's function. Similarly, Lady Wisdom has taken the role of a guide for the people of God within the history of Israel (Wis 10:10, 17–18).[100] Philo's symbolic explanation of Wisdom as a "dove" suggests that the Spirit descending as a dove at Jesus' baptism in John 1:32–33 offers yet another close association between Wisdom and Spirit.[101] We have already drawn attention to the illustration of the Enochic Son of Man, in whose person dwells "a spirit of wisdom" (1 En. 49:3).[102] Based on this data, it is apparent that some Jews were depicting God's personified wisdom as either synonymous with or at the very least strongly associated with the Spirit of God. This is a reasonable conclusion to draw because both "spirit" and "wisdom" functioned in similar ways to articulate how the God of Israel frequently interacted with his creation.[103] These authors portray Lady Wisdom as pouring out the Spirit, convicting the ungodly, and giving guidance and enlightenment to the righteous. Each of these points resurfaces in the Fourth Gospel's characterization of incarnate Wisdom, who is closely aligned with the Spirit of God's activity among the community of disciples.[104]

CONCLUSION

This chapter began by noting how the Matthean Jesus embodied Lady Wisdom's invitation for disciples to come to learn from her and take upon her yoke. Our goal was to ascertain to what degree the Gospel of John depicts Jesus in an analogous manner. The results of our inquiry indicate that Wisdom Christology heavily saturates several key facets of the relationship between Jesus and those who believe in him. We first

---

100. O'Day and Hylen, *John*, 159, draw attention to the way in which the guiding Paraclete takes on the role of God's wisdom. O'Day, "Gospel of John," 773, has also pointed out that the verb "to lead" (*ago*) characterizes the Paraclete in John and Lady Wisdom in Wis 9:11; 10:10

101. Schroer, *Wisdom*, 140, who points to Philo, *Her.* 126–28.

102. See chapter 2.

103. McGrath, *John's Apologetic Christology*, 52, who cites Dunn, *Christology in the Making*, 266.

104. Brown, *Introduction to the Gospel of John*, 263; Ringe, *Wisdom's Friends*, 87–88.

observed that the ways in which Jesus forms a community of disciples exhibit noticeable traces of influence from earlier portrayals of Lady Wisdom gathering a group of followers. Second, we examined six significant encounters between Jesus and women and found that each of these stories, in their own way, builds upon the foundation of characteristics and traits belonging to Wisdom that the author of the Fourth Gospel applies to Jesus. Furthermore, we gleaned that these women take upon the role of maidens of Wisdom (Prov 9:3), a position that elevated them among the disciples in ways that are hard to overlook. Third, we drew attention to a key emphasis present in the community of disciples, namely the love that they have for one another and for incarnate Wisdom. Within this community defined by reciprocating love, we located yet another indication of Wisdom's impact with the underscoring of our fourth finding—the status of "friends" that the disciples come to acquire in their obedience to the Johannine Jesus. Next, we explored evidence indicating that Jesus' invitation to his followers that they should abide in him is indebted to several sapiential texts where disciples of Wisdom long to dwell with her. Finally, we observed the distinctive christological portrayal in the Gospel of John that strongly associates Jesus and the Spirit—the Spirit that continues Jesus' ministry among the disciples after his departure. We then recalled how the authors of Jewish wisdom literature often identified or closely related Wisdom and the Spirit of God. The close association of these two attributes provided the context for the Johannine Jesus to assure that his disciples were to receive the Spirit. Our study concentrating on the wisdom themes present within Jesus' interactions with his believing disciples yielded some of the clearest parallels to earlier wisdom texts, thus allowing us to further sketch the extent to which Wisdom Christology pervades the Gospel of John.

9

Reflections and Conclusions

As WE REFLECT ON the fruits of our labors, it is important to take stock of how the Fourth Gospel compares to the earlier works of the New Testament that advocate for a Wisdom Christology. In the Synoptic tradition, the portrayal of Jesus in terms of God's wisdom is certainly evident in Q, Matthew, and Luke, with Mark possessing only a few possible allusions. Within the Pauline corpus of letters, some works express a dominant Wisdom Christology (e.g., 1 Corinthians, Colossians), while others only apply wisdom themes to Jesus in a few passages (e.g., Romans, 2 Corinthians, Galatians, Ephesians). The opening of the Letter to the Hebrews contains several clear parallels to the Jewish wisdom tradition, but outside of the first chapter these passages are practically absent. This survey indicates that while Wisdom Christology is unmistakably apparent in the Synoptic Gospel traditions, the Pauline corpus, and the Letter to the Hebrews, the portrayal of Jesus as Wisdom is unevenly divided. None of these works expresses a full-fledged Wisdom Christology.

When we compare these earlier works to the Gospel of John, the emphasis shifts dramatically.[1] Our study has demonstrated that the Johannine Jesus is incarnate Wisdom and that this christological presentation permeates all twenty-one chapters of the Fourth Gospel.[2] Martin Scott's assessment of Wisdom's influence comes to a similar conclusion,

---

1. Dunn, *Parting of the Ways*, 227, remarks, "the Fourth Gospel has gone beyond anything which we have so far read in Christian writing of the period to bring out the full significance of Wisdom Christology."

2. Pace Hurtado, *Lord Jesus Christ*, 384, who suggested that the divine-name tradition is more influential within the Gospel of John than the Jewish wisdom traditions.

which is worth hearing here: "Her role is not merely influential, but more accurately *fundamental*: the Fourth Gospel's Christology is nothing short of a *Sophia* Christology."[3] Within the Prologue, which serves as the introduction to the rest of the narrative, we counted twenty parallels with the Jewish wisdom tradition. The Wisdom Christology that the author presents in the Johannine Prologue persists with the main characters in the Fourth Gospel's plot. This includes Jesus' relationship with his God, his controversial encounters with his opponents, his dialogues with prominent female disciples, and even with the wider community of believing followers. Wisdom Christology is interwoven into every aspect of Jesus' mission, including his teachings, summons to others, offers of the life of the age to come, provision of abundant food and drink, and even in the distinctly Johannine signs. Other christological titles, such as the Son of Man, Messiah, and "unique son," receive further clarity when we acknowledge how the author infuses them with the influence of personified wisdom traditions. All these points are even more remarkable when we remind ourselves that the noun "wisdom" is completely absent from the Gospel of John. The concept of wisdom, however, makes up the very essence of the Fourth Gospel's testimony.[4]

A crucial concern that I implicitly maintained while organizing the data for the Wisdom Christology in the Gospel of John is a tendency that scholars often describe as "parallelomania."[5] This term refers to the interpretive inclination to see connections between ancient texts in an uncritical, simplistic manner. Just because two passages sound similar does not necessarily prove that one directly influenced the other. The interpreter must provide a sound and persuasive argument for each occurrence of dependence between texts. Since my study depends upon the influence of several strands of Jewish wisdom literature upon the Christology in the Gospel of John, I was aware that my readers would only find my position convincing if I was able to demonstrate the legitimacy and high probability of this proposed influence.[6] I have taken several methodological steps in order to reasonably guide this study while attempting to set aside

3. Scott, *Sophia*, 241 (emphasis original).

4. Dunn, *Jesus according to the New Testament*, 66–67. Sidebottom, *Fourth Gospel*, 19, concludes from the sheer number of wisdom parallels apparent within the Fourth Gospel's Wisdom Christology that the author "undoubtedly belonged to some branch of Wisdom school."

5. The pivotal study of this term is Sandmel, "Parallelomania," 1–13.

6. Moeller, "Wisdom Motifs," 98, confesses to a similar admission at the conclusion of his study of the parallels between Jewish wisdom literature and the Gospel of John.

my own biases (which I openly acknowledge that I possess regarding this topic). First, I have been careful to ascertain which Jewish wisdom texts the author of the Gospel of John could have reasonably had access to, resulting in a direct source of influence upon his Wisdom Christology. The wisdom passages within the Hebrew Bible (Job, Psalms, Proverbs) fit into this category. I also think that it is extremely probable that the Greek texts within the deuterocanonical collection (Sirach, Baruch, Wisdom of Solomon) were available based on their demonstrable impact upon the Fourth Gospel. In chapter 2 I drew attention to two Qumran texts (1Q20 and 11Q5) that were probably not directly accessible to the author of the Gospel of John. I share the same hesitation with the writings of Aristobulus and Philo Judaeus. The *Parables* of 1 Enoch offers attractive insights into how some apocalyptically minded Jews could conceive of a figure called "Son of Man" in terms of personified wisdom, but I do not see any evidence that the Fourth Gospel had direct access to the *Parables*. Of course, most of the Tannaitic and Amoraic literature postdates the Gospel of John, while nevertheless offering insight into the trajectories of how some wisdom concepts took a different direction than what we observe in Christian circles. My arguments have shown that the various places within the Fourth Gospel that depict Wisdom Christology exhibit influences from not just one of these Jewish wisdom texts, but from several of them, whether directly impacting the portrayal of Jesus with a citation or highly probable allusion, or indirectly by showing that these sort of ways of thinking about Wisdom were "in the air" among exegetes interested in the topic.[7] Furthermore, I have given considerable effort to bridge the gap between critical scholarship on the Fourth Gospel's Wisdom Christology and nonspecialist readers of the Bible by documenting which scholars acknowledge the impact of Jewish wisdom texts upon various passages of the Fourth Gospel. By taking these important methodological steps, I am confident my readers will find this study to be innocent of widespread parallelomania.

Why Wisdom's Personification Matters

We would do well to take this opportunity to reflect on the implications of a full-fledged portrayal of Jesus Christ as Lady Wisdom's embodiment.

---

7. Sandelin, *Wisdom as Nourisher*, 180, concludes similarly that the author of the Fourth Gospel has utilized the images of personified wisdom to illustrate the Johannine Jesus "in a free and creative manner."

What does this mean when we think critically about the person of Jesus as he is portrayed in the Gospel of John? The answer lies in the definition of personified wisdom. The Jewish wisdom texts to which the Gospel of John is heavily indebted repeatedly expressed wisdom as YHWH's wise interactions with and instruction to his creation. When the sages said that God made the world with his wisdom, they were conveying the idea that the creation was wisely ordered, structured, and meaningfully purposed. When these same Jewish sages invited their readers to "acquire wisdom," they sought to encourage those interested in wisdom to take hold of the wise instructions of God that contain knowledge and understanding. When several Jewish authors came to identify exceptional human figures with God's wisdom, this characterization aimed to underscore the figures in question as incarnating the wise and ordered purposes of Israel's God. We observed that the concept of personified wisdom shares many of the qualities and traits with God's word—the often-personified utterance and speech belonging to YHWH. All these points merge in the Johannine Prologue, where we find the personified word/wisdom becoming flesh and dwelling among humanity. To understand and believe in the Johannine Jesus as the incarnation of the wisdom of God is to regard this noteworthy human being as the locus of God's wise intentions and ordered instructions for his creation. To be sure, Jesus as incarnate Wisdom speaks forth the commands and orders of the Father as the authorized agent, but he accomplishes this task in the capacity of a man, a genuine member of humanity. The Gospel of John frequently stresses the true humanity of incarnate Wisdom, calling Jesus a human being more frequently than the gospels of Matthew, Mark, and Luke combined.[8] There is absolutely no hint or suggestion that the humanity of the Johannine Jesus is some sort of impersonal human nature assumed by a preexisting divine nature belonging to the *logos*.[9] In order to appreciate the human Jesus within the Fourth Gospel, we must take seriously the context set forth by the many strands of Jewish wisdom literature, rather than starting with the conclusions of the ecumenical church councils of the fourth and fifth centuries and then reading those dogmatic precepts back into

---

8. Robinson, *Priority of John*, 368. The number of times that the NT gospel writers designate Jesus as a human being are: Matthew (3), Mark (2), Luke (7), and John (16). This data flies directly in the face of those scholars who argue that the Fourth Gospel presents the highest Christology of the four NT gospel accounts. If we want to responsibly speak of the Fourth Gospel's high Christology, it would be more appropriate to label it as a *high human Christology*.

9. See especially Nemes, *Trinity and Incarnation*, 163–64.

the first century CE.[10] The Jesus whom we find in the Gospel of John is a first-century Jew, so we must interpret him, his words, and his actions within his first-century Jewish context.[11]

The Preexistence of the Johannine Jesus

If the Johannine Jesus is an authentic human being, how does Wisdom Christology contribute to the topic of the preexistence of Jesus? This is an important question since the nature of the Johannine Jesus' preexistence directly pertains to who Jesus is as a figure in history. Having established within several Jewish wisdom texts that preexisting Wisdom is a personification—rather than a conscious female divine person alongside YHWH—then the question of determining what sort of preexistence the author of the Gospel of John had in mind begins to yield some fruit.[12] Preexisting as a poetic personification is not the same as literal preexistence. In other words, the portrayal of Jesus as the incarnation of the Wisdom that preexisted alongside God does not indicate that the son of God personally and consciously existed before his birth. Now, it must be said that the Johannine Jesus often looks back at the career of preexisting Wisdom and, recognizing that he is the embodiment of Wisdom, speaks of his ministry as continuing what Wisdom started. Jesus draws a conscious, direct line from himself back to Lady Wisdom in several statements, but this is part and parcel with Wisdom Christology.[13] When the sages who compiled the book of Proverbs presented the Woman of Substance as the incarnation of personified wisdom, there is no indication that these Jewish women existed with YHWH before he created the heavens and the earth. When Ben Sira followed in the footsteps of the theology of Proverbs and presented Simon the high priest as incarnate Wisdom, no

---

10. Fuller, "Incarnation," 57, makes the case that Nicene and Chalcedonian definitions should not be used as presuppositions for New Testament exegesis.

11. See Manns, "Jewish Approach," 279: "Taking the Jewishness of Jesus seriously means . . . to study the literary and linguistic background of the gospels."

12. Dunn, *Early Christians*, 76, notes that sometimes interpreters will try to get around Wisdom being a personification by describing it with a term common in fourth-century trinitarian controversies, a hypostasis. Dunn rightly remarks that this sort of qualifying the Wisdom of God is historically anachronistic, as it imports a meaning onto the wisdom of God that was completely alien to those steeped in the Jewish wisdom tradition. This protest was already been made over a hundred years ago by Moore, "Intermediaries in Jewish Theology," 55.

13. Dunn, *Parting*, 220.

reader thought that Simon was consciously alongside God in the beginning. When the author of the Genesis Apocryphon characterized Sarah, Abraham's wife, as the human incarnation of Lady Wisdom, he was not thinking that Sarah personally preexisted her birth. In the first century, Philo explicitly identified both Sarah and Rebekah (and to a lesser extent, Leah and Zipporah) with the very same wisdom that the God of Israel used to wisely create the universe. Readers of the Gospel of John familiar with just one of these earlier portrayals of personified wisdom's incarnation would recognize exactly what is going on in the Prologue, for it is in Jesus that Wisdom has now made her definitive and permanent abode. On this particular point, James Dunn offers an appropriate summary:

> For while we can say that divine wisdom became incarnate in Christ, that does not mean that Wisdom was a divine being, or that Christ himself was pre-existent with God, but simply that Christ was (and is) the embodiment of divine Wisdom, that is, the climactic and definitive embodiment of God's own creative power and saving concern.[14]

The data presented in this book points to the realization that the Gospel of John—rather than exhibiting a high divine Christology—presents a *high human Christology*.[15]

The God of the Gospel of John

Having identified the primary Christology within the Fourth Gospel as Wisdom Christology—the portrayal of Jesus Christ in terms of personified wisdom—what sort of conclusions can we draw regarding the understanding of another important actor in the narrative: the God of Jesus? Although the Gospel of John is a Greco-Roman biography of Jesus, the God of Israel plays a massively prominent role by commissioning Jesus as an agent, by sharing with Jesus the prerogatives of God, and by anointing Jesus for the role of Israel's kingly Messiah. Recognizing that God has sent Jesus as his agent is crucial to knowing God, as we observe in John 17:3: "This is the life of the age to come, that they may know you, the only true God, and Jesus Christ whom you have sent." In other words, it is not sufficient to simply know the Father, whom Jesus addresses as

---

14. Dunn, *Christology in the Making*, 212.

15. John deserves a place at the table with the three Synoptic Gospels, which Kirk, *Man Attested By God*, has argued in great detail represent a high human Christology.

the only true God; one must also acknowledge that the true God has authorized Jesus as his agent. According to the Johannine Jesus, his own father is the only true God. The God of the Gospel of John is—according to Jesus—the God and Father of Jesus (20:17). The presentation of God within the Fourth Gospel is in continuity with Jewish monotheism, which worshipped God as one.[16] This unitarian understanding of God was shared by both Jesus and his Jewish opponents (5:44; 8:54).[17] As the God of Jesus, the Father is self-evidently greater than the son, a point that Jesus openly admits (14:28).[18] Although the Wisdom Christology within the Fourth Gospel offers a portrayal of Jesus that is highly empowered and highly authorized, he nevertheless remains distinct from God, and the two are never collapsed into a single being.[19] Just as it is important to set the Johannine Jesus in the context of the heritage of Jewish wisdom literature, the God of Jesus must also be placed in the context of traditional Jewish monotheistic understandings.

Clement of Rome

One final point that deserves our attention is the legacy of Wisdom Christology in the understanding of the church in the centuries following the composition of the Gospel of John. We may offer a brief survey here of how those Christian writers who chose to discuss their understanding of Wisdom Christology within the surviving works. We may begin with Clement of Rome, who authored *1 Clement* sometime towards the end of the first century CE. *1 Clement* appears to show no discernable awareness of the Gospel of John, but we do find evidence that Clement identified Jesus with Lady Wisdom.[20] Clement of Rome draws upon Matthew's gospel in order to portray Christ as Wisdom and recapitulates it with a summons to come, listen to Jesus, and learn from his teaching.[21]

In *1 Clement* 36 Christ is depicted with the assistance of a citation from Heb 1:3–4, which echoes back to descriptions of personified wisdom

16. Robinson, *Twelve More*, 175; Thompson, *God of the Gospel of John*, 228
17. McGrath, *Only True God*, 60.
18. Culpepper, *Gospel*, 95.
19. Thompson, *God of the Gospel of John*, 235.
20. Douglas, *Early Church Understandings*, 55. I draw quite heavily upon the work of Douglas in this section.
21. 1 Clem. 22.1, alluding to Matt 11:28–30 which itself owes dependance to Sir 51:19–28.

in Wisdom of Solomon.[22] We may discern further evidence of Clement's Wisdom Christology in chapters 57–58. He encourages his readers to adopt a humble and submissive stance towards their presbyters, resulting in a positive reputation in Christ's flock and possession of the hope of Christ. Clement immediately follows up this admonition with a reference to Wisdom: "For thus says his all-virtuous Wisdom," accompanied by a lengthy quote of Lady Wisdom's entire speech from Prov 1:23–33.[23] After the citation from Proverbs reached it conclusion, Clement summons the readers to an obedient stance: "For this reason, we should be obedient to [Christ's] most holy and glorious name, fleeing the dangers foretold by Wisdom" (58.1). When God is portrayed as Creator, Clement attributes God's wisdom and understanding to the creative acts: "you are wise when you create and understanding when you establish what exists."[24] These seem to be a few of the various ways that the true God is depicted as the Maker of all things, and there are passages where even the word of God functions as the creative speech.[25] Clement not only presupposes a Wisdom Christology but there is evidence that he possesses a wisdom soteriology as well.[26] Clement's presentation of Jesus as Wisdom demonstrates an early Christian reception of Wisdom Christology that regards God's wisdom as a personification, rather than as a conscious person.[27]

The Didache

The *Didache*, otherwise known as "The Teaching of the Twelve Apostles," is an early second-century document containing several ethical guidelines intended for Christian communities of faith. The compiler of this work, known as the Didachist, begins by giving attention to the "teaching of the Lord" that leads to the path of life, rather than to the path of death.[28] This

22. E.g., 1 Clem. 36.2 notes that Jesus is the "reflection/radiance" (*apaugasma*) by taking a description of Lady Wisdom in Wis 7:26 and applying it to Christ. The same literary move occurs in Heb. 1:3. On Clement's use of Wisdom of Solomon, see Bushur, "Early Christian Appropriation," 74.

23. 1 Clem. 57.3–7. A similar association between Wisdom and Jesus might have been intended by Clement in 13.1, but it is far from conclusive evidence.

24. 1 Clem. 60.1, which could be drawing on a number of passages where YHWH creates with his wisdom and understanding—e.g., Prov 3:19; Jer 10:12; 51:15.

25. See 1 Clem. 27.4; 33.3

26. Douglas, *Early Church Understandings*, 56.

27. O'Boyle, *Wisdom Christology*, 184.

28. *Did.* 1.1–2.

description of the instruction of Jesus may echo back to several passages in Proverbs where Lady Wisdom teaches her followers to take the path of life and not the path that leads to destruction.[29] Additionally, those who heed the commands of Jesus are taking on "the entire yoke of the Lord" (6.2), a statement that reminds us of Wisdom's yoke in Sirach 51:23–27 and, more importantly, the yoke of Jesus in Matt 11:29–30. If the *Didache* is drawing upon Jesus' words in Matt 11:29–30 (where Matthean Jesus speaks about the woke of Wisdom), then this strongly suggests that the Didachist, like Matthew, possessed a Wisdom Christology.

We may gain further insight into the Didachist's Christology by examining the prayers of the Eucharist in chapter 9. When the cup is to be blessed, the author offers a prayer in which the Father receives praise "for the holy vine of David, your child" (9.2). Several scholars argue that this reference to the vine refers to Lady Wisdom as the vine in Sir 24:17–19, a passage that, as we demonstrated, helped give shape to a title of the Johannine Jesus: "the True Vine" (John 15:1–5).[30] Additionally, the *Didache* applies to Christ several other traits of Wisdom, such as giver of bread, knowledge, life, immortality, and the role of nourisher. There is no indication that the Didachist attributes to Christ a personal preexistence, especially in light of Christ being characterized as an offshoot of David's family lineage and as a child of the Creator. The author of the *Didache* appears to, therefore, present his Wisdom Christology in continuity with that which we observe in the New Testament—a Christology where Jesus is the embodiment of the personified wisdom of God.[31]

Justin Martyr

Justin, a second-century philosopher-turned-Christian theologian, offers some explicit connections between Jesus and Lady Wisdom.[32] In his *Dialogue with Trypho*, Justin argues for the conscious preexistence of Jesus

---

29. Douglas, *Early Church Understandings*, 59, points to Prov 3:18; 8:8, 34–35; 9:6; and Wis 9:9, 11. Varner, *Didache*, 57, likewise draws attention to the two ways in Proverbs 1–9.

30. Sandelin, *Wisdom as Nourisher*, 194–98; Betz, "Eucharist in the Didache," 266; Douglas, *Early Church Understandings*, 60; Feuillet, *Johannine Studies*, 87.

31. Sandelin, *Wisdom as Nourisher*, 222, argues extensively that the prayers over the meals in *Didache* 9–10 originally stressed personified wisdom.

32. Collins and Collins, *King and Messiah*, 177, acknowledge that Justin adapted aspects of Middle Platonic philosophy and used them to explain his theology of how God created the material world.

by referring to him as "the word and wisdom and power and glory of him who begot him."[33] Justin unpacks what he means by his identification of Jesus as God's wisdom by providing a lengthy quotation from personified wisdom's speech in Prov 8:21–30. Later, Justin declares that Solomon called the son of God "Wisdom" and that the son was begotten before all of God's works, which draws again on the portrayal of wisdom in Proverbs 8.[34] Justin recounts how Trypho essentially agrees with this assessment of Wisdom in *Dialogue* 63, and Justin continues to cite Proverbs 8 extensively to identify Jesus with Wisdom in *Dialogue* 126. Furthermore, Justin repeatedly attributes Wisdom's trait as the first-begotten of God to Jesus in both his *First* and *Second Apology*.

It seems, however, that Justin does not regard the preexisting wisdom that became incarnate in Jesus as a personification, but rather as an independent, conscious agent alongside but subordinate to God the Father.[35] Byron Shafer echoes this reading of Justin's Christology: "[Justin] seems to have been the first Christian apologist explicitly to interpret the Wisdom-passage Proverbs 8:22 as an identification of Christ."[36] Justin's redefinition of personified wisdom is due to the dominance of his Middle Platonic *logos* Christology, which had taken steps far beyond the portrayals of the personified word expressed in the Hebrew Bible and Jewish wisdom literature.[37]

Origen

When it comes to examining the Wisdom Christology in the third-century works of Origen, there is some added complexity to the work of interpretation. Origen is articulating his own christological understanding as a direct response to the Monarchians and their view of the *logos*.[38] As a response to the Monarchians, Origen elected to highlight "Wisdom" as the primary referent for Christ. As a proponent of Jesus's subordination to the Father, which was the orthodox position for the first three

33. *Dial.* 61.
34. *Dial.* 62.
35. Johnson, "Jesus, the Wisdom of God," 289; O'Boyle, *Wisdom Christology*, 186–87.
36. Shafer, "Wisdom Christology," 57.
37. On the non-Jewish influences upon Justin's *logos* Christology, see especially Hillar, *From Logos to Trinity*, 138–169; Daley, "Beginning," 153–55.
38. Waers, "Wisdom Christology and Monarchianism," 105. In my discussion of Origen, I draw heavily from Waers's scholarship.

centuries CE, Origen makes the argument that Wisdom Christology is more valuable that *logos* Christology: "The saying then stands, first, 'In the beginning was the Logos;' we are to place that full in our view; but the testimonies we cited from the Proverbs led us to place Wisdom first, and to think of Wisdom as preceding the Word which announces her. We must observe, then, that the Logos is in the beginning, that is, in Wisdom, always."[39]

In another important work, *On Principles*, Origen notes that Christ is referred to by many different names, one of which is "Wisdom" based upon the evidence Origen cites from Prov 8:22–25.[40] In fact, Origen applies the title "Wisdom" to Jesus over fifty times in his collective works, often by giving preference to Wisdom's role over the role of the *logos*. We can be sure that Origen understands Jesus as the agent of the Father when he cites Ps 104:24 thus: "so all things came into being in accordance with the structures of things that were to exist, as previously defined by God in his Wisdom; 'for in Wisdom he made all things.'"[41] In an admission of what he and others in his circle understand, Origen writes, "We believe . . . that God's Wisdom entered a woman's womb, was born as an infant, and wailed like crying children."[42] Although he clearly distinguishes Wisdom from the Father as distinct beings, Wisdom nevertheless is a conscious, preexisting being for Origen, not a personification of God's wise attribute.[43]

Closing Thoughts

In sum, the Christian pilgrimage of Lady Wisdom saw her transformation from being a preexisting *personification* that became flesh in the human Jesus (Gospel of John, Clement of Rome, *Didache*) to becoming an actual preexisting *person* alongside the Father in heaven (Justin, Origen). This major development from Wisdom as a personification to a real entity[44] would, of course, lead to the heated christological controversies of

---

39. Origen, *Comm. Jo.* 1.42.
40. *Princ.* 1.2.1.
41. *Comm. Jo.* 1.22. I owe this insight to Daley, "Beginning," 157.
42. *Princ.* 2.6.2.
43. Johnson, "Jesus, the Wisdom of God," 290; Hanson, *Christian Doctrine of God*, 48; Shafer, "Wisdom Christology," 57.
44. See e.g., Haight, *Jesus, Symbol of God*, 257, 475–76.

the fourth and fifth centuries CE.[45] During this period, key figures like Marcellus,[46] Hilary,[47] Athanasius,[48] and Gregory of Nyssa[49] were more interested in proof-texting than engaging in serious exegesis of the Jewish wisdom texts, as evidenced by their attribution of the wisdom of God in Proverbs 8 to *the incarnate Christ*, rather than to preexistent Wisdom. My hope, however, is that by recognizing the figure of Jesus that we find on the pages of the Gospel of John as personified wisdom made flesh, we too might walk along the wise paths of Wisdom that lead to the life of the age to come. If my readers find encouragement from this volume to venture forth in the ways of Wisdom incarnate, I will regard my literary efforts as meaningful.

---

45. For a detailed history of Wisdom Christology from Athanasius to the medieval period, see esp. O'Boyle, *Wisdom Christology*, 193–208; Shafer, "Wisdom Christology," 57–59.

46. Hanson, *Christian Doctrine of God*, 227, 232.

47. Hanson, *Christian Doctrine of God*, 475.

48. Hanson, *Christian Doctrine of God*, 424, 434, 457.

49. Hanson, *Christian Doctrine of God*, 727.

Bibliography

Achtemeier, Paul J., Joel B. Green, and Marianne Meye Thompson. *Introducing the New Testament: Its Literature and Theology.* Grand Rapids: Eerdmans, 2001.

Alexander, Philip. "'In the Beginning': 'Rabbinic and Patristic Exegesis of Genesis 1:1." In *The Exegetical Encounter between Jews and Christians in Late Antiquity*, edited by Emmanouela Grypeou and Helen Spurling, 1–29. Jewish and Christian Perspectives 18. Leiden: Brill, 2009.

Allen, Leslie C. *Psalms 101–150.* WBC 21. Waco, TX: Word, 1983.

Anderson, Gary. "The Interpretation of Genesis 1:1 in the Targums." *CBQ* 52 (1990) 21–29.

Anderson, Paul N. "The Having-Sent-Me Father: Aspects of Agency, Encounter, and Irony in the Johannine Father-Son Relationship." *Semeia* 85 (1999) 33–57.

Anthonioz, Stéphanie. "Amon (אָמוֹן) in Prov 8:30: A Linguistic, Comparative, and Historical Approach." *Antiguo Oriente* 20 (2022) 73–93.

Aristotle. *Poetics, On the Sublime, On Style.* Translated by Stephen Halliwell et al. LCL. Cambridge, MA: Harvard University Press, 1995.

Ashton, John. "The Transformation of Wisdom: A Study of the Prologue of John's Gospel." *NTS* 32 (1986) 161–86.

———. *Understanding the Fourth Gospel.* 2nd ed. Oxford: Oxford University Press, 2007.

Aune, David E. "Chiasmus." In *The Westminster Dictionary of New Testament and Early Christian Literature and Rhetoric*, edited by David E. Aune, 93–96. Louisville: Westminster John Knox, 2003.

Bachmann, Veronika. "Jesus Ben Sira 24: On Wisdom, Who Has Found an Earthly Dwelling Place." *European Judaism* 54:1 (2021) 91–98.

Bailey, Kenneth E. *Jesus through Middle Eastern Eyes: Cultural Studies in the Gospels.* Downers Grove, IL: IVP Academic: 2008.

Balentine, Samuel E. *Job.* Smyth & Helwys Bible Commentary. Macon, GA: Smyth & Helwys, 2006.

Barclay, William. *The Gospel of John.* Vol. 1, *Chapters 1–7.* Rev. ed. Philadelphia: Westminster, 1956.

Barton, George A. "On the Jewish-Christian Doctrine of the Preexistence of the Messiah." *JBL* 21:1 (1902) 78–91.

Barrett, C. K. "'The Father Is Greater than I' John 14:28: Subordinationist Christology in the New Testament." In *Essays on John.* Philadelphia: Westminster, 1982.

———. *The Gospel according to St. John: An Introduction with Commentary and Notes on the Greek Text*. 2nd ed. Philadelphia: Westminster, 1978.
Bauckham, Richard. *Jesus and the God of Israel: God Crucified and Other Studies on the New Testament's Christology of Divine Identity*. Grand Rapids: Eerdmans, 2008.
———. *Son of Man*. Vol. 1, *Early Jewish Literature*. Grand Rapids: Eerdmans, 2023.
Bautch, Kelly Coblentz. "Enoch, First Book of." In *NIDB*, 2:262–265. Nashville: Abingdon, 2007.
Beasley-Murray, Gordon R. *John*. 2nd ed. WBC 36. Nashville: Thomas Nelson, 2000.
Beentjes, Pancratius C. "Full Wisdom Is from the Lord." In *The Wisdom of Ben Sira: Studies on Tradition, Redaction, and Theology*, edited by Angelo Passaro and Giuseppe Bellia, 139–54. DCLS 1. Berlin: de Gruyter, 2008.
———. "Philo of Alexandria and Greek Ben Sira." In *Canonicity, Setting, Wisdom in the Deuterocanonicals*, edited by Geza G. Xeravita et al., 63–78. DCLS 22. Berlin: de Gruyter, 2014.
Beirne, Margaret M. *Women and Men in the Fourth Gospel: A Discipleship of Equals*. JSNTSup 242. London: Sheffield Academic, 2003.
Bekken, Per Jarle. *The Lawsuit Motif in John's Gospel from New Perspectives: Jesus Christ, Crucified Criminal and Emperor of the World*. NovTSup 158. Leiden: Brill, 2015.
Berlin, Adele. "The Wisdom of Creation in Psalm 104." In *Seeking Out the Wisdom of the Ancients: Essays Offered to Honor Michael V. Fox on the Occasion of His Sixty-Fifth Birthday*, edited by Ronald Troxel et al., 71–83. Winona Lake, IN: Eisenbrauns, 2005.
Bernard, J. H. *A Critical and Exegetical Commentary on the Gospel according to St. John*. Vol. 1. ICC. Edinburgh: T. & T. Clark, 1928.
Betz, Joannes. "The Eucharist in the Didache." In *The Didache in Modern Research*, edited by Jonathan A. Draper, 255–70. Leiden: Brill, 1996.
Bhaldraithe, Eoin de. "The Johannine Prologue: Structure and Origins." *ABR* 58 (2010) 57–71.
Boer, Martinus C. de. "The Original Prologue to the Gospel of John." *NTS* 61 (2015) 448–67.
Boismard, M. E. *St. John's Prologue*. Translated by Carisbrooke Dominicans. London: Blackfriars Publications, 1957.
Borg, Marcus. *Meeting Jesus Again for the First Time*. San Francisco: HarperOne, 1994.
Borgen, Peder. *Bread from Heaven: An Exegetical Study of the Concept of Manna in the Gospel of John and in the Writings of Philo*. Johannine Monograph Series 4. Eugene, OR: Wipf & Stock, 2017.
———. "God's Agent in the Fourth Gospel." In *Religions in Antiquity: Festschrift E. Goodenough*, edited by Jacob Neusner, 137–48. Leiden: Brill, 1968.
———. "The Gospel of John and Hellenism: Some Observations." In *Exploring the Gospel of John: In Honor of D. Moody Smith*, edited by R. Alan Culpepper and C. Clifton Black, 98–123. Louisville: Westminster John Knox, 1996.
———. *The Gospel of John: More Light from Philo, Paul and Archaeology: The Scriptures, Tradition, Exposition, Setting, Meaning*. NovTSup 154. Leiden: Brill, 2014.
Bowley, James E. "Aristobulus." In *The Eerdmans Dictionary of Early Judaism*, edited by John J. Collins and Daniel C. Harlow, 378–79. Grand Rapids: Eerdmans, 2010.
Boyarin, Daniel. *Border Lines: The Partition of Judaeo-Christianity*. Philadelphia: University of Pennsylvania Press, 2004.

Brant, Jo-Ann A. *John*. Paideia Commentaries on the New Testament. Grand Rapids: Baker, 2011.

Brewer-Boydston, Ginny. "'They Walk in Wisdom or Folly': The Intensification of Wisdom and Folly from the Book of Proverbs to the Dead Sea Scrolls." *PRS* 39:4 (2012) 319–34.

Brown, Raymond E. *The Death of the Messiah. From Gethsemane to the Grave: A Commentary on the Passion Narratives in the Four Gospels*. 2 vols. ABRL. New York: Doubleday, 1994.

———. *The Gospel according to John: I–XII*. AB 29. Garden City, NY: Doubleday, 1966.

———. *The Gospel according to John: XIII–XXI*. AB 29A. Garden City, NY: Doubleday, 1970.

———. *An Introduction to New Testament Christology*. New York: Paulist, 1994.

———. *An Introduction to the Gospel of John*. Edited by Francis J. Moloney. ABRL. New York: Doubleday, 2003.

Brown, William P. "Proverbs 8:22–31." *Interpretation* 6:3 (2009) 286–88.

Bruce, F. F. *The Gospel and Epistles of John*. Grand Rapids: Eerdmans, 1983.

Brueggemann, Walter. *Theology of the Old Testament: Testimony, Dispute, Advocacy*. Minneapolis: Fortress, 1997.

Bultmann, Rudolf. *The Gospel according to John: A Commentary*. Translated by G. R. Beasley-Murray et al. Philadelphia: Westminster, 1971.

Burkes, Shannon. "Choosing Life in Ben Sira and Baruch." *JSJ* 30:3 (1999) 254–76.

Burnett, F. W. "Wisdom." In *DJG*, 873–77.

Bushur, James G. "The Early Christian Appropriation of Old Testament Scripture: The Canonical Reading of Scripture in 1 Clement." *CTQ* 83:1 (2019) 63–83.

Camp, Claudia V. *Wisdom and the Feminine in the Book of Proverbs*. BLS 11. Sheffield: The Almond, 1985.

Capes, David B. "Preexistence." In *DLNT*, 955–61.

Carson, D. A. *The Gospel according to John*. Grand Rapids: Eerdmans, 1991.

Carter, Warren. *John: Storyteller, Interpreter, Evangelist*. Peabody, MA: Hendrickson, 2006.

———. *John and Empire: Initial Explorations*. New York: T. & T. Clark, 2008.

———. "The Prologue and John's Gospel: Function, Symbol, and the Definitive Word." *JSNT* 39 (1990) 35–58.

Casey, Maurice. *From Jewish Prophet to Gentile God: The Origins and Development of New Testament Christology*. Louisville: Westminster John Knox, 1991.

Ceresko, Anthony R. *Introduction to Old Testament Wisdom: A Spirituality for Liberation*. Maryknoll, NY: Orbis, 1999.

Charlesworth, James H. "Lady Wisdom and Johannine Christology." In *Light in a Spotless Mirror: Reflections on Wisdom Traditions in Judaism and Early Christianity*, edited by James H. Charlesworth and Michael A. Daise, 92–133. Harrisburg, PA: Trinity, 2003.

Clark, Douglas K. "Signs in Wisdom and John." *CBQ* 45 (1983) 201–9.

Clarke, Ernest G. *The Wisdom of Solomon*. Cambridge: Cambridge University Press, 1973.

Clifford, Richard J. *Proverbs: A Commentary*. OTL. Louisville: Westminster John Knox, 1999.

———. *The Wisdom Literature*. Interpreting Biblical Texts. Nashville: Abingdon, 1998.

Clines, David J. A. *Job 21–37*. WBC 18A. Nashville: Thomas Nelson, 2006.

Cohen, Shaye J. D. *From the Maccabees to the Mishnah*. LEC 7. Philadelphia: Westminster, 1987.
Cohen, Shaye J. D., et al., eds. *The Oxford Annotated Mishnah: A New Translation of the Mishnah with Introductions and Notes*. 3 vols. Oxford: Oxford University Press, 2023.
Collins, Adela Yarbro. "Aristobulus: A New Translation and Introduction." In *OTP*, 2:831–42.
Collins, Adela Yarbro, and John J. Collins. *King and Messiah as Son of God: Divine, Human, and Angelic Messianic Figures in Biblical and Related Literature*. Grand Rapids: Eerdmans, 2008.
Collins, John J. *Between Athens and Jerusalem: Jewish Identity in the Hellenistic Diaspora*. New York: Crossroad, 1982.
Coloe, Mary L. *John 1–10*. Wisdom Commentary 44A. Collegeville, MN: Liturgical, 2021.
———. *John 11–21*. Wisdom Commentary 44B. Collegeville, MN: Liturgical, 2021.
———. "The Structure of the Johannine Prologue and Genesis 1." *ABR* 45 (1997) 40–55.
Corley, Jeremy. *Ben Sira's Teaching on Friendship*. BJS 316. Providence, RI: Brown University, 2002.
———. "Intertextual Study of Proverbs and Ben Sira." In *Intertextual Studies in Ben Sira and Tobit*, edited by Jeremy Corley and Vincent Skemp, 155–82. CBQMS 38. Washington, DC: Catholic Biblical Association of America, 2005.
Cory, Catherine. "Wisdom's Rescue: A New Reading of the Tabernacle Discourse (John 7:1–8:59)." *JBL* 116:1 (1997) 95–116.
Coutsoumpos, Panayotis. "The Difficulty of ΜΟΝΟΓΕΝΗΣ ΘΕΟΣ in John 1,18: A Reassessment." *Biblica* 98:3 (2017) 435–46.
Cowan, Christopher. "The Father and Son in the Fourth Gospel: Johannine Subordination Revisited." *JETS* 49:1 (2006) 115–35.
Crenshaw, James L. "The Book of Sirach: Introduction, Commentary, and Reflections." In *NIB*, 5:601–867.
Crowe, Brandon D. "The Chiastic Structure of Seven Signs in the Gospel of John: Revisiting a Neglected Proposal." *BBR* 28:1 (2018) 65–81.
Cullmann, Oscar. *The Christology of the New Testament*. Translated by Shirley C. Guthrie and Charles A. M. Hall. Rev. ed. Philadelphia: Westminster, 1963.
———. *The Johannine Circle*. Translated by John Bowden. Philadelphia: Westminster, 1976.
Culpepper, R. Alan. "The Christology of the Johannine Writings." In *Who Do You Say That I Am? Essays on Christology*, edited by Mark Allan Powell and David R. Bauer, 66–87. Louisville: Westminster John Knox, 1999.
———. *The Gospel and Letters of John*. Interpreting Biblical Texts. Nashville: Abingdon, 1998.
———. "The Pivot of John's Prologue." *NTS* 27:1 (1980) 1–31.
Daley, Brian E. "'The Beginning of His Ways': Christ as God's Personified Wisdom in the Early Greek Fathers." *GOTR* 63 (2018) 147–72.
Davies, Margaret. *Rhetoric and Reference in the Fourth Gospel*. JSNTSup 69. Sheffield: Sheffield Academic, 1992.

Davies, W. D. "Reflections on Aspects of the Jewish Background of the Gospel of John." In *Exploring the Gospel of John: In Honor of D. Moody Smith*, edited by R. Alan Culpepper and C. Clifton Black, 43–64. Louisville: Westminster John Knox, 1996.

Davis, Ellen F. *Proverbs, Ecclesiastes, and the Song of Songs*. Westminster Bible Companion. Louisville: Westminster John Knox, 2000.

Deutsch, Celia M. *Lady Wisdom, Jesus, and the Sages: Metaphor and Social Context in Matthew's Gospel*. Valley Forge, PA: Trinity, 1996.

Devillers, Luc. "Le prologue du quatrième évangile, clé de voûte littérature johannique." *NTS* 58:3 (2012) 317–30.

Di Lella, Alexander A. "Fear of the Lord as Wisdom: Ben Sira 1,11–30." In *The Book of Ben Sira in Modern Research: Proceedings of the First International Ben Sira Conference, 28–31 July 1996 Soesterberg, Netherlands*, edited by Pancratius C. Beentjes, 113–33. BZAW 255. Berlin: de Gruyter, 1997.

———. "God and Wisdom in the Theology of Ben Sira." In *Ben Sira's God: Proceedings of the International Ben Sira Conference, Durham – Ushaw College, 2001*, edited by Renate Egger-Wenzel, 3–17. BZAW 321. Berlin: de Gruyter, 2002.

Dillon, Richard. "Wisdom Tradition and Sacramental Retrospect in the Cana Account (Jn 2,1–11)." *CBQ* 24:3 (1962) 268–296.

Dodd, C. H. *The Interpretation of the Fourth Gospel*. London: Cambridge University Press, 1953.

Domeris, William R. "The Confession of Peter According to John 6:69." *TynBul* 44:1 (1993) 155–67.

Douglas, Sally. *Early Church Understandings of Jesus as the Female Divine: The Scandal of the Scandal of Particularity*. LNTS 557. London: Bloomsbury T. & T. Clark, 2016.

Dunn, James D. G. "Christology as an Aspect of Theology." In *The Christ & the Spirit*, vol. 1, *Christology*, 377–87. Grand Rapids: Eerdmans, 1998.

———. *Christology in the Making: A New Testament Inquiry into the Origins of the Doctrine of the Incarnation*. 2nd ed. Grand Rapids: Eerdmans, 1989.

———. "Christology (NT)." In *ABD*, 1:979–91.

———. *Did the First Christians Worship Jesus? The New Testament Evidence*. Louisville: Westminster John Knox, 2010.

———. "Incarnation." In *The Christ & the Spirit*, vol. 1, *Christology*, 30–47. Grand Rapids: Eerdmans, 1998.

———. *Jesus according to the New Testament*. Grand Rapids: Eerdmans, 2019.

———. "Let John Be John." In *Das Evangelium und die Evangelien*, edited by Peter Stuhlmacher, 309–39. Tubingen: Mohr, 1983.

———. *Neither Jew nor Greek: A Contested Identity*. Christianity in the Making 3. Grand Rapids: Eerdmans, 2015.

———. "New Testament Christology." In *The Christ & the Spirit*, vol. 1, *Christology*, 3–29. Grand Rapids: Eerdmans, 1998.

———. *New Testament Theology: An Introduction*. Library of Biblical Theology. Nashville: Abingdon, 2009.

———. *The Parting of the Ways: Between Christianity and Judaism and Their Significance for the Character of Christianity*. London: SCM, 1991.

———. *The Theology of Paul the Apostle*. Grand Rapids: Eerdmans, 1997.

———. *Unity and Diversity in the New Testament: An Inquiry into the Character of Earliest Christianity*. 3rd ed. London: SCM, 2006.

Ehrman, Bart D. *The Apostolic Fathers*. Vol. 1. LCL. Cambridge, MA: Harvard University Press, 2003.

———. *The Orthodox Corruption of Scripture: The Effect of Early Christological Controversies on the Text of the New Testament*. New York: Oxford University Press, 1993.

Ellis, Teresa Ann. *Gender in the Book of Ben Sira: Divine Wisdom, Erotic Poetry, and the Garden of Eden*. BZAW 453. Berlin: de Gruyter, 2013.

Epp, Eldon Jay. "Wisdom, Torah, Word: The Johannine Prologue and the Purpose of the Fourth Gospel." In *Current Issues in Biblical and Patristic Interpretation*, edited by Gerald F. Hawthorne, 128–46. Grand Rapids: Eerdmans, 1975.

Evans, Craig A. "Evidence of Conflict with the Synagogue in the Johannine Writings." In *John and Judaism: A Contested Relationship in Context*, edited by R. Alan Culpepper and Paul N. Anderson, 135–54. RBS 87. Atlanta: SBL, 2017.

———. "The Genesis Apocryphon and the Rewritten Bible." *Revue de Qumran* 13:49–52 (1988) 153–65.

———. *Word and Glory: On the Exegetical and Theological Background of John's Prologue*. JSNTSup 89. Sheffield: Sheffield Academic, 1993.

Feuillet, André. *Johannine Studies*. Translated by Thomas E. Crane. Staten Island: Alba House, 1965.

Fischel, Henry A. "Wisdom in the World of Midrash." In *Aspects of Wisdom in Judaism and Early Christianity*, edited by Robert L. Wilken, 67–101. Notre Dame, IN: University of Notre Dame Press, 1975.

Fletcher-Louis, Crispin H. T. "The Cosmology of P and Theological Anthropology in the Wisdom of Jesus Ben Sira." In *Of Scribes and Sages: Early Jewish Interpretation and Transmission of Scripture*, edited by Craig A. Evans, 1:69–113. London: T. & T. Clark, 2004.

Fox, Michael V. *Proverbs 1–9: A New Translation with Introduction and Commentary*. AB 18A. New Haven, CT: Yale University Press, 2000.

———. *Proverbs 10–31: A New Translation with Introduction and Commentary*. AB 18B. New Haven, CT: Yale University Press, 2009.

Freed, Edwin D. "Egō Eimi in John 1:20 and 4:25." *CBQ* 41:2 (1979) 288–91.

———. "'EGŌ EIMI' in John VIII. 24 in the Light of its Context and Jewish Messianic Belief." *JTS* 33:1 (1982) 163–67.

———. *The New Testament: A Critical Introduction*. 3rd ed. London: Wadsworth, 2001.

Friend, Helen S. "Like Father, Like Son: A Discussion of the Concept of Agency in Halakah and John." *ATJ* 21 (1990) 18–28.

Fuller, Reginald H. *The Foundations of New Testament Christology*. New York: Scribner, 1965

———. "The Incarnation in Historical Perspective." *ATR*, Supplementary Series 7 (1976) 57–66.

Gammie, John G. "From Prudentialism to Apocalypticism: The Houses of the Sages amid the Varying Forms of Wisdom." In *The Sage in Israel and the Ancient Near East*, edited by John G. Gammie and Leo G. Perdue, 479–97. Winona Lake, IN: Eisenbrauns, 1990.

———. "Spatial and Ethical Dualism in Jewish Wisdom and Apocalyptic Literature." *JBL* 93:3 (1974) 356–85.

Gaston, Thomas E. "Does the Gospel of John Have a High Christology?" *HBT* 36 (2014) 129–41.

———. *Dynamic Monarchianism: The Earliest Christology?* 2nd ed. Nashville: Theophilus, 2023.
Gathercole, Simon. "Wisdom (Personified)." In *The Eerdmans Dictionary of Early Judaism*, edited by John J. Collins and Daniel C. Harlow, 1339. Grand Rapids: Eerdmans, 2010.
Geyer, John. *The Wisdom of Solomon: Introduction and Commentary*. London: SCM, 1963.
Gilbert, Maurice. "Ben Sira, Reader of Genesis 1–11." In *Intertextual Studies in Ben Sira and Tobit*, edited by Jeremy Corley and Vincent Skemp, 89–99. CBQMS 38. Washington, DC: Catholic Biblical Association of America, 2005.
Girard, Marc. "La composition structurelle des sept 'signes' dans le quatrieme evangile." *Sciences Religieuses* 9 (1980) 315–24.
Goldingay, John. *Biblical Theology: The God of the Christian Scriptures*. Downers Grove, IL: IVP Academic, 2016.
———. *Psalms*. Vol. 3, *Psalms 90–150*. Baker Commentary on the Old Testament Wisdom and Psalms. Grand Rapids: Baker Academic, 2008.
Gordley, Matthew E. "The Johannine Prologue and Jewish Didactic Hymn Traditions: A New Case for Reading the Prologue as a Hymn." *JBL* 128:4 (2009) 781–802.
Gottlieb, Fred. "The Creation Theme in Genesis 1, Psalm 104 and Job 38–42." *JBQ* 44:1 (2016) 29–36.
Grant, Deena E. "Reinterpretation of Scripture in the Hymn to the Creator." *TC* 16 (2001) 1–10.
Habel, Norman C. *The Book of Job: A Commentary*. OTL. London: Westminster, 1985.
Hadas-Lebel, Mireille. *Philo of Alexandria: A Thinker in the Jewish Diaspora*. Translated by Robyn Fréchet, edited by Francesca Calabi and Robert Berchman. Studies in Philo of Alexandria 7. Leiden: Brill, 2012.
Haenchen, Ernst. *John 1: A Commentary on the Gospel of John, Chapters 1–6*. Translated and edited by Robert W. Funk. Hermeneia. Philadelphia: Augsburg Fortress, 1980.
———. *John 2: A Commentary on the Gospel of John, Chapters 7–21*. Translated and edited by Robert W. Funk. Hermeneia. Philadelphia: Augsburg Fortress, 1988.
Haight, Roger. *Jesus, Symbol of God*. Maryknoll, NY: Orbis, 2002.
Hamerton-Kelly, Robert G. *Pre-Existence, Wisdom, and the Son of Man: A Study of the Idea of Pre-Existence in the New Testament*. SNTSMS 21. Cambridge: Cambridge University Press, 1973.
Hanson, Anthony Tyrrell. *The New Testament Interpretation of Scripture*. London: SPCK, 1980.
Hanson, R. P. C. *The Search for the Christian Doctrine of God: The Arian Controversy, 318–381*. Grand Rapids: Baker Academic, 1988.
Harrington, Daniel J. *Jesus Ben Sira of Jerusalem: A Biblical Guide to Living Wisely*. Collegeville, MN: Liturgical, 2005.
Harris, Elizabeth. *Prologue and Gospel: The Theology of the Fourth Evangelist*. JSNTSup 107. Sheffield: Sheffield Academic, 1994.
Harris, J. Rendel. *The Origin of the Prologue of St. John's Gospel*. Cambridge: Cambridge University Press, 1917.
Henderson, Ruth. "The Inter-Textual Dialogue between Deuteronomy 4, 30 and Job 28:12–20 in Baruch 3:9—4:4." In *Studies on Baruch: Composition, Literary Relations, and Reception*, edited by Sean A. Adams, 43–59. DCLS 23. Berlin: de Gruyter, 2016.

Hengel, Martin. *Studies in Early Christology*. Edinburgh: T. & T. Clark, 1995.
Hillar, Marian. *From Logos to Trinity: The Evolution of Religious Concepts from Pythagoras to Tertullian*. Cambridge: Cambridge University Press, 2012.
Himes, Paul Aaron. "Loving Wisdom: The Ἀγαπάω-Φιλέω Exchange in John 21:15–17 as an Allusion to LXX Proverbs 8:17." *BBR* 30:3 (2020) 379–402.
Himmelfarb, Martha. "The Wisdom of the Scribe, the Wisdom of the Priest, and the Wisdom of the King According to Ben Sira." In *For a Later Generation: The Transformation of Tradition in Israel, Early Judaism, and Early Christianity*, edited by Randal A. Argall et al., 88–99. Harrisburg, PA: Trinity, 2000.
Holladay, Carl R. *A Critical Introduction to the New Testament: Interpreting the Message and Measning of Jesus Christ*. Nashville: Abingdon, 2005.
Horne, Milton P. *Proverbs-Ecclesiastes*. Smyth & Helwys Bible Commentary. Macon, GA: Smyth & Helwys, 2003.
Hossfeld, Frank Lothar, and Eric Zenger. *Psalms 3: A Commentary on Psalms 101–150*. Translated by Linda M. Maloney. Hermeneia. Minneapolis: Fortress, 2011.
Hurtado, Larry W. *Lord Jesus Christ: Devotion to Jesus in Early Christianity*. Grand Rapids: Eerdmans, 2003.
———. *One God, One Lord: Early Christian Devotion and Ancient Jewish Monotheism*. 2nd ed. London: T. & T. Clark, 1998.
———. "Pre-Existence." In *DPL*, 743–46.
Irons, Lee, et al. *The Son of God: Three Views of the Identity of Jesus*. Eugene, OR: Wipf & Stock, 2015.
Isaac, E. "1 (Ethiopic Apocalypse of) Enoch." In *OTP*, 1:5–90.
Johnson, Elizabeth A. "Jesus, the Wisdom of God: A Biblical Basis for Non-Androcentric Christology." *ETL* 61 (1985) 261–94.
———. "Wisdom Was Made Flesh and Pitched Her Tent among Us." In *Reconstructing the Christ Symbol: Essays in Feminist Christology*, edited by Maryanne Stevens, 95–117. New York: Paulist, 1993.
Jones, Scott C. *Rumors of Wisdom: Job 28 as Poetry*. BZAW 398. Berlin: de Gruyter, 2009.
Jonge, Marinus de. *Jesus: Stranger from Heaven and Son of God: Jesus Christ and the Christians in Johannine Perspective*, edited by Wayne A. Meeks. SBLSBS 11. Missoula, MT: Scholars, 1977.
Kealy, Sean P. *The Wisdom Books of the Bible: Proverbs, Job, Ecclesiastes, Ben Sira, Wisdom of Solomon: A Survey of the History of Their Interpretation*. Lewiston, NY: Edwin Mellen, 2012.
Kee, Howard Clark. *Jesus in History: An Approach to the Study of the Gospels*. 2nd ed. New York: Harcourt Brace Jovanovich, 1977.
Keener, Craig S. *The Gospel of John: A Commentary*. 2 vols. Peabody, MA: Hendrickson, 2003.
Kim, Sang-Hoon. *Sourcebook of the Structures and Styles in John 1–10: The Johannine Parallelisms and Chiasms*. Eugene, OR: Wipf & Stock, 2014.
King, Sheri D. "Wisdom Became Flesh: Analysis of the Prologue to the Gospel of John." *CurTM* 40:3 (2013) 179–87.
Kirk, J. R. Daniel. *A Man Attested by God: The Human Jesus of the Synoptic Gospels*. Grand Rapids: Eerdmans, 2016.
Kittel, Gerhard. "λέγω, λόγος, κτλ." In *TDNT*, 4:69–192.

Klausner, Joseph. *The Messianic Idea in Israel From Its Beginning to the Completion of the Mishnah.* New York: Macmillian, 1955.
Klein, Michael L., ed. *The Fragment-Targums of the Pentateuch according to Their Extant Sources.* Translated by Michael L. Klein. Analecta Biblica. Rome: Biblical Institute, 1980.
Knibb, Michael A. "Enoch, Similitudes of (1 Enoch 37–71)." In *The Eerdmans Dictionary of Early Judaism,* edited by John J. Collins and Daniel C. Harlow, 585–87. Grand Rapids: Eerdmans, 2010.
Kobel, Esther. *Dining with John: Communal Meals and Identity Formation in the Fourth Gospel and its Historical and Cultural Context.* BIS 109. Leiden: Brill, 2011.
Koester, Craig R. *Symbolism in the Fourth Gospel: Meaning, Mystery, Community.* 2nd ed. Minneapolis: Fortress, 2003.
Kolarcik, Michael. "The Book of Wisdom: Introduction, Commentary, and Reflections" In *NIB*, 5:435–600. Nashville: Abingdon, 1994.
Köstenberger, Andreas J., *John*. BECNT. Grand Rapids: Baker Academic, 2004.
Kovalishyn, Mariam Kamell. "Wisdom in the New Testament." In *The Oxford Handbook of Wisdom and the Bible,* edited by Will Kynes, 173–86. Oxford: Oxford University Press, 2021.
Kruse, Colin G. *The Gospel according to John: An Introduction and Commentary.* TNTC. Grand Rapids: Eerdmans, 2003.
Kümmel, Werner Georg. *Introduction to the New Testament.* Translated by Howard C. Kee. Rev. ed. Nashville: Abingdon, 1973.
———. *The Theology of the New Testament according to Its Major Witnesses: Jesus-Paul-John.* Translated by John E. Steely. Nashville: Abingdon, 1973.
Kuschel, Karl-Josef. *Born before All Time? The Dispute over Christ's Origins.* New York: Crossroad, 1992.
Kwon, JiSeong, "Wisdom Incarnate? Identity and Role of אשת־חיל ('the Valiant Woman') in Proverbs 31:10–31." *JESOT* 1:2 (2012) 167–88.
Kysar, Robert. *John, the Maverick Gospel.* Atlanta: John Knox, 1979.
Ladd, George E. *A Theology of the New Testament.* Grand Rapids: Eerdmans, 1974.
Laporte, Jean. "Philo in the Tradition of Wisdom." In *Aspects of Wisdom in Judaism and Early Christianity,* edited by Robert L. Wilken, 103–41. Notre Dame, IN: University of Notre Dame Press, 1975.
Lee, Dorothy A. "Beyond Suspicion? The Fatherhood of God in the Fourth Gospel." *Pacifica* 8 (1995) 140–54.
———. *The Symbolic Narratives of the Fourth Gospel: The Interplay of Form and Meaning.* Sheffield: Sheffield Academic, 1994.
Lincoln, Andrew T. *The Gospel according to Saint John.* BNTC. Peabody, MA: Hendrickson, 2005.
Lindars, Barnabas. *The Gospel of John.* New Century Bible Commentary. Grand Rapids: Eerdmans, 1972.
Lipscomb, Anthony I. "'She Is My Sister': Sarai as Lady Wisdom in the Genesis Apocryphon." *JSJ* 50 (2019) 319–47.
Loader, William. "The Central Structure of Johannine Christology." *NTS* 30:2 (1984) 188–216.
———. *The Christology of the Fourth Gospel: Structure and Issues.* BET 23. Frankfurt: Peter Lang, 1989.

Longman, Temper, III. *Proverbs*. Baker Commentary on the Old Testament Wisdom and Psalms. Grand Rapids: Baker Academic, 2006.

———. "Woman Wisdom and Woman Folly." In *Dictionary of the Old Testament: Wisdom, Poetry & Writings*, edited by Temper Longman III and Peter Enns, 912–16. Downers Grove, IL: IVP Academic, 2008.

Lucas, Ernest C. *Proverbs*. Two Horizons Old Testament Commentary. Grand Rapids: Eerdmans, 2015.

Lund, Nils W. "The Influence of Chiasmus upon the Structure of the Gospels." *ATR* 13:1 (1931) 27–48.

Macaskill, Grant. *Revealed Wisdom and Inaugurated Eschatology in Ancient Judaism and Early Christianity*. JSJSup 115. Leiden: Brill, 2007.

Machiela, Daniel A. *The Dead Sea Genesis Apocryphon*. Edited by Florentino Garcia Martinez. STDJ 79. Leiden: Brill, 2009.

Mack, Burton. L., and Roland. E. Murphy. "Wisdom Literature." In *Early Judaism and Its Modern Interpreters*, edited by Robert A. Kraft and George. W. E. Nickelsburg, 371–410. Atlanta: Scholars, 1986.

MacRae, George W. "The Fourth Gospel and Religionsgeschichte." *CBQ* 32:1 (1970) 13–24

Maher, Michael. "Some Aspects of Torah in Judaism." *ITQ* 38:4 (1971) 310–25.

Manns, Frédéric. "A Jewish Approach to the Gospel of John: Part One, a Methodological Approach." *Antonianum* 87:2 (2012) 259–79.

Martin, James D. *Proverbs*. Old Testament Guides. Sheffield: Shefield Academic, 1995.

Mattila, Sharon Lea. "Wisdom, Sense Perception, Nature, and Philo's Gender Gradient." *HTR* 89:2 (1996) 103–29.

Mazzinghi, Luca. *Wisdom*. IECOT. Stuttgart: W. Kohlhammer, 2019.

McCann Jr., J. Clinton. "The Book of Psalms." In *NIB*, 4:639–1280.

McCreesh, Thomas P. "Wisdom as Wife: Proverbs 31:10–31." *RB* 92:1 (1985) 25–46.

McGrath, James. *John's Apologetic Christology: Legitimation and Development in Johannine Christology*. SNTSMS 111. Cambridge: Cambridge University Press, 2001.

———. *The Only True God: Early Christian Monotheism in Its Jewish Context*. Urbana: University of Illinois Press, 2009.

———. *What Jesus Learned from Women*. Eugene, OR: Cascade, 2021.

McHugh, John F. *John 1–4*. ICC. New York: T. & T. Clark, 2009.

McIlhone, James P. "Jesus as God's Agent in the Fourth Gospel: Implications for Christology, Ecclesiology, and Mission." *Chicago Studies* 44 (2005) 295–315.

McKinlay, Judith E. *Gendering Wisdom the Host: Biblical Invitations to Eat and Drink*. JSOTSup 216. Sheffield: Sheffield Academic, 1996.

McNamara, Martin. *Targum Neofiti 1: Genesis*. The Aramaic Bible: The Targums. Collegeville, MN: Liturgical, 1992.

Meier, John P. *A Marginal Jew: Rethinking the Historical Jesus*. Vol. 2, *Mentor, Message, and Miracles*. ABRL. New York: Doubleday, 1994.

Meyer, Paul W. "'The Father': The Presentation of God in the Fourth Gospel." In *Exploring the Gospel of John: In Honor of D. Moody Smith*, edited by R. Alan Culpepper and C. Clifton Black, 255–73. Louisville: Westminster John Knox, 1996.

Meyers, Carol L., et al., eds. *Women in Scripture: A Dictionary of Named and Unnamed Women in the Hebrew Bible, the Apocryphal/Deuterocanonical Books, and the New Testament*. Boston: Houghton Mifflin, 2000.

Michaels, J. Ramsey. *The Gospel of John*. NICNT. Grand Rapids: Eerdmans, 2010.
Moeller, Henry R. "Wisdom Motifs and John's Gospel." *BETS* 6 (1963) 92–100.
Moloney, Francis J. *The Gospel of John*. Sacra Pagina 4. Collegeville, MN: Liturgical, 1998.
Moore, G. F. "Intermediaries in Jewish Theology." *HTR* 15 (1922) 41–55.
Morris, Leon. *The Gospel according to John*. NICNT. Grand Rapids: Eerdmans, 1971.
Mulder, Otto. *Simon the High Priest in Sirach 50: An Exegetical Study of the Significance of Simon the High Priest as Climax to Praise of the Fathers in Ben Sira's Concept of History of Israel*. JSJSup 78. Leiden: Brill, 2003.
Muraoka, Takamitsu. *Wisdom of Ben Sira*. OBO 302. Leuven: Peeters, 2023.
Murphy, Roland E. *Proverbs*. WBC 22. Nashville: Thomas Nelson, 1998.
———. *The Tree of Life: An Exploration of Biblical Wisdom Literature*. New York: Doubleday, 1990.
———. *Wisdom Literature: Job, Proverbs, Ruth, Canticles, Ecclesiastes, and Esther*. FOTL 13. Grand Rapids: Eerdmans, 1981.
Myers, Alicia D. *Characterizing Jesus: A Rhetorical Analysis of the Fourth Gospel's Use of Scripture in its Presentation of Jesus*. London: T. & T. Clark, 2012.
Nemes, Steven. *Trinity and Incarnation: A Post-Catholic Theology*. Eugene, OR: Cascade, 2023.
Newsom, Carol A. "The Book of Job: Introduction, Commentary, and Reflections." In *NIB*, 4:317–637.
Nickelsburg, George W. E., and James C. VanderKam. *1 Enoch 2: A Commentary on the Book of 1 Enoch, Chapters 37–82*. Hermeneia. Minneapolis: Fortress, 2011.
Niehoff, Maren R. *Philo of Alexandria: An Intellectual Biography*. ABRL. New Haven, CT: Yale University Press, 2018.
Novakovic, Lidija. *John 1–10: A Handbook on the Greek Text*. BHGNT. Waco, TX: Baylor University Press, 2020.
———. *John 11–21: A Handbook on the Greek Text*. BHGNT. Waco, TX: Baylor University Press, 2020.
O'Boyle, Aidan. *Towards a Contemporary Wisdom Christology: Some Catholic Christologies in German, English and French 1965–1995*. Tesi Gregoriana Serie Teologica 98. Rome: Gregorian University Press, 2003.
O'Day, Gail R. "The Gospel of John: Introduction, Commentary, and Reflections." In *NIB*, 9:491–865.
O'Day, Gail R., and Susan E. Hylen. *John*. Westminster Bible Companion. Louisville: Westminster John Knox, 2006.
Oh, Dong Woo. "Name Theology in John 1:14." *NovT* 64 (2022) 210–28.
Painter, John. "Christology and the History of the Johannine Community in the Prologue of the Fourth Gospel." *NTS* 30 (1984) 460–74.
———. *The Quest for the Messiah: The History, Literature and Theology of the Johannine Community*. 2nd ed. Nashville: Abingdon, 1993.
Pauw, Amy Plantinga. *Proverbs and Ecclesiastes: A Theological Commentary on the Bible*. Louisville: Westminster John Knox, 2015.
Paxson, James. *The Poetics of Personification*. Literature, Culture, Theory 6. Cambridge: Cambridge University Press, 1994.
Perdue, Leo G. "Cosmology and the Social Order in the Wisdom Tradition." In *The Sage in Israel and the Ancient Near East*, edited by John G. Gammie and Leo G. Perdue, 457–78. Winona Lake, IN: Eisenbrauns, 1990.

---. *Proverbs*. Interpretation. Louisville: John Knox, 2000.

---. *Wisdom & Creation: The Theology of Wisdom Literature*. Nashville: Abingdon, 1994.

---. *Wisdom Literature: A Theological History*. Louisville: Westminster John Knox, 2007.

Perkins, Pheme. "The Gospel According to John." In *The New Jerome Biblical Commentary*, edited by Raymond E. Brown et al., 942–85. Englewood Cliffs, NJ: Prentice Hall, 1990.

Perriman, Andrew. *In the Form of a God: The Pre-Existence of the Exalted Christ in Paul*. Studies in Early Christology 1. Eugene, OR: Cascade: 2022.

Phillips, Peter M. *The Prologue of the Fourth Gospel: A Sequential Reading*. London: T. & T. Clark, 2006.

Plutarch. *Lives VII: Demosthenes and Cicero, Alexander and Caesar*. Translated by Bernadotte Perrin. LCL 99. Cambridge, MA: Harvard University Press, 1919.

Pope, Marvin H. *Job: Introduction, Translation, and Notes*. AB 15. Garden City, NY: Doubleday, 1965.

Potterie, Ignace de la. "Je suis la Voie, la Vérité et la Vie (Jeann 14,6)." *NRT* 88 (1966) 907–42.

Pryor, John W. "Jesus and Israel in the Fourth Gospel—John 1:11." *NovT* 32:3 (1990) 201–18.

Rad, Gerhard von. *Old Testament Theology*. Vol. 1. Translated by D. G. G. Stalker. New York: Harper & Row, 1962.

---. *Wisdom in Israel*. Translated by James D. Martin. London: SCM, 1972.

Reider, Joseph. *The Book of Wisdom: An English Translation with Introduction and Commentary*. New York: Harper & Brothers, 1957.

Reiterer, Friedrich Vincenz. "The Interpretation of the Wisdom Tradition of the Torah within Ben Sira." In *The Wisdom of Ben Sira: Studies on Tradition, Redaction, and Theology*, edited by Angelo Passaro and Giuseppe Bellia, 209–32. DCLS 1. Berlin: de Gruyter, 2008.

Richardson, Alan. *An Introduction to the Theology of the New Testament*. New York: Harper, 1958.

Ridderbos, Herman N. *The Gospel according to John: A Theological Commentary*. Translated by John Vriend. Grand Rapids: Eerdmans, 1997.

Ringe, Sharon H. *Wisdom's Friends: Community and Christology in the Gospel of John*. Louisville: Westminster John Knox, 1999.

Robert, André, and André Feuillet. *Introduction to the New Testament*. Translated by Patrick W. Skehan. New York: Desclee, 1965.

Robinson, John A. T. *The Priority of John*. Edited by J. F. Coakley. Oak Park: Meyer Stone, 1987.

---. "The Use of the Fourth Gospel for Christology Today." In *Christ and Spirit in the New Testament*, edited by Barnabas Lindars and Stephen S. Smalley, 61–78. Cambridge: Cambridge University Press, 1973.

---. *Twelve More New Testament Studies*. London: SCM, 1984.

Rogers, Jessie. "'It Overflows Like the Euphrates with Understanding': Another Look at the Relationship between Law and Wisdom in Sirach." In *Of Scribes and Sages: Early Jewish Interpretation and Transmission of Scripture*, edited by Craig A. Evans, 1:114–21. London: T. & T. Clark, 2004.

Rybolt, John E. *Sirach*. Collegeville Bible Commentary 21. Collegeville, MN: Liturgical, 1986.
———. *Wisdom*. Collegeville Bible Commentary 20. Collegeville, MN: Liturgical, 1986.
Saldarini, Anthony J. "The Book of Baruch: Introduction, Commentary, and Reflections." In *NIB*, 6:927–82. Nashville: Abingdon, 2001.
Sandelin, Karl-Gustav. *Wisdom as Nourisher: A Study of an Old Testament Theme, Its Development within Early Judaism and Its Impact on Early Christianity*. Åbo: Åbo Akademi, 1986.
Sanders, J. A. "The Modern History of the Qumran Psalms Scroll and Canonical Criticism." In *Emanuel: Studies in Hebrew Bible, Septuagint, and Dead Sea Scrolls in Honor of Emanuel Tov*, edited by S. Paul et al., 393–411. Boston: Brill, 2003.
———. *The Psalms Scroll of Qumran Cave 11 (11QPSa)*. DJD 4. Oxford: Clarendon, 1965.
Sandmel, Samuel. "Parallelomania." *JBL* 81:1 (1962) 1–13.
Sanford, John A. *Mystical Christianity: A Psychological Commentary on the Gospel of John*. New York: Crossroad, 1994.
Schäfer, Peter. *The Origins of Jewish Mysticism*. Princeton, NJ: Princeton University Press, 2011.
Schechter, Solomon. *Aspects of Rabbinic Theology: Major Concepts of the Talmud*. 4th ed. New York: Schocken, 1987.
Schipper, Bernd U. *Proverbs 1–15*. Translated by Stephen Germany. Hermeneia. Minneapolis: Fortress, 2019.
Schmidt, A. Jorden. *Wisdom, Cosmos, and Cultus in the Book of Sirach*. DCLS 42. Berlin: de Gruyter, 2019.
Schnackenburg, Rudolf. *The Gospel according to St. John*. 3 vols. New York: Crossroad, 1990.
Schneiders, Sandra M. *Written That You May Believe: Encountering Jesus in the Fourth Gospel*. 2nd ed. New York: Crossroad, 1999.
Schroer, Silvia. *Wisdom Has Built Her House: Studies in the Figure of Sophia in the Bible*. Translated by Linda M. Maloney and William McDonough. Collegeville, MN: Liturgical, 2000.
Schüssler Fiorenza, Elisabeth. *In Memory of Her: A Feminist Theological Reconstruction of Christian Origins*. New York: Crossroad, 1998.
———. *Jesus: Miriam's Child, Sophia's Prophet: Critical Issues in Feminist Christology*. 2nd ed. London: Bloomsbury T .& T. Clark, 2015.
Schweizer, Eduard V. "Zum religionsgeschichtlichen Hintergrund der Sendungsformel." *Zeitschrift für die neutestamentliche Wissenschaft und die Kunde der älteren Kirche* 57:3–4 (1966) 199–210.
Scott, Martin. *Sophia and the Johannine Jesus*. JSNTSup 71. Sheffield: Sheffield Academic, 1992.
Shafer, Byron E. "Wisdom Christology." *Bangalore Theological Forum* 41:1 (2009) 52–78.
Shaw, Karen L. H. "Wisdom Incarnate: Preaching Proverbs 31." *JEHS* 14:2 (2014) 44–53.
Sidebottom, E. M. *The Christ of the Fourth Gospel in Light of First-Century Thought*. London: SPCK, 1961.
Sinnott, Alice. *The Personification of Wisdom*. SOTSMS. London: Ashgate, 2017

Skehan, Patrick W., and Alexander A. Di Lella. *The Wisdom of Ben Sira: A New Translation with Notes, Introduction, and Commentary.* AB 39. New York: Doubleday, 1987.
Sly, Dorothy. *Philo's Perception of Women.* BJS 209. Atlanta: Scholars, 2010.
Smith, D. Moody., Jr. *John.* ANTC. Nashville: Abingdon, 1999.
Snaith, John. *Ecclesiasticus.* CBC. Cambridge: Cambridge University Press, 1974.
Stanton, Graham. *The Gospels and Jesus.* 2nd ed. Oxford: Oxford University Press, 2002.
Sterling, Gregory E. "The Interpreter of Moses: Philo of Alexandria and the Biblical Text." In *A Companion to Biblical Interpretation in Early Judaism,* edited by Matthias Henze, 415–35. Grand Rapids: Eerdmans, 2012.
———. "Philo." In *The Eerdmans Dictionary of Classical Judaism,* edited by John J. Collins and Daniel C. Harlow, 1063–70. Grand Rapids: Eerdmans, 2010.
Strack, Hermann Leberecht, et al. *A Commentary on the New Testament from the Talmud & Midrash.* 3 vols. Bellingham, WA: Lexham, 2022.
Strawn, Brent A. "*Bĕ-rē' šît,* 'With 'Wisdom,' in Genesis 1.1 (MT)." *JSOT* 46:3 (2022) 358–87.
Suggs, M. Jack. *Wisdom, Christology, and Law in Matthew's Gospel.* Cambridge, MA: Harvard University Press, 1970.
Talbert, Charles H. *The Development of Christology During the First Hundred Years and Other Essays on Early Christian Christology.* NovTSup 140. Leiden: Brill, 2011.
———. *Reading John: A Literary and Theological Commentary on the Fourth Gospel and the Johannine Epistles.* New York: Crossroad, 1992.
Teh, Abigail Ramos. "Images of Personified Wisdom." *Landas* 22:1 (2008) 103–61.
Thomas Aquinas. *Commentary on the Gospel of John Chapters 1–5.* Translated by Fabian Larcher and James A. Weisheipl. Washington, DC: Catholic University of America Press, 2010.
Thompson, Marianne Meye. *The God of the Gospel of John.* Grand Rapids: Eerdmans, 2001.
———. *John: A Commentary.* NTL. Louisville: Westminster John Knox, 2015.
———. "John, Gospel of." In *DJG,* 368–83.
———. "Thinking about God: Wisdom and Theology in John 6." In *Critical Readings of John 6,* edited by R. Alan Culpepper, 221–46. BIS 22. Leiden: Brill, 1997.
Tibbertsma, Trevor. "The Ambiguous Way to Wisdom in Baruch 3,9—4,4." *Biblische Notizen Bar* 188 (2021) 83–99.
———. "Bright Ecological Wisdom in Baruch 3:33–35." *JSP* 30:3 (2021) 156–65.
Tobin, Thomas H. "Logos." In *ABD,* 4:348–56.
Treier, Daniel J. *Proverbs and Ecclesiastes.* Brazos Theological Commentary on the Bible. Grand Rapids: Brazos, 2011.
Tropper, Amram. "Wisdom in Rabbinic Interpretation." In *The Oxford Handbook of Wisdom and the Bible,* edited by Will Kynes, 205–18. Oxford: Oxford University Press, 2021.
Urbach, Ephraim. *The Sages: Their Concepts and Beliefs.* Translated by Israel Abrahams. Jerusalem: Hebrew University Magnes Press, 1975.
Uusimaki, Elisa. "Tree of Wisdom: Visual Piety in Sir 24 and John 15." In *Theology and Anthropology in the Book of Sirach,* edited by Bonifatia Gesche et al., 203–17. SCS 73. Atlanta: SBL, 2020.
Verner, William. *The Way of The Didache: The First Christian Handbook.* Lanham, MD: University Press of America, 2007.

Villiers, P. G. R. de. "Revealing the Secrets: Wisdom and the World in the Similitudes of Enoch." *Neotestamentica* 17 (1983) 50–68.
Von Wahlde, Urban C. *The Gospel and Letters of John.* 3 vols. ECC. Grand Rapids: Eerdmans, 2010.
Vries, Pieter de. "The Targumim as Background of the Prologue of the Gospel According to John." *Journal of Biblical Theology* 1:4 (2018) 97–122.
Wacker, Marie-Theres. *Baruch and the Letter of Jeremiah.* Wisdom Commentary 31. Collegeville, MN: Liturgical, 2016.
Waers, Stephen E. "Wisdom Christology and Monarchianism in Origen's Commentary on John." *GOTR* 60:3–4 (2015) 93–113.
Wainwright, Elaine M. *Shall We Look for Another? A Feminist Rereading of the Matthean Jesus.* Maryknoll, NY: Orbis, 1998.
Wallace, Daniel B. *Greek Grammar beyond the Basics.* Grand Rapids: Zondervan, 1996.
Waltke, Bruce K. *The Book of Proverbs: Chapters 15–31.* NICOT. Grand Rapids: Eerdmans, 2005.
Webster, Jane S. "Sophia: Engendering Wisdom in Proverbs, Ben Sira, and the Wisdom of Solomon." *JSOT* 78 (1998) 63–79.
Weder, Hans. "Deus Incarnatus: On the Hermeneutics of Christology in the Johannine Writings." In *Exploring the Gospel of John: In Honor of D. Moody Smith,* edited by R. Alan Culpepper and C. Clifton Black, 327–45. Louisville: Westminster John Knox, 1996.
Whybray, Roger N. *The Intellectual Tradition in the Old Testament.* BZAW 135. Berlin: de Gruyter, 1974.
Willett, Michael E. *Wisdom Christology in the Fourth Gospel.* San Francisco: Mellen Research University Press, 1992.
Williams, Catrin H. *I Am He: The Interpretation of "Anî Hû" in Jewish and Early Christian Literature.* WUNT 113. Tübingen: Mohr Siebeck, 2000.
Wilson, Lindsay. *Proverbs: An Introduction and Commentary.* TOTC 17. Downers Grove, IL: IVP Academic, 2018.
Wilson, Walter T. *The Wisdom of Sirach.* ECC. Grand Rapids: Eerdmans, 2023.
Winston, David. *The Wisdom of Solomon: A New Translation with Introduction and Commentary.* AB 43. Garden City, NY: Doubleday, 1979.
Witherington, Ben, III. *Jesus the Sage: The Pilgrimage of Wisdom.* Minneapolis: Fortress, 1994.
———. *John's Wisdom: A Commentary on the Fourth Gospel.* Louisville: Westminster John Knox, 1995.
Witte, Markus. "Key Aspects and Themes in Recent Scholarship on the Book of Ben Sira." In *Texts and Contexts of the Book of Sirach,* edited by Gerhard Karner et al., 1–31. SCS 66. Atlanta: SBL, 2017.
Wolde, E. J. van. "Separation and Creation in Genesis 1 and Psalm 104, A Continuation of the Discussion of the Verb ברא." *VT* 67:4 (2017) 611–47.
Wright, Benjamin G., III. "'Fear the Lord and Honor the Priest': Ben Sira as Defender of the Jerusalem Priesthood." In *The Book of Ben Sira in Modern Research: Proceedings of the First International Ben Sira Conference, 28–31 July 1996 Soesterberg, Netherlands,* edited by Pancratius C. Beentjes, 189–222. BZAW 255. Berlin: de Gruyter, 1997.

Yoder, Christine Roy. "Personified Wisdom and Feminist Theologies." In *The Oxford Handbook of Wisdom and the Bible*, edited by Will Kynes, 273–86. Oxford: Oxford University Press, 2021.

———. *Proverbs*. AOTC. Nashville: Abingdon, 2009.

———. *Wisdom as a Woman of Substance: A Socioeconomic Reading of Proverbs 1–9 and 31:10–31*. BZAW 304. Berlin: de Gruyter, 2000.

Zerwick, M., and M. Grosvenor. *A Grammatical Analysis of the Greek New Testament*. Roma: Gregorian & Biblical, 2016.

Ziener, Georg. "Weisheitsbuch und Johannesevangelium." *Biblica* 38:4 (1957) 396–418.

Zurawski, Jason M. "The Wisdom of Solomon." In *The Oxford Handbook of the Apocrypha*, edited by Gerbern S. Oegema, 335–51. New York: Oxford University Press, 2021.

Author Index

Achtemeier, Paul J., 49n2, 62n67, 70n105, 77n132, 156n67
Alexander, Philip, 44, 44n179
Allen, Leslie C., 14n17
Anderson, Gary, 44n179, 57n36, 61n60
Anderson, Paul N., 90n28, 90n30, 92n43, 94n59, 109n24, 109n25, 116n45, 138n14, 169n8, 209n88
Anthonioz, Stéphanie, 18n37
Aristotle, 162, 162n1
Aquinas, St. Thomas, 61n61, 63n73, 64n75, 91n34, 108n20, 108n21, 109n23, 125n77, 129n95, 141n21, 175n26, 181n35, 195n39, 197n45
Ashton, John, 76n129, 90n29
Aune, David E., 55n27

Bachmann, Veronika, 128n90
Bailey, Kenneth E., 194n29
Balentine, Samuel E., 12n7
Barclay, William, 58n46
Barton, George A., 82n2
Barrett, C. K., 58n41, 61n61, 70n102, 71n111, 94n60, 148n41
Bauckham, Richard, 17n32, 39n159, 40n161, 86n15, 181n34
Bautch, Kelly Coblentz, 39n159
Beasley-Murray, G. R., 56n28, 65n82, 125n78, 128n89, 141n22, 144n29

Beentjes, Pancratius C., 22n61, 23n62, 35n124
Beirne, Margaret M., 53n14
Bekken, Per Jarle, 141n24, 167n5
Berlin, Adele, 14n16
Bernard, J. H., 54n18, 58n41, 60n55, 63n68, 63n73, 65n82
Betz, Joannes, 221n30
Bhaldraithe, Eoin de, 53n17
Boer, Martinus C. de, 57n38, 60n54, 62n62
Boismard, M. E., 55n26
Borg, Marcus, 69n99
Borgen, Peder, 36n130, 91n36, 91n40, 91n41, 92n42, 92n44, 92n46, 93n51, 94n55, 114n35, 115n40, 118n51, 120n61, 128n89, 128n90, 135n4, 137n12, 145n33, 145n34, 146n37, 181n36
Bowley, James E., 21n55
Boyarin, Daniel, 56n30, 57, 57n37, 58n41, 58n42, 62n63, 64n74, 64n76, 65n79, 65n84
Brant, Jo-Ann A., 56n32, 58n41, 63n73, 67n92, 94n57, 209n90
Brewer-Boydston, Ginny, 34n115
Brown, Raymond E., 10n29, 49, 49–50n3, 56n28, 56n32, 63n73, 64n77, 65, 65n82, 65n83, 65–66n84, 69–70n101, 70n105, 70n106, 92, 92n45, 102n2, 106n15, 107n18, 111n30, 113n33, 113n34,

115n37, 115n38, 116n44,
125n78, 128n90, 136n6,
144n30, 145n33, 147n39,
152n53, 153n56, 163n57,
169n11, 171n13, 172n16,
174n21, 174n23, 174n24,
177n31, 187n3, 189, 189n9,
189n12, 190n16, 192n24,
199n49, 206, 206n76,
206n78, 211n104
Brown, William P., 18n36
Bruce, F. F., 56n28
Bruggemann, Walter, 12n4
Bultmann, Rudolf, 50, 50n6
Burkes, Shannon, 12n5, 24n75,
27n95
Burnett, F. W., 53n17, 62n64, 63n69,
65n81, 68–69n96
Bushur, James G., 220n22

Camp, Claudia V., 19n46
Capes, David B., 82–83, 83n4
Carson, D. A., 56n28
Carter, Warren, 50, 50n5, 51n8,
56n32, 58n44, 61n56, 61n61,
62n64, 63n69, 63n73, 64n77,
65n81, 66n89, 70n105,
71n109, 71n112, 76n127,
79n135, 110n29, 120n61,
135n4
Casey, Maurice, 49n2
Ceresko, Anthony R., 23n62, 56n32,
103n7, 115n41, 118n54,
151n51, 154n59
Charlesworth, James H., 56n32,
58n44, 61n56, 62n64, 62n67,
65n82, 69–70n101, 89n26,
116n44, 120n60, 125n75,
127n84, 128n88, 147n39,
156n66, 188n7, 204n65,
206n79, 207n81
Clark, Douglas K., 128n92
Clarke, Ernest G., 30n107
Clifford, Richard J., 17n34, 69n99,
103n6
Clines, David J. A., 12n4
Cohen, Shaye J. D., 35n124, 36n134

Collins, Adela Yarbro, 21n56,
22n58, 59n51, 62n64, 62n67,
71n110, 221n32
Collins, John J., 21n55, 28n98
Coloe, Mary L., 50, 50n7, 56n32,
57n36, 61n61, 62n63, 62n64,
64n77, 66n89, 68n94, 70,
70n104, 70n105, 75n123,
102n5, 115n42, 116n43,
119n55, 119n58, 119n59,
120n60, 122n65, 123n66,
124n70, 125n76, 127n84,
136n7, 143n27, 144n29,
147n40, 152m52, 155n63,
171n12, 173n20, 177n32,
187n5, 188n8, 191n17,
195n37, 195n38, 198n47,
199n50, 201n57, 203n62,
205n69, 206n72, 206n76
Corley, Jeremy, 206n71, 210n95
Cory, Catherine, 49n2, 171, 171n14
Coutsoumpos, Panayotis, 71n110
Cowan, Christopher, 94n61
Crenshaw, James L., 22n60
Crowe, Brandon D., 128n92
Cullmann, Oscar, 53n17, 65n84,
69n99
Culpepper, R. Alan, 49n1, 50n3,
52n9, 53n17, 55, 55n24,
55n26, 68–69, 69n97,
74n121, 106n16, 128n91,
198n47, 219n18

Daley, Brian E., 222n37, 223n41
Davies, Margaret, 58n45, 65n78,
65n84, 144n29, 147n40,
152n53, 176n29
Davies, W. D., 52n13,
Davis, Ellen F., 18n39
Deutsch, Celia M., 185n1
Devillers, Luc, 76n129
Di Lella, Alexander A., 23n67,
24n71, 24n74
Dillon, Richard, 56n35, 63n71,
69n101, 76n127, 92n48,
109n25, 118n52, 119n56,
138n16, 144n29, 189, 189n9,

AUTHOR INDEX 243

192n24, 193n26, 205n68, 206n73, 206n79, 208n83, 208n84, 210n94, 210n99
Dodd, C. H., 49n1
Domeris, William R., 157n71, 158n73
Douglas, Sally, 53n14, 219n20, 220n26, 221n29, 221n30
Dunn, James D. G., 4n9, 5n10, 5n11, 6n17, 23n64, 37n140, 46n186, 47, 47n188, 47n190, 57n38, 61n61, 67n91, 68n93, 68n95, 76n129, 79, 79n136, 83n4, 84, 84n10, 93, 93n50, 98n75, 115n37, 116n44, 125n79, 127n85, 128n87, 128n91, 135n4, 138n16, 140n20, 144n29, 144n31, 147n39, 149n45, 150n47, 168n7, 169n9, 210n93, 211n103, 213n1, 214n4, 217n12, 217n13, 218, 218n14

Ehrman, Bart D., 75n123
Ellis, Teresa Ann, 23n66, 25n81
Epp, Eldon Jay, 13n11, 41n166, 49n1, 54n21, 71n112, 74n119, 74n120, 74n122
Evans, Craig A., 32, 32n112, 71n108, 93n52

Feuillet, André, 113n34, 128n88, 128n90, 144n31, 207n80, 221n30
Fischel, Henry A., 44, 44n183
Fletcher-Louis, Crispin H. T., 25, 25n83
Fox, Michael V., 19n44, 19n45, 22n61
Freed, Edwin D., 49n2, 141n23, 176n30
Friend, Helen S., 90n30
Fuller, Reginald H., 68–69n96, 93n52, 105n13, 109n24, 146n38, 160n78, 181n34, 217n10

Gammie, John G., 14n13, 83n9
Gaston, Thomas E., 56n28, 56n30, 61n57, 76n128, 94n56, 137n9
Gathercole, Simon, 25n82
Geyer, John, 30n108
Gilbert, Maurice, 24n73
Girard, Marc, 128n92
Goldingay, John, 14n15, 17n30
Gordley, Matthew E., 54n18
Gottlieb, Fred, 14n14
Grant, Deena E., 33n113

Habel, Norman C., 12n7, 13n9
Hadas-Lebel, Mireille, 35n125, 37–38n148, 38, 38n151
Haenchen, Ernst, 53n16, 56n28, 61n56, 65n81, 68–69n96, 69n100, 70n102, 75n123, 96n67
Haight, Roger, 223n44
Hamerton-Kelly, Robert G., 83, 83n5
Hanson, Anthony Tyrrell, 113n32
Hanson, R. P. C., 223n43, 224n46, 224n47, 224n48, 224n49
Harrington, Daniel J., 23n64
Harris, Elizabeth, 36n134, 68–69n96, 75n123, 146n37
Harris, J. Rendel, 49, 49n1
Henderson, Ruth, 27n91
Hengel, Martin, 4n8
Hillar, Marian, 222n37
Himes, Paul Aaron, 204, 204n66
Himmelfarb, Martha, 24n78
Holladay, Carl R., 65n84
Horne, Milton P., 19n44, 19n45, 20n50
Hossfeld, Frank Lothar, 14n18
Hurtado, Larry W., 2n5, 53n17, 61n58, 83, 83n6, 213n2

Irons, Lee, 82n2
Isaac, E., 39n159

Johnson, Elizabeth A., 13n9, 37n139, 59n49, 103n7, 104–

105n11, 116n44, 117n49, 120n61, 128n91, 144n29, 148n41, 171n13, 174n24, 191n18, 193n26, 222n35, 223n43
Jones, Scott C., 12n3, 13n9
Jonge, Marinus de, 90n27

Kealy, Sean P., 95n64
Kee, Howard Clark, 76n129
Keener, Craig S., 52, 52n10, 56n31, 71n110, 82n2, 87n17, 91, 91n33, 92n49, 93n51, 97n73, 108n19, 116–117n47, 118n50, 119n57, 120n62, 123n66, 124n72, 130–131n96, 135n3, 136n8, 139n18, 139n18, 148n41, 169n10, 172n15, 172n18, 174n23, 178n33, 181n37, 187n3, 188n6, 192n23, 194n30, 200n51, 209n88, 209n91, 210n93, 210n97, 210n99
Kim, Sang-Hoon, 55n25
King, Sheri D., 68n93
Kirk, J. R. Daniel, 25n82, 218n15
Kittel, Gerhard, 41n166
Klausner, Joseph, 83n8
Klein, Michael L., 44n178
Knibb, Michael A., 39n159
Kobel, Esther, 115n41
Koester, Craig R., 125n78, 145n33, 146n38
Kolarcik, Michael, 29n103, 128n93
Köstenberger, Andreas J., 76–77n130
Kovalishyn, Mariam Kamell, 76n129, 131n97
Kruse, Colin G., 61n56
Kümmel, Werner Georg, 49n2, 58n47, 113n33, 143n26
Kuschel, Karl-Josef, 21n57, 64n77, 68n93
Kwon, JiSeong, 20n49
Kysar, Robert, 56n32

Ladd, George E., 53n17, 93n53
Laporte, Jean, 37n140, 37n141, 38, 38n152, 39n157
Lee, Dorothy A., 90n28, 105n12, 116n46, 144n28, 193n25
Lincoln, Andrew T., 52n11, 54n20, 58n41, 60n53, 62n65, 63n71, 65n82, 68–69n96, 69–70n101, 74n121, 90n30, 93n52, 94n58, 125n78, 128n88, 143n27, 144n30, 144n31, 147n39, 156n67, 164n3
Lindars, Barnabas, 68–69n96
Lipscomb, Anthony I., 31n111, 32, 32n112
Loader, William, 90n30, 97, 97n70
Longman III, Tremper, 2n4, 17n33, 17n34, 20n49
Lucas, Ernest C., 20, 20n52
Lund, Nils W., 55n26

Macaskill, Grant, 40n162
Machiela, Daniel A., 31n110
Mack, Burton. L., 2–3, 3n6
MacRae, George W., 50n3
Maher, Michael, 42n171, 42n172
Manns, Frédéric, 53n17, 65n84, 70n105, 76n126, 116n44, 128n88, 128n90, 206n79, 217n11
Martin, James D., 17n29, 19n40
Mattila, Sharon Lea, 34n117
Mazzinghi, Luca, 28n97
McCann Jr., J. Clinton, 14n15
McCreesh, Thomas P., 19m44
McGrath, James, 68n93, 74n121, 75n123, 87n16, 87n19, 90n28, 93n52, 137n9, 137n13, 144n29, 148n41, 174n23, 195, 195n41, 211n103, 219n17
McHugh, John F., 56n28, 58n41, 64n77, 69n99, 75n123, 76n125, 117n49, 125n73, 126n82, 136n6, 189n10,

193n26, 193n27, 194n32,
  195n35
McIlhone, James P., 91n35, 93n51,
  159n74, 209n90
McKinlay, Judith E., 20n49, 24n77,
  26n87
McNamara, Martin, 44n180
Meier, John P., 143n27
Meyer, Paul W., 110n29, 167n4
Meyers, Carol L., 12n1, 13n10,
  15n21, 20n49, 23n65, 27n91,
  30n109, 76n129, 194n29
Michaels, J. Ramsey, 49n2
Moeller, Henry R., 214n6
Moloney, Francis J., 58n46, 58n47,
  67n90, 75n123, 94, 94n61,
  103n8
Moore, G. F., 57n38, 217n12
Morris, Leon., 61n58, 63n70,
  123n66, 128n90, 148n41
Mulder, Otto., 25n79
Muraoka, Takamitsu, 23n70
Murphy, Roland E., 2–3, 13n9,
  13n12, 16n25, 16n26, 20n47,
  45n185
Myers, Alicia D., 56n31

Nemes, Steven, 27n94, 29m101,
  108n21, 176n29, 216n9
Newsom, Carol A., 12n2, 12n3
Nickelsburg, George W. E., 40,
  40n160, 41n164, 126n80
Niehoff, Maren R., 36n133
Novakovic, Lidija, 58n46

O'Boyle, Aidan, 21n54, 48n193,
  52n11, 79n133, 85n14,
  89n25, 107n18, 115n37,
  118n52, 119n59, 120n61,
  144n30, 147n39, 148n42,
  150n46, 151n51, 154n59,
  156n67, 189, 189n11,
  206n75, 206n79, 208n84,
  208n85, 220n27, 222n35,
  224n45
O'Day, Gail R., 50, 50n4, 58n44,
  87n20, 97n71, 144n29,
  153n55, 155n60, 192n22,
  195n37, 196n43, 198n46,
  199n49, 202n58, 211n100
Oh, Dong Woo, 69n100

Painter, John, 49n1, 52n9, 53n17,
  164n2, 175n27, 176n30
Pauw, Amy Plantinga, 20, 20n51
Paxson, James, 2, 2n3
Perdue, Leo G., 13n10, 20, 20n49,
  20n50, 20n53, 23n69,
  24–25n78
Perkins, Pheme, 61n57, 64n77,
  65n82, 90n31
Perriman, Andrew, 5n12
Phillips, Peter M., 58n45, 58n46,
  68–69n96
Plutarch, 54, 54n22
Pope, Marvin H., 12n4
Potterie, Ignace de la, 152n53
Pryor, John W., 54n23, 64n75,
  64n76

Rad, Gerhard von, 16n24, 23n63
Reider, Joseph, 29n105
Reiterer, Friedrich Vincenz, 24n72
Richardson, Alan, 69n99, 83n4
Ridderbos, Herman N., 49n2
Ringe, Sharon H., 19n44, 64n77,
  68–69n96, 71n109, 71n112,
  72n114, 74n121, 93n52,
  103n7, 104–105n11, 124n72,
  127n83, 128n87, 146n38,
  148n41, 149n44, 152n54,
  154n59, 156n67, 193n26,
  196n42, 206n76, 211n104
Robert, André, 58n44, 114n36,
  210n96
Robinson, John A. T., 56n29, 59n51,
  93, 93n54, 97n71, 108n21,
  110n28, 172n17, 173n19,
  176n29, 216n8, 219n16
Rogers, Jessie, 23n69
Rybolt, John E., 22n60, 28n99,
  29n105

Saldarini, Anthony J., 26n88, 190n15
Sandelin, Karl-Gustav, 18n38, 22n61, 23n68, 37n141, 38n153, 39n157, 115n40, 124n70, 125n74, 158n72, 215n7, 221n30, 221n31
Sanders, J. A., 33n113
Sandmel, Samuel, 214n5
Sanford, John A., 194n31
Schäfer, Peter, 35n124
Schechter, Solomon, 42n169, 42n170
Schipper, Bernd U., 102m4
Schmidt, A. Jorden, 24n73, 24n74, 24–25n78, 25, 25n82, 25n84
Schnackenburg, Rudolf, 54, 54n19, 63n72, 64n77, 65n80, 69n101, 75n123, 85n12, 115n39, 124n71, 155n62, 187n3, 206n76
Schneiders, Sandra M., 52n12, 196n43
Schroer, Silvia, 20n49, 104–105n11, 115n37, 124n72, 126n82, 142n25, 144n29, 211n101
Schüssler Fiorenza, Elisabeth, 10, 10n28, 50n7, 81n1, 88n21, 93n52, 102n3, 116n44, 126n82, 144n29, 148n41, 171n13, 191n19, 193n26, 193n28, 196n43, 202n59, 203n64, 206n79
Schweizer, Eduard V., 5n14, 117n48
Scott, Martin, 52n11, 53n17, 58, 58n43, 59n50, 61n61, 62n65, 63n68, 65n81, 65n84, 68n96, 69n101, 70n105, 71n112, 72n115, 73n118, 77n131, 79n135, 107n17, 116n44, 149n43, 152n53, 192n20, 194n34, 195n36, 195n40, 197n44, 200n52, 213–214, 214n3
Shafer, Byron E., 84n11, 104–105n11, 111n30, 136n5, 147n39, 160n77, 223n43, 224n45

Shaw, Karen L. H., 20n49
Sidebottom, E. M., 61n57, 63n71, 71n112, 89n24, 113n33, 120n63, 128n90, 129n94, 135n2, 156n64, 174n21, 183n38, 204n67, 205n68, 206n77, 210n98, 214n4
Sinnott, Alice, 12, 13n8, 22n60, 23n64, 28n97, 28n98, 28n100, 29n103, 29n104, 30n106, 47, 47n192
Skehan, Patrick W., 24n76, 25n80, 125n75
Sly, Dorothy, 37n141, 38, 38n154, 38n156
Smith. Dustin R., 82n2
Smith Jr., D. Moody, 52n12
Snaith, John, 24n73
Stanton, Graham, 49n2
Sterling, Gregory E., 34n116, 35n124
Strack, Hermann Leberecht, 82n3
Strawn, Brent A., 42n168, 44, 44n178, 44n181
Suggs, M. Jack, 185n1

Talbert, Charles H., 49n2, 56n35, 58n41, 59n48, 61n61, 62n66, 63n69, 63n73, 64n77, 65n81, 66n89, 70n102, 70n105, 71n112, 76n127, 117n49
Teh, Abigail Ramos., 15n21
Thompson, Marianne Meye, 52n9, 58n45, 64n77, 76–77, 77n131, 86n15, 87, 87n18, 90n30, 91n33, 92n42, 92n47, 95, 95n65, 97n74, 106n14, 109n24, 110n26, 110n27, 110n29, 124n67, 124n68, 124n71, 139n17, 144n30, 146n38, 183n39, 205n70, 206n76, 219n16, 219n19
Tibbertsma, Trevor, 27n92, 28n96
Tobin, Thomas H., 21n57, 22n59, 29n101, 37n141, 49n2, 56n32, 58n44, 61n56, 62n64,

62n67, 63n73, 64n77, 65n81, 66n85, 70n105
Treier, Daniel J., 15n20, 17n31, 20n49
Tropper, Amram, 42n167, 43n177

Urbach, Ephraim, 43n173, 43n174
Uusimaki, Elisa, 155n61

Varner, William, 221n29
Villiers, P. G. R. de, 41n165
Von Wahlde, Urban C., 56n28, 56n32, 57n40, 59, 59–60n52, 63n73, 69–70n101, 71n112, 72n116, 75n123, 95n63, 118n54, 128n90, 156n66, 174n24, 194n31
Vries, Pieter de, 44n180, 56n34

Wacker, Marie-Theres, 26n89, 27n90, 27n93
Waers, Stephen E., 222n38
Wainwright, Elaine M., 185n1
Wallace, Daniel B., 58n46
Waltke, Bruce K., 19n41
Webster, Jane S., 29n101
Weder, Hans, 76n130
Whybray, Roger N., 14n13
Willett, Michael E., 21n54
Williams, Catrin H., 108, 108n22, 137n11
Wilson, Lindsay, 17n30, 69n98
Wilson, Walter T., 25, 25n85

Winston, David, 29n105, 159, 159n75
Witherington III, Ben, 20n49, 28n98, 45n185, 47, 47n191, 56n31, 56n32, 57n38, 63n71, 65n82, 69–70n101, 71n109, 79, 79n134, 85n13, 88n22, 93, 93n51, 95n62, 95–96n66, 96n68, 97n72, 101n1, 102n5, 103n9, 104n10, 104–105n11, 110n27, 112n31, 116n44, 118n53, 118n54, 123n66, 124n70, 125n78, 127n86, 137n10, 138n14, 139n19, 144n30, 146n38, 147n39, 148n41, 149n44, 151n48, 152n52, 156n66, 156n67, 158n73, 160n76, 171n13, 174n23, 176n30, 187n4, 189n13, 189–190n14, 191n18, 193n25, 195n39, 200–201n56, 208n82, 208n85, 209n87, 210n93, 210n96, 210n97
Witte, Markus, 23n64
Wolde, E. J. van, 14n14
Wright III, Benjamin G., 26n86

Yoder, Christine Roy, 16n28, 18n35, 19n40, 19n42, 20n48, 20n49, 22n61, 45, 45n184

Zerwick, M., 58n46
Ziener, Georg, 130–131n96
Zurawski, Jason M., 28n97

Ancient Document Index

OLD TESTAMENT

Genesis
1	14n14, 24n73, 56, 56n30, 57, 57n38, 60, 61, 62
1:1	42, 43, 44n179, 56n28, 56n34, 60
1:1 LXX	56
1:2–3	63
1:3	14
1:20	62
1:24	62
1:26–27	62
2:7	145
2:7 LXX	210n92
3:5 LXX	203, 203n62
3:20	151
3:22–24	17
12:13	32
15:10	37
22:2	7n23
28:12	135

Exodus
16:4	36, 144, 146
40	71

Numbers
16:3–5	157n70
21:18	195

Deuteronomy
6:4	44
18:15–22	109n25, 168
18:15–19	109
18:15–18	169
18:18	109n25
18:20	169
33:2–3	157n70

2 Samuel
7:14	122n64
15:20	71n113

1 Kings
3	30
3:9	122
3:13	16n27
3:28	142n25
4:29–34	142n25

2 Kings
4:9	157n70

2 Chronicles
1:11–12	16n27

Job
10:13	57
11:6–7	113
23:14	57
27:11	57

Job (continued)

28	12, 13, 24, 27, 27n91, 29n104, 75, 111, 153
28:1–28	54
28:1–11	12
28:12–28	12, 179
28:12	2n2, 12
28:14	12
28:20	2n2, 12, 111
28:21	12, 179
28:22	12
28:23–27	85, 179
28:23	12, 111, 153
28:24–27	13
28:25	210n9
28:26–27	56n33
28:27	13, 111
28:27 LXX	76
28:28	1, 2n2, 13, 111

Psalms

2:4	15–16n23
2:7	7n23, 122n64
19	23n69
23:6	2
25:10	71n113
33:6	14, 29, 60
33:9	60
36:9	125n73
40:11	71n113
43:3	2
57:10	71n113
85:10	2
89:1	71n113
89:2	71n113
89:5	157n70
89:7	157n70
89:14	71n113
89:24	71n113
89:33	71n113
89:49	71n113
96:6	2
103:24 LXX	73
104	14, 14n14, 24
104:24	1, 5, 14, 29, 44, 56n33, 61, 73, 223
106:16	157n70
107:20	59
119	23,69
147:15	59

Proverbs

1–9	15, 15n19, 19, 68, 221n29
1	15, 169, 170, 182
1:2–4	15
1:2–3	66
1:7	2n2
1:8–9	200
1:8	15, 66, 200, 200n53
1:10	66, 200n53
1:15	66, 200n53
1:20–33	15, 29n104, 54, 173, 182
1:20–31	65
1:20–28	103n7, 189
1:20–23	97, 169
1:20–21	15, 102, 106
1:20	15n20
1:21	102
1:22	111, 165
1:23	16, 104, 111, 124, 150, 165, 210, 210n95, 210n96
1:23–33	220
1:24–32	165
1:24–28	106
1:24–27	182
1:24–25	8, 15, 169
1:26–27	15, 169
1:28–30	15
1:28–29	1
1:28	16, 106, 107, 165, 167, 174, 178
1:28 LXX	174
1:29–30	111
1:29	97
1:30	165
1:31–32	15, 174
1:32–33	170
1:32	182

ANCIENT DOCUMENT INDEX 251

1:33	7n25, 16, 150, 165, 182	6:20	200
		7:1	200n53
2:1–12	16	7:4	32
2:1–13	16	7:7–9	102–103
2:1	66, 200n53	7:25–26	165
2:2	2n2, 66	8	23n70, 45, 57, 75, 85, 114n35, 115, 165, 179, 182, 187n4, 222
2:6–11	16		
2:6	2n2, 111, 140		
2:10–13	63, 147		
2:10–11	16, 140	8:1–36	29n104, 54
2:10	16, 111	8:1–11	150
2:15–19	16	8:1–3	102, 106
3	16, 42, 152	8:1	102
3:1	66, 200n53	8:2–3	17, 102n2, 179
3:11	66, 200n53	8:3	19
3:12	66	8:4–36	24n71
3:13–18	31	8:5	2n2
3:13–15	198	8:6–8	17
3:13	2n2, 141n21	8:6	7n25
3:14–15	16, 31	8:7	72, 113
3:14	19	8:8–9	111
3:15	19, 32	8:8	221n29
3:16	5n13, 16, 151, 151	8:10–11	199
3:17	16, 152	8:10	17, 115
3:18	17, 62, 155, 203, 221n29	8:12	2n2, 111
		8:13	151
3:19	2n2, 5, 17, 220n24	8:14	17, 122
3:19–20	1, 2n2, 17, 29, 61, 111	8:15–16	122, 142
		8:15	182
3:21–23	153	8:16	182
3:21–22	200	8:17–18	5n13, 17
3:21–22 LXX	72	8:17	179, 197, 202, 204
3:21	17, 200n53	8:17 LXX	197, 204n66
4:4–5	104	8:18	70, 85
4:5–6	201, 204	8:19	19
4:5	2n2	8:20	153, 165
4:6–8	199	8:21–30	222
4:7–9 LXX	72	8:21	17, 204
4:10	200n53	8:22–31	17, 56n33, 69n98
4:11	104, 153	8:22–30	85
4:11 LXX	104	8:22–25	223
4:13	113	8:22–23	57
4:18	63	8:22–23 LXX	56
4:19	165	8:22	18, 35n125, 42, 43, 56, 56n34, 57, 106, 222
4:20	200n53		
5:1	66		
6:1	200n53	8:23	18
6:3	200n53	8:24	18, 56

Proverbs (continued)

8:25	18
8:26	18, 56
8:27	18, 57, 106
8:28	18
8:28	18
8:30–31	19, 75, 85, 86, 89
8:30	7, 18, 58, 85, 106
8:32–36	18
8:32–35	113, 165
8:32–34	7n25, 148, 182
8:32	66, 115, 153
8:33–35	150
8:33	17
8:34–35	149, 221n29
8:34	115, 199
8:35–36	183
8:35	62, 62n65, 115, 148, 151, 157, 181, 197
8:36	165
9	18, 115, 144, 151, 165
9:1–12	151
9:1–6	23n67, 23n68, 29n104, 127, 144, 165, 189, 192, 197
9:1	18, 19
9:2–3	192
9:2	18
9:3–6	115n38, 150, 195
9:3	18, 19, 102n2, 199, 203, 212
9:4–6	127n86
9:5–6	115
9:5	18, 19, 42, 115, 124, 124n70, 127, 193n25
9:6	18, 127, 221n29
9:10	1, 97, 140
9:11	151
9:13–18	18, 151, 165
9:15	153
9:17	18
9:18	18, 151
10:11	125n73
13:14	125n73
14:6	174
14:6 LXX	174
14:27	125n73
15:33	140
16:16	199
16:22	125n73
18:4	125, 125n73
19:14	20
23:23	72, 199
30:3 LXX	104
31	20, 21n54, 24n77, 25, 39
31:1–9	19n43
31:10–31	15, 15n19, 19, 19n43, 20, 31, 32, 33, 68, 192
31:10	19, 199
31:12	19
31:13	19
31:14	19
31:15	19
31:16	19
31:23	19
31:25	19
31:27	19

Ecclesiastes

1:13	142n25

Song of Songs

4:15	125n73

Isaiah

1:15	15n22, 15–16n23
5:1–7	154
11:2	142n25
42:1	7n23
50:2	15n22
51:9	2
55:11	59, 105, 106
65:12	15n22
66:4	15n22

Jeremiah

6:9	154
7:13	15n22

10:12	5, 17n30, 29, 34, 61, 220n24	1:2-3	24
11:10-11	15n22	1:4	24, 57
11:11	15-16n23	1:9-10	107
17:23	15n22	1:9	24, 57
29:19	15n22	1:10	23, 64n75
51:15	5, 17n30, 29, 61, 220n24	1:12	23
		1:14	140
		1:16	23, 140, 155, 193n27

Ezekiel

15:1-6	154
15:4-6	154
15:6	154
17:5-10	154
19:10-14	154
19:12	154
19:14	154
36:25-27	121

1:17	23, 23n67
1:18	23, 140
1:19	111
1:20	140, 155
1:26	22, 204
1:27	140
1:30	140
2:1	66, 189, 200n54
3:1-2	189
3:1	66, 200n54
3:12	200n54
3:17	66, 189, 200n54
4:1	66, 189, 200n54
4:10-11	66
4:11-6:17	206n71
4:11-17	206
4:11-14	89
4:11	23, 67, 189
4:12-16	201
4:12	23, 113, 197, 204, 206, 206n74
4:13	70
4:14	23, 23n66, 59, 76, 140, 197, 197n45, 204
4:15	23
4:16	67, 166
4:17-19	166
4:18	140
4:19	107
4:24-25	72
6:7-10	206n71
6:7	206
6:8-10	206
6:12	7n26
6:18-31	23
6:18-22	66
6:18	189, 200n54
6:19	193n27, 207

Daniel

4:17	157n70
7	92n48, 134, 181
7:9	92n48
7:13-27	134
7:13-14	181
12:2	150

Hosea

5:6	15n22, 15-16n23

Micah

3:4	15n22

Zechariah

9:9	141

APOCRYPHA

Sirach

1:1-10	23, 54
1:1	24, 58

Sirach (continued)

6:20–22	179
6:20	166
6:21	166
6:22–24	7n25
6:22	179
6:23	200n54
6:24–28	202
6:24–27	179
6:24–25	208
6:26–31	166
6:26	153
6:27–28	153, 180
6:29–31	70
6:32	66, 200n54
7:26	7n26
7:29	7n26
8:4	76
10:28	200n54
11:10	200n54
14:11	200n54
14:24–25	208
14:26–27	208
14:26	155
14:27	155
15:1–2	66
15:1	67
15:2	23, 200n55
15:3	23, 125, 128, 175n26
15:4	67, 201
15:7	65
16:24	200n54
16:25	210n95
18:15	200n54
19:20	140
21:1	200n54
21:13	125n73
23:7	200n54
23:25	156
24	23, 23n70, 27, 69, 92, 95, 116, 124n70, 125, 155n61
24:1–34	54, 115
24:1–33	29n104
24:1–23	67
24:1	25
24:3	24, 107
24:4–8	65
24:4	24
24:5–6	143n27
24:5	91n34
24:6	24, 189
24:7–9	194
24:7–8	24
24:7	69
24:8–12	74, 189
24:8	23, 24, 69, 92, 95, 156n64
24:9	24, 57
24:10	25, 70, 95
24:11	95, 197
24:12	95
24:12–17	24
24:12	25
24:13	25
24:14	25
24:15	25
24:16	72, 155
24:17–22	155
24:17–21	23n68
24:17–19	221
24:17	72, 156, 156n64
24:18–21	128
24:19–21	109n25, 193n27
24:19	23, 115, 150, 189
24:20–21	150
24:20	115
24:21	116, 128, 193n25, 194n32
24:22	24, 116, 150
24:23	23, 41n166
24:25–31	126n80
24:25–27	63, 147
24:25–26	111
24:25	125, 153
24:26	125, 195
24:27	112, 125
24:29	125
24:30–34	104, 125, 195
24:30–32	124n70
24:32	63, 147
31:22	200n54
32:24	67

33:3	67	3:29–4:1	5n15
37:21	72	3:29–30	170
37:27	200n54	3:29	136n6
38:9	200n54	3:31	27, 65
38:16	200n54	3:32–4:4	190
40:28	200n54	3:32–35	27
41:6	200n54	3:35	170
41:14	200n54	3:36–4:1	170
42:14	195	3:36–37	27, 65, 194
43:31	76	3:36	112, 117
43:33	24, 76	3:37–4:1	70, 74, 180
45:2–6	157n70	3:37	102n2, 117
45:6	157n70	4	26
50	25, 39, 52	4:1–2	41n166, 63n70, 112
50:1–24	24, 68	4:1	27, 62, 113, 117
50:1–21	95	4:2	63, 147, 194
50:5	25		
50:8	25		
50:9	25		
50:10	25		
50:12	25		
50:15	25		
50:20	25		
50:25–26	195		
51:19–28	185, 189, 219n21		
51:23–27	9, 221		
51:23	185, 187n4, 189n14, 208		
51:25–27	185, 187n4		
51:26	208		

Wisdom of Solomon

1:3	210n98
1:4–5	157
1:4	208
1:6–7	6n21, 73, 210
1:6	30
1:7	30
1:9	210
1:14	29
2:23	29
3:9–11	72
4:27	210n98
5:5	173n20
5:6	153, 166
5:7	166
5:13–14	119
5:15	119
6	187n4
6:4–5	122
6:9–10	104
6:9	122
6:12–16	190
6:12–13	190n16, 205
6:12	63, 180
6:13	140, 208
6:14	102n2, 108n21, 129n95
6:16	102n2, 177, 189, 190n16, 208

Baruch

3	26
3:9–4:4	29n104, 54, 170
3:9	26, 170, 190
3:10–12	65, 112
3:10–11	26
3:12–13	190
3:12	8, 27, 126, 170
3:14	27, 63, 147, 170, 190
3:15	27, 170, 180
3:20	27, 112, 180
3:21	65
3:22–35	180
3:23	27
3:28	190

Wisdom of Solomon (*continued*)

6:17–20	122
6:17–18	120, 205
6:18–20	62
6:18–19	113, 118
6:18	180
6:22	56n33, 57, 72, 113
7–9	97n72
7	142
7:7	30, 98, 142, 210
7:8–11	142
7:11	193n27
7:12	29, 66, 142, 200n55
7:14	98, 193n27
7:15–22	112
7:15	143
7:21	104, 140
7:22–8:1	54
7:22–24	159
7:22–23	30
7:22	29, 30, 71, 75, 98, 112, 157, 190–191, 210
7:23–24	30
7:25–26	30
7:25	59, 70, 88n22, 140
7:26	6n20, 59, 63, 101n1, 140, 147, 220n22
7:27	28, 30, 98, 108n20, 149, 157, 191, 206, 211
7:28	191, 197, 205, 208
7:29	63
7:30	63
8:1	30, 65
8:2–16	143
8:2	29, 149, 208
8:3	7n24, 29, 89
8:4	89, 112, 113
8:5	29, 120
8:6	29, 98
8:7	29, 120
8:8	112, 129n94
8:9	89, 150, 208
8:10	71
8:13	62, 118
8:16	29, 120, 150
8:17–18	150
8:21	117
9:1–4	92n48
9:1–3	122
9:1–2	6n19, 28, 61, 62, 98
9:2–3	183
9:2	30, 191
9:4	7n22, 30, 92, 107, 117, 123
9:9–11	95
9:9–10	113, 157
9:9	30, 56n33, 58, 112, 221n29
9:10–12	143
9:10–11	70, 85
9:10	5n14, 30, 65, 88n22, 92, 92n49, 107, 112, 123
9:11	123, 211n100, 221n29
9:12	123
9:16–18	113
9:16–17	135n2, 136n6
9:17–18	93
9:17	5n14, 117, 120n63, 135n3, 157, 210
9:18	62, 104
10–19	28
10	29
10:1–21	98
10:1–2	191
10:1	29n105
10:2	89
10:4	30, 191
10:5	29n105, 191
10:6–11:1	191
10:6	29n105
10:9–10	103n9
10:10–12	194
10:10	29n105, 123, 158, 191n17, 211, 211n100
10:13	29n105, 30
10:14	123

ANCIENT DOCUMENT INDEX 257

10:15–16	129
10:15	29n105
10:17–18	211
10:17	153, 166
10:20	158
11–19	128
11:1	130, 158
11:4	126
11:5–14	130
11:15–20	130
12:1	30
13:3	29
14:2	29
14:5	143n27
16:1–4	130
16:5–14	130
16:5–7	120
16:7	136n7
16:13	118
16:15–29	130
17:1–18:4	130
18:5–25	130
18:14–16	29
19:1–9	130

PSEUDEPIGRAPHA

1 Enoch

37–71	39, 40n161, 134
42	40, 65, 170, 171, 171n12
42:1–2	54, 65, 70, 137
42:1	40, 107, 171
42:2	40, 107, 171
42:3	40
48–49	40
48:1	40, 126, 126n80, 164n3
48:7	40, 138
48:10	164n3
49:1	41, 71, 126, 164n3
49:3	40, 138, 211
49:4	41, 138

NEW TESTAMENT

Matthew

11:2	8
11:25–27	9
11:28–30	9, 185, 219n21
11:29–30	221
12:42	8
13:19–23	53
23:34–36	8
23:37–39	9

Mark

1:11	7
1:24	157n69
1:45	53
2:2	53
6	7
6:2	8
9:3	7
9:7	7

Luke

1:1–4	54n22
2:40	9
2:52	9
4:34	157
5:1	53
7:31–35	8
7:35	10
8:11	53
10:21–22	9
11:31	8
11:49–51	8
13:33–36	9
21:15	10

John

1–12	188
1:1–18	50, 55
1:1–5	63

John (continued)

Reference	Pages
1:1	56n28, 57n36, 57n38, 59, 60, 81, 86
1:1–2	55, 57, 75
1:2	59
1:3	55, 60, 64, 74
1:4–5	55, 61, 73, 114, 182
1:4	62n62, 63n70, 147, 151
1:5	63, 64n76, 147
1:6–8	55, 63
1:6	83
1:7–8	64
1:9–11	55, 64, 67
1:9	64, 67
1:10–13	64n76
1:10–12	209n86
1:10–11	183
1:10	64, 68, 166
1:11–12	163
1:11	64, 64n76, 65, 68, 166
1:12–13	55, 55n26, 66, 67, 67n92, 167, 184, 186
1:12	55n26, 66, 66n85, 67, 73, 173n20
1:13	55n26
1:14	55, 67, 67n92, 69n99, 69n100, 70, 71, 75, 156n64, 158
1:15	55, 72, 73n117, 83, 84
1:16	55, 73
1:17	55, 74, 75–76n124
1:18	55, 58, 75, 81, 86, 107, 139, 158, 200–201n56
1:19–34	189n14
1:28	101
1:30	84
1:31–34	209n91
1:32–33	209, 211
1:35–51	190
1:35–43	189
1:37	187
1:38–39	187
1:38	103
1:39	103, 189
1:41	121, 141
1:43–49	187
1:43	101
1:45	74n122
1:46	189
1:47	108, 189
1:49	121, 122, 134, 141
1:51	135, 187, 191n17
2:1–11	101, 126, 192
2:1	192n21
2:4	175n25
2:9	175
2:11	128, 129
2:13–25	101
2:13–22	70
2:24–25	108, 112
3	158
3:2	101, 103
3:3–7	135
3:3	120
3:5–8	209
3:5	120
3:8	175
3:9	121
3:11–12	139
3:12	135, 135n2
3:13	135, 135n3
3:14–16	120, 136n7
3:14	136
3:15	136
3:16–17	93
3:16	87, 116, 117, 117n48, 158, 159, 180
3:17	90, 93, 158
3:18	159
3:19	163, 181
3:20	163
3:32	139
3:34	90, 139
3:35	86
3:36	119
4:1–42	193

ANCIENT DOCUMENT INDEX 259

4:1–3	101	6:5–6	109, 175
4:1	112	6:7	175
4:4–42	101	6:14–15	109
4:7–9	123	6:14	128, 175
4:10	116, 123	6:15	112, 141
4:11	175	6:19–20	143
4:14	123	6:24–25	175
4:15	124	6:25–71	102
4:17–19	108	6:26	128, 129, 143
4:25–26	176n30	6:27	127, 137
4:25	108, 121, 141	6:29	90
4:26	108, 141, 176n30	6:30	129
4:32–33	175	6:32	105, 116, 144
4:34	94, 95	6:33	119
4:39	108	6:34–35	105
4:48	129n94	6:35	113, 114n35, 127, 128, 144
4:54	129	6:37	115, 119
5–11	174	6:38–40	95
5	86, 108	6:38	94, 105, 144
5:1–15	101, 129	6:39	92n44, 118
5:16–47	102	6:40	118
5:17	108	6:41–42	144
5:18	86, 172, 174n22	6:41	114n35
5:19	94, 108	6:44–45	115
5:20–29	118	6:44	92n44, 118
5:20	87, 108, 118	6:48	114n35
5:21	119	6:50–51	144
5:22–24	109	6:51–56	144
5:22	181	6:51	105, 114, 114n35
5:23	181	6:53–58	127
5:23	91	6:53	137
5:24	119	6:54	118, 119
5:25–27	87	6:57	128
5:26–27	89n23, 118, 183	6:63	209
5:26	181	6:65	115
5:27	137	6:66	156
5:28–29	118, 181	6:68	119
5:30	91, 94, 95, 109, 181, 209n89	6:69	157
5:36	91	6:70–71	112, 158
5:38	90	7	146, 167
5:39	74n122	7:1–8:59	171
5:40	115	7:1	171, 174n22
5:42	109	7:5	200
5:43	167	7:7	163
5:45–46	74n122	7:10–11	172
6	143, 158	7:11	174n22
6:1–14	102, 127, 129	7:12	163

John (*continued*)

7:14–8:59	102
7:14–18	172
7:16–17	103
7:16	91
7:17	209n89
7:19–23	74n122
7:19–20	172
7:19	174n22
7:20	174n22
7:25	172, 174n22
7:28–30	176
7:28–29	109
7:28	103, 163, 167, 167n6, 209n89
7:30	167, 174n22, 175
7:31–32	167
7:31	163
7:32	163
7:33–34	176
7:33	106, 164, 167
7:34	106, 174, 174n22, 176n28
7:35–36	106, 176
7:36	174n22, 174n23, 176n28
7:37–39	115, 126n80
7:37–38	124
7:37	115
7:39	124, 209
7:40–43	164
7:42	74n122
7:44	164
7:49–51	74n122
8:12	114, 146, 147, 182
8:13	182
8:14	176
8:16–18	182
8:17	74n122
8:20–21	172
8:20	103, 175
8:21	174n22, 174n23
8:26	91, 139
8:28–29	109
8:28	94, 137, 139, 209n89
8:29	113
8:37	172, 174n22
8:40	172, 174n22
8:42	209n89
8:55	109
8:58–59	176
8:59	172
9	164
9:1–10:21	102
9:1–41	146, 168
9:3	139
9:5	146
9:10–12	177
9:11	113
9:13–15	164
9:16	129, 164
9:18–21	168
9:22	141, 168
9:35	137, 177n31
9:39	177, 182
9:40–41	177, 182
10	164
10:1–3	187
10:3	187, 188, 203
10:4	187, 188
10:7–9	114
10:7	148
10:9	148, 187
10:10	119, 148, 149
10:11–18	149
10:14–15	149
10:14	203
10:15	109, 149, 164, 187
10:16	149, 188
10:17–18	149
10:17	87
10:18	87, 94, 164
10:20	164
10:22–42	102
10:25	96
10:27–31	177
10:27–28	96
10:28–31	172
10:28	119
10:29	97
10:30	96, 188
10:32	94, 139
10:33–36	173
10:33	87

ANCIENT DOCUMENT INDEX 261

10:34	74n122	12:44–50	102
10:36	90	12:44	102
10:38	97	12:49–50	91, 139
10:39	173, 174n22, 174n23, 177	12:49	209n89
		13–17	51, 186
11:1–44	196	13	101
11:1–2	198	13:1	175
11:3	196	13:3	89n23, 105, 174n23
11:5	196		
11:8	173, 174n22	13:13–15	188
11:9–10	146	13:13	103, 205
11:11	205n69	13:14–15	198
11:14–37	102	13:14	103
11:20	197	13:16	93
11:24	118	13:20	93n51
11:25–27	177	13:23	200n56
11:25–26	114, 151	13:28–29	127n86
11:25	118, 196	13:31–17:26	188
11:27	122, 141, 196	13:31	137
11:28	103	13:33	178, 189
11:29	197	13:34–35	203
11:36	196	14–16	51
11:43	118	14:2–4	152
11:47–53	173	14:2–3	178
11:47	129	14:4–6	178
11:51–52	173n20	14:5	152
11:53	177	14:6	114, 139, 152, 153
11:54	173, 177	14:7	110n29, 139
11:56	174n22	14:9	97, 110n29, 139
12:1–8	196, 198	14:10	97, 110n29, 209n89
12:3	198		
12:4–6	198	14:12	106
12:7–8	198	14:15	188, 203, 205
12:13	121, 141	14:17	209
12:14–36	102	14:19	76
12:15	121, 141	14:21–23	188
12:23	134, 137	14:21	203
12:27	175	14:23	188
12:31–32	178	14:24	110n29
12:31	182	14:26	124, 209
12:32–34	137	14:27	188
12:32	92n44, 137n12	14:28	94, 94n60, 106
12:34	74n122, 134	14:31	203
12:35–50	168	15	114, 155n61
12:35–36	147	15:1–17	207
12:35	178	15:1–11	154
12:36	178	15:1–5	221
12:42	168	15:1	154

John (continued)

15:4–5	154
15:4	155, 207n80
15:5	114, 207n80
15:6	154, 207n80
15:7	155, 207n80
15:9	88, 207, 207n80
15:10	88, 109, 203, 207, 207n80
15:12–13	188
15:12	203
15:13–15	188, 191, 206
15:13–14	205
15:14	188, 203
15:15	139, 205
15:16	207n80
15:25	74n122
15:26	124, 209
16:1–2	168
16:3	168
16:5–6	179
16:7	106
16:8–9	209
16:8	210n98
16:10	106
16:11	182
16:13–15	124
16:13	209
16:14	209
16:16	179
16:17–18	179
16:19	109, 174n23
16:20–22	188
16:20	179
16:21	175
16:22	179
16:28	105, 107
16:30	110
16:32	199n48
16:33	89n23
17	110
17:1–26	84
17:1	175
17:2	89n23
17:3	88, 90, 110, 119, 119n56, 141, 167n6, 218
17:5	84, 85, 85n13
17:6–14	188
17:6	139
17:8	110
17:11	97
17:17	188
17:19	188
17:21	90, 96
17:22	96, 188
17:23	88, 96
17:24	85, 88
17:25–26	88
17:25	110
17:26	139
18:4	110
18:19–20	102
18:19	103
18:31–32	74n122
18:33	121, 141
18:36–37	142
18:36	121
18:37	121, 142
18:38	121
19:3–7	122
19:3	121, 142
19:6–7	168
19:7	169
19:12	142
19:14	121
19:15	169
19:19	121, 142
19:21	121, 142
19:25–27	199
20:1–18	201
20:15	202
20:16	104, 202, 203
20:17	106, 202, 203n62
20:21–23	209
20:22	210, 210n92
20:28	110n29
20:29	193
20:30–31	51
20:30	129
20:31	67, 122, 133, 141, 165, 187, 196
21	51, 104, 104n10
21:1–11	127
21:5	188n8

ANCIENT DOCUMENT INDEX 263

21:15–17	204
21:17	112
21:25	104

Romans

8:3	5n15
10:6–8	5n15

1 Corinthians

1:24	4
1:30	4
8:6	4, 5n10
10:4	5

2 Corinthians

4:4	5n13
4:6	5n13

Galatians

4:4–6	5n14

Ephesians

1:6	5n16
1:8–10	5n16
1:12	5n16
1:22–23	5n16
3:10	5n16
3:17–19	5n16
4:10	5n16

Colossians

1:9–10	6n18
1:15–20	5, 6
1:28	6n18
2:3	6
2:9	6n18
3:16	6n18

Hebrews

1:1–2	6n19
1:1–4	6
1:2	6
1:3–4	219
1:3	6, 220n22
1:4	6

~

DEAD SEA SCROLLS

1Q20	31, 33, 215
19–20	68
19	31
19.15–17	31
19.18–20	32
20.2–7	31
20.2–6	32
20.6	32
20.7	32
20.9–10	32
20.26–27	32

11Q5	33, 34, 215
9	33
10	33
10–11	33
13–14	33, 34

~

PHILO

Cher.

9–10	37n148
41	38n155
49	34n118
127	36n136

Cong.

9	37n147
12–13	37n146
22–33	38n156
36–37	38n153
170–174	145
174	36n132, 145n35

Det.

54	34n118, 35n126, 61n59, 66n88, 200n55
115–116	35n120, 66n87
117	126n81
124	37n142

Deus

142–143	153–154, 154n58

Ebr.

30–31	34n118, 200n55
31	35n125
59–62	37n142
112	35n122
112–113	126n81, 195n35

Fug.

51	34n118, 38n152
97	37
109	34n118, 35n127, 61n59, 66n88, 200n55
166–167	37n145
166	38n153
195	194n33

Her.

52–53	151n49
61–62	37n148
126–128	211n101
205	35n128, 66n86

Leg.

1.65	36n137
2.49	35n119, 66n87
2.82	37n143
3.10	35n128
3.52	151n50
3.161–162	145n36
3.162	36n131

Legat.

369	92n46

Mut.

259	36n129, 144–145, 145n32
264	38n149

Post.

77–78	38n155
135	38n156
136	194n33
146	38n152

Praem.

59–61	35n121

QG

2.62	66n86
3.21–22	37n148
4.73	38n150
4.97	38n152
4.98	194n34
4.101	194n34
4.107	194n34
4.145	37n145

Sacr.

8	36n135

Somn.

1.70	66n86
1.190	66n86
2.170–171	156n65
2.242	35n123, 36n138
2.270–271	126n81
2.190–192	156n65

❦

TARGUMIC TEXTS

Frg. Tg. on Genesis

1:1	43, 44n179, 57, 61
28:10	124n68

Tg. Neof. on Genesis
1:1   44, 44n179, 57, 57n36

Tg. Ps–J. on Genesis
28:10   124n68

RABBINIC WRITINGS

m. 'Abot
2:7   42n172
3:14   43n177, 74n119

m. Sukkah
4:9–10   124n69

m. Ter.
4:4   92n43

m. Qidd.
3:1   92n43

b. B. Qam.
70a   92n44, 137n12
113b   91n41

b. Ber.
5.5   91n38

b. 'Erub.
31b–32a   92n43

b. Git.
32   181n36

b. Ned.
72b   91n37

b. Qidd.
42a   92n43

43a   91n39, 181n36

b. Sanh.
111b   181n36

'Abot R. Nat.
31 (8b)   75–76n124

Genesis Rabbah
1:1   74n119
1:4   43, 74n119
8:2   43n176, 74n119
54:1   42, 74n119
70:19   124n68
78:1   91n41

Sipre Deuteronomy
84a   42

GRECO-ROMAN WRITINGS

Aristotle
Poetics
6   162

Plutarch
Alexander
1:1–3   54n22

EARLY CHRISTIAN WRITINGS

Apostolic Constitutions
7.34.6   44n182

1 Clement

13.1	220n23
22.1	219n21
27.4	220n25
33.3	220n25
36	219
36.2	220n22
57–58	220
57.3–7	220n23
58.1	220
60.1	220n24

Origen
Comm. Jo.

1.22	223n41
1.42	223n39

Princ.

1.2.1	223n40
2.6.2	223n42

Justin Martyr
Dialogue with Trypho

61	222n33
62	222n34

Didache

1.1–2	220n28
6.2	221
9–10	221n31
9	221
9.2	221

Eusebius
Praeparatio Evangelica

13.12.10–11	21n56
13.12.12	22n58

www.ingramcontent.com/pod-product-compliance
Lightning Source LLC
Chambersburg PA
CBHW071245230426

43668CB00011B/1588